WALTER BENJAMIN AND ART

WALTER BENJAMIN STUDIES SERIES

Series Editors: Andrew Benjamin, Monash University, and Beatrice Hanssen, University of Georgia.

Consultant Board: Stanley Cavell, Sander Gilman, Miriam Hansen, Carol Jacobs, Martin Jay, Gertrud Koch, Peter Osborne, Sigrid Weigel and Anthony Phelan.

A series devoted to the writings of Walter Benjamin – each volume will focus on a theme central to contemporary work on Benjamin. The series aims to set new standards for scholarship on Benjamin for students and researchers in Philosophy, Cultural Studies and Literary Studies.

Walter Benjamin and Romanticism (2002), edited by Beatrice Hanssen and Andrew Benjamin.

Walter Benjamin and Art

Edited by Andrew Benjamin

continuum
LONDON • NEW YORK

Continuum
The Tower Building   15 East 26th Street
11 York Road   New York
London SE1 7NX   NY 10010

British Library Cataloguing-in-Publication Data
A catalogue record for this book is available from the British Library.

ISBN: HB: 0–8264–6729–6
      PB: 0–8264–6730–X

Library of Congress Cataloging-in-Publication Data
Walter Benjamin and Art/edited by Andrew Benjamin.
    p.cm. – (Walter Benjamin sudies series) Includes bibliograpical references and index.
ISBN 0-8264-6729-6 – ISBN 0-8264-6730-X (pbk.)
    1. Benjamin, Walter, 1892–1940. Kunstwerk im Zeitalter seiner technischen Reproduzier barkeit.
2. Benjamin, Walter, 1892–1940 – Aesthetics. 3. Art and Society. I. Benjamin, Andrew E. II. Series.
PT2603. E455K868 2004
834ʹ. 912—dc22
200456178

Typeset by Fakenham Photosetting Ltd, Fakenham, Norfolk
Printed and bound in Great Britain by Cromwell Press, Trowbridge, Wiltshire

Contents

Acknowledgements

Earlier versions of a number of these papers appeared in the following publications. All were revised for this publication.

Rebecca Comays' 'Materialist Mutations of the *Bilderverbot*', in ed. David Michael Levin, *Sites of Vision: The Discursive Construction of Vision in the History of Philosophy* (Cambridge, MA: MIT, 1997).

Fabrizio Desideri, *Il fantasma dell'opera: Benjamin, Adorno e le aporie dell'arte contemporanea* (Il Melangolo: Genova, 2002).

Howard Giland, 'Reception in Distraction', in Kevin McLauglin and Philip Rosen (eds), *Benjamin Now: Critical Encounters with* The Arabs Project, *boundary 2*, 30. 1 (2003): 51–66.

Robert Kaufman, 'Aura, Still', *October* 99 (2002): 45–80.

Detlef Mertins, 'Walter Benjamin and the Tectonic Unconscious', in *The Optic of Walter Benjamin*, ed. Alex Coles (London: Black Dog Press, 1999).

Abbreviations

AP *The Arcades Project*, trans. Howard Eiland and Kevin McLaughlin (Cambridge, MA: Belknap, 1999).

C *The Correspondence of Walter Benjamin 1910–1940*, ed. Gershom Scholem and Theodor W. Adorno, trans. Manfred R. Jakobson and Evelyn M. Jakobson (Chicago, IL: The University of Chicago Press, 1994).

CC Theodor W. Adorno and Walter Benjamin, *The Complete Correspondence 1920–1940*, ed. Henri Lonitz, trans. Nicholas Walker (Cambridge, MA: Harvard University Press, 1999).

GB *Gesammelte Briefe*, ed. Christoph Gödde and Henri Lonitz (Frankfurt am Main: Suhrkamp, 1995 and following years).

GS *Walter Benjamin: Gesammelte Schriften*, eds. Rolf Tiedemann and Hermann Schweppenhäuser (Frankfurt am Main: Suhrkamp, 1974ff.).

OT *The Origin of the German Tragic Drama*, trans. John Osborne (London: Verso, 1998).

SW *Walter Benjamin, Selected Writings*, ed. Michael W. Jennings (Cambridge, MA: Belknap, 1997–2003).

Introduction

ANDREW BENJAMIN

Central to any discussion of the work of art in the contemporary period, and this will be the case whether those discussions are situated within philosophy, literary criticism, art history, or cultural studies, is Walter Benjamin's text 'The Work of Art in the Age of its Technological Reproducibility'. There were three versions of the German text and a contemporary French translation by Pierre Klossowski.[1] The text was first drafted in 1935 and rewritten between that date and 1939.[2] The history of the text's production provides an important glimpse into the contested relation between art and politics in the late 1930s. More exactly, the final version provides a way into an understanding of the role of art in any analysis of fascism as well as in finding possible avenues of response to its emergence. It should be noted that Benjamin's essay is concerned as much with a diagnosis as it is in the argument that shifts in technical production generate interpretive possibilities that could not be easily recuperated by fascism. On one level the text's history is vital to any sustained investigation of Benjamin's project. Nonetheless, the text has had a profound influence on approaches to art that far outweighs its historical particularity. As such the text demands both contextualizing approaches, as well as others that acknowledge its impact and relevance beyond the hold of its initial setting. (Both are at work in this collection.)

While there are many aspects of Benjamin's essay that can be privileged, one of the most compelling concerns the relationship between, on the one hand, the history of artistic production in terms of the history of techniques and technological development, and, on the other, the concomitant effect of that development on the concepts and categories through which art is to be understood. In other words, while artistic practice may have a history, that history has a profound impact on the understanding and thus interpretation of art in any one period. What is given centrality therefore is no longer art as occupying a transcendent realm. Techniques open upon different ways of thinking both the history of art and equally any philosophy of art. Here would be the most radical point of departure from the other essay that has come to dominate contemporary discussions of art – though it should be added that it is a domination felt more acutely within philosophy than elsewhere – namely Heidegger's *The Origin of the Work of Art*.[3] Heidegger's project was to 'discover the essence of art'.[4] Benjamin will continually argue that what is essential inheres in the changes within the techniques pertaining to art's production. Points of affinity and separation between Heidegger and Benjamin cannot ignore questions of production.

Working from Benjamin's essay, it can be argued that changes in production have two results that need to be noted. The first is explicit. The history of technical development provides the framework within which contemporary production within the visual arts is to be understood. The second is implicit. Accepting these shifts does not mean abandoning the art of the past. Indeed the contrary is the case; the art of the past is given an after-life by the occasion of its 'now' possible reinterpretation in terms of the changes on a conceptual level demanded by developments on the technical. Art lives on through its reworking. Technical development – as opposed to mere speculative invention – sets the measure.

The project of this collection of essays is to use Benjamin's text as a way of opening up questions within the practice of art. The term 'practice of art' is to be given as broad an extension as possible, i.e. as moving from the philosophical to criticism passing through the necessity of the political. Hence not only is there the need to view Benjamin's essay refracted through the advent of the digital, it is also necessary to reconsider it within the differing modalities of music, photography, literature and architecture amongst others. Each of these reconsiderations allows the potential of the essay to be investigated. This occurs since fundamental to the essay's project is the resistance to any attempt to develop either an essentialist conception of art – a conception that would be constrained to refuse both generic distinctions and therefore fail to see them as sites of differing forms of technical innovation and development – or, secondly, allowing art any place within a large philosophical concern that would, as a consequence, efface the plurality of media through which it operates. Working for Benjamin means that art takes on a different quality.

Attempting to provide an introductory summary of the texts presented here is not an integral part of the project. Another element needs to be noted in advance. While Walter Benjamin's text has an almost lapidary quality, its argumentative and stylistic elegance has not been fashioned in order to generate simple copies. While canonical in terms of allowing contemporary debates to be staged around the complex interconnections between art, philosophy and politics, and while there are principles, perhaps even allegiances that the text envisages, there is no one disciplinary position or approach that these principles or allegiances demand. While it is essential to write in the wake of Benjamin's text – hence the concession to its canonical nature – it is also impossible to remain strictly Benjaminian. The latter is the case precisely because Benjamin's *œuvre*, while establishing directions, resists any straightforward formulation in terms of an unequivocal theory.

In sum, therefore, this collection represents a sustained attempt to interrogate Benjamin's text first by putting it to use and second by investigating its utility by situating its concerns within larger philosophical, critical and political contexts.[5]

1

RECEPTION IN DISTRACTION

HOWARD EILAND

I take my title from a passage near the end of Benjamin's essay on the technological reproducibility of the work of art. Benjamin italicizes the sentence: '*Reception in distraction* [Die Rezeption in der Zerstreuung] – *the sort of reception which is increasingly noticeable in all areas of art and is a symptom of profound changes in apperception – finds in film its true training ground* [Übungsinstrument]' (*GS* 1.2:505/*SW* 4:269).[1] I would like, in what follows, to highlight a certain inconsistency (if I can put it that way) in Benjamin's handling of the concept of distraction, a variance in his attitude towards the concept, and I would like to show how two separate attitudes involved here – one prominently exemplified in his writings on Brecht and the other in the 'Work of Art' essay – are both reflected in *The Arcades Project*. I shall refer, provisionally, to the first of these attitudes as 'negative', and the second as 'positive', but it should be kept in mind that, especially in the case of the 'Work of Art' essay and *The Arcades*, the notion of distraction operates in a peculiarly slippery manner, such as very likely makes this one of the more elusive of Benjaminian *topoi*. It is at its slipperiest where it bears on the theory of montage.

The 'negative' view of distraction is enunciated in Benjamin's discussion of Brecht's epic theatre in two pieces from the early 1930s: the magazine article 'Theatre and Radio', from 1932, and the famous (possibly unde-livered) lecture from 1934, 'The Author as Producer' ('*Der Autor als Produzent*'). In both texts Benjamin distinguishes epic theatre from the big-city 'theatre of convention', which, in its complementary functions of cultivation and distraction, *Bildung* and *Zerstreuung* (the latter might also be translated here as 'entertainment'), caters to a 'sated class', as he says, 'for which everything it touches becomes a stimulant' (*GS* 2.2:697/*SW* 2:778). In the epic theatre, on the other hand, a certain concrete pedagogics takes the place of sensationalism; *Schulung* replaces *Bildung* (that is, 'training' – the training of expert judgement – replaces 'culture'), and instead of distraction there is 'group formation' (*Gruppierung*), which refers to the formation of both a well-informed audience and a highly trained ensemble of performers on the basis of a set of shared social and political concerns translated on the stage to a series of radically distinct, thought-provoking 'actions' – what Brecht calls the 'knotting' of the incidents.[2] *Zerstreuung* thus has the sense of '*divertissement*' here, of complacent diversion. Rather than such a bald appeal to the emotions – above all, to the capacity for empathy, for identifying with characters – epic theatre engenders critical distance; rather than soothing or warming its audience, it seeks to astonish them through the well-known 'alienation effect', which, by making ordinary objects and actions seem strange, renders them conspicuous and encourages audience and actor alike to reflect on them. Discovery through alienation – 'communication by alienation' (*ST*, p. 169/*BT*, p. 202) – these are Brecht's formulas for the new experimental theatre which he and others (like the directors Meyerhold and Piscator) have established, one where the development of plot gives way to the 'lightning-like' (*GS* 2.2:530) illumination of situations and where performance becomes critique. As Benjamin puts it in the first of two essays entitled 'What is Epic Theatre?' (dating from 1931), 'The discovery of situations is accomplished by means of the interruption of sequences' (*GS* 2.2:522). Benjamin lays emphasis on the principle of interruption, which, with its 'retarding character' (a term derived from Schlegel and Novalis [*GS* 1.1:99/*SW* 1:172]), makes for the distinctively punctuated, intermittent rhythm of Brechtian drama. Whether by means of the sudden intervention of song, the use of captions, or what Brecht calls the gestic conventions of the actors, this interruption of sequences creates gaps which undermine the audience's illusion of a 'world' on the stage and make room for critical reflection, including the possibility of imagining, as Brecht says, 'a different set of political and economic conditions' (*ST*, pp. 242–3/*BT*, p. 86) under which the actions on stage might take place. In this way the stage is converted from a *Bannraum*, a magic space, a space for working spells, to an *Ausstellungsraum* or exhibition space (*GS* 2.2:520), and the merger of artistic and political projects is realized.

In 'Theatre and Radio' and 'The Author as Producer', Benjamin explicitly connects the Brechtian discovery of the 'gestus' – the element of a gesture, action, or word which conveys a particular attitude on the part of a character towards other human beings – to the 'restoration of the method of montage decisive in radio and film' (*GS* 2.2:698/*SW* 2:778). On the stage of the epic theatre, declares Benjamin, this technological process – namely, montage – becomes a human one. The principle of interruption, which is as central to the method of montage as it is to the alienation effect, has here a pedagogic function and not just the character of a stimulus. It brings the action to a halt, occasioning surprise, and hence compels the spectator to adopt an attitude towards the situation in question, and the actor towards his or her role. One of the most important responsibilities of the actor, Benjamin suggests in 'What is Epic Theatre?', is the spacing out of his actions, so as to make them, he says, 'quotable' (*GS* 2.2:529, 536). Brecht himself, writing in 1930, contrasts conventional dramatic theatre with epic theatre in terms very close to these. Dramatic theatre is distinguished by 'growth', 'linear development', 'evolutionary determinism' (i.e., the 'fate' of central characters), by the fact that 'one scene makes another'; epic theatre is distinguished by 'montage', 'curves', 'breaks' (*Sprünge*), and by the fact that 'each scene [is] for itself' (*ST*, p. 20/*BT*, p. 37). For the productions of epic theatre Brecht insists on 'a radical separation of the elements'. This means, for example, that 'words, music and setting must become more independent of one another' (*ST*, p. 21/*BT*, p. 38), but in referring to 'elements' Brecht also has in mind single incidents, movements of figures or groups, sound effects, even single sentences and exclamations (*ST*, pp. 165–6, 230/*BT*, pp. 200–1, 214, 100–1). The separate constellations of the action, he maintains, and even the distances between them have dramatic significance (*ST*, p. 230/*BT*, p. 214). In theory at least, the spacing out of the elements, their emerging disparateness, makes for a recurrent shock effect – a hallmark of montage – and it is this shock-engendered form, by means of which situations are set off against one another, that creates a transitory space in which contradictions in social conditions can present themselves and society's causal network can be traced. The individual gestus, which as such is always a social gestus, at the same time figures in an historical discourse; in Benjamin's interpretation (in the first version of 'What is Epic Theatre?'), it discloses the actuality of 'dialectics at a standstill' (*GS* 2.2:530) – a central category of *The Arcades Project*, begun some four years earlier. The dialectically charged gestus is the rock of astonishment on which the stream of things breaks (*GS* 2.2:531) – notice that the 'standstill' at issue here is not anything simply static;[3] to vary the metaphor, the gestus is an eddy formed in reflecting the currents of history at a particular point in space and time. Brecht calls it a 'nodal point', an emergent knot of tension at which the situations of the story collide to reveal specific social forces at work or to unmask the crisis of authority. In his didactic, indeed combative intention (deliberately opposed to the process of catharsis that has marked traditional theatre since Aristotle), the radical montage of elements works against the goal of 'fusion', whether this be understood in terms of the generation of a dominant mood, or atmosphere, or in terms of the empathic identification with characters on the stage. In Brechtian parlance, montage counteracts the 'witchcraft' (*Magie*), the 'hypnosis', the 'fog', the state of 'trance' (*Entrückung*) induced in the spectators of bourgeois theatre – a state which Brecht compares to that of sleepers dreaming restlessly with their eyes open (*ST*, pp. 142–3/*BT*, p. 187), and which we might liken to the 'strange stare' and 'spell-stopped' stance of the characters in Shakespeare's *Tempest* who come under the influence of Prospero's art. 'My high charms work', observes Prospero, 'And these, mine enemies, are all knit up/ In their distractions'. Here is a classical locus for the conception of distraction as not just counter-productive but actually stupefying.[4] What for the bourgeois is a salutary diversion from his 'troubles' is for Brecht, in the 1930s, a form of 'drug trafficking', a 'sordid intoxication' and bondage. In place of the theatre as witches' caldron or sirens' isle, he establishes the theatre as laboratory, which seeks to induce clarified emotion and pleasurable knowledge. There, be it noted, the method of montage is *opposed* to that of distraction.

Now, in his attitude towards the idea of intoxication – *Rausch*, of course, is a pivotal term in Nietzsche's later philosophy – Benjamin parts company with Brecht. This will be immediately apparent to any reader of *The Arcades Project* who remembers the emphasis placed on the anamnestic intoxication of the *flâneur* wandering the streets at all hours, on the gambler's presence of mind in the intoxication of play, or on the enchantment of the collector who both loses himself and renews himself in gazing on his object (M1,5; O12a,2; H1a,2). All these instances of 'intoxicated experience' (*rauschhafte Erfahrung* [M1a,2]) – with which Benjamin, at one point, implicitly conjoins Baudelaire's evocation of the 'religious intoxication of great cities' (J34a,3; cf. J84a,1) – point towards a more complex conception of the problem of *distraction* than we get in the essays on Brecht, or indeed from Brecht himself.[5] Being carried away – which is what distraction and intoxication have in common, and which is what links them, classically, to the concept of madness – does not necessarily exclude a certain profane illumination (*GS* 2.2:297ff./*SW* 2:209ff.).

This more complicated attitude, as I indicated at the outset, is developed in Benjamin's most famous essay, 'The Work of Art in the Age of its Technological Reproducibility', which focuses the problem in the workings of film. In the third version of the essay, with which he was occupied from 1936 to 1939, and which expands the discussion of distraction, Benjamin quotes the author Georges Duhamel, who voices a complaint made often enough by critics of the cinema during the second and third decades of its commercial existence: 'I can no longer think what I want to think. My thoughts have been replaced by moving images' (*GS* 1.2:503). Indeed, comments Benjamin, the train of associations in the person wishing to contemplate one of these images is immediately *interrupted* by new images, and this, Benjamin goes on to say, constitutes the shock effect of film, 'which, like all shock effects, seeks to induce heightened attention [*Geistesgegenwart*, meaning also 'presence of mind']'. One may think here not only of the Brechtian alienation effect – which, as we have seen, aims to sharpen attention by means of interruption – but also of the practised vigilance required to follow such things as big-city traffic, trading on the floor of the stock exchange, or collective jazz improvisation.[6] For Benjamin, such high-speed vigilance is as much a defining feature of modern experience as distraction itself is. In other words, when he asserts that reception in distraction is becoming increasingly noticeable in all areas of art today, and is moreover a symptom of profound changes in human 'apperception' (such as unsettling the possibility of relaxed contemplation, of mentally 'dwelling'), he is offering both a description and a challenge.[7] Reception in distraction is conditioned, first of all, by the dynamics of modern technology, by the technologization of things – the accelerated pace of life, the rapid transitions of modern media, the press of commodities and their programmed obsolescence, and so on. At the same time, it is a covert measure of the ability to perform new tasks of apperception, for *successful* reception in distraction presupposes that a mastery of certain tasks has become habitual. What is at stake here, it would seem, is a dialectical mode of reading that effectively masters the technological apparatus – as the film actor masters the recording devices on the set – with the aid of the apparatus itself. The actor places the apparatus in the service of his triumph over it; this triumph of what appears to the audience to be the actor's humanity is a product of the use which the actor makes of his own self-alienation in the face of the camera. His mastery therefore presupposes, as well as promotes, an interpenetration of nature and technology, *physis* and *techne*. His and the audience's humanity is vindicated insofar as it is absorbed by, and in turn absorbs, the apparatus – which puts our humanity to the test.

The essay on technological reproducibility makes it evident that distraction, in a properly modern context, must itself be understood dialectically – that is to say, beyond the simple opposition of distraction and concentration (or, in Brecht's terms, distraction and recognition). The challenge, Benjamin suggests (in a notational schema to the 'Work of Art' essay entitled 'Theory of Distraction' [*GS* 7.2:678-9/*SW* 3:141–2, written ca. 1935–6])[8] is to appreciate 'the values of distraction', which he associates with a convergence of educational value and consumer value (*Lehrwert* and *Konsumwert*) in a new kind of learning (*eine neue Art des Lernens*). In this positive attitude towards the production and experience of distraction, he is anticipated by his colleague Siegfried Kracauer. To be sure, Kracauer's discussion of the Berlin *Lichtspielhäuser* (or picture palaces) of the mid-1920s, with their incorporation of film-screenings into a revue-like show involving a series of production numbers, and with their 'homogeneous cosmopolitan audience ... addicted to distraction [*Zerstreuungssüchtig*]',[9] appears at first to echo the viewpoint represented by Duhamel in Benjamin's 'Work of Art' essay: the interior design of the *Lichtspielhäuser*, as well the character of their programmes, serve 'to rivet the viewers' attention to the peripheral, so that they will not sink into the abyss. The stimulations of the senses succeed one another with such rapidity that there is no room left between them for even the slightest contemplation' (314/326). Nevertheless, Kracauer argues, what the audience encounters in 'the fragmented sequence of splendid sense impressions' is its own fragmented reality. In their motley parade of 'externalities', these shows convey a momentary sense, at least, of the disorder of society – unless, that is, the motley has been concealed beneath a contrived appearance of 'artistic unity', which in fact is usually the case. In Kracauer's view, this evasion of the truth of fragmentation implicit in the discontinuous revue form is part of a more general failure on the part of film producers: namely, their subordination of the revolutionary potential of cinematography – which includes its ability to reveal the most hidden facets and unexpected stations of ordinary existence – to the obsolete conventions of bourgeois theatre. Putting an original spin on what was by then a familiar demand for a cinema freed from the influence of theatre, Kracauer calls for 'a kind of distraction that exposes disintegration instead of masking it' (317/328). Such distraction would have a '*moral* significance' (315/326).

Kracauer does not himself use the term 'montage' in connection with the revue form that occasions a positive idea of distraction. But we have only to recall the references to 'music hall and circus' in Eisenstein's discussion of the 'montage of attractions' to grasp the pertinence of the term here. Eisenstein's conception of montage, of course, develops out of his work as set designer and director in the Moscow Proletkult Theatre in the early 1920s, where he experimented with multiple planes of action on the stage, mounting several scenes simultaneously and cross-cutting between them, where he sought to obviate conventional perspective by disjoining and foregrounding all the elements of the composition or by employing several perspectives at once (as in a cityscape), and where he came to regard acting itself as a form of montage insofar as a character's gestures and movements are meant to *epitomize* an extended emotional and intellectual process within a particular person. On the stage, 'the "montage of attractions" ... turned each episode of the play into a separate "number" and gathered them into a unified "montage" on the pattern of a music-hall programme'.[10] As applied to the continuously changing flow of imagery in the motion picture (there is, of course, a paradox hiding in this term), the montage of attractions necessitated a dynamic composition in time, a construction in transformation, through which the various individual 'cells' of the action would compose a rhythmic whole in the collision of sequences. In other words, 'there is no lack of composition' where montage is in force, 'but the composition does not take precedence over the detail'.[11] Imbued with the modernist principle that 'perceiving is building', Eisenstein could herald an 'entirely new era of constructive possibilities' made possible by 'the magic power of montage',[12] a power historically conditioned, as he says, since the forms it assumes in the movies reflect contradictions and conflicts within actual events. The main outlines of what he called 'montage thinking',[13] as it operates in both horizontal and vertical dimensions, could be traced in virtually all the contemporary arts, though film remained the model for such thinking. With this invocation of the exemplary status of the cinematic medium – a position not uncharacteristic of the heyday of montage aesthetics in the 1920s – we are back again to Benjamin's theory of distraction, which is also a theory of perception, and the key role played by film in habituating 'the masses' to this new mode of experience and this new architectonics. To cite once more the programmatic language of Benjamin's 'Work of Art' essay: the cinema is the authentic *Übungsinstrument*, or training device, for the sort of reception in distraction which is coming into being in all areas of contemporary art, and which is symptomatic of a new kinetic apperception, one opened out and agitated, as it were, jolted. What makes film instrumental in the cultivation of such a decentred reception is, it is now clear, the metamorphic mechanism of montage.[14] Montage is no longer opposed to distraction, as in the essays on Brecht, but is its vehicle.

The opposition now would seem to be between *mere* distraction and, shall we say, productive distraction – between distraction as a skewing of attention, or as abandonment to diversion, and distraction as a spur to new ways of perceiving. In either case, a certain wandering or dispersion makes itself felt. As I suggested at the beginning of this chapter, both ideas of distraction can be found in *The Arcades Project.* The negative view is reflected in passages concerned with commodity fetishism, specifically with the world exhibitions and with the entertainment industry. In section III of the Exposé of 1935, we are told that the world exhibitions that began to be organized in Europe after 1850 'open a phantasmagoria which a person enters in order to be distracted [*um sich zerstreuen zu lassen*]. The entertainment industry makes this easier by elevating the person to the level of the commodity. He surrenders to its manipulations while enjoying his alienation from himself and others' (*GS* 5.1:50–51/*AP*, p. 7). Several of the Brechtian themes (they are Marxian themes as well, of course) are noticeable here, in particular the association of distraction with complacent self-surrender in a crowd and willingness to be manipulated by the apparatus; this makes for alienation in a negative sense, an oblivious, morally paralysing estrangement from oneself and others. The experience is one of being mastered by the apparatus – Benjamin may also be thinking, in this regard, of the fascist mass rallies of his own day – instead of mastering it for the good of humanity. The Exposé goes on to connect the 'enthronement of the commodity' to, first, the art of Grandville – whose illustrations turn the whole of nature into a display of luxury goods, thus caricaturing the fatal 'lustre of distraction' that emanates from the commodity – and, secondly, to the conception of the *Gesamtkunstwerk*, or total work of art, that finds its chief representative, at this period, in Wagnerian opera. Whereas Grandville's satire encourages critical awareness of the technologized cult of commodities, the *Gesamtkunstwerk* would 'seal art off from the developments of technology' and, with its solemn rites, conceal from its audience the fact of its own commodification. The techniques of distraction serve here – as in the world exhibitions that pave the way to the entertainment industry – to 'abstract from the social existence of human beings'. Even Baudelaire 'succumbs' to the 'rage' for Wagner (*GS* 5.1:56/*AP*, p. 11).

Of course, the arcades themselves – these showplaces of nineteenth-century 'industrial luxury', with their corridors of shop windows and their sundry allures (including the allure of prostitutes) – are dedicated to the 'distraction that transfigures the commodity'. In this 'strange zone', as Louis Aragon puts in his *Paysan de Paris* (that Surrealist travel guide which helped

inspire *The Arcades Project*), *all* is distraction (*tout est lapsus*) – 'lapse of attention as well as of inattention'.[15] Carried along by the relentless 'current of
objects' (*Paysan*, p. 60/*Peasant*, p. 47), knowingly absorbed in a 'cult of the
ephemeral' (21/14), as celebrated in this modern-archaic 'underwater world'
(52/40), Aragon's narrator confesses himself the 'master-slave of his vertigos'
(125/102). 'Everything distracts me indefinably, except from my distraction
itself [*tout me distrait indéfiniment, sauf de ma distraction même*]. A feeling
akin to nobleness of heart prompts me to exalt this surrender, and my ears
are closed to the reproaches you make me' (12/7–8). What is striking about
these passages from Aragon is the way they blithely transcend our duality of
positive and negative distractions. The most ordinary or workaday objects
– and we are treated, in his distracted prose, to phantasmagoric inventories
of such objects, as encountered in strolls through the Passage de l'Opéra (a
display of sponges, a target pinned on the back of an old telephone directory
at a gunsmith's, an emerald-coloured skin lotion bearing the name *Velouté
Naturel*, a sombre, oak-panelled hairdressing salon for men) – the most
fugitive of distractions are grist to his philosophic mill and engine of his
exaltations. There is no opposition here between entertainment as an end in
itself and the education of apperception, or indeed between intoxication and
education:

> Some everyday object ... plunged me into ... mystery. I loved this intoxi-
> cation which I knew how to put into effect ... The way I saw it, an object
> became transfigured: it did not so much manifest an idea as constitute
> that very idea. Thus it extended deeply into the world's mass. (*Paysan*, pp.
> 140–1/*Peasant*, pp. 113–14)

The same analytic revelling in material and commercial ephemera, in a
half-submerged world of things (*Dingwelt*), is a defining feature of *The
Arcades Project*. Just as the film prop becomes an actor while the film actor
becomes a prop, and just as objects in films (like objects in fairy tales) take
on a life of their own, so the physical spaces and furnishings and milieux of
Benjamin's arcades evince a ghostly animation, like creatures of a lost world.
They wear a face. Benjamin does not explicitly call attention to the positive
value of distraction in *The Arcades Project*, as he does in the 'Work of Art'
essay, but he repeatedly demonstrates it through his cultural physiognomics,
his widely diffused researches into the historical 'rags' and 'refuse' of the
nineteenth century (N1a,8). And, like Aragon, he conjures an 'intoxicated
experience' of city life that, in its often startling concreteness, counteracts
the propensity for 'abstraction from the social existence of human beings',
the propensity attributed to the commodity in the Exposé of 1935. No
doubt we have come up against the famous Benjaminian ambivalence at this
point – in particular, the ambivalence towards commodity fetishism and
'the crowd'. But the simultaneity of positive and negative valorizations of

distraction and intoxication is also, presumably, a function of the 'ambiguity of the arcades' (R2a,3). In Benjamin's presentation, they are *both* laboratory and atmosphere.

I mentioned a little earlier the leading role played in the *The Arcades Project* by the figures of *flâneur*, gambler, and collector. In the case of each of these nineteenth-century types, Benjamin applies a peculiarly double-edged formula: the *flâneur* is characterized, once again, by 'anamnestic intoxication', a recollection not dulled but heightened by intoxication; the gambler by an intoxicated presence of mind, a divinatory reading of his chances that is entirely obedient to bodily reflex; and the collector by an entranced absorption in his chosen object that allows him to see through it to a profile of the historical epoch from which it derives, that makes of his object in its showcase a 'magic encyclopedia' of that epoch (H2,7; H1a,2). Benjamin's usage of the term *Zerstreuung* is double-edged in another sense. There is an ontological distraction as well as an epistemological one. Meditating the task of the collector, Benjamin writes: 'Perhaps the most deeply hidden motive of the person who collects can be described this way: he takes up the struggle against dispersion [*Zerstreuung*]. Right from the start, the great collector is struck by the confusion, by the scatter [*Zerstreutheit*] in which the things of the world are found' (H4a,1). To the things in their primordially strewn state the collector brings his distraught concern, historically informed as it is. It is much the same with the *flâneur*, as he wanders aimlessly, senses primed, through the labyrinth of streets and neighbourhoods, gathering news of 'what has been' through the medium of building styles or place-names, and with the gambler, as he gives himself up to the flow of the game, dispelling all gravity, in order to come to a decision at the last possible moment. All three are at home, relatively speaking, in the world's scatter. They are touched and inspired by it. They spend themselves and expand themselves in being dispersed to the current of objects. And their reception in distraction, like that of the movie audience, is not merely visual but tactile, or visceral; it involves their whole sensorium, as illuminated by memory (for the experience in 'intoxicated experience' is long experience [*Erfahrung*]). Their struggle against dispersion succeeds only by dint of studious abandonment to it, and this is the source of their presence of mind as something bodily.

The ontological scatter that is accessible to an intensively scattered perception bespeaks a crisis of the object, a crisis of meaning. What I referred to above as the technologization and commodification of things (involving, as it does, the unmooring of metaphysical substance) can be seen as a manifestation of this crisis. From an aesthetic point of view, it is a crisis of form, entailing, for the modern artist, the challenge of discovering a form commensurate with the entropic or centrifugal tendency of modern experience, with what in fact resists integration and closure. An articulation of dispersion, a dis-integrated form, a meaning in shock: is this not a possible purchase on

what is meant by 'literary montage' in *The Arcades Project* (N1a,8)?[16] To be
sure, this project as a whole, with its persistent documentary intention and
its improvisatory arrangement of materials (an arrangement dictated mainly,
it appears, by the course of Benjamin's studies), would seem to combine the
most concrete sort of content with the most indeterminate sort of form. But
perhaps it can be said that the montage of fragments (excerpts and reflections) which Benjamin has assembled in this text – assuming that it *is* a text,
at least *de facto*, and not just a notebook – does work soberly to mirror the
scatteredness of things, especially of things perceived in an urban environment, and, as it were, *en passant*. The centrifugal tendency would be an
element of the work itself, complementary to a constellatory tendency. For it
is not by any means simple scatter that we find here; the historical objects of
Benjamin's collection, with their store of 'secret affinities' (R2,3), are sprung
together, so to speak, in thematic arcs, and tend to communicate with one
another, intermittently, through a multitude of channels. They tell a story,
for one thing, a story about the life and death of an architectural form,
about the entrance of the artist into the marketplace and into the cycles of
class warfare, about the technological and administrative transformation of
the modern city, about the dream life of an epoch as manifest in its cultural
products, most generally about the interpenetration of past and present in
the field of the 'dialectical image'. This spatiotemporal interpenetration – by
virtue of which the present, as dreamt once by the past, awakens from the
past it itself dreams – conditions the key motif of 'precursors' in the text
(that is, the anticipations and afterlives of cultural innovations), as well as
the key motif of superimpositions. It is worth noting, in this regard, how
often Benjamin returns to instances of superimposition in his evocation of
nineteenth-century interiors and street scenes, museums and exhibitions,
illustrations and window displays. Such effects play a part in what he calls
'the masks of architecture' (F1a,1). The *flâneur* sees – or rather feels – the
ghosts of earlier times and places haunting the streetcorners and building
facades he passes by (M1,1; M2,4); the collector, in gazing into the distances
of his object, summons up the various stages of its history (H2,7); the
hashish eater is witness to 'the colportage phenomenon of space', a myriad
of phantasmal figures and happenings from the past populating the room he
inhabits (M1a,3); the man who waits encounters an image of the expected
woman superimposed on that of some unknown woman (M°,15); the young
Marcel, at the opening of Proust's great novel, quoted by Benjamin towards
the end of Convolute K, finds a whole series of remembered rooms in which
he had formerly slept whirling madly through the darkness of the bedroom
in which he awakens one night in a state of disorientation (K8a,2).[17] In these
and many other passages of *The Arcades* (and this is true of the *Berliner
Kindheit um Neunzehnhundert* [Berlin Childhood around 1900] in a somewhat different sense), we meet with 'a past become space' (*GS* 5.2:1041/ *AP*,
p. 871), a past embedded in things, as the etymon is embedded in a word.

Memory is spatialized, at such moments, in more or less perceptible image-strata, something as in cinematic superimposition, or photomontage. One might also think of it as a collage effect, or a sort of palimpsest, through the translucencies of which the present is inscribed as the 'essence of what has been' (D°,6).[18] In the experience of a single passage, understood as a threshold in space and time, there may be a coexistence and coming-to-terms of distinct events, or levels of an event, including our reception of the passage in what Benjamin names 'the now of recognizability', that critical moment of interpretation at which a particular historical object attains to legibility, is actualized in a particular reading (N3,1).[19] In other words, the montage operates on both horizontal and vertical planes of language, of image space,[20] drawing the attention through various sequences as well as into the depths. We can thus see how a richly diversified diffusion factor – not unallied to the apperception of 'modern beauty' – is built into the compositional tendency of the work itself.

No doubt this makes for a peculiarly distracted reading experience, even if we read the text straight through from beginning to end. We make our way through the maze of passages like a *flâneur* at the mercy of his sensations: with a little practice, we start to pick up echoes and to sense the approach of apparitions as we focus in on some detail, which has suddenly come to life amid the shadows and the dust. Through the kaleidoscope of distractions, a manifold historical object, image of a past in the present, flashes into recognition: a facet reflecting that 'constellation of awakening' which Benjamin, at one point, posits as the basic tendency of his 'unfinishable' project on the arcades (N1,9; m2,1). In the dialectic of awakening that governs the thought of this strange ongoing reclamation project, we come awake only to the degree that we penetrate the dream. At issue here is 'that dream we name the past' (K1,3).

2

THE TIMING OF ELECTIVE AFFINITY: WALTER BENJAMIN'S STRONG AESTHETICS

JOANNA HODGE

The dialectical image is that form of the historical object that meets Goethe's demands on the object of analysis: it exhibits a true synthesis. It is the primal phenomenon [*Urphänomen*] of history.

(N9a,4)

Goethe here perfected the portrait of the writer as 'genius'. For if the great writer is someone who transforms his inner life into a matter of public interest from the very outset and simultaneously makes the questions of the day into matters of immediate concern for his own personal thought and experience, then it is in Goethe's youthful works that we find this type of the great writer in unmatched completeness.

(*GS* 2.2:709/*SW* 2:164)

I INTRODUCTION: BENJAMIN *CONTRA* DERRIDA

This chapter is constructed around an exposition of three antinomies, two set out in the writings of Walter Benjamin, and one to be developed in this introduction to account for the curious dissonance between the writings of Benjamin and the responses they evoke in Jacques Derrida's writings.[1] The two antinomies discussed by Benjamin provide a frame for adducing the antinomy between Benjamin and Derrida, and for exploring the relation between Benjamin's writings and Kant's aesthetics. This third antinomy provides a preliminary orientation for those who are perhaps more familiar with Derrida's responses to Benjamin than with the writings of Benjamin himself. Benjamin's writings pose formidable difficulties in both reading and exposition and I shall briefly indicate what I take to be the major obstacles preventing an adequate response to them, making it tempting to accept Derrida's readings as expositions, which Derrida himself would never claim them to be. The three critical difficulties posed by Benjamin's writings are their internal architecture; the complex relation to a notion of theology, on which Derrida's readings throw some light; and Benjamin's relation to Goethe. This last, to be discussed in the second part of the chapter, turns on Goethe's and Benjamin's preoccupation with a category of expressionlessness, retrieved from the writings of Spinoza. Underpinning all of these there is Benjamin's relation to Kant's philosophy, which I shall argue is a constant for Benjamin's writings.

In the 1930s, when he might appear to have moved furthest away from philosophy and most of all from philosophy as system, the Kantian distinctions between concept and idea, and between moral and epistemological issues are still in play in Benjamin's writings, and the notion of antinomy is emphatically deployed, in the context of a rethinking of the idea of progress. This then takes up and develops the notion of synthesis mentioned in the first of my two exergues, concerning Goethe's contribution to a thinking of the dialectical image. The second exergue introduces Benjamin's estimation of the significance of Goethe, as a marker for this notion of a strong aesthetics: one for which there is no gap between the specific configurations of human sensibility and the aesthetic processes of innovation and judgement. The second section of the chapter introduces an antinomy concerning art, through a discussion of Benjamin's shifting relation to Goethe. The third antinomy, concerning time, is explored in the third section with the assistance of a differentiation between Kant and Benjamin on the scope of aesthetics. Since Kant is the inventor of the notion of antinomy in this sense, it is especially suitable to lead up in this way to a discussion of Benjamin's borrowing from Kant's critical system. The chapter, after this introduction concerning theology and an antinomy constituting the differences between Benjamin and Derrida's writings, consists in two main parts: a discussion of Benjamin's reception of Goethe, led by this opening citation from *The Arcades Project*; and a discussion of the implied contrast between the strong aesthetics of my title and the notion of weak messianism, advanced by Benjamin in the 'Historical Philosophical Theses' of 1940. The proposal is to read Benjamin's writings as aligned to Kant's aesthetics rather than to Derridean messianism.

The part concerned with Benjamin's reception of Goethe focuses on a parallel between Goethe's enthusiasm for Spinoza and Benjamin's enthusiasm for Rosenzweig. It will set on one side the apparent opposition between Benjamin and Goethe, introduced in the conclusion to the *Origin of German Tragic Drama*, where Benjamin displaces Goethe's emphasis on a role for the symbol in art, privileging instead the disseminations of allegory. When Goethe affirms and Benjamin denies priority to the symbol for the purposes of artistic analysis, they are not, I suggest, addressing themselves to a single neutral content. Indeed, the citation concerning the dialectical image makes it clear that in the refinement of that notion, it is to Goethe rather than to some theorist of allegory that Benjamin appeals. It would be a task for another occasion to show how what Goethe proposes under the endorsement of the notion of the symbol, and what Benjamin endorses through the notion of dialectical image can be thought together without sacrificing Benjamin's affirmation of allegory. Indeed it may be that the disputation of the role of symbol is directed not so much at the work to which Goethe puts it but rather to its re-affirmation in the reception of Goethe. This suggests a process of emergence for Benjamin's distinctive mode of enquiry, out of the academic writings of 1917–1926, arriving at the affirmation of allegory, but not abandoning the Kantian infrastructure of inquiry, nor yet the commitment to theological categories. The works of Goethe and of Kant in and of themselves might be thought to present two halves of an antinomy to be resolved by Benjamin's writings, but this will not be explored here.[2]

There are three main writings between 1917 and 1926: the doctoral dissertation *The Concept of Criticism in Early German Romanticism*; the study of Goethe's *Elective Affinities*; and the study *The Origin of German Tragic Drama*, which was intended by Benjamin to provide his *venia legendi*, his access to an academic career. I shall not be discussing the last of these in any detail. Walter Benjamin, born 1892, died 1940, moved through a number of career options, driven on from one to another by the economic and political crises of his day. This tempts his less perspicacious readers to split his work up into phases. He is at first a gentleman scholar, until the Weimar inflation eroded his inheritance; he is then political journalist, until National Socialism in Germany rendered his writings unpublishable; he is the exiled intellectual, until the occupation of Paris by the Nazis; and, at the end, he is martyr to the cause of intellectual self-determination. His reworking of theology remains, however, curiously illegible. There is however an invariant in his writings which puts in question the customary supposition that his writings fall into these distinct phases: a literary theological phase, aiming towards an academic career; a political critical phase, aiming towards a political engagement; and a final theological melancholy phase, tending towards self-immolation. This is the recasting of theology. The famous image, the chess-playing automaton, from the 'Historical Philosophical Theses', marks the return of theology in his writings, after attempts to convince Adorno amongst others of his political critical soundness. For the deployment of theological categories remains suspect to the emphatically secularized interests of such analysis. However, only through these categories can his theoretical commitments be made sense of, for these theological categories provide him with the wherewithal to disaggregate time into discrete constituent parts, which forms the kernel of his thinking.

The first of the historical theses invokes the chess-playing machine, which wins the intellectual debate in the name of historical materialism by using theological categories. This is to be understood as combining, without merging, the theological preoccupations of his youthful writings, with his Marxist critiques of both bourgeois and fascist political orders, and his intellectual commitments, as coterminous one with the other. The first thesis famously runs:

> There was once, we know, an automaton constructed in such a way that it could respond to every move of a chess player with a countermove that would ensure the winning of the game. A puppet in Turkish attire and with a hookah in its mouth sat before a chessboard placed on a large table. A system of mirrors created the illusion that this table was transparent on all sides. Actually, a hunchbacked dwarf – a master at chess – sat inside and guided the puppet's hand by means of strings. One can imagine a philosophic counterpart to this apparatus. The puppet called 'historical materialism', is to win all the time. It can easily be a match for anyone if it enlists the services of theology, which today, as we know, is small and ugly and has to keep out of sight. (*SW* 4:389)

Benjamin deploys theological categories to disturb and delimit the liberal consensus concerning the nature of progress and of time. He deploys Marxist categories to demonstrate the inextricability of artworks from their historical and temporal indices. These two operations are inseparable from one another and constitute his strong aesthetics. For in each case there is a critique of an emptying out of time, as simply the medium for realizing cumulative progress in human affairs, and of the evacuation of historical specificity in the name of eternal aesthetic value. Here then there emerges a challenge concerning a secret complicity between the natural and the human sciences preventing an adequate thinking of time and temporality, instead fetishizing it as linear succession and eternity respectively.

Benjamin's deepening interest in the possibility of a Jewish theology is in part a response to Franz Rosenzweig's *The Star of Redemption* (1921) but is also in response to the writings of Hermann Cohen.[3] What is most significant about Rosenzweig's book for Benjamin's purposes is the rigorous separation of a moment of creation, from those of manifestation or revelation, and of redemption. This provides Benjamin with a model for a thinking of time as discontinuous. Whereas for Christianity the revelation of Christ provides the believer with an understanding of the connections between divine creation, the coming of messiah as redeemer, and the grounding of redemptive hope in that revelation, the theology developed by Rosenzweig is concerned with charting discontinuity, between the differential times of fulfilment, in creation, of revelation and of redemption, understood as quite distinct one from the other. There is no entry of divinity into profane time and no possibility here for the construal of a rationalist theology. Thus the distinctions which are constitutive for Christian theology, between rationalist theology, negative theology, and mystical theology are not constitutive for the theological thinking invoked by Benjamin: for there never was a rationalist theology in the Jewish tradition, except as providing a mythological underpinning for the iron fist of persecution. This is a theology of discontinuous temporalities and withheld unifications.

While the contrast implied in my title between strong aesthetics and weak messianism assists identification of Benjamin's take on Kant, the notion of weak messianism also invokes the Derrida reading of Benjamin. Derrida refers to Benjamin in his discussion of weak messianism in *Spectres of Marx: The State of the Debt, the Work of Mourning, and the New International* (1993) and also in his essay on Religion from 1994, 'Faith and Knowledge: The Two Sources of "Religion" at the Limits of Reason Alone', the title of which combines the titles of Bergson's and Kant's discussions of religion.[4] Derrida has returned to readings of Benjamin on a number of occasions since 1978; and their differences can be understood only in the context of this series of encounters and in the context of a conflict concerning the inheritance of Kant in the twentieth century. The latter, the conflict concerning Kant, and not the former, Derrida's reading of Benjamin, is my theme here.[5] The relations to be foregrounded between Benjamin and Goethe, and between Benjamin and Kant, serve as a frame for an analysis of Benjamin's notions of hope and redemption, his work of retrieval of theological categories, and his distinctive deployment of them in relation to non-religious contents.[6] Indeed it is Benjamin's retrieval of these theological categories to which Derrida objects and with which many of Benjamin's readers find it hard to come to terms.

The differences between Benjamin and Derrida may then be summed up aphoristically as the one engaged in theology without religion and the other by religion without theology. Of religion Benjamin writes in notes from 1919 to 1920:

> 5A: What is at issue here is not the 'realization' of divine power. On the one hand, this process is the supreme reality; on the other, divine power contains its reality in itself (Bad terminology).
> B: The question of 'manifestation' is central.
> C: 'Religious' is nonsense. There is no essential distinction between religion and religious denomination, but the latter concept is narrow and in most contexts peripheral. (*SW* 1:227)

In his 'Religion' essay, from 1994, by contrast, Derrida writes of two names for a duplicity in the origins of religion: the messianic, as a category of divine revelation, and the Platonic *chora*, in the register of Greek theogony:

> First name; *the messianic or messianicity without messianism. This would be the opening to the future or to the coming of the other as the advent of justice, but without horizon of expectation and without prophetic prefiguration. The coming of the other can only emerge as a singular event when no anticipation sees it coming, when the other and death – and radical evil – can come as a surprise at any moment.*[7]

It is worth noting here that the notion of radical evil here invoked makes reference to Kant's discussion of evil in *Religion Within the Bounds of Reason Alone*. This splitting of the phenomena under investigation into two distinct registers, as evoked by the two distinct names, is a device characteristic of Derrida's strategy of putting in question the unifiability of the series of phenomena under discussion, in this case, the phenomena constituting the domain of religion. His use of the term 'name' here contrasts to Benjamin's continuing use of the Kantian terms, idea and concept, with the implication of a philosophically determinate distinction between them. In his early essay on language, Benjamin deploys the notion of naming to quite other ends, to set up a distinction between univocal Adamic naming and the disseminations of natural languages.

Derrida deploys the notion of weak messianism against the phenomenological notion of a given horizon, within which what there is appears. The notion of a given horizon posits, as weak messianism does not, a thinking of the future in conjunction with the thinking of present and past. Benjamin, however, has no commitment to any such notion of a horizon. In 'Marx and Sons', clarifying the differences opening up between his theoretical concerns and those of Benjamin, Derrida adduces the following, in a response to the papers addressed to him:

> For I do not believe, as Hamacher and Jameson do, that the continuity between the Benjaminian motif and what I am attempting is determinant – or, above all, that it is sufficient to account for what is going on here. One should not be too quick to recognize and identify things, even supposing that Benjamin's purpose were, in itself, sufficiently clear and identifiable for one to be able to identify something else with it. I do not mention the possibility of this discontinuity with Benjamin in order to lay claim to some sort of originality but simply to clarify in programmatic fashion a number of points.[8]

Thus Derrida too appears to be of the view that the relation between his and Benjamin's writings is by no means straightforward, and, as I hope to show, Benjamin has other, quite distinct theoretical concerns. As a marker for these differences, Derrida characteristically here finds a duplicity of irresolvable slippages of meaning, between Greek theorizings of origins and the messianic religions. Benjamin by contrast sets about defining antinomies presented in extant theorizing, in order to propose a transformative thinking of their resolution.[9] The lines of dispute between Derrida and Benjamin permit a re-evaluation of the status and impact of theological categories in philosophy, making it possible to put on one side the Hobson's Choice of either accepting these categories as doctrine for the faithful or engaging in the futile gesture of atheistical rejection. Benjamin's deployment of the theological categories creation, revelation, and redemption is one in which there is no overarching salvation history and no single unifying account of a horizonal temporality in which all times are brought into relation one with another. The effect of a disaggregation of a unified time, which Derrida achieves by rewriting *différence* as *différance* and by insisting on the differences between the finite time of unfinished history and the non-finite time of Hegelian speculative philosophy, Benjamin accomplishes by insisting on the differences between thinking these theological categories from the stance of the messiah who died on the cross, and the messiah as Elijah who will come and make whole the contract between God and his people.

II BENJAMIN AND GOETHE: ON EXPRESSIONLESSNESS

In the study *The Concept of Criticism in Early German Romanticism*, Benjamin takes up the tradition of German Romanticism and of German idealism, but in a context where he can recast the constitutive categories of that thinking independently from any endorsement of one true religion, Christianity.[10] This perhaps is the key to his admiration for Goethe. Kant is at pains to separate the moment of philosophical critique from that of formulating doctrine, and from that of theological conceptualization, thus freeing the philosophical conceptualization for deployment in non-doctrinal non-dogmatic contexts. Goethe goes one step further in his enthusiasm for Spinozan pantheism. Each, Kant and Goethe, thus makes available a theory of knowledge and indeed an account of art, which do not render them subordinate and inferior to a divine knowledge and a divine creativity. This context of reading also inflects Benjamin's responses to the Hegelian and Marxist traditions, which are marked by a running together of theological, philosophical and political motifs, in a way which accords with Benjamin's own skill in pursuing hybrid inquiry. Hegel and Marx already deploy theological categories in relation to analysis of the supposedly secular world; Benjamin continues the strategy of releasing those categories from their mooring in religious ritual and doctrine. There is here a thematizing of hope, without faith, by contrast with Derrida's interest in thematizing faith, without theology, in, for example, *The Gift of Death*.[11] The concluding line of the Goethe study runs: 'Only for the sake of the hopeless ones have we been given hope' (*SW* 1:356). This invention of a theology without faith, centred on a hope against hopelessness, suggests a different take on the challenge to think the Holocaust in relation to theology.[12]

Benjamin's correspondence reveals the impact on him of a reading of Franz Rosenzweig's *The Star of Redemption* (1921), published the year after Rosenzweig's study of Hegel, *Hegel and the State* (1920). *The Star* is most remarkable philosophically for its undoing of the unifications imposed by Hegel on the categories of theology, philosophy, art, and everyday life, instead thinking incommensurabilities between the domains of metaphysics, meaning, and metaethics. There is a marked return here from Hegelian triumphalist philosophizing to the incompleteness of infallibility marked up in the Kantian system, with its delimitation of the scope of knowledge, which starkly contrasts to the announcement in Hegel's *Phenomenology of Spirit* (1807) of a fulfilment of meaning in the notion of absolute knowledge. Benjamin's appreciation of Rosenzweig underpins the greater confidence of his treatment of theological motifs in the 'Elective Affinities' essay, by contrast to their deployment in the *Concept of Criticism*. A similar kind of impact may be read into Goethe's responses to Spinoza, which provided a basis for Goethe's affirmation of a philosophy of nature, separate from and in contrast to the religions of his day. It would be a task for another place to compare and contrast the reception of Spinoza in Hegel's philosophical system and in Goethe's implied philosophy of nature. Of Spinoza, Goethe writes in *Dichtung und Wahrheit*:

> After seeking through the world in vain, to find a means of cultivation for my unusual nature, I at last fell upon the *Ethics* of this philosopher. It would be impossible for me to render an account of how much I drew from my perusal of the work itself and how much I myself read into it. Enough that I found in it a sedative for my passions, and that it seemed to open out for me a free and boundless view of both the sensible and the moral world. But what especially riveted me to him, was the utter disinterestedness, which glowed in his every sentence.[13]

And in a bravura gesture, characteristic of Benjamin himself, Goethe denounces Bayle for his remarks on Spinoza, in the famous dictionary, 'a work as valuable for its learning and acumen, as it is ridiculous for its gossip and scandal'.[14] Spinoza's impact on Goethe may then be likened to that of Rosenzweig on Benjamin, in providing an emphatic disruption of constraints on thinking. There are then elective affinities between Goethe and Spinoza, between Benjamin and Rosenzweig, and between Benjamin and Goethe to be traced out.

The notion of an elective affinity is rendered emblematic by the title of Goethe's novel from 1809, *Die Wahlverwandschaften*: 'elective affinity', or 'chosen relationships'. This novel was the focus for a detailed study and critique composed by Benjamin, between 1921 and 1923. In this study, Benjamin sets about producing a form of immanent reading of literary texts, by contrast to the approach of Gundolf's book on Goethe, so vividly denounced by Benjamin in his notes towards a review: 'He remains satisfied with stretching out some fragile strands of linkage between Goethe and aspects of modern literature while the significance of Goethe for the most distinctive and deepest task of contemporary life remains completely closed to him' (*SW* 1:98). Benjamin denounces Gundolf's use of literary historical context and biographical details as simple obfuscation, occluding any actual response to what happens in the texts themselves and rendering the notion of history impenetrable. This then establishes a first and important principle in the construction of Benjamin's writings: he is almost always polemically engaged in opposition to some style of writing which he identifies as inept, obfuscatory, meretricious, or downright misleading. Gundolf was the leading literary critic of the day, a professor at Heidelberg, and in setting himself in opposition to him, Benjamin was engaging in a high-risk strategy well designed for bringing to an end his hopes for academic recognition.

A discussion of Goethe is indicated by Goethe's place in the earlier study, *The Concept of Criticism in Early German Romanticism*; as indeed is a discussion of the novel form, which is identified in early Romanticism, as discussed by Benjamin, as the highest form of its reflective methodology, in pursuit of a schema for the infinitude of art and of its unity. The version submitted and accepted *summa cum laude* by the philosophy faculty at the University of Bern did not include the section on Goethe, added as a critical, indicative afterword, for circulation among his friends and peers. In the suppressed section of the essay, Benjamin sets out an antinomy for the concept of art, between two accounts of the work of art: the early German Romantic view, as reconstructed by Benjamin, and a view attributed by him to Goethe. The contrast is held in place by the affirmation in early German Romanticism of an idea of art, as an a priori of a method, privileging an endless task of perfecting its forms and genres; by contrast to Goethe's insistence on a privilege to an ideal of art, as its realization in a perfected content. Benjamin sums up the antinomy in the following way:

> The Romantics defined the relation of artworks to art as infinity in totality – which means that the infinity of art is fulfilled in the totality of works. Goethe defines it as unity in plurality – which means that the unity of art is found again and again in the plurality of works. This infinity is that of pure form; this unity is that of pure content. (*SW* 1:183)

A pure content is one which exhausts the meaning intentions from which it arises, and is thus, in Spinoza's sense, expressionless. Benjamin then claims, again in the part of the thesis not submitted, that the fundamental systematic question of the philosophy of art is a questioning of this relation between the idea of pure form and the ideal of pure content in art, to which he returns in *The Origin of German Tragic Drama*.

Benjamin's epigraph to the *Concept of Criticism* suggests his solution to this problem: the Romantic synthesis concerning art is no synthesis: it is still only an aggregate. The citation is from Goethe, and it runs: 'Above all, the analyst should inquire or rather train his eye to see whether he has really found a mysterious synthesis or is only dealing with an aggregate, a juxtaposition ... and to see how this all might be modified' (*SW* 1:116). Benjamin characteristically adds a crucial clue by returning to the context of this citation in a footnote, 145 in the German, 149 in the English, in the course of his discussion of reflection. I shall cite this lengthy footnote as a whole. It is attached to the remark: 'What in Fichte holds true of the "I", in Novalis holds true for the natural object and becomes the central tenet of his philosophy of nature at that time' (*SW* 1:147–8). Benjamin identifies in Goethe's thinking a notion of an empirical observation of nature as providing a privileged route to knowledge of what there is. The footnote then reads:

> This perception bears on Goethe as well. Clearly the ultimate intention of his regard for nature does not at all coincide with the romantic theory in question from which he stood removed. Nevertheless considered from other perspectives, Goethe's work displaces a concept of experience [*Empirie*] which is very close to the Romantic concept of observation. 'There is a tender empiria that conforms intimately to its object and that, through identification with it, becomes its true and proper theory. Such heightening of the spiritual faculty, however, bespeaks a highly cultivated age.' Goethe, *Werke* (Weimar, 1887–1914) part 2, vol. 2, pp. 128 ff. This 'empiricism' grasps what is essential in the object itself; therefore, Goethe says: 'The highest thing would be to understand that everything factual is already theory. The blue of the sky reveals to us the fundamental law of chromatics. Only one must not look for anything behind the phenomena; they are themselves the doctrine' (*Werke,* part 2, vol. 2, p. 131). By virtue of its self-awareness, the phenomenon is the lesson for the Romantics, too. (*SW* 1:192)

Thus in the second half of the footnote Benjamin identifies Goethe as refusing a distinction between empirical observation and an essential determination in some other register. This then provides a second principle for making sense of Benjamin: he is perfectly content to approve of his sources selectively. In this case taking up Goethe's emphasis on an observational empiricism as not opposed to essentializing critique, while rejecting the emphasis in his writings on the symbol, which has led him contrarily to be aligned with romanticism. This return to Goethe to theorize phenomena might also be taken to be an oblique critique of the move in Husserlian phenomenology towards an idealism, which sacrifices the absolute priority of pre-predicative experience. Goethe's writings give Benjamin access to such a pre-predicative experience which is not susceptible to any displacement in favour of a return to a platonism, repressed or explicit.

The reason neither Benjamin nor Goethe fit into the systems of classification of their day is that they are engaged in a double subversion: of the distinction between art and nature (*physis* and *techne*); and of the distinction between criticism and observation (*Kritik* and *Beobachtung*). Benjamin states his case thus in the *Concept of Criticism* and it provides the clue to his enthusiasm for Goethe:

The task for the criticism of art is knowledge in the medium of reflection that is art. All the laws that hold generally for the knowledge of objects in the medium of reflection also hold for the criticism of art. Therefore criticism when confronting the work of art is like observation when confronting the natural object: the same laws apply, simply modified according to their different objects. (*SW* 1:151)

Through the notion of elective affinity Benjamin sets out a notion of singular unities, in which conjunctures of discrete particulars are bound together by a reconfiguration of the relation of space and time, such as to constitute both a unique object of aesthetic attention and a unique capacity for judgement of it, in the formation of a specially attuned sensibility, capable of responding to it. This foregrounds a thinking of a permeable relation between natural history and human self-determination, between nature and art. At this point it is important to turn to Benjamin's reception of Kant, for it is from Kant that Benjamin borrows the notion of antinomy, through which he poses the tension between Goethe's and early romantic concepts of art.

III BENJAMIN AND KANT

My title, as already remarked, implicitly juxtaposes two terms: the implicit notion of weak messianism, discussed by Derrida in his responses to Benjamin, and a new notion of strong aesthetics. This latter will be identified here as the distinctive feature of Benjamin's analyses which as often remarked consist in a curious hybrid of art criticism, aesthetic theory, conceptual analysis, and history of philosophy. There is an evolving relation between these genres of writing in Benjamin's writings, which will now be construed in terms of the emergence of this strong aesthetics. This style of aesthetics combines a thinking of the changing nature and status of artworks and a meditation on the changing nature and significance of time and temporality, by grounding both in an interaction between cultural activity and a transformation of human sensibility: the crossover from natural history to artistic activity and back. It achieves this result by deploying theological categories. Thus Benjamin's analysis takes up the dual positioning of the notion of aesthetics as both an account of artworks and an account, at least in Kant's critical system, of the formal status of time and space in relation to human understanding of phenomena in the world. It is thus necessary to reconsider the status of the transition from Kant's thinking of space and time in formal terms, in the transcendental aesthetic of the first *Critique*, to the re-determination of time in the third *Critique* as the moment of the arrival of the new, as the moment of dislocation or interruption, in the dizzying sensation induced by experiencing sublimity, and as the infinite horizon within which purposiveness plays itself out. In Husserl's terms, the first *Critique* provides a formal indication of the notion of time, which then gets recast as a materially given fulfilment in the third *Critique*.[15]

The status of theological categories for philosophy has been one of disrepute, with a long struggle dating from Descartes' *Meditations on First Philosophy* (1641) to put the thinking of the perfections of divine conceptuality on one side and thus to make room for the fallibilism of human reasoning. Indeed the reinstallation of theological categories can be understood as against the grain of the whole enterprise of modern philosophy. Kant's *Critique of Pure Reason* (1781) can be seen as yet another staging post in this struggle, whereby purposiveness is released from its embedding in a notion of divine providence. Benjamin's disruption of the Kantian system upsets Kant's careful containment of theological categories. This disruption is the other side of the bringing together of the themes of time and space as discussed in the first *Critique* and the themes of time and space as deployed in the third *Critique*, the *Critique of Judgement* (1790). There is then in the first half of the third *Critique* a discussion of aesthetics in the more familiar terms as the mode of access to artworks. Benjamin develops a challenge to the division between formal and substantive aesthetics, in the division between the transcendental aesthetics of the first *Critique* and the material aesthetics of the third *Critique*. He also poses the possibility of reversing the privilege usually granted to the determinations of time in the first *Critique*, over those of the third *Critique*.

Kant accepts from the Greeks a notion of aesthetics as the study of systems of sensation, and then, in line with the pattern of analysis distinctive of the first *Critique*, he sets out the formal conditions of possibility for the deployment of the faculty. This may be understood as a move necessitated by the enterprise of combining Greek philosophical categories, *aesthesis*, *noesis*, *phainesthai*, within a framework of a commitment to the Christian four last things: heaven, hell, death, and judgement. The dissonance between these two registers is one of the many aspects of the Kantian system to which Derrida draws attention. Thus sensation is grounded by Kant in an analysis of the pure forms of intuition, time and space, and to this he gives the title 'transcendental aesthetics'. This is then supplemented by two further determinations of aesthetics, as an account of the binding of the drives (*Triebfeder*) in the second *Critique*, and that of the third *Critique*. The determination of aesthetics in the second *Critique* releases the thinking of time from the constraints of finitude imposed on it in the first *Critique*, thus making possible a thinking, if not a conceptualization, of the immortality of the soul and the non-finite status of divine judgement. This makes possible a schematization of concepts of reason in relation to the requirements of this non-finite freedom, from which Kant deduces the typology, or model, of morally informed judgement. This of course is a morally informed judgement grounded in, but not deduced from, a commitment to the articulations of the categorical imperative in divine judgement, the Ten Commandments, and Christ's reformulation of them in the new commandment of the Gospels, as given by a certain lawyer, in Luke 10.27. The problem posed by the palimpsest effect of the New Commandments, overlaying the Old Commandments, is one explored by Derrida in his careful negotiations with Kierkegaard's texts in *The Gift of Death*.

In the third *Critique* Kant introduces the notions of aesthetic and teleological judgement, alongside the notions of logical and practical judgement analysed in the first two critiques. Aesthetic judgement he again splits in two, as empirical and pure judgement, along the lines set out in the first *Critique* of separating out the empirical exercise of judgement from its transcendental conditions as formal possibility. One remark from section 14 of the *Critique of Aesthetic Judgement* will suffice to indicate the kind of distinction in play:

> Aesthetic judgements, just like theoretical (i.e. logical) ones, can be divided into empirical and pure. Aesthetic judgements are empirical if they assert of an object or way of presenting it as agreeable or disagreeable: they are pure if they assert that it is beautiful. Empirical aesthetic judgements are judgements of sense (material aesthetic judgements): only pure aesthetic judgements (since they are formal) are properly judgements of taste.[16]

Benjamin disputes the division of empirical judgement from their empirical conditions and he disputes the division in the Kantian system into the determinations of the objects of science, through the categories of understanding, and the determinations of moral imperatives, through the concepts of reason. He thus puts in question the need for Kant to resolve the hiatus between these two registers of thought in the analysis of judgement in the third *Critique*. Judgement will come to play a different role for Benjamin, as a determination of time.

The key concept in the third *Critique* is that of purposiveness, which Kant discusses in two phases:

> This is the basis for dividing the critique of judgement into that of aesthetic and that of teleological judgement. By the first I mean the power to judge formal purposiveness (sometimes called subjective purposiveness) by the feeling of pleasure or displeasure; by the second I mean the power to judge the real (objective) purposiveness of nature by understanding and reason.[17]

In place of purposiveness, Benjamin will propose a conception of standstill, immobilization, for in this notion there comes available an affirmation, without merging, of the parallel processes of producing a unity in an artwork and of a determination of a unique specification of the relation between time and space. For Benjamin the catastrophe is continuation: 'The concept of progress should be grounded in the idea of catastrophe. That things "just keep on going" is the catastrophe. Not something that is impending at any particular time ahead, but something that is always given' (*AP* N9a,1). It is worth noting the deployment of the terms 'concept' (*Begriff*) and 'idea' (*Idee*), which retains the Kantian determination of the difference between concepts, as thought with determinate content, and ideas, as regulative principles. Benjamin's thus is an immanent rewriting of Kant's critical system, working some strands of it against other strands, rather than a challenge from the outside. This is Benjamin's distinctive mode of reading: inhabitation of the text of the other, with partial citation working to shift the conceptual apparatus in line with a shifting configuration of thinking, as responsive to changing historical conditions. For Benjamin, unlike Kant, endorses the notion of historical a prioris; and, unlike Husserl, abandons all formal a priorism in favour of Goethean realized contents. Indeed his writings can be seen as an exploration of the consequences of such a move.

Later in the *Passagenwerk*, Benjamin elegantly aligns the thought of the eternal return with a diagnosis of the mythological status of belief in an idea of progress and arrives at a sketch of his own undertaking: the development of a dialectical concept of historical time:

> The belief in progress in an unending perfectibility, an unending task in moral thinking and the representation of the eternal return are complementary. They are insoluble antinomies. With respect to which the dialectic concept of historical time is to be developed. By contrast to this, the representation of eternal return is just as flat a rationalization as the belief in progress is accused of being and the idea of progress is just as much a form of mythological thinking as the representation of eternal return. (D10a,5)

This provides a clue to his relation to Kant: for this is Kant's notion of antinomy, transformed for Benjamin's rather different purposes. In his essay 'Resentment Begins at Home: Nietzsche, Benjamin and the University', Irving Wohlfarth identifies the critique of Nietzsche at work already in the essay on Goethe's *Elective Affinities*.[18] He discusses how for Benjamin the Nietzschean image of Apollo the destroyer is a mask for an affirmation of a beautiful appearance, leaving art in place as a harmonious moment in conflict with the chaos of lived history. Wohlfarth points out how it is against this sham disruption that Benjamin mobilizes Goethe's exploration of the category of the expressionless moment, anatomized by Goethe in his *Elective Affinities*, and commented on by Benjamin:

> The expressionless is the critical violence, which while unable to separate semblance from essence in art, prevents them from merging. It possesses

this violence as moral dictum. In the expressionless the sublime violence of the true appears as that which determines the language of the real world according to the laws of the moral world. For it shatters whatever still survives as the legacy of chaos in all beautiful semblance: the false, errant totality – the absolute totality. Only the expressionless completes work, by shattering it into a thing of shards, into a fragment of the true world, into the torso of the symbol. (*GS*1.1: 181/*SW* 1.1:340)

It is the reading of Goethe, which gives Benjamin access to this Spinozan category of expressionlessness; and a violent appropriation of Goethe, and a transformation of Kantian critique are here emphatically brought together. It is important to note the manner in which Benjamin here simultaneously deploys the Kantian categories of a phenomenal realm of known relations and a moral realm of the categorical imperative, but displaces them by proposing an alternative account of their mediation to that offered by Kant in the third *Critique*. Benjamin proposes in place of the power of judgement, constructed out of a certain combination of faculties, and in place of the reflection, preferred by the early Romantic critics, the violence of destruction, in a conjugation of times designed to release the future from barbarity.

Here it is important to understand this expressionlessness, as invoking the Spinozan notion of substance, one which is fully expressed in its attributes, with no remainder, as analysed in the *Ethics* (1677). In the expressionless moment, there is no exteriority, no remainder, no time to come. This is a modality of existence for which there is no relation of a core essence to an exteriorized appearance, or semblance, which may or may not do justice to the core. Expressive power is reduced to zero by already having been actualized in the system of relations in which the existent consists. Benjamin then hypothesizes a molecularized Spinozan substance, each self-contained and complete in itself and this is Goethe's conception of the artwork, as excavated by Benjamin. In the contemporary essay 'The Task of the Translator', Benjamin writes concerning expressionlessness:

> In this pure language – which no longer means or expresses anything but is, as expressionless and creative Word, that which is meant in all languages – all information, all sense and all intention finally encounter a stratum in which they are destined to be extinguished. This very stratum furnishes a new and higher justification for free translation; this justification does not derive from the sense of what is to be conveyed, for the emancipation of this sense is the task of fidelity. (*SW* 1:261)

Language and by extension the artwork is the medium of revelation of truth, whereby what resists articulation momentarily becomes comprehensible for the reader or observer equipped to respond to the configuration presented in the artwork. In this moment of transient comprehension there is a standstill of historical time.

The notion of time invoked by weak messianism, the messianic, is one of interruptability. The time of historical process is interrupted, brought to a standstill, such that the 'then' of lost time may be brought into a now of recognizability. But this weak messianism remains agnostic concerning the nature of a time thus inaugurated, as a time of fulfilment. This version of messianism, then, confronted by the epistemological problems of explaining the thinkability of fulfilled time, and of thinking the temporality of the transition from fallen, dispersed time to fulfilled completed time, affirms instead a formal conception of time as limit and indication, of possibility of fulfilment, by contrast to a conception of time to be excavated from Benjamin's writings which transforms this formal indication of possible fulfilment into the performative register. This is the task of writing, which Benjamin undertakes anew with each of his writing projects. This is a molecular theology which will also have destroyed all other theologies, for in this analysis, the splitting of an actual world from a moral world is smashed in a revelation of morality as actual; and the splitting of a harmonious artwork from a scarcely concealed notion of the real world as a meaningless flux of forces, is similarly dissolved in favour of a true world as a fragmentation of the symbol.

The constitutive conceptual difference here is between a messianism transgressing Kant's delimitations, and a notion of messianism caught in the Kantian gesture of distinguishing between the task of critical delimitation of the scope of concepts and doctrinal exposition of the content of what can be known. This latter supposes that conceptual determination is practicable, indeed in Kant's view is only practicable, independently from ontological determination. By contrast to this weak messianism, Benjamin proposes a critical writing which performs a momentary retrieval of the past, in a 'now' of recognizability, on which he places an explicit temporal restriction:

> The dialectical image is a lightning flash. The Then must be held fast as it flashes its lightning image in the Now of recognisability. The rescue that is thus – and only thus – effected, can take place only for that which in the next moment is irretrievably lost. (N9,7)

Benjamin's achievement is to have formulated a kind of judgement, subordinating the formal analyses of time and of the concept to the temporal determinacy and finitude of the occasion for the singular judgement concerning specific aesthetic phenomena. A relation across time takes precedence in the constitution of an ephemeral meaning, which dissolves temporal continuity in favour of ontological coherence and comprehensibility. In this molecular theology, what there is exists only in the brief moment of naming, and then dissolves again as its conditions of existence and therefore its nameability cease to pertain.

CONCLUSION

Derrida and Benjamin in their differences concerning weak messianism rehearse an argument concerning the Kantian inheritance: are the lines of incommensurability drawn between the various deployments and combinations of the faculties, sensation and understanding, understanding and reason, reason and imagination, imagination and sensation; or should the lines of incommensurability be recast not in terms of faculties, and their distinct employments, but in terms of temporal differentiation itself? Derrida and Benjamin affirm a need for such a recasting but then disagree on the potential thereby released for a redeployment of theological categories. Derrida remains suspicious of the religious commitments appertaining to these categories. Benjamin is the more sanguine. Here a key question is whether or not Judaism is supposed in the twentieth century to have arrived at a formulation of a distinctive theology. If so, then a Christian monopoly on theology is at an end, and theological categories cease to carry their sectarian Christian commitments. Franz Rosenzweig's *The Star of Redemption* can be thought both to have inaugurated such a theology and to have suffered almost instant eclipse in the destruction of the tradition of European Jewry, in which alone such an innovation can be made sense of.

A truly Benjaminian task would be to retrieve that inauguration and to demonstrate the non-sectarian possibilities for theology. The three incommensurable temporal determinations of Rosenzweig's *Star* are those of an ever-enduring creation; of an ever-renewed birth of the soul; and the performance of an eternal future in redemption. Access to them is achieved through remembrance, a memory defined as cleansed of resentment. These ontologically differentiated notions of eternity contrast to the formal, limitless void of the scientific horizon and of the Kantian experience of sublimity. For Benjamin, the thinking of the temporality of incommensurability and of discontinuity makes the time of innovation and transformation the pivotal point for thematizing time, by contrast to a time of repeatability, of succession and unlimited dimensions, affirmed in the study of the natural sciences. In place of the empty time of a succession of 'now' points, in which physical events are supposed to take place, there is the full time of meaning coextensive with, and inseparable from, the transformation of understanding taking place there. The analysis of sensation in response to an artwork then is inseparable from and co-implicates an understanding of and receptivity to time and space as singular topologies in which the world is made anew, through which meaning and order flash up for a moment in time and then are lost: for the first and only time, and only temporarily there emerges an ordering of a chaos, which then returns. It is Kafka's door, which was meant for just one person and now is shut. There is then here the indicated abolition of the distinction between analysing transcendental conditions and identifying empirical givens; transcendental conditions on this account are unique to, and vary with, the determinability of meaning.

This is a world constantly brought into existence, and constantly abolished again, by its creator God.

3

MATERIALIST MUTATIONS OF THE BILDERVERBOT

REBECCA COMAY

Why should only idealists be permitted to walk a tightrope, while materialist tightrope walking is prohibited?

Walter Benjamin, quoted by Gershom Scholem

I SECULARIZATIONS

No idealist, but only a materialist deliverance from myth.

Benjamin, 'Karl Kraus'

What could be at work in the Marxist rendition of the theological prohibition of images? In *Negative Dialectics*, Theodor Adorno explicitly binds the by-now familiar critique of representation (mediation, mediatization, the society-of-the-spectacle) to the secular imperative to 'grasp the object itself' (*die Sache zu begreifen*) in its corporeal truth. Such a 'grasp' would seem to re-inflect the theological longing for redemption along decidedly a-theological lines:

> It is only in the absence of images that the full object could be conceived. Such absence concurs with the theological ban on images. Materialism brought that ban into secular form by not permitting Utopia to be positively pictured; this is the substance of its negativity. At its most materialistic, materialism comes to agree with theology. Its great desire would be the resurrection of the flesh, a desire utterly foreign to idealism, the realm of the absolute spirit.[1]

I propose to use this startling passage – a formulation which seems to announce nothing less than the recoil of the ascetic ideal upon itself – as a starting point to re-examine the well-rehearsed debate between Adorno and Benjamin.

What are we to make of this unholy marriage of theology and materialism? It will in any case be more than a question of finding vague parallels or surreptitious borrowings (an easy dig at Marxism as chiliastic 'creed' or 'dogma', a familiar nod towards the Jewish return-to-history): a question not of compatibility nor of complicity, but rather of an 'agreement' forged precisely where the antithesis would seem most intractable. For according to such a refunctioning of the monotheistic prohibition, the apparent mortification of the senses would come to signal not the familiar pay-off of supersensuous fulfilment – the sublime passage from physical blindness to spiritual insight (Oedipus, Teiresias) – but rather the vindication of the body itself at the very point of its most irreparable disfiguration. At its limit, then, materialism is said to absorb or reinscribe theology precisely in speaking of a restitution beyond every idealizing compensation and in this sense intransigently unconsoling.

How does the iconoclastic imperative get attached here to the promise of resurrection? And how would each or both, together or apart, withstand the temptation of otherworldliness? If the redemption of the suffering body precludes any representation or mediation of its singularity, this could only imply a kind of return outside the restricted economy of a salvation predicated on the compensatory exchange of commensurable abstractions. It would thus imply something other than the spiritual metamorphosis of a body raised to divine immortality, rationality, and *apatheia*. It would, in short, indicate the persistence of matter in its utterly unreconciled alterity.

Such redemption would therefore suggest something other than the *theiosis* of the perfected individual formed in the image of the incorruptible divine. This latter notion would inevitably substitute for the banished idol the essentialized image of an incorporeal God. Spiritual insight would redeem the blindness of corporeal vision.[2] 'Image of the invisible' (Colossians 1:15), the apparition of Christ would present the possibility of a vision ultimately purified of sensuous immediacy and thus the very promise of spirit's victory over dead matter. The transfiguration of the Pauline grain of wheat – 'sown in humiliation, raised in glory' (1 Corinthians 15:44) – presupposes the divine *oikonomia* of a redemption mimetologically secured through the figure of Christ as *imago Dei* and thus guaranteed to humanity precisely as bearer of the heavenly 'stamp', 'seal', or imprint.[3]

What would it mean to articulate the *Bilderverbot* without recourse to the sublimated mimetology of idealism? And what would a non-transfiguring resurrection begin to look like? It would be tempting but misleading here to quickly confront a 'Christian' with a 'Jewish' eschatology – Ezekiel's dry bones pitted against the spiritual body of St. Paul, the mended pot of the Sanhedrin[4] pitted against Augustine's recast statue – in order to mark the essential terms of opposition. The philosophical challenge of thinking a non-reconciling restitution remains nonetheless pressing.

'Redemption', as Benjamin writes (the allusion is here to Kafka), 'is no reward or recompense for existence but the last way out' ('*die Erlösung ist keine Prämie auf das Dasein, sondern die letzte Ausflucht*' (*GS* 2.2:423/*SW*

2:804)). At stake here is not the return of spiritual commensuration but rather a rupture all the more radical in being premised on an imperceptible difference – a 'slight adjustment' ('*eine Geringes zurechtstellen*' (*GS* 2.2:432/ *SW* 2:811)) – between this world and the next. Whatever the 'weakness' of the Messianic power (*GS* 1.2:694/*SW* 4:390) – the angel of history cannot linger, cannot awaken the dead, cannot make whole what has been smashed, and so on (*GS* 1.2:697–8/*SW* 4:392) – the very identification of the Messianic with the domain of transience or 'downgoing' (*GS* 2.1:204) [5] (the Nietzschean overtone is unmistakable) would suggest that redemption cannot be thought beyond or apart from the eternal return of bodily remnants or remainders, without totalizing compensation. If the dead cannot be revived this is no doubt for the same reason that they cannot be said to properly or securely die: 'Even the dead are not safe from the enemy if he wins' (*GS* 1.2:695/*SW* 4:391).[6] Our permanent *rendezvous* or assignation with 'past generations' (*GS* 1.2:694/*SW* 4:390) indicates precisely the tenacity of dead matter as that which haunts the plenitude of the living present. 'Living on' (*Überleben*) becomes thus the perpetual obsolescence that at once both defines and subverts tradition.

Adorno will evoke Kafka somewhat similarly (in *Prisms*). If the theory of the 'unsuccessful death' (Odradek, Gracchus) 'is the sole promise of immortality ... permit[ted] to survive the ban on images',[7] the very possibility of redemption would hinge precisely on the fact that it inevitably comes too late. Thus the famous litany of missed opportunities: philosophy's failure to have sublated itself in practice (*Negative Dialectics*), the bourgeoisie's inability to 'find a successor' (*Prisms*, 273/260), the necrology of art announced in the *Aesthetic Theory*. This guilty longevity – the flipside of Kantian deferral – testifies precisely to an imperative all the more urgent for being announced too late. 'The resurrection of the dead would have to take place in the auto graveyards' (*Prisms*, pp. 273/260).

Benjamin's dilemma

In the notoriously hermetic preface to his *Trauerspielbuch*, Benjamin identifies the regime of vision – *Schau*, *Anschauung*, the phenomenological projection of horizons – as the acquisitive or 'possessive' operation of the subject seeking confirmation in what it knows (*GS* 1.1:215/*OT*, p. 35). Famously, truth is said to resist this. Non-intentional and non-relational, truth, according to Benjamin's formula (which in this respect resembles that of Levinas), 'is not an unveiling [*Enthüllung*] that destroys the mystery but a revelation [*Offenbarung*] which does it justice' (*GS* 1.1:211/*OT*, p. 31).[8] It has become somewhat conventional to read here a continuation and radicalization of a certain tendency within both orthodox and heterodox Judaism towards an attenuation of any positive concept of revelation: the rabbinic emphasis on aurality (the 'voice from Sinai'), the kabbalistic emphasis on the divine name. In short: the hermeneutic excess of interpretation over meaning, and thus the demystification of every authoritative disclosure.

The predominance of language over vision, according to a convention, would suggest a certain privilege of Symbolic over Imaginary and thus the foreclosure of every fantasy of fusion. Visualization invites identification and thus inevitably the spectre of idolatrous confusion: the heterogeneity of the absolute requires a denunciation of 'beautiful appearance' (*schöner Schein*) as the renunciation of the appropriative order of the Same.

Benjamin will speak, indeed, of sacrifice. Beauty is to be immolated – but simultaneously seeks 'refuge' – on the 'altar of truth' (*GS* 1.1:211/*OT*, p. 31). The priority of 'truth' to 'beauty' in this context (Hermann Cohen is never distant[9]) will elsewhere provoke an extended invocation of a certain sublime (*GS* 1.1:181/*SW* 1:340): Kant, Novalis, the familiar 'fable' of the 'veiled image' of Isis, whose unveiling is said to be fatal – shattering, even castrating (*zusammenbrechend*) – for the inquirer (*GS* 1.1:216/*OT*, p. 37).[10]

The prohibition at work here is by no means a simple one. If Benjamin will invoke a traditional enough trope of truth-as-woman – inaccessible invisible inexpressible object of an impossible desire – this is not to reinstate mystery cults under the rubric of iconoclasm. That would be only to reduce the *Bilderverbot* to a simple esotericism – 'some enigmatic cruelty in actual meaning' (*GS* 1.1:216/*OT*, p. 36) – and thus ultimately to reify the lost object as simple positivity.

For the exposure of the truth here – the object neither 'veiled' (*verhüllt*) nor 'unveiled' (*enthüllt*) but rather the object itself in its 'being-veiled' (*GS* 1.1:195/ *SW* 1:351) – implies simultaneously both a 'surrender' (*GS* 1.1:184/*SW* 1:342) and an 'escalation of appearance (*Schein*) in a final and most extreme form' (*GS* 1.1:186/*SW* 1:344). The loss in representational or intentional mediacy would involve a corresponding gain in 'presentational' (*darstellende*) intensity whereby what is relinquished is enhanced, and this according to the very measure of its own negation. The very sacrifice of the aesthetic – Benjamin speaks in a related context of Proust's 'sacrifice' of character, plot, play of the imagination, and so on (*GS* 2.1:314/*SW* 2:239) – would be accompanied and indeed counterbalanced by the expansion of a certain 'image sphere' (*Bildraum*) in which language itself, as it will happen, comes to the fore.

The very kernel of the dispute between Benjamin and Adorno lies just here. For would not such a 'sublime' sacrifice appear to involve a compensatory logic familiar at least since Kant and Hegel: less is more, *qui perd gagne*, the slave logic of recuperative self-denial? How to redeem such a sacrifice from the rationalist calculus identified by Adorno and Horkheimer as the dialectic of *Aufklärung* – the mythic circle of renunciation and reward? What will prevent Benjamin's version of the 'saving of the phenomena' from reverting into a simple legitimation of the existent?

This will be precisely Adorno's final question to Benjamin.

II BEFORE THE LAW

In breaking a statue one risks becoming a statue ...

Jean Cocteau, Le sang d'un poète

How can a prohibition against images be enunciated? Is there not something profoundly contradictory about the very representation of the law forbidding representations of the absolute? Would not the law inevitably transgress itself in its own pronouncement? Would it not, indeed, stimulate the very iconophilia that it prohibits – this according to the irreducible imbrication of law with desire, proscription with enjoyment – and thus undermine itself in its very enunciation?

The issue here involves somewhat more than the double bind attendant on every law in its self-universalizing force and promise. Hegel had already identified that initial problem, a logical one, in his chapter on 'Force and the Understanding': this is the paradox of a law rendered vacuous by its formal repeatability and hence binding power.[11] It involves more, too, than the performative self-contradiction of a pronouncement delegitimating itself precisely by virtue of its own legality. To pronounce the *Bilderverbot* is itself to assume legislative authority – thus to identify with the origin of the law even if only in order to speak of it and on its behalf – in this sense committing self-idolatry precisely in order to restrict or limit it, contaminating transcendence in the very effort to protect its purity, assuming the essential guilt it would deter. *Follow me/do not follow me ...* Is not the *Bilderverbot* in this respect the most self-transgressive of all laws? Invoked in order to be violated – does it not indeed exemplify the ultimate impossibility of the law as such? There is, however, more than one way of responding to such an impossibility.

At issue here is not only the familiar psychoanalytic point (regarding the return of the repressed as neurotic symptom), nor only the Foucaultian one (concerning the positive productivity of the law in its very negativity). One might remark with equal cogency – this will be my essential argument – that if every prohibition both incites and requires a corresponding transgression, it is also conversely the case that through its apparent self-infraction the law only binds us closer (although to what remains undetermined). In this case the law's very inability to authorize itself may testify equally to an even deeper, if perhaps ultimately inscrutable, prohibition – but perhaps equally to the claim of an unspeakable desire.

Perhaps something more than dialectical reciprocity is at work in such a chiasmus of law-and-transgression. Perhaps in this doubly contaminating movement of self-deregulating regulation and self-regulating deregulation another relationship both to the law and to the image may begin to announce itself.

Ambiguity is the imagistic appearance of the dialectic, the law of the dialectic of the standstill.

Benjamin, 'Paris – the Capital of the Nineteenth Century'

Since Kant, if not indeed since Longinus, it has become habitual to remark on the 'meta-sublime' nature of the very law announcing the essential incommensurability between law and manifestation – the Second Commandment here taken to be not only the paradigmatic statement about the sublime but the very paradigm of a 'sublime utterance'[12] – suggesting the ultimate aporia of a law exemplifying itself precisely in pronouncing the impossibility of every example. Thus the Biblical warning regarding every possible (inevitable) reification of the law. Moses' smashing and rewriting of the tablets at Sinai expresses precisely the necessity of the second-degree iconoclasm necessary to sustain the law by mitigating its eidetic self-evidence, thus marking its origins in a prior event of self-erasure and hence its irreducible inscription within the domain of history. The replacement set – no longer identified as 'God's handiwork' (Exodus 32:16) but inexorably marked as substitute or simulacrum, writing rather than 'engraving' – as such signifies the impossibility of any immediate relation to the original. This announces the originary doubling of the law as the permanent imbrication of law and interpretation. 'It is from an already destroyed word that man learns the demand that must speak to him.'[13]

But if the law thus incorporates its own infraction as the very condition of its own articulation, it holds equally that every adherence is marked by a corresponding violation. The smashing of the tablets anticipates the pulverizing of the golden calf, which in turn in its literalizing aggressivity only confirms the charismatic power of the idol. The accusation of idolatry in this sense typically presupposes (as Hegel points out in his analysis of Enlightenment's crusade against superstition) a 'not very enlightened'[14] assumption regarding the relationship between finite being and the absolute, and for this reason mystifies the very act of demystification as a 'new serpent of wisdom raised on high for adoration'.[15]

And so on. The point is not simply a formal or logical one, nor is the issue quaintly theological. It exposes a risk which affects every radical politics. For the very renunciation of images threatens precisely to determine the future as a tabula rasa or blank slate receptive to the arbitrary projections of the present day. 'Homogeneous empty time' would be reinstated. The old 'geometrical conception of the future' – Bataille's expression – would be re-established. Even setting aside the familiar paradoxes accompanying the notion of a utopia determined essentially as the very absence of determination – the conventional picture of a world without pictures – the danger of abstraction remains ineluctable.

How to avoid a relapse into indeterminate negativity and thus immediacy? Does not every *Bilderverbot* presuppose the familiar Platonic series of bifurcations – essence/appearance, original/copy, truth/ideology – and hence a prolongation of the ascetic ideal?

Much would seem to be at stake here.

Politically: how to resist reifying negativity itself as the very consolation which is being denied?

Theologically: how to resist invoking negative theology as the symmetrical obverse of dogmatic fundamentalism?

We will not yet be able to name the law under which we stand.

Benjamin, *'Gedanken über Gerhart Hauptmanns Festspiel'*

There are, one might say, mythical and non-mythical articulations of the dilemma. That is: the inevitable circle of law-and-transgression can be entered in a variety of fashions. If, to introduce Benjamin's terms, the regime of fate is defined by the compulsive circle of guilt-retribution-guilt which turns the 'guilt context of the living' (*GS* 1.1:138/*SW* 1:307) into the nightmare of a 'never ending trial' (*GS* 2.2:412/*SW* 2:796) – from the tragic cycles of Greek drama to the protracted vertigo of Kafka's *Prozess* – such a regime also harbours an essential 'ambiguity' (*Zweideutigkeit*) (*GS* 2.1:199/ *SW* 1:249) which may conceal unexpected resources.

According to the terms of the 'Critique of Violence', the mythical origin of the law (cf. *GS* 2.1:154/*SW* 1:71–2) suggests 'the ultimate undecidability of all legal problems' (*GS* 2.1:196/*SW* 1:247) and eventually points to the inability of the law itself to determine practice. Thus Kafka's 'new attorney' no longer practises but only 'studies' law (*GS* 2.2:437/*SW* 2:815) – an impasse which will eventually receive its starkest formulation in Kafka's notion of a trial in which guilt is perpetuated even or especially in every effort at self-exculpation, as indeed in the very judgment which would delimit or contain it. 'Does it not turn the judge into the defendant?' (*GS* 2.2:427/*SW* 2:807). If this suggests (to Scholem's unease)[16] a final indeterminacy regarding the status of the law in its 'purest' or most paradigmatic form as a Last Judgment (now indefinitely protracted and hence de-finalized owing to its complicity with its object), perhaps no firm distinction can be sustained (at least by way of any tribunal of judgment or 'critical' discrimination) between the mythic cycle of retribution and the divine justice which would 'only expiate' (*GS* 2.1:199/*SW* 1:249).

Adorno has rehearsed the problem with irritating rigour. The inescapable imbrication of myth and enlightenment implies the persistence of superstition in the very 'taboo' which would eliminate it and as such the inevitable relapse of every demythologization into yet another demonology. The 'blank' purity of a world from which idols have been eliminated not only 'assumes the numinous character' of a reality still governed by fear and trembling,[17] but moreover represses the mimetic impulse without which happiness as such – the very possibility of reconciliation – remains unthinkable. Thus the inevitable inscription of the law forbidding representation within the logic of self-preservation. (Exodus 33:20: '... No man may see me and live.') Absence itself can in this sense become a defence or fetish. 'The destruction of illusion does not produce truth but only one more piece of ignorance, an extension of our "empty space", an increase of our desert.'[18]

Every move from here can be predicted. Every abstract or undialectical *Bilderverbot* both assumes and stimulates prudish fantasies of purity which only serve to reinforce the mystification under contestation while providing the familiar comforts of self-mortification. The mistakes of others are, as usual, for Adorno, instructive. From Kierkegaard to, yes, finally, Schönberg, a slavish adherence to the law satisfies a priggish need for punishment while releasing a stream of phantasmagorical productions. Thus Adorno's infamous diagnoses. Kierkegaard's longing for 'imageless presence' expresses the (class-based) asceticism which would – in its eagerness to repudiate every finite semblance obstructing the 'infinite good of happiness' – only reinscribe the latter within a sacrificial calculus of 'goods' or acquisitions, and would in this way mistake the 'emptiness of the concept' for the desired gratification.[19] Veblen's desire for a clean slate is found to be a variation on this. The 'splendidly misanthropic' invective against the regime of kitsch or spectacle (*Prisms*, 77/79) presupposes as the price of its insight a Platonizing blindness with respect to the world of 'deceptive appearances'; this only reproduces the puritanical fantasy of a fresh start regulated by the bourgeois 'idol' of production (*Prisms*, 83/83). Ditto (*mutatis mutandis*) the curmudgeonly abjection – resentful, crypto-Christian – of a Huxley. 'His anger at false happiness sacrifices the idea of true happiness as well' (*Prisms*, 105/103). Not even Adorno's Schönberg in the end will be exempted. Schönberg's 'entanglement in the aporia of false transition' (*Prisms*, 170/164) will symptomatically betray itself, in *Moses and Aaron*, in a neo-Wagnerian monumentalism which will eventually elide the caesura between myth and monotheism and thus undermine the opera's own iconoclastic momentum: 'Moses and the Dance around the Golden Calf speak a single language'.[20]

And so on. It is not my interest here either to reprimand Adorno for his unkindness or to rehearse the familiar litany of counter-accusations regarding Adorno's own malingerings in the 'grand hotel abyss' of abstract negation. If there is something painfully self-revealing about Adorno's portrait of the raging penitent rubbing himself raw against the prison-bars of self-denial, the point is less to procure from Adorno a corresponding auto-critique (such confessions are not hard to extract, and tend in any case to neutralize themselves) than to consider the specific demand here placed on thought. Adorno himself formulates the dilemma with precision:

How is potentiality to be conceived if it is not to be abstract and arbitrary, like the utopias dialectical philosophers proscribed? Conversely, how can the next step assume direction and aim without the subject knowing more than what is already given? If one chose to reformulate Kant's question, one could ask today: *how is anything new possible at all?* (*Prisms*, 95/93)

It is around just this point that relations between Adorno and Benjamin will eventually become a little tense.

Adorno will finally force the question on Benjamin. Will Benjamin's version of Messianism evade the dilemma here presented as being quite irresistible? Will the dialectical image ultimately escape the antithesis between abstract negativity and the idolatry of the given? The question will also in the end be Horkheimer's. Does Benjamin's 'atheological theology' overcome the antinomy between positivism and otherworldliness? Is every image of the past condemned to confirm the present precisely by insisting on the possibility of redemption?

Both Adorno and Horkheimer will finally charge Benjamin with utopianism. Horkheimer convicts Benjamin of 'idealism': to form a dialectical image of the past is to occlude its 'closure' – 'the slain are really slain' – and thus to smuggle in some kind of eschatological horizon of consolation (*GS* 2.3:1332f.). Adorno, as we will see, charges positivism: to form any image of the future is inevitably to reify the present and thus to garnish the status quo with its ultimate apologia. Each will therefore come to diagnose Benjamin's problem as that of 'insufficient dialectics'. Too much theology on the one hand, not enough on the other: the symmetrical accusations typify what will indeed soon enough become the standard chorus of reproaches. 'Janus-faced', 'two tracked',[21] Benjamin's project will be found to fall 'between two stools'[22] – a graft as awkward as the stitching of a 'monk's cowl' onto the withered body of historical materialism.[23]

III   ILLUSION OF A FUTURE

A prophet facing backwards.

Friedrich Schlegel

An early text of Benjamin's presents the problem 'figuratively' (*in einem Bilde*) (*GS* 2.1:203/R, p. 312). If the disjunction between theology and materialism implies simultaneously a reciprocity, this means, at once, both a foreclosure of every progressivist, secular eschatology and a vindication of its deepest claims. 'Nothing historical can relate itself on its own to anything Messianic.' Such a notion relates not only to the apocalyptic mystical strand of Judaism (as glossed by Scholem), but equally (something often overlooked by Benjamin's readers) to a certain rationalist tradition running from the Babylonian Talmud through Maimonides and beyond.[24] This means that a

cataclysmic rupture divides the profane order of history (*olam hazeh*) from
the kingdom of God (*olam haba*).

'From the standpoint of history', the Kingdom of God – redemption – 'is
not the goal [*Ziel*], but the end [*Ende*]' (*GS* 2.1:203/*R*, p. 312). Every teleological determination of history reduces to a narrowly instrumentalist or
reformist series of improvements and adjustments – the opposition between
a Lenin and a Bernstein in this sense immediately collapses – only sanc-
tioning the hegemony of the present day.

Thus the familiar catalogue of renunciations – the historian as the prophet
facing backward (Schlegel), the modern Orpheus who now stands to re-lose
his Eurydice by looking ahead (Jean Paul). 'Accursed is the rider who is
chained to his nag because he has set himself a goal for the future' (Kafka's
bucket-rider) (*GS* 2.2:436/*SW* 2:814–815). The angel of history catches not
even a glimpse of the future to which his back is turned (*GS* 1.2:697f/*SW*
4:392). The 'destructive character' who 'clears away' without a constructive
'vision' of the future leaves 'for a moment, at least, empty space [*leere Raum*]
in which "ways" or "crossroads" might open up' (*GS* 4.1:397f/*SW* 2:541–2).
No image, similarly, inspires the revolutionary: neither 'the ideal of liberated
grandchildren' nor the utopia 'painted in the heads' of the Social Democrats
(*GS* 1.2:700/*SW* 4:394). The long view of historicist prognostication must
thus contract to the lightning flash of historical materialist intervention.

Benjamin explicitly links such a renunciation to the iconoclastic imperative of Judaism: 'we know that the Jews were prohibited from investigating
the future' (*GS* 1.2:704/*SW* 4:397). The messianic moment – 'Messianic
power' in the 'weak' sense (*GS* 1.2:694/*SW* 4:390) – remains as inscrutable
as ultraviolet rays. 'Whoever wants to know how a "redeemed humanity"
would be constituted, under what conditions it would be constituted, and
when one can count on it, poses questions to which there is no answer. He
might as well ask about the colour of ultraviolet rays' (*GS* 1.3:1232).

Kant avec Marx

The image (yes) presented by Benjamin's first thesis on history indicates the
complexity of the issue. Whatever the nature of the entanglement between
'theological' dwarf and 'historical materialist' puppet – collusion, codepen-
dence, unsublatable contradiction – the figure itself invokes the very spectre
of idolatry if only in order to demystify it. The automaton is in any case considerably less automatic than the animated images of Daedalus. To celebrate
the unfettered progress of the 'apparatus' – Social Democracy, from one
side, Stalinism, from the other – is in itself to fall prey to the transcendental
illusion which would hypostatize the absolute as already there.

Kant and Marx awkwardly join forces. The error of utopian socialism
would be precisely to blur the critical border between the 'realm of necessity'
and the 'realm of freedom' – the vocabularies of Kant and Marx curiously

coincide here – thereby contaminating the very ideal of communism with the empirical categories of the present day. Every effort to write 'recipes for the cookshops of the future'[25] is guilty of this. Hegel saw this clearly in the preface to the *Philosophy of Right* when he rejected the popular demand to 'give instruction' (*Belehren*)[26] – to construct the world 'as it ought to be' – as presupposing an undialectical collapse of the critical gap between *Sein* and *Sollen*, constative and performative, thus introducing the spectre of unmediated abstraction.

For Marx such a collapse marked the secret complicity between ideology and utopia. The 'chimerical game' of painting 'fancy pictures of the future structure of society'[27] could only whitewash the existent precisely by 'leaving out the shadows'.[28] For Kant such a collapse would introduce the illegitimate miscegenation of a theoretical noumenology. To the 'magic lantern of phantoms' projected by natural theology[29] would correspond the commandeering gaze which would 'behold' or 'prove'[30] what should remain properly conjectural. Presumptive insight (*Einsichtsfähigkeit*) would thereby usurp the place of the 'weak glimpse' (*schwache Blick*) of reason.[31] The reduction of the law (freedom) to the conditions of phenomenality could only reduce action to the 'lifeless' gesticulations of a 'puppet' governed by fear and trembling. Hypertrophic enlightenment would in this way come to signify nothing but the tutelage of a mortified nature.

In either case the result is fetishism: to depict redemption as a logical extension of the present is effectively to confuse potentiality with facticity, freedom with necessity, and thus only to confirm one's own immersion in the imaginary. Every 'ideal of liberated grandchildren' (*GS* 1.2:700/*SW* 4:394) cannot fail, in this sense, to function ideologically. The very faith in a better future secretly sanctifies the given by offering placating pictures which would only distract the viewer from the most urgent imperatives of the day. To honour the false god of progress is precisely to fall victim to the 'system of mirrors' creating the optical illusion of 'transparency', Enlightenment, or clear sight. If theology today 'has to keep out of sight' (dwarfish, 'small and ugly') (*GS* 1.2:693/*SW* 4:389), this is ultimately because its promise contains the still unredeemed possibility of a happiness unrepresentable within the perspective of the present day.

Everything Benjamin writes, from the earliest exhortations to the youth movement through to the final 'Theses on the Philosophy of History' – thus the entire uneasy trajectory from hyperidealism to Messianism – will reiterate this basic point.

The Kantian commitments of the early writings establish the essential problematic. If the task of 'youth' is to keep open the critical 'abyss' (*Kluft*) (*GS* 2.1:31) between the absolute and the apparent, any premature sighting of the Idea is tantamount to the 'deadly sin' (*GS* 2.1:32) of naturalizing *Geist* by hypostatizing its incarnation as already or even foreseeably accomplished.

This would be the theological hubris of the 'great seer' (*der große Schauender*) (*GS* 2.1:32). Benjamin will target under an identical censure the otherwise contradictory conciliations proposed, variously, by German classicism, by the *Wandervogel,* and by the instrumentalism haunting Weimar, from the academic *Berufsgeist* to the progressivist optimism of *Der Anfang* – each of which will be convicted of a veritable 'idolatry of *Geist*' (*GS* 3:320) in its sterile affirmation of the existent.

Nietzsche had already identified the modern military state as the newest idol: a 'horse of death' masquerading in the name of life itself, and thereby 'clattering in the finery of divine honours'.[32] Thus, for the young Benjamin (already traumatized from the outset), the degradation of the Idea into the 'spirit of 1914' and the harnessing of the youth movement to the patriotic ratification of the status quo.

A certain optical conceit would indeed seem from beginning to end to mark the ideology of 'life' as that which prolongs by dissimulating the mortified condition of a fallen nature. Every gaze into the 'blue distance' (*GS* 2.2:620) – from the Romantic *Fernsicht* to the *schauendes Bewußtsein* of a Jung or Klages – would placate the viewer with the consolation of unattainable ideals all the more enticing for being eternal and thus present in their very absence.

Was not such an illusionistic distance precisely the 'urbanistic ideal' (*GS* 5.1:56/*AP*, p. 11) of the Second Empire?[33] Haussmann's boulevards would entice the spectator with the long perspectival vistas promising an infinitely deferred gratification (while at the same time effectively forestalling insurrection by preventing the building of barricades). The Eiffel Tower would offer a secure vantage point from which the spectactor could admire his progress, reiterating the general point underlying the architecture of all the nineteenth-century world expositions ('modern festivals' (G16,5) enabling the workers to gape at the very machinery which was rendering them superfluous), thereby confirming the Saint-Simonian 'fairy-tale that *progrès* is the prospect of the very near future (U4a,1). The glass architecture of the arcades would foster the illusion of the outside on the inside, promising a visual exteriority while in fact reinforcing the immanence of the exterior (meanwhile new technologies of artificial lighting would be turning the street itself into a domestic *intérieur*[34]), and would in this way mollify the demand for transcendence by providing the gratification of a good view. The crowds making their daily 'pilgrimage' (A2,2) to these 'enchanted grottoes' (a°,2) of consumerism would enjoy the spectacle of goods whose very appearance of availability only underscores the scopophilic regime of private property – 'look, don't touch' (G16,6) – while the peepshow panoramas were to provide the visual sensation of a progressive movement securely contained and oriented within the private confines of a box.

It is no coincidence that the cruciform structure of the arcades will be observed by Benjamin to resemble church architecture (A10a,1). If the arcades are seen to preserve perspectival space with the same tenacity as cathedrals (c°,2), this is ultimately because the phantasmagoria of progress here would involve nothing less than a generalized fantasy of resurrection. Dead things promise to come alive within these enchanted 'temples' (A2,2). Vision would seek to confirm itself through the specular return of a gaze emanating from a universe packaged as merchandise, whose inviting glances exemplify the 'theological caprices' of which Marx speaks. Thus Benjamin's re-articulation of the classic chapter on commodity fetishism: 'things' acquire speech, glance, personality – the anthropomorphic features stripped from a by now thoroughly reified humanity – in a chiastic transfer whereby the transfer of 'life' as such passes essentially by way of the eyes. Hence the multiplication of optical devices designed to prop up the subject's faltering sense of sight. 'The opticians' shops were besieged' (Y4,1). The phantasmagoric gaze of the object becomes one more prosthetic extension designed to confirm the eidetic powers of the subject[35] whose own ocular anxieties meanwhile betray themselves in obsessive fantasies of an uncanny non-reciprocity and non-simultaneity, as in Baudelaire's images of jewel-eyed statues, blank-eyed prostitutes, eyes gleaming as vacantly as mirrors (c°,2) or as shop windows – '*tes yeux illuminés ainsi que des boutiques*' (GS 1.2:649/SW 4:341). 'Jugendstil sees in every woman not Helena but Olympia' (S9a,2).

Vision would falsely promise here to fulfil the ego's fantasy of an immanence which would elide the temporal gap or non-identity at work in all experience. This is the ideological aspect of the idealist 'apotheosis of existence' (GS 1.1:337/OT, p. 160), exemplified by Weimar classicism and theorized as the reconciliation of finite and infinite in the visual plasticity of the symbol – interpreted, as always, Hegelian-wise[36] – as the 'sensuous embodiment of the idea' (GS 1.1:341/OT, p. 164). If such an incarnation of the noumenal involves a spiritual animation of nature and specifically the latter's self-representation, delimitation and perfection in the human – henceforth securely installed (*eingestellt*) along the sacral course of *Heilsgeschichte* (GS 1.1:337/OT, p. 160) – such a logic of substitution (*Stellvertretung*) (GS 1.1:341/OT, p. 165) involves a fundamental distortion (*Entstellung*) (GS 1.1:337/OT, p. 160) underwritten by a politics of 'domination' and 'usurpation' (GS 1.1:336/OT, p. 159) whereby not only allegorical distance is occluded but with it the radical transience and suffering of a finite nature (GS 1.1:343/OT, p. 166).

Such an occlusion would severely restrict the potential space of every action. In its 'seamless transition' from phenomenal to noumenal (the 'limitless immanence of the ethical world in the world of beauty'), the humanist apotheosis of the perfected individual would constrict the 'radius of action' to a mere 'radius of culture' (*Bildungsradius*) (GS 1.1:337/OT, p. 160), would misconstrue particularity (*das Einzelne*) (GS 1.1:343/OT, p. 166) as abstract inwardness or individuality (*Individuum*) (GS 1.1:337/OT, p. 160) – would, in short, condemn the ethical subject to the 'unmanly' posturings of the

beautiful soul. The beautiful images or 'constructions' (*Gebilde*) of the symbolic would efface the (Kantian) 'abyss' (*Abgrund*) dividing 'visual being
[*bildliche Sein*] from meaning' (*GS* 1.1:342/*OT*, p. 165) – phenomenon
from noumenon – and would thereby erase the 'jagged line of demarcation'
which etches the traits of nature's untransfigured countenance as 'untimely,
sorrowful, unsuccessful' (*GS* 1.1:343/*OT*, p. 166): the line of death.

In such a consoling vision of a transfigured nature, the 'enigmatic question' (*Rätselfrage*) is suppressed regarding human existence in its (historic)
specificity as tied inexorably to a fallen, transient nature (*GS* 1.1:343/*OT*,
p. 166). Such occlusion will ultimately define the barbarism underwriting
every 'document of civilization' (*GS* 1.2:696/*SW* 4:392) – the secret link
between humanism and militarism, 'the unity between Weimar and Sedan'
(*GS* 3:258). The seven-headed hydra of the *Geisteswissenschaften* ('creativity, empathy, timelessness, re-creation, *Miterleben*', etc.), with its vitalist
identifications and its 'lecherous urge for the big picture' (*GS* 3:286)
– historicism's 'bordello' (*GS* 1.2:702/*SW* 4:396) – would institutionalize
itself in the 'sacred groves' of 'timeless poets' (*GS* 3:289) and 'eternal
values' (*GS* 3:286), in a fanatic 'exorcism of history' (*GS* 3:289) which
would entrench the hegemony of 'Western man' under the cover of a uni-
versality posited as already there. It is in this sense that classicism is said
to culminate in the 'Germanic soteriology' (*GS* 3:254) whose 'Rettung'
(*GS* 3:257) (Benjamin's scarequotes) of the dead as *Vorbilder* (*GS* 3:255)
– objects of empathic identification – adds up to the *sauve qui peut* of a
triumphant nationalism. This would occlude the persistence of inherited
power relations through an appeal to the presumed continuities of race or
caste.

It is no coincidence here that such a soteriology is said to be orchestrated by 'seers whose visions appear over dead bodies' (*GS* 3:259). This
is the empathic gaze which would find spiritual return in a past reani-
mated as ancestral prototype or precursor – so too equally Benjamin's
eventual definition of aura as the inanimate object's ability to return the
gaze[37] – an idealizing revival of the dead which inevitably accrues to the
profit of the survivors in their triumphal march through the continuum
of time.

IV   *BILDERFLUCHT*: CRITICAL RESUSCITATIONS

Re(sus)citations

This is not to exclude the possibility of another gaze, another resurrection.
In the face of the 'blooming, blazing vision' (*blumenhaft flammende Blick*)
of neo-classicist revival, Benjamin opposes the (yes, still fertile) gaze of a
theoria which would again summon back the dead – not, this time, for adulation, but for interrogation.

We must stand ... by the inconspicuous [*unansehnlichen*] truth, the laconism of the seed, of fruitfulness, and thus of theory, which leaves behind the spell of vision [*Schau*]. If there are timeless images, there are certainly no timeless theories. Not tradition, but only originality [*Ursprünglichkeit*], can decide this. The genuine image may be old, but the genuine thought is new. It is of today. This today may be derelict, granted. But be that as it may, one must seize it firmly by the horns, if one is to be able to pose questions of the past. It is the bull whose blood must fill the pit, if the spirits of the departed are to appear [*erscheinen*] at its edge. (*GS* 3:259)

What exactly is the distinction introduced here between 'vision' and 'theory'? A temporal one, to begin with. Whatever the apparent continuities between flower and seed, between 'image' and 'appearance', there is (to be) a fundamental opposition between mythic violence, which would efface time by occluding the position of the present (thereby surreptitiously securing it), and the sacrifice which would vindicate the present precisely by exposing the latter's vulnerability and responsibility to – its 'secret rendez-vous' with (*GS* 1.2:694/*SW* 4:390) – the past.[38]

On this distinction rests the difference between 'tradition' and 'originality'. The former, we might gloss, aims at re-sur-rection: the spiritual transfiguration, exaltation, and uplifting of the dead as 'cultural treasures' (*GS* 1.2:696/*SW* 4:391) within the homogeneous continuum of mythic time. The latter aims at re-sus-citation: the solicitation or summoning of the dead as *Abhub* or unsublatable remainder within the fractured discontinuum of a history brought to a caesura or Messianic standstill. The measure of 'originality' is thus not the abstractness of a new beginning staked out within the historicist 'stream of becoming' (*GS* 1.1:226/*OT*, p. 45). It will express itself rather according to the diphasic 'rhythm' of a finite repetition whereby the past is restored or cited as radically 'imperfect' and 'incomplete' (cf. *GS* 1.1:226/*OT*, p. 45).

'Vision' thus sees a face: the specular return-to-self of the viewing subject as it narcissistically constructs itself through the consoling tête-à-tête with the beautified or transfigured other. 'Theory' sees a mask: the stain of the death's head whose vacant stare marks the radical alterity or non-coincidence of viewer and viewed, look and gaze (the Lacanian framework would seem here indispensable),[39] and as such the annihilation or traumatic wounding of the self-conscious subject hostage to the claim of an immemorial past. Such non-coincidence marks the scene of history as *facies hippocratica*, non-recuperable alterity, the one-way street of irredeemable transience and suffering.[40] 'It is as something incomplete and imperfect that objects stare out [*starren*] from the allegorical structure' (*GS* 1.1:362/*OT*, p. 186).

Symbolic resurrection – 'vision' – thus calls up the dead as object of consumption: the mourned object devoured or introjected as host or food for thought. Allegorical resuscitation – 'theory' – throws up the dead as indigestible remainder and untimely reminder, the persistent demand of unsublimated matter. Thus the appearance of the returning spirits as vampires feeding at the present's trough.

Resurrection, as we read in the essay on Leskov, is in this sense to be conceived less as an idealizing transfiguration than as a radical disenchantment (*Entzauberung*): humanity's liberation from the 'nightmare' of mythic immanence (*GS* 2.2:458/*SW* 3:157–8). Such a demystification cannot assume a (mythic) opposition between myth and enlightenment. The operative distinction would seem to work rather within the interstices of myth itself, at the point where myth points towards its own exterior or buried entrails. These are the little 'tricks' folded into the apparently seamless fabric of mythic identity – the 'liberating magic' of the fairy-tale's reassuring happy ending – Kafka's 'proof that inadequate, even childish measures may serve to rescue one' (*GS* 2.2:415/*SW* 2:799).

Theatres of Redemption

The only break from the spell of the imaginary is thus by way of a thoroughgoing immersion. If (as Adorno has insisted) every abstract foreclosure of images elicits a hallucinatory return (as symptom or delirium), it is perhaps conversely the case (this is now what we must consider) that a certain intensification of images may open a breach or rupture within the seamless continuum of mythic *immanence*, and thus indeed point precisely to the *imminence* of what is radically unforeseen. To wit: the apparent violation of the *Bilderverbot* may indeed attest to its most productive power.

Iconophilia itself (or its appearance) may indeed thus come to assume iconoclastic proportions. Writing of the Baroque extravaganza – the *folie du voir*[41] of a culture outdoing 'even the Egyptians' (*GS* 1.1:350/*OT*, p. 174) in effects of specularity – Benjamin perceives in the 'eruption of images' of the stage-world a style nothing short of 'sublime' (*GS* 1.1:349/*OT*, p. 173). The allegorical detachment of appearance from signification – the 'abyss separating visual being from meaning' (*GS* 1.1:342/*OT*, p. 165) – intensifies ocular possibilities so as to heighten the eschatological tension between immanence and transcendence, thereby 'securing for the latter the greatest conceivable rigour, exclusivity, and relentlessness' (*GS* 1.1:359/*OT*, p. 183). It is indeed the very profusion of images which will here block any fantasy of premature reconciliation.

If it is part of the very logic of modernity to convert every prohibition of images into yet another image of prohibition – thus the dazzle of negative signposts cluttering the urban landscape of *One-Way Street* ('Post no bills!', 'Caution: Steps!', 'No Vagrants!', 'Protect these Plantings!') – it will take 'heroic' (cf. *GS* 1.2:577/*SW* 4:44) measures to negotiate the aporia of such a specularity without term.

One-Way Street presents the by now familiar aporia vividly. Here the 'imperial panorama' of progress is seen only to prolong the claustrophobia of the interior. Thus the vista of a 'glorious cultural future' as ultimate domestic phantasm: a consoling 'mirage' projected against the 'folds of dark drapery' which mask and reinforce the confinement of the present day (*GS* 4.1:98/*SW* 1:453). Not even the most sublime landmarks would remain intact. Mountaintops are shrouded. 'A heavy curtain shuts off Germany's sky' (*GS* 4.1:99/*SW* 1:453). It would be clearly no escape here to appeal to the presumed neutrality of a 'critical standpoint', 'prospect' or 'perspective' (*GS* 4.1:132/*SW* 1:476). Such a perspective could only smuggle in the optical illusion of the panorama, would intensify the phantasmagoria in the very effort to see through it, would therefore reinforce immanence precisely in the claim to externality or transcendence. This is the nightmare of total theatre – Proust's aquarium,[42] if not indeed Aragon's[43] – the no-exit or 'dead end' (as *One-Way Street* was originally baptised) of our spectacular modernity:

> It is as though one were trapped in a theatre and had to follow the events on stage whether one wanted to or not, had to make them again and again, willingly or unwillingly, the subject of one's thought and speech. (*GS* 4.1:98/*SW* 1:453)

The 'way out' here can be figured, indeed properly staged, only as a dramatic pause within the phantasmagoria of total vision. If every premature attempt to quit the circle secretly prolongs what it would abandon (cf. *GS* 4.1:85f./*SW* 1:445), any rupture will require a certain collaboration with mythic forces and will thus assume an infinitely ambiguous guise. 'Costume Wardrobe' presents the scene of redemption as nothing more and nothing less than a theatrical occurrence:

> Again and again, in Shakespeare, in Calderon, battles fill the act, and kings, princes, attendants and followers 'enter, fleeing'. The moment [*Augenblick*] in which they become visible to spectators brings them to a standstill. The flight of the *dramatis personae* is arrested by the stage. Their entry into the visual field [*Blickraum*] of non-participating and truly impartial persons allows the harassed to draw breath, bathes them in new air. The appearance on stage of those who enter 'fleeing' takes from this its hidden meaning. Our reading of this formula is imbued with expectation of a place, a light, a footlight glare [*Rampenlicht*], in which our own flight through life may be likewise sheltered in the presence of onlooking strangers. (*GS* 4.1:143/*SW* 1:484)

Redemption – breath, here, as always – is thus figured within the *Blickraum* or *Bildraum* of consummated visibility. The decentring of the gaze (the transformation of spectator to potential spectacle) is here presented as a reversal without empathic reciprocity or symmetry. A Brechtian distance characterizes the position both of viewing subject and of object viewed.

This is the 'cunning' (GS 5.2:1213/AP, p. 907) – 'teleological' – whereby the dream, intensifying itself, pushes forward towards its own awakening.

There will, then, 'still be a sphere of images [*Bildraum*], and, more concretely' – for this very reason – 'of bodies [*Leibraum*]' (*GS* 2.1:309/*SW* 2:217). If the modern epoch, despite or because of its hypertrophic specularity, represents the ultimate laming or maiming of the imagination (*GS* 1.2:611/*SW* 4:316), it is the image alone that will come to redeem a body and a body politic fractured irreparably by the force of time. The expulsion of 'moral metaphor from politics' (*GS* 2.1:309/*SW* 2:217) – the elimination of the social-democratic *gradus ad parnassum* (*GS* 2.1:308/*SW* 2:216) – requires precisely the 'opening' or elaboration of a competing image sphere through which alone the body reconfigures itself in time.

This is not the project of aesthetic *Bildung*. In this version of a materialist last judgment, the suffering body submits to a 'dialectical justice' (Benjamin's rewriting of the Hegelian Bacchanalian revel) according to which 'no member remains unrent [*unzerissen*]' (*GS* 2.1:309/*SW* 2:217). The reconstitution of a new *physis* (*GS* 2.1:310/*SW* 2:217) or 'new body' (*GS* 4.1:148/*SW* 1:487) for the corporeal collective (*leibliche Kollektivum*) (*GS* 2.3:1041) involves the shattering of every fantasy of aesthetic harmony or immanence. If Benjamin here announces the onset of a veritable 'slave revolt of technology' (*GS* 3:238), this is not to be confused with the ascetic consolation which would (as in futurism) vitalistically sublate or aestheticize the mortified conditions of a damaged life. This is therefore not the resurrection of a body or a body politic spiritualized within the eternal community of mankind. If it is a fissured, epileptic (*GS* 4.1:148/*SW* 1:487) body which is to enter the final court of judgement, this is precisely so as to repel every mythic solidarity suggested by the 'idol' of a 'harmoniously and perfectly formed humanity' – the 'phantom of the unpolitical or "natural" man' (*GS* 2.1:364/*SW* 2:454). 'The subject of history: not mankind [*die Menschheit*] but the oppressed' (*GS* 1.3:1244). To 'work at important locations in the sphere of images' is precisely to protect the revolutionary impulse from degenerating into a 'bad poem on springtime' (*GS* 2.1:309/*SW* 2:217): this is the 'organization of pessimism' of which Benjamin writes.

It could indeed be argued that Benjamin's familiar series of salvage operations (romanticism, surrealism, Proust, Baudelaire, Brecht, Kafka, film, photography, and so on) will be directed precisely towards that kernel in the imaginary which defies idealization, and which thus negotiates an opening to the unforeseen. The Biblical *Bilderverbot* is thus refunctioned as a *Bilderflucht* (J54,2): a flight *from* the mythical image *to* the dialectical image divested of all consoling force. Benjamin's 'dialectical optic' will pit image against image.

Whatever else may be at work in brushing cultural history against the grain of historicist (self)-misunderstanding – Goethe against Gundolf, Romanticism against *Sturm und Drang*, Kafka against Brod, cinema against Riefenstahl, Mickey Mouse against Disney, surrealism against the musty 'spiritualism' which would collapse the visionary impulse into the occultism of mystagogues and mediums (*GS* 2.1:298/*SW* 2:209) – whatever the force and legitimacy of Benjamin's specific rewritings, it will in each case be a question of a retrieval rather than a repression of ocular possibilities, and as such the vindication of an imaginary burdened by the essential 'ambiguity' that announces the very 'law' of the refurbished dialectic (*GS* 5.1:55/*AP*, p. 10).

If it is within the world-theatre that Kafka's 'hope for the hopeless' is to be realized (*GS* 2.2:415/*SW* 2:799) – fake sky, paper wings: Adorno will indeed come to suspect this (*GS* 2.3:1177f) – this is precisely because the only 'way out' (as in the *Report to an Academy*) is by recapturing the last vestige of a repressed mimetic impulse (*GS* 2.2:423/*SW* 2:804). 'The mimetic and the critical faculties can no longer be distinguished' (*GS* 2.3:1050). If Proust's frenetic search for images will involve the 'vice' ('one is tempted to say, theological') of obsequious curiosity,[44] this will indeed come to imply the inevitable enmeshment of every image of redemption within the 'enchanted forest' (*Bannwald*)' (*GS* 2.1:313/*SW* 2:239) of mythic guilt.

All of which will lead soon enough to the predictable charges: bewitchment, cooptation, identification with the aggressor.

V *BILDERSTREIT*: ADORNO CONTRA BENJAMIN

Mosaics

It is with the abortive *Passagenwerk* – 'the theatre of all my conflicts and all my ideas' (*GB* 3:503/*C*, p. 359) – that the issues first come to a head. Benjamin will be observed playing sorcerer's apprentice, mesmerized by what he would subvert. Specifically: if it is the ocular regime of modernity which presents the face of history as sheer monstrosity – not only an 'oversized head' (G°,17) but indeed (as Marx also observed[45]) a 'Medusa head' (*GS* 1.2:682) – Benjamin will be found to be petrified by what he sees.

By 1935 Adorno will indeed accuse him of capitulating to the force of capital. Panoramatic representations of the panorama, kaleidoscopic representations of the kaleidoscope – the montage technique is here found not only to mime that of surrealism, but effectively to adopt what will be for Adorno the latter's irremediably conciliatory position. A cryptic affirmation, *Behauptung*, would be detected in the physiognomic determination of Paris as *Hauptstadt der neunzehnten Jahrhunderts*, head or capital of the nineteenth century (a title 'privately' translated into French by Benjamin (*GB*

5:83–4/*C*, p. 482) and eventually discarded), which would be thus transfigured as nothing less than the proscribed figure of utopia. Paris, decapitated site of missed revolutionary opportunities,[46] would be reinstated to centre stage so as indeed to provide the alluring scene or spectacle of redemption. *Caput mortuum* would be thus figured or transfigured as – precisely, face.

It is not simply that Benjamin will aggressively rely on images to tell a story (cf. N11,4); nor just that what begins as an 'album' (*GS* 5.2:1324) will soon collapse under its own weight into a 'rubble field' (*GB* 4:112/*C*, p. 396) of Bouvard-and-Pécuchet-esque proportions; nor even that the specific images to be culled here – the familiar shopping list: arcades, ragpickers, balconies, and the rest – will for Adorno bear an irredeemably consumerist stamp.

Nor is it only (although this is not irrelevant) a question of the respective commitments of Adorno and Benjamin as cultural critics – high culture vs. mass culture, music vs. photography, aural vs. visual, and all the rest. If Adorno's complaint will come eventually to crystallize in the notorious assault on film culture as mass hypnosis, it is perhaps less the specific example of the medium which is significant here than the actual logic underlying the attack. If Benjamin will be rebuked, following the artwork essay, for the 'romantic anarchism' (*GS* 1.3:1003) which would hypostatize the 'actually existing consciousness of actually existing workers' (*GS* 1.3:1005) and thereby pre-empt revolution precisely by prefiguring it – the charge essentially reproduces Lenin's reproach to Luxemburg – it is important to consider the specific assumptions here at work. Underpinning what will be an otherwise conventional jeremiad linking media culture to mass idolatry (from Baudelaire's 1859 *Salon*[47] to Jacques Ellul) is a confrontation over the nature of memory and the specific temporality of the historical imagination.

The very conception of the dialectical image is here at stake. Benjamin's 'stereoscopic' (cf. N1,8) glance into the untimely constellation of an unrealized past and a regressive present will be condemned as doubly affirmative insofar as it would symmetrically entrench both, according to Adorno, within a shared horizon of conciliation. In short: any image of a 'redeemed humanity' glimpsed from within the phantasmagoric dream sleep of modernity could only transgress the *Bilderverbot* and thereby inevitably recycle ideology as utopia.

Benjamin's citation of Michelet ('*Avenir! Avenir!*') is here decisive: 'Chaque époque rêve la suivante' (*GS* 5.1:46/*AP*, p. 4). Benjamin reads here the crucial ambiguity of every image – the 'law of dialectic at a standstill' (*GS* 5.1:55/*AP*, p. 10) – the intertwining of regression and utopia visibly at work in every time. 'In the dream in which every epoch sees in images the epoch which is to succeed it, the latter appears coupled with elements of prehistory – that is to say, of a classless society' (*GS* 5.1:46/*AP*, p. 4). Adorno reads in such a coupling the monstrous complicity of nostalgia and otherworldliness. Klages married to Fourier: a 'linear' relationship to the future spun from the cocoon of collective consciousness, a hallucinatory wish fulfilment destined only to accommodate the present by posing undialectically as the truth (*C*, p. 495).[48] In short: in succumbing to the 'spell of bourgeois psychology' (*Br* 2:674/*C*, p. 497) Benjamin will not only divert psychoanalysis along Jungian lines but indeed disregard Freud's emphatic denial of all prophetic significance to the work of dream.[49] 'Every epoch not only dreams the next' but in so doing presses 'dialectically' (*GS* 5.1:59/*AP*, p. 13) and with 'cunning' (*GS* 5.2:1213/*AP*, p. 907) towards its own awakening. This is Benjamin's Proustian refunctioning of Hegel's *List der Vernunft*: the 'Trojan horse' (K2,4) installed within the dream sleep of nineteenth-century mass culture. Adorno, perhaps the better Freudian here, would see the essential purpose of the dream to prolong our dogmatic slumbers, and thus reads Benjamin as apologist of continuity or consummated 'immanence' (*Br* 2:672f./*C*, p. 495f.). The dialectical image would in this way forfeit its 'objective liberating power' and so resign itself to the sterile reproduction of *das Nächste*.

Adorno will be neither the first nor the last to accuse Benjamin of idolatry. By 1938, the montage-effect will represent the ultimate disintegration of the Mosaic imperative into the concatenations of sheer mosaic – a 'superstitious enumeration of materials' (*Br* 2:787/*C*, p. 583) which in its 'ascetic' abstention from conceptual elaboration would 'demonically' (*Br* 2:783/*C*, p. 580) restrict itself to a pious 'incantation' (*Beschwörung*) of the bare facts (*Br* 2:786/*C*, p. 582).

The status of 'theory' as such is on the line. From the beginning it will have been for Benjamin a question of refunctioning the 'tender empiricism' of a Goethe (*GB* 3:332 and *GS* 1.1:60/*SW* 1:148). 'Everything factual is already theory' (*C*, p. 313).[50] This will come to apply, *mutatis mutandis*, to the neo-Platonic saving of the phenomena proposed in the preface to the *Trauerspielbuch* ('The value of fragments of thought is all the more decisive the less immediate their relationship is to the underlying idea' (*GS* 1.1:208/*OT*, p. 29)); to the artless art of the vanished storyteller ('it is half the art of storytelling to keep a story free from explanation' (*GS* 2.1:445/*SW* 3:148)); and to the 'technique' presented by the *Passagenwerk* ('Method of this work: literary montage. I need say nothing. Only show' (N1a,8)). Whatever the shift – Benjamin himself describes it as nothing short of 'total revolution' (*vollkommenen Umwälzung*) (*GB* 5:88/*C*, p. 486) – between the earlier 'metaphysical' (Benjamin's word) problematic and the cultural materialist agenda of the late work, the micrological commitment to the object would persistently forswear every claim of a panoptic theory and thus any stable or consistent totalization of what appears. If the 'saving of the phenomena' coincides here (as always) with the 'presentation of ideas' (*GS* 1.1:215/*OT*, p. 35), this is precisely because the phenomena are to be divested of any self-subsistent or 'integral' unity or intactness, and submitted to the fracturing, dispersive and reintegrative, but also constantly self-revising, combinatorial of thought (*GS* 1.1:213/*OT*, p. 33). This marks the fundamental continuity, whatever Adorno suspected, between the philosophical mosaic of the *Trauerspielbuch* and the much maligned (by Adorno) 'surrealist method'.

Nothing less than life itself turns out to be at stake here. The issue ultimately concerns the very possibility of resuscitation. A 'hopeless fidelity to things' (*GS* 1.1:333/*OT*, p. 156) will require nothing less than a descent to the 'ashes': a turn to the most recalcitrant or 'heavy' remnant of unsublimated matter (*GS* 1.1:334/*OT*, p. 157). If Benjamin's version of 'theory in the strictest sense' (*C*, p. 586) risks the appearance of a certain empiricism, this is precisely out of a theological ambition to 'let what is "creaturely" speak for itself' (*GB* 2:232/*C*, p. 313): that is, to restore precisely by abstaining from ventriloquizing or anthropomorphically representing the voice of a fallen nature and thus indeed of a history-now-mortified-as-second-nature.[51] This is the critical alchemy (*GS* 1.1:126/*SW* 1:298) or 'philosopher's stone' promised by the 'constructive' method (*GB* 5:142/*C*, p. 507) – hope for the hopeless (cf. *GS* 1.1:201/*SW* 1:356) – the allegorical gaze directed towards that which in its very transience and ruination figures precisely as the cipher of resurrection (cf. *GS* 1.1:405f/*OT*, p. 232). 'In the monad', writes Benjamin, 'everything that was mythically paralysed [*in mythischer Starre lag*] as textual evidence comes alive' (*GB* 6:185/*C*, p. 588).

Benjamin's rewriting of Goethe is crucial.[52] If Benjamin will insist for his presentation on a sense of 'heightened visuality [*gesteigerte Anschaulichkeit*]' (N2a,6) exceeding both the 'shabbiness' of Marxist historiography and the 'cheapness' of the bourgeois kind (*GS* 5.2:1217/*AP*, p. 911), the ultimate model for such a pictorial method is to be derived from Goethe's morphological studies (O°73). As with the *Urpflanze*, the revelation of the general in the detail involves a certain 'unfolding' – 'like a leaf', writes Benjamin (N2a,4) – in this case, of the specific temporal constellation (never stable) within which every 'small individual moment' (N2a,6) is to be inscribed.

But what is announced here as a 'transposition' or 'translation' (*Übertragung*) of the morphological principle of observation from the 'pagan context of nature into the Jewish contexts' – plural – 'of history' (N2a,4) would seem to obey a familiar enough logic of translation according to which the original (and indeed the original concept of the originary) will by no means remain intact. Whatever else is at work in Benjamin's 'transfer' of attention from an organic nature to a nature-history stripped of all immanent fulfilment, it becomes clear that the concepts of both nature and history will have been radically transformed.

Goethe's 'genial synthesis'[53] of essence and appearance would have not only involved the 'ideal symbol' (*GS* 6:38) – timeless, total, instantaneous – but would have moreover privileged the domain of biological 'life' itself as the specific object of 'irreducible perception' (*GS* 6:38). Benjamin's montage principle, in contrast, will not only introduce allegorical distance or non-simultaneity into the 'wooded interior' (*GS* 1.1:342/*OT*, p. 165) of the monad but will, moreover, and for this very reason, force a fundamental revision of the very concept of 'life' itself.

If the micrological embrace of lumpen particularity involves as its 'truly problematic' assumption the desire to 'give nothing up' (N3,3) – to consider nothing irredeemably lost or beneath consideration – this is precisely out of a conviction, nothing less than theological, regarding the 'indestructibility of the highest life in all things' (N1a,4). Such an appeal to life will pre-empt any fixed antithesis between living and dead – positive and negative, forward and backward, or, for that matter, destruction and construction ('and so on *in infinitum*') (N1a,3) – just as it will preclude any organicist or 'vulgar naturalist' (N2,6) theodicy, whether along progressive-evolutionary or regressive Spenglerian lines (N1a,3).

The familiar figures of cameraman and surgeon again converge here (as in the artwork essay [*GS* 1.2:495f/*SW* 4:263]) to initiate the caesura or cut to be inflicted on the historical corpus as living corpse.[54] Whatever the nature of the historical materialist 'operation' – freezing the image, choosing the angle, adjusting the lighting, clicking the shutter (*GS* 1.3:1165) – it is only within the 'darkroom of the lived moment' (*GS* 2.3:1064) (equally the *camera obscura* of ideology[55]) that the full 'development' of the image is to be achieved. This is in any case to be the distinguished from the 'bourgeois' gape (*Schauen*) mesmerized by the spectacle of history as a display of 'colourful images' (*GS* 1.3:1165). 'A constant shift in visual perspective' (*Verschiebung des Gesichtswinkels*) eventually presents every negative as positive according to a theology of 'historical *apokatastasis*' (N1a,3) – the heretical source is Origen (cf. *GS* 2.2:458/*SW* 3:159) – until at the 'high noon of history' (N15,2), and out of the 'dialectical nuances' (N1a,4) of the messianic optic ('light for shade, shade for light' [*GS* 1.3:1165], and so on), 'life springs anew' (N1a,4). 'As flowers turn their heads towards the sun, what has been strives to turn – by dint of a secret heliotropism – toward that sun which is rising in the sky of history. The historical materialist must be aware of this most inconspicuous of all transformations' (*GS* 1.2:695/*SW* 4:390).

Adorno, notwithstanding, will suspect here an unsublimated naturalist residue – if not, in fact, something like the 'neo-paganism' parodied by Baudelaire. If the constructive method will be attacked for collapsing the precarious dialectic of concept and intuition, rationality and mimesis, universal and particular, this is because, like every empiricism, it will be found to bear the stain of a reason which would mask its own domination over the very object it would claim to let speak. Underpinning the theoretical modesty which abstains from conceptual intervention would be the secret hubris of a rationality intent on mastering the very nature that it would redeem. This is Odysseus, strapped to the mast, entranced by a siren song whose ultimate charm will amount to nothing more than the self-seduction of his own controlling ego.[56] Thus the 'philosopher's stone' would cloak arrogance as humility. It will indeed be Benjamin's own project which will stand ultimately convicted of self-sanctification.

> Gretel once joked that you lived in the cavelike depths of your *Arcades* and therefore shrank in horror from completing the work because you feared having to leave what you built. So let us encourage you to allow us into the holy of holies. I believe you have no reason to be concerned for the stability of the shrine, or any reason to fear that it will be profaned. (*Br* 2:788/*C*, p. 583)

I want to love and perish that an image not remain a mere image

Nietzsche, Thus Spoke Zarathustra

It is perhaps unnecessary here to recite at length the familiar chorus of defences: what is 'dialectical' about the image is, for Benjamin, precisely what should preclude any assimilation into the continuum of mythic time. The specific historicity of the image would exclude equally both nostalgia and prognostication, and would as such undermine any evidential or pictorial relation to what might come. As already effectively past, or on the verge of disappearing (*GS* 1.2:590) – the model of monetary inflation is never distant (cf. *GS* 2.2:620) – the image disturbs all contemplative reconstruction and so too every consoling blueprint of what might be. Jung and Fourier would here be symmetrically deflected.

As the memory of a lost future and the anticipation of a future absence – 'sadness for what was and hopelessness towards what is to come' (*GS* 1.2:586) – the image in fact expresses the rigorously traumatic structure of all experience. The logic of latency would introduce a fundamental anachrony to the image such that any and every anticipation of redemption – the 'classless society' – would appear as at once not only radically precipitate but indeed properly legible only posthumously if not, indeed, too late. If the much-trumpeted *Auseinandersetzung* (*GS* 5.2:1160) with Jung, Klages, and company never properly as such transpires (indeed it is tempting to blame Adorno himself as much as anyone for this deferral), it becomes clear that any image of *Urgeschichte* could point only to an 'origin' fractured by a retroactivity which would pre-empt all retrieval and thus equally every secure vision of a future or consummated end. If in the dialectical image the mutual illumination between past and present is typically characterized as both 'flashlike' (N2a,3) and 'explosive' (O°56), this is because what is ruptured here is both the immanence of every epoch and the immanence of subjectivity, whether of an individual or of a phantom collectivity hypostatized in Jungian garb.

'The place where one encounters [the image] is language' (N2a,3). If the 'authentic image' is the 'read image' – the familiar Barthesian problematic opens up here[57] – this is precisely because the 'point' (*Punktum*) of legibility involves the recognition of the now-time of interpretation in its most 'critical, dangerous' responsibility towards the past (N3,1). Such punctuality would indeed shatter (*zerspringen*) any timeless plenitude of truth and thus every contemplative relationship to what appears.

The temporal structure of the image converts seeing into reading, image into text. If what is essential about the image is that it is 'not seen before being remembered' (*GS* 1.3:1064), every prophecy would inevitably become but the guilty prophecy of a present that cannot fail to come too late (cf. N13,1). 'Hell is nothing that awaits us but this life here' (Strindberg) (N9a,1). This will in fact define the essential shape of Benjamin's iconoclasm. 'To worship the image of divine justice in language … that is the genuinely Jewish somersault' by which the mythic spell is to be broken (*GS* 2.1:367/*SW* 2:244).

Conjurations

Nor need we now rehearse the inevitable ripostes and rejoinders. If Adorno's somewhat hysterical rhetoric of exorcism follows a predictable enough logic of conjuration – demonology/counter-demonology[58] – it will not take much to expose Adorno's own secret reliance on the phantasmagoria he would seek to 'liquidate' (*Br* 2:784/*C*, p. 580). Thus the frantic appeal to 'mediation' as the magic wand which is to 'break the spell' (*Br* 2:786/*C*, p. 582) of a 'satanic' (*Br* 2:783/*C*, p. 579) positivity.

The charges are by now familiar: Adorno the 'devil' (Lyotard), Adorno the 'witch' (Agamben), Adorno the drunk, hooked on the 'mysticism of the dialectical reversal' (Bürger).[59] Does not the invocation of the 'total process' (*Gesamtprozess*) (*Br* 2:785/*C*, p. 582), to 'development' (*Durchführung*) (*Br* 2:783/*C*, p. 580), to 'more dialectic' – more thoroughgoing, indeed perhaps more continuous dialectic, *durchdialektisieren* – does not this demand for mediation threaten precisely to reinstate a historicist continuity of the most orthodox Lukacsian sort?[60] Hegel contra Schelling? Does not the demand for theoretical elaboration threaten to reinvest the 'contents of consciousness' with the occult properties which are specifically to be avoided? 'Restoration of theology' (Adorno's request) (*Br* 2:676/*C*, p. 498) as so much more German ideology?

More to the point: does not the very accusation of apologetics assume a linear temporality of the *noch nicht*? Would not the charge of premature reconciliation arrogate to itself the very standard of fulfilment which it would thereby withhold? Would not the very allegation of positivism essentially indict itself in appealing to the proscribed standpoint of totality?

Things are complicated. It is indeed possible to argue here (as

Benjamin almost does) that Adorno's own version of 'theory' – whether as the esoteric redemption of the phenomena (*Ideologiekritik*) or as the boot-strapping of a philosophical Münchhausen – itself assumes the angelic standpoint or 'waxen wings' (*GB* 6:184/*C*, p. 587) of the detached observer. If there is, to be sure, a certain vanguardist conceit in Adorno's 'carpings' (*Br* 2:683/*C*, p. 503) (most clearly marked in his response to the artwork essay[61]), Adorno himself is the first to insist that the price of theoretical success would be not only practical failure but indeed a theoretical blindspot premised precisely on the repression of that original guilt.

If there is a wilful stupidity here – Adorno stubbornly mistakes the dream-image for the dialectical image thereby inviting all the inevitable refutations and rejoinders – the misprision is revealing in that it points to a specific antinomy not yet properly addressed.

It may indeed be that Adorno's suspicions in the end, and despite every-thing, retain a certain cogency. Perhaps both Benjamin and Adorno share a certain fantasy of premature reconciliation. Perhaps such a fantasy is a necessary one. Suspended between the 'desert' of the nineteenth century (J33,2) and the 'icy desert of abstraction',[62] the struggle between Moses and Aaron would seem unbearably long.

Does Benjamin's commitment to a fracturing of totality inevitably reinstate it at a higher level? If there is something resembling histori-cism in the indiscriminacy of the montage, this is precisely insofar as it would risk arrogating to itself the divine perspective – the 'equal value' of Leopold von Ranke's *unmittelbar zu Gott*, Hermann Lotze's 'miraculous vision' – from which alone redemption in the strict sense is to be thought.[63] Does *Rettung* here confuse itself with *Erlösung*?[64] If the determination to give nothing up is, as Benjamin himself concedes, 'truly problematic' (N3,3), this is perhaps not automatically due to a simple empiricism or intuitionism but rather (which may, however, in the end not be so very different) to the secret hubris that would anticipate the perspective of a memory accessible exclusively to God (cf. *GS* 4.1:10/*SW* 1:254). Is the heap or aggregate of images structured by the regulative ideal of the totality?

If, 'to be sure' (*freilich*) – strange concession – 'it is only to a redeemed humanity that the past becomes citable in each and every one of its moments' (*in jeder ihrer Momente*: admittedly, not 'all' but 'each and every' in its singularity) (*GS* 1.2:694/*SW* 4:390), does the historian here turn into the chronicler who would assume the very reconciliation which would by that very token be rendered void? Does the 'weak Messianic power' secretly claim an omnipotence which would subvert even a partial intervention into the past? Whatever the distinction between the con-soling universal history of historicism and the 'esperanto' proper to the

Messianic (*GS* 1.3:1239), does not the historical materialist risk both, and precisely in the same measure, insofar as he would surreptitiously occlude and thereby hypostatize the present conditions of both thought and deed? If 'every second' becomes 'the narrow gate through which the Messiah might enter' (*GS* 1.2:704/*SW* 4:397) – yes, 'the' Messiah – how is this different from the homogenizing abstractness which would efface the absolute singularity of the revolutionary event? Does the leap into the 'open air' of history (*GS* 1.2:701/*SW* 4:395) inevitably reinforce the very confinement it would circumvent? Abstract negativity as the secret positivism of the day?[65]

If to make such a charge (as Adorno arguably could have done) is in itself equally to risk being tarred with the brush of a complacent historicism – to charge premature reconciliation is in itself to assume it, and so on – this in itself points to the inextricable interlocking of two 'torn halves of a freedom' (as Adorno himself was famously to characterize the stand-off in another context) to which 'they do not, however, add up' (*GS* 1.3:1003). Is Adorno equally guilty of that abstract negativity which would inevitably (Hegel) embrace the present in the exquisite gratification of its own despair? Is this then the interminable stand-off between the beautiful soul and its impatiently naive adversary?

It is perhaps not a question of decision here. However one is to (mis)construe the terms of the *Auseinandersetzung* – autonomous art vs. mass culture, concept vs. intuition, transcendence vs. immanence, consciousness-raising vs. redemptive criticism, scientific vs. utopian socialism, rationalism vs. romanticism, Moses vs. Aaron, Jeremiah vs. Ezekiel (the oppositions are not unrelated, but by no means identical) – the very persistence of the antinomy points in itself to something irresolvable for thought.

Whatever the differences, in the end, between negative dialectics and dialectics at a standstill, the entanglement in itself points to a permanent antinomy facing thought. If both Adorno and Benjamin inevitably transgress the *Bilderverbot* in their most strenuous efforts to honour it, this in itself points to an impatience founded in the radical non-synchronicity of every time. The logic of latency could mean nothing other than the risky venture of an image that cannot fail to come 'too early' – but equally 'too late'. There is in this sense always a little Fourier mixed into every imagination. It may indeed be, for this reason (as Franz Rosenzweig was to have insisted[66]), that false Messianism inevitably comes to define not only the obstacle but equally the very possibility of redemption. Shooting the clocktowers (cf. *GS* 1.2:702/*SW* 4:395) would at the very least shatter any illusion that either redemption or indeed its image could ever come on time. That should equally preclude any easy ontologizing of the issue which would efface the specific urgency of an imperative all the more pressing for appearing inevitably too late.

It would in this light be tempting but scarcely sufficient to conclude here, as Adorno winds up *Minima Moralia,* with the observation that 'beside the demand thus placed on thought, the question of the reality or unreality of redemption itself hardly matters'.[67]

4

IS THERE AN ANSWER TO THE AESTHETICIZING OF THE POLITICAL?

PETER FENVES

I offer the following remarks with one reservation: a sense that, at a certain point, this reflection on a passage in Walter Benjamin's 'The Work of Art in the Age of its Technical Reproducibility' succumbs to a temptation that has no place in either commentary or critique, as Benjamin understands these terms – a scholarly temptation that has acquired a rather grand term in German: *Rechthaberei*, which is to say, wanting to be right by showing where someone else went wrong. There are few texts in which commentators have more thoroughly indulged in this temptation than the 'artwork' essay, as a few recent volumes largely devoted to the exposition of its errors demonstrate with sufficient clarity. And the answer I give to the question posed in my title seems to succumb to the same temptation. For in response to the question 'is there a solution to the aestheticizing of the political?' I say 'no'. The degree to which 'no' is an expression of *Rechthaberei* is for others to decide. In any case, it appears to contradict the famous last words of Benjamin's 'Artwork' essay, which I quote as a prefatory remark here:

> Humanity, which was once a spectacle for the Olympian gods, has become one for itself. Its self-alienation has reached such a level that it can experience its own annihilation as an aesthetic enjoyment of the highest order. Thus it stands with the aestheticization of the political perpetuated by fascism. Communism answers it with the politicizing of art. (*GS* 7.1:384)[1]

I

The concluding words of Benjamin's essay, like its opening section, allude to a famous claim: 'Humanity poses for itself only such tasks as it is able to solve.'[2] Thus writes Marx in a crucial passage from the famous Preface to the *Critique of Political Economy* in which he concludes his most explicit formulation of historical materialism. According to the schema Marx presents in these preliminary pages of his critical project, at certain historical moments, which are charged with revolutionary potential, the social relations of production begin to 'fetter' the forces of production they have hitherto supported; these regressive relations can then be sustained only by further intensification of class conflict – and in any case (such at least is the supposition or hope), not for long. The 'Artwork' essay takes its point of departure from the prolegomena to historical materialism contained in the Preface to the *Critique of Political Economy*. Whereas Marx's treatise concerns itself primarily with the foundation of human affairs, Benjamin's essay turns its attention to 'higher' and therefore derivative spheres. And from the perspective of classical German aesthetics, this means, above all, the work of art. The critical passages of Benjamin's essay are therefore those that address the question: Upon what, after all, is the work of art founded? And the answer to this question is bound up with the earlier question: Under what condition – if any – can humanity solve its self-assigned tasks?

Marx's confident claim that 'Humanity poses for itself only such tasks as it is able to solve' is an allusion as well, for it self-consciously retrieves and rescinds the opening pronouncement of the only previous critical project comparable to his own in terms of its breadth and scope:

> Human reason has the peculiar fate that in one species of knowledge it is burdened by questions it cannot dismiss, for they are given as tasks by the nature of reason itself, which, however, cannot be answered, for they overstep all power of human reason.[3]

Thus writes Kant at the opening of the Preface to the first edition of the first *Critique*. The 'species of knowledge' in question is that of metaphysics, and the inability of human reason to accomplish certain tasks it inevitably sets for itself generates what Kant calls 'transcendental semblance' (*transzendentaler Schein*). Semblance of this kind cannot be simply demystified, for it belongs to the very structure of finite rationality and is therefore inseparable from the means and ends of demystification. Properly understood *as* unsolvable, however, unanswerable questions assume the form of *infinite* tasks – precisely what Marx denies. In the case of Benjamin's essay, such reflections would mean something like this: any definitive answer to the aestheticizing of the political mistakes the task for a problem that can be definitively resolved; together, the two answers – here called 'aestheticizing of politics' and 'politicizing of art' – would constitute an antinomy, which, following the same shadow of an argument, derive from a common misconception: that the world can be grasped independently of the manner and mode in which it is perceivable – or, to use Benjamin's lexicon, independently of 'the human perceptual apparatus' (*GS* 7.1:381). Comprehending this misconception yields the infinite task of gradually adapting to, and therefore entering into, this very condition: the absence of a world above and beyond the apparatus in which it is perceivable.[4]

II

That Benjamin's essay moves in a similar direction gives some indication that the previous remarks are not entirely removed from the field of its argumentation, even if they are quite remote from the desperate circumstances of its composition. From the perspective of these circumstances the phrase 'aestheticizing of the political' can be readily understood in the following manner: certain regimes conceive themselves as works of art, the primary materials of which – namely human beings, organized into a *Volksgemeinschaft* – are nothing more than inert matter at the disposal of form-giving political artists, who, in making their *Gesamtkunstwerke*, need worry about the fate of their material as little as Wagner need concern himself with the sentiments of his singers. There are doubtless those who have accurately deployed the phrase 'aestheticizing of the political' in this manner: as a description of those regimes that purge politics of legal and moral standards by more or less explicitly proffering aesthetic ones in their stead.

Not only does Benjamin *not* pose the question in this manner, however; he could not do so given his point of departure, for – and this is nowhere presented more succinctly than in the Preface to Marx's *Critique of Political Economy* – political categories do not correspond to legal or moral ones. This is a premise of historical materialism, which is usually expressed by saying that the legal functions of a particular social formation are as much a part of the superstructure as its moral codes and mythological creatures. Even if the final section of Benjamin's essay parenthetically proposes that the aestheticizing of the political corresponds to a time in which the 'masses' are deprived of their rights and are given the opportunity for 'expression' instead, the rights in question cannot be identified either with the positive rights guaranteed by a particular regime or the natural rights that, according to some legal theorists, are either the source of its legitimacy or the rationale for revolt. The rights to which Benjamin refers are, rather, altogether extralegal: more exactly, the right to alter 'the relations of ownership' (*GS* 7.1:382), which is to say, the right to something other than positive rights or their putatively natural foundations. By making use of the questionable term 'right' in this context, Benjamin aligns himself with – and at the same time subtly distances his line of argument from – those who develop the phrase 'aestheticizing of the political' in order to answer a lingering question: How is it possible for certain social relations, in particular those of advanced capitalism, to sustain themselves when they ought to be fettering the further development of productive forces? 'The right to alter the relations of ownership' functions in Benjamin's essay as a *political right*, which, however, is only another way of naming the same problem: a 'right' outside the order of positive law and yet removed from the sphere of nature as well. The categories and criteria of the political – whatever these may be, and Benjamin for good reason remains silent about them here – enjoy a relative independence from those of positive or natural legality, and this independence, which betrays itself in exceptional circumstances, makes the question posed by its aestheticizing far more difficult, far less open to answers that take the reassuring form: shape political affairs according to legal norms.

The independence of political from legal criteria is, moreover, the source of its proximity to aesthetics, understood as a particular philosophical discipline first created and developed in the context of classical German, that is to say, Leibnizian metaphysics. And here, for better or worse, is a little *Rechthaberei*: the last sentence of the penultimate section of Benjamin's essay (in all but the final version) is wrong – not necessarily in what it says about film but in what it asserts about aesthetics. It reads: 'Thus [film] shows itself from here on out as, for the time being, the most important object of that theory of perception, which, among the Greeks, was called aesthetics' (*GS* 7.1:381). Many commentators have more or less strenuously rejected Benjamin's account of film. I decline to take sides in this debate. I do, however, object to his account of the word *aesthetics*. Of course, the term ultimately derives from the Greek verb *aesthesnesthai* according the model of word-formation that has given rise to a large number of technical terms, including the word *technical* itself. It was not, however, among the ancient Greeks that the term developed in this manner but, rather, among certain Germans of the eighteenth century, especially Alexander Baumgarten, who invented *aesthetics* as a technical term for a particular branch of metaphysics.[5] 'The excellent analyst Baumgarten' (A21; B35), to cite the first footnote in Kant's own Transcendental Aesthetic, does not appear among the dozen or so *Deutsche Menschen* whose letters Benjamin edits and briefly discusses while writing and revising the 'artwork' essay. Nor does Benjamin mention Baumgarten in conjunction with his rediscovery of Carl Gustav Jochmann, whose largely forgotten treatise 'On the Retreat of Poetry', as Benjamin retrospectively realized, served as a prolepsis of his own philosophical-historical inquiry into the fate of art. Nevertheless, despite this curious lacuna, it is possible to identify certain affinities between Baumgarten's and Benjamin's inquiries into the 'human perceptual apparatus' that each conducts under the rubric of 'aesthetics'. And from the perspective of the reception of their respective inquiries, the term *affinity* fails to do justice to this relation; *identity* is better, for in both cases the 'aesthetica' they propose have been widely recognized and largely repudiated, often in the very same gesture.

Here is not the place for a broad exploration of the relation between Baumgarten's massive *Aesthetica* and Benjamin's miniature one – and not only because Benjamin neglects to mention his predecessor. This much can be stated, however: something in Baumgarten's invention of the technical term *aesthetics* corresponds to Benjamin's attempt to develop entirely new terms for the study of both artwork and the human sensorium at large, and this correspondence is nowhere more apparent than in the place where Benjamin overlooks Baumgarten's innovation. For Benjamin, the theory of perception called 'aesthetics' must henceforth acknowledge the indispensable function of *distraction*, for Baumgarten, that of *confusion*. Indeed, *Zerstreuung* ('distraction'), as Benjamin presents this term, may even be considered a translation and intensification of *Confusion*, as Baumgarten understands it. Whereas Benjamin makes a case for distraction in 1935, Baumgarten does the same with confusion exactly two hundred years earlier – and thereby invents aesthetics as a discipline devoted, on the one hand, to the critique of taste and, on the other, to the analysis of the human perceptual apparatus. According to Baumgarten's groundbreaking *Philosophical Meditations Pertaining to Poetry* (1735), poetry – the study of which holds a principal place in the new science of aesthetics – consists in the perfection of distinct yet confused perceptions: distinct, because the object of perception is distinguishable from every other; confused, because the concept under which this object falls eludes poet and reader alike. Distinct yet confused perceptions are particularly apt for the representation of spatio-temporal individuals, however, since the objects of perception can be distinguished from other things but cannot be analysed into their constituent elements. However persuasive the analysis of an 'aesthetic' object, there always remains, to quote Leibniz, an element of '*je ne sais quoi*'. In this sense, aesthetics makes room for what the 'higher' science of rational metaphysics scorns: *singularities*, which appear to be different from everything else, although no one can say either how or why. By granting themselves the joy of confusion, without suffering any loss in the ability to make distinctions – quite the contrary – those whom Baumgarten calls 'aestheticians' enter into a relatively independent sphere of knowledge: a 'lower' sphere in comparison to that of rational cognition, to be sure, but one that nevertheless enjoys a dignity of its own. This sphere can also be described in terms Benjamin invents for the purpose of avoiding the terminology of aesthetics developed in the wake of Baumgarten's innovation: the 'lower' sphere of aesthetics arises, namely, in conjunction with the 'decline' of the aura.

III

Without entering into a lengthy engagement with the specific terms with which Benjamin elucidates the idea of the auratic 'decline', this much can be said: the aura consists in the appearance of another spatio-temporal nexus in relation to our own. 'What is the aura, properly speaking [*eigentlich*]?', Benjamin asks in a rare use of the rhetorical question. Answer, 'a peculiar web made of space and time [*ein sonderbares Gespinst aus Raum und Zeit*]: the one-time appearance of a distance, no matter how near it may be' (*GS* 7.1:355).[6] The peculiarity of this ghostly web – *Gespinst* verges on *Gespenst* – consists in its violation of those principles of space and time to which Kant gives canonical expression at the opening of his critical project. According to the Transcendental Aesthetic, closeness can never be predicated of 'a distance' – not even once. This is not to say, however, that singularity is always an altogether illegitimate predicate, wholly without 'objective validity'; it is illegitimate only in relation to objects of possible knowledge. Whereas the Transcendental Aesthetic of the first *Critique* can be called the metaphysical ratification of auratic decline, the Critique of Aesthetic Judgement moves in the opposite direction: towards the disclosure of a sphere in which the category of singularity can be delicately applied to things that seem to appear. Take a palace, for example – or, more exactly, 'the palace I see before me' (Ak, 5:204): insofar as the palace alone is the subject of my capacity to judge, without regard to any thoughts I might entertain of its function and purpose, the only possible point of reference for my reflective power of judgement is my own state of mind, which is to say, my feeling of pleasure or displeasure. However far it may be from my – or indeed from Kant's – range of experience, the example of the palace is not chosen arbitrarily; on the contrary, it is drawn from the first example of 'a beauty' to which Kant refers in the *Critique of Judgement* and the very example through which he first elucidates the categorial 'quality' of the aesthetic mode of judgement: namely disinterest, which is to say, disregard for the actual, spatial-temporal existence of the object represented in the singular presentation that serves as the subject of our 'power of judgement'. In the light of the vast squander of labour poured into the institution of palaces – or, as Kant, ventriloquizing Rousseau, writes, in the light of 'the vanity of the great who waste the sweat of the people on such superfluous things' (Ak, 5:204) – this disregard is no small accomplishment.

That the palace is a politically charged example – especially in the fall of 1790, when the third *Critique* was first published and certain palaces came under siege – goes without saying. If, as Kant famously proposes, one of the defining features of beauty is 'purposiveness without purpose' (Ak, 5:236), the palace can also be seen to exemplify its exact inversion: social non-purposiveness with an unmistakable political aim, namely demonstrating who's in charge. The aristocracy may have no valid function – this is a point Kant increasingly stresses as he grows older[7] – but the products its members install can still be judged to be beautiful; indeed, they are exemplary in their beauty for precisely this reason. Yet Kant never goes beyond such suggestions. Politics for him has no right to claim independent criteria and must, instead, be made into a matter of purely legal norms. Such is the point of *Toward Perpetual Peace* and the source of his ever-more bitter polemic against 'practical politicians'. Kant therefore refrains from doing what he suggests: politicizing aesthetics. And the form of politicization from which he abstains is discernible in the first example of aesthetic judgement: beauty would be the promise of palaces without power.

The same is not true of Kant's successors, however, a large number of whom propose, invert, and subvert the following thesis: the domain of aesthetic experience is that of non-domination. Inaugurated as an emancipation of perception from its subjection to the 'higher' cognitive faculties, developed in the light of the circular and self-grounding liberality of the 'liberal arts', aesthetics could claim to be a prolegomena for the project of universal human liberation – indeed, an indispensable propaedeutic for anyone who wishes to pursue this project without installing regimes that are even more domineering than the ones they replace. Such a politicizing of aesthetics, which turns beauty into the unambiguous appearance of freedom, can be answered by reversing its terms: the domain of aesthetics is a symptom and agent of domination – not an immediate enthralment to princes and palaces perhaps, but a mediated subjection to those economic and bureaucratic powers that constitutively conceal their modes of mastery. And the mediated character of such domination makes it all the more insidious: not only is freedom lacking, but so too is the chance of recognizing its absence. New forms of art can then be charged with the task of making the absence of freedom recognizable by subverting their own aesthetic impulses, and an aesthetic theory can develop, in turn, as a second-order propaedeutic for the project of liberation – a negative 'aesthetic education' that takes its point of departure from those self-conscious semblances of autonomy which uneasily retain the rubric of 'fine art'. This proposal, which still maintains an uneasy place for beauty, can then be negated in turn: without freedom and without a valid claim to liberation from the semblance of freedom – this is the desolate domain of aesthetics, if this word remains viable. It is as though the exemplary palace in the third *Critique* were no longer an example of 'a beauty' but were, instead, the provocation of a sublimity that whispers 'no, no, no': 'you cannot take charge; you cannot make good on your impotence; and you cannot silently rescue this double negation by way of a relentlessly negative dialectics'. From Schiller through Adorno to Lyotard, the politicizing of aesthetics follows something like this course.

IV

All of this supposes, however, that one is in command of the term 'politicizing'. In the light of Benjamin's 'artwork' essay, its counterpart can be defined in a fairly concise manner: 'aestheticizing' consists in the transformation of something into an object that is grasped and evaluated from two incompatible yet reinforcing perspectives: that of self-interested expression and that of self-alienated enjoyment. Neither perspective is concerned with artworks *per se*, only with the interests and emotions of its audience. In this sense, the first victim of aestheticizing is, as Heidegger suggests in a series of contemporaneous lectures, artwork itself.[8] Benjamin proposes something similar – without supposing, however, that this thesis were the opening bid of a 'grand politics' that would revive the era and aura of great art. And it is in response to this question – what is to come of art*work* in the absence of its aura? – that the question of its counterpart, namely 'politicizing', can be effectively posed. What Benjamin offers in this context is the following passage, which contains his definitive renunciation of aesthetic autonomy (I apologize for the clumsiness of the translation, which exacerbates the uncharacteristic awkwardness of the original):

> At the very moment in which the criterion of genuineness fails to apply to the production of art, the entire social function of art rolls over. Into the place of its founding in ritual, its founding in another praxis has to step [*hat zu tritt*]: namely, its founding in politics. (*GS* 7.1:357)

With this underlined but unexplained passage, Benjamin turns to other topics: the distinction between cultic-value and display-value in some versions of the essay, the early days of photography, in others. What remains unexplained and unchanged is the awkwardness of the passage itself, especially in its second version: being founded in politics '*has* to step in place' of being founded in ritual. That Benjamin struggled with the tense in which to formulate this precarious step cannot be doubted: in the first version of the essay the sentence in question is in the past (*GS* 1.2:442), whereas in the third version it is in the present (*GS* 1.2:482); and in the second, in the imperative. At no other juncture in the essay – and, to my knowledge, at no other place in Benjamin's entire corpus – is he so uncertain as to which verb form should be used: '*ist getreten*' ('has stepped') indicates an event that has been completed; '*tritt*' ('steps') something taking place now or forever; and '*hat zu treten*' ('has to step') a causal connection, a metaphysical axiom, or a principle of practical reason. Aesthetics may declare its autonomy – and in the very person of Adorno, it does so for the purpose of Benjamin's edification – but artwork cannot stand on its own: it must be grounded in some other practice. And this 'must' must somehow be integral to the very workings of 'artwork', so much so that, regardless of what anyone means by the term *artwork*, it says: 'grounded in a founding praxis' or, in other words, 'derivative'. The axiom with which Benjamin begins his inquiry, 'Artwork has in principle always been reproducible' (*GS* 7.1:351), perhaps even derives from its irreducible derivativeness. Which is to say: the predicate by which artworks appear to distinguish themselves from other things – 'singularity' – cannot, properly speaking, belong to them; nor does it belong to the practice upon which all artwork, according to Benjamin, was initially founded, namely ritual. In terms of Benjamin's essay there is only one remaining term: politics, the nature of which cannot be determined in advance of its entrance. If, however, politics, unlike the artwork of any era, can indeed be called singular, for this very reason it cannot unambiguously be said to *appear* as such.

Insofar as every thematization either presupposes a rule or reflexively suggests one, a practice consisting of unhallowed singularities cannot be thematized – and Benjamin avoids doing so. Instead of using the phenomenological term *thematization*, however, it would be better to remain within the lexicon of the essay and say: *politicization*, the formulation of a practice in accordance with a rule or reflexively suggesting one. From this perspective it is legitimate to make a further assertion: whereas the work of art is the first casualty of aestheticization, the practice of politics is the primary victim of politicization.

V

Benjamin never says this – and for good reason: politics appears to be inconceivable without politicization. The same cannot be said of its counterpart: an aesthetics without aestheticization is at least conceivable, and Benjamin offers his early study of 'Two Poems of Friedrich Hölderlin' as a contribution to what he calls 'pure aesthetics' (*GS* 2.1:105). By contrast, the inconceivability of politics without politicization – the inconceivability of a pure politics, one might say, or, taking a cue from the title of an earlier essay that Benjamin completed but apparently lost, the inconceivability of 'true politics [*die wahre Politik*]'[9] – draws politics into a particularly tense relation with aesthetics, as the placeholder for singularity in the era of auratic decline. Under the rubric of aesthetics, singularity appears as sheer presentation – as, for example, the presentation of a palace in eighteenth-century Königsberg, which, despite its royal name, had none. And under the same rubric, an object can acquire the label 'autonomous', insofar as the criterion for its judgement is supposed to be drawn from no power other than that of judgement itself. If, however, the criterion of the political is indeed irreducible to those of the legal order, as the doctrine of historical materialism maintains; and if, as Benjamin indicates, politics is a *new* founding praxis, irreducible to, and independent of the constitutively recursive practice of ritual; then something similar can be said of politics: its criteria can have no source other than the sheer novelty or, better still, the total topicality of the founding praxis itself. Each case of political praxis cannot even be considered *a* case of politics but is, instead, insofar as the praxis is political, another foundation irreducible to anything previously associated with this term. Herein, at best, lies the elective affinity between politics and aesthetics: neither is entirely free of laws, and yet neither is bound to them either. And herein, at worst, lies the danger of politics as a *founding* praxis: it can represent its foundational character in legal terms and therefore present itself as the only supreme order to which every sphere of life is immediately and ultimately subordinate. For the best and for the worst, in short, the praxis called 'politics' resembles the theory of perception called 'aesthetics' under the condition of auratic decline.

All the techniques of Benjamin's effort – from its concern with technical reproducibility through its reflections on mimesis to its dense theory of compact masses – aim to show that this resemblance is nothing other than semblance, which, however, cannot be simply dispelled by means of a categorical demarcation: here is politics, here aesthetics. Hence, Benjamin's approval of the Brechtian programme of politicizing art, which happens in any case; hence, also his pursuit of the task to which this programme owes its origin: doing away with the conditions under which politics resembles aesthetics and aesthetics politics. Only by doing away with the last trace of the auratic, in other words, can the semblance be undone. Such a task cannot fail to assume the appearance of a certain 'nihilism' – and it cannot afford to be anything other than infinite.

Once again, Benjamin does not speak in this manner. Neither term enters the lexicon of his essay: neither 'nihilism', with which he enigmatically concludes the so-called 'Theologico-Political Fragment', nor 'infinite task', which was one of the Kantian terms Benjamin analysed and reconfigured in conjunction with his 'Program for the Coming Philosophy'. Instead, Benjamin offers the following account of the tasks in question: 'The tasks that are posed to the human perceptual apparatus at historical turning points simply cannot be solved by way of mere optics, thus by contemplation. Under the guidance of tactile reception, they are gradually mastered by habituation' (GS 7.1:381). The quotations from Kant and Marx with which this chapter began are pertinent here as well. From Marx: 'Humanity poses for itself only such tasks as it is able to solve.' From Kant: '[Certain questions], which are given as tasks by the nature of reason itself, cannot be answered.' For Benjamin, the questions can be answered, the tasks solved – but not by us: not by those engaged in contemplation, still less by 'human reason', and not even by 'humanity' at large. The 'not us' is, in this sense, the primary subject of reflection; its name, for the purpose of this particular essay, is 'the masses', which solves the tasks at hand without knowing what it is doing, indeed without realizing that there are tasks in the first place, and above all, without recognizing itself as such: as 'the masses'. For the masses are, as such, unrecognizable; there is no concept under which they can be made into a unity, the elements of which share some characteristic in common. One of the manners in which this feature of the masses can be expressed gives shape to the concluding paragraphs of Benjamin's essay: the masses are 'distracted' (zerstreut); in other words, there is no unity of consciousness. The same can be said in another manner, however: not in terms of discrete numbers but in terms of the Kantian table of categories, the masses are infinite; they are – or it is – 'not one'. This 'no one' can, however, gain the semblance of unity under one condition: when its elements, despite their diversity, are in spatial proximity to one another. The masses are then, in Benjamin's term, 'compact'. Non-compact masses, by contrast, do not appear to be so: they – or it – do not appear to be masses at all. Only a non-compact mass can be, strictly speaking, *zerstreut* ('dispersed'). And for the same reason, only non-compact, dispersed, or 'diasporic' masses are 'really' the masses: constitutively inconsistent pluralities, the elements of which cannot be grasped as 'one'. The tasks of the non-compact masses are infinite in turn – once again, not because they take an infinite amount of time but because only a dispersed 'no one' can accomplish them.

VI

The model of a task that can be solved only by those who are no longer conscious of what they are doing is one of the earliest undertakings human beings are asked to perform on their own: learning how to walk. Only insofar as I can walk while distracted, without knowing my way around, can I be said to have definitively mastered the art of walking. In the language of the 'artwork' essay, the foundational praxis of politics appears in precisely this manner: as the act of taking a step. To cite once again a passage I discussed above: 'At the very moment in which the criterion of genuineness fails to apply to the production of art, the entire social function of art rolls over. Into the place of its founding in ritual, its founding in another praxis has to step [*hat zu tritt*]: namely, its founding in politics.' Beyond being a 'foundation' – emphasized by the threefold repetition of the term *Fundierung* in a single, short sentence – the praxis of politics, according to this remarkable passage, takes a step: more exactly, a step *in place*, which runs counter to progress and regress alike. The act of taking a step is generally thought to be based on something; indeed, of all practices, none is perhaps more dependent upon a ground that it cannot provide for itself. According to this passage in the 'artwork' essay, however, a foundation takes a step, namely the new founding of art in 'politics'. In the tradition to which Benjamin alludes when he mistakenly attributes the term *aesthetics* to the Greeks, a similar idea appears under a very different name: that of a highest being, whose own immobility is the source of all movement. Political theology has perhaps never had a more subtle formulation.

No wonder Benjamin could not settle on the exact formulation for the step in question. And no wonder he minimized the role of optical reception, for this step, perhaps like our first, is vertiginous. A glimpse of the awkward situation Benjamin describes in an unusually awkward way, still more the contemplation of its abyssal dimensions, would doubtless make even the most agile pedestrians think twice – or once: there is neither a way nor a place to go. (This situation is more like walking on ice than water, and in Benjamin's account of Moscow in winter, this is every novice's first task, so much so that, every year, the city transforms its inhabitants into children: 'walking wants to be learned anew on the thick, smooth ice of these streets' (*GS* 4.1:318). It may be for this reason – rather than for reasons of 'politics' as the term is generally understood – that Benjamin retains a certain loyalty to the October Revolution.) Politicization, then, could be understood as the process by which the awkwardness of the critical step is rectified, given guardrails, and turned into a recognizable programme, which connects starting points and final destinations, premises and conclusions. Benjamin's attraction to Parisian *passages* follows in turn: these elaborate arcades, which draw the exterior into the interior and project the inside onto the outside, betray the process of politicization in a particularly powerful manner. Instead of providing exercise and training for a step unlike any other, a work of art – in this case, a certain form of urban architecture – offers pedestrians the appealing spectacle of planned perplexity. Or, in Baumgarten's words: the *passages* offer confusing yet distinct perceptions. Or in still other words: they aestheticize what might otherwise be a 'political' step. In this regard, politicizing and aestheticizing go hand in hand.

VII

That the awkward step Benjamin proposes is not a step anyone could accomplish on his or her own is clear – and hardly surprising, since, if it were possible for one to take this step on one's own, it would no longer be a matter of politics. Instead, it would be another kind of concern: an aesthetic, ethical, or religious problem, let us say, comparable to a torturous yet unremarkable 'leap of faith' (if I may be allowed to draw on Kierkegaard's questionable enumeration of 'spheres', which Adorno's *Construction of the Aesthetic* may have impressed again on Benjamin's thought). That this step cannot be formulated as a programme for common action is also clear – and equally unsurprising: the concept of politics as a foundation that steps in place of another has as little to do with programmes as it does with progress. Least of all does the step consist in a plan behind which a group of elements fall into line. Perhaps this is ultimately why Benjamin makes the much-disputed pronouncement that the concepts he introduces into the discourse of art are 'completely unusable for the purposes of fascism' (*GS* 7.1:350). Still, certain questions remain unanswered, among which the following may be the most insistent, inasmuch as it gives an indication of the manner in which many others might be addressed: When does this all happen? When, in other words, does the founding of art in the praxis of politics take its step? Only on the basis of an answer to this question could Habermas's famous objection be answered, namely that Benjamin gives no historical grounds for the 'de-ritualizing of art'.[10] That Benjamin worried about this question – not, however, about Habermas's – is evident from the tense change in the formulation of the passage under consideration: whereas the first version indicates 'earlier', the third version implies 'now or forever', and the second says 'perhaps never – but necessarily nevertheless'. This remarkable diffidence does not mean, however, that, from the perspective of Benjamin's essay, there is no definitive answer to the question. On the contrary, the preceding sentence, which remains unaltered throughout all the extant variations, contains one:

> At the very moment in which the criterion of genuineness fails to apply to the production of art, the entire social function of art *rolls over*. Into the place of its foundation in ritual, its foundation in another praxis has to step: namely, its founding in politics.

The answer to 'when' is, therefore: '*in dem Augenblick*', 'at the very moment', more literally 'in the blink of an eye' – which, upon reflection, is a surprising turn of phrase, especially since the essay everywhere else emphasizes the very qualities to which the Kierkegaardian term *Augenblick* opposes: gradualness, adjustment, habituation, and tactile receptivity. The social function of art rolls over; the founding of art in politics has stepped, steps, or has to step in the place of its founding in ritual. Despite the temporal uncertainty of this event, one thing is certain: the change from one 'foundation' to another takes place in the blink of an eye, without any transitional steps. And this moment, this *Augenblick*, ironically attracts the very category that vanishes *for artwork* at this very moment, namely singularity. For this moment is like no other: it is less a moment 'in' history than an epoch-making moment. 'Before' and 'after' the moment, artwork is founded; *at* the moment, by contrast, it is not. This 'not' should not, however, be understood to mean that artwork is somehow autonomous for a brief shining moment; rather, artwork as a whole rests on the movement-in-place of its foundation. In the light of the moment in which the step in place takes place, 'for the time being, the most important object of that theory of perception, which, among the Greeks, was called aesthetics' (*GS* 7.1:381), namely film, can be seen to consist in a massive groping in the dark, which corresponds to a task that is at once tactile and tactical: learn how to move about in the absence of any synopsis of the site. Nevertheless, for better or worse, the infinitude of the non-compact, dispersed masses that adapts itself to the absence of any synopsis of its space of action means that there is no answer to the aestheticizing of the political – only a task that no one, in the strict sense, can accomplish.

5

BENJAMIN OR HEIDEGGER: AESTHETICS AND POLITICS IN AN AGE OF TECHNOLOGY

BEATRICE HANSSEN

Hannah Arendt's personal reflections about Walter Benjamin indicate that she may have been the first postwar critic to establish close affinities between her former teacher Martin Heidegger and the German-Jewish refugee, Walter Benjamin, whom she befriended in the 1930s while directing the Paris office of the Youth Aliya. 'Without realizing it,' Arendt observed, 'Benjamin actually had more in common with [Heidegger]' than 'he did with the dialectical subtleties of his Marxist friends'; for, like the Freiburg existentialist, he '[listened] to the tradition that does not give itself up to the past but thinks of the present'.[1] During Benjamin's relatively short lifetime other such comparisons to the author of *Being and Time* had been made, the most perplexing one perhaps on the occasion of the publication of the long essay he devoted to Goethe's *Elective Affinities*. Much to Benjamin's dismay, one unfriendly reviewer likened the impenetrability of his language to Heidegger's so-called philosophical opacity. To be sure, Benjamin never wrote *The Jargon of Authenticity*. That task was left to his friend Adorno, whose negative dialectical journey would come into its own as he disengaged himself from the tradition of phenomenology – Husserl's phenomenology as well as Heidegger's existentialist philosophy, developed in *Being and Time*. Still, Benjamin's growing uneasiness with, and political aversion to, Heidegger's 'philosophy of being' motivated him to distinguish his own emerging theory of the dialectical image from the flawed historicity of Heideggerian philosophy, as is evident in a cryptic note of *The Arcades Project*.[2] Moreover, in a 1930 letter to Scholem, Benjamin reported that, together with his Marxist playwright-friend Bertolt Brecht, he planned to convene a critical reading group, whose sole purpose was to demolish Heidegger's thought. Although this group to all appearances never materialized, Benjamin's reference to the planned meeting leaves no doubts as to his political view of Heidegger.[3]

It is all the more remarkable, therefore, that Benjamin's own disclaimers regarding his so-called Heideggerian *ethos* have failed to stop several commentators, critics and interested readers from constructing sometimes problematic analogies and parallels between the writings of these two thinkers. Moving often on shaky ground, such attempts at analogizing seem animated by the same willingness to collapse political and philosophical differences that already emerged in Arendt's postwar recollections of Benjamin. One connection that has fascinated commentators and critics alike is the fact that both Heidegger and Benjamin drafted essays on the work of art at about the same historical moment in time: the year 1935. Heidegger's essay was entitled 'The Origin of the Work of Art', Benjamin's 'The Work of Art in the Age of Technological Reproducibility'.[4] However, such instances of 'identity-thinking', based on textual similarities between both essays, seem strange given that, even on a superficial reading, their points of departure and the conclusions drawn by both authors appear wholly at odds with one another.

This chapter aims to avoid such interpretive analogizing, not, to be sure, to deny the connections that might exist between both texts and authors, but rather, to argue that an awareness of these thinkers' differences is necessary to appreciate the profound disparity in the ethico-political and aesthetic choices that both made. For, what makes the comparison between both authors not a fruitless exercise but a necessary task is precisely the historical moment – or now-time (*Jetztzeit*) – at which both essays were written. Living under the dictatorship of National Socialism – for Benjamin a 'permanent state of exception' – one thinker composed his lecture while holding a professorship in philosophy at the University of Freiburg; the other, while living on borrowed time, as an expatriate German-Jewish critic in Parisian exile. An appreciation of their profoundly different historical circumstances must accompany the critical evaluation of their philosophical differences. Such an interpretive vantage point, it will be argued, may be necessary if the question of how politics, art, and philosophy relate to one another is not to lose its meaning.

In November of 1935, Heidegger presented an early lecture version of 'The Origin of the Work of Art' in Freiburg (and again in Zürich in 1936), about a year and a half after he had stepped down from his position as rector of the Albert-Ludwigs-University of Freiburg (February 1934).[5] According to the apologetic text Heidegger submitted to the university in November of 1945, his 1934 renunciation of the post was motivated by the clash between his own 'spiritual' understanding of the 'movement' (*die Bewegung*, or National Socialism), the racial politics of Rosenberg, and the turn the party had taken in the wake of Hitler's elimination of SA leader Ernst Röhm.[6] Benjamin, by contrast, wrote his artwork essay while living in financial hardship in exile, finding in Horkheimer and Adorno two responsive if sometimes highly critical interlocutors. Practising 'philosophy on the streets', Benjamin turned public space into his private study, as he roamed the arcades, cafés and boulevards of the French capital or conducted research

in the *Bibliothèque nationale.* Wandering from one unsteady dwelling place
to the next, he jotted down his reflections in small, often borrowed rooms,
amid the packed or unpacked books he carried in suitcases across Europe.
Considering the dire political situation of the time, it is at least remarkable
that both authors selected the work of art as the privileged medium through
which they chose to formulate a revolutionary response to the historical
upheavals. For that both thinkers considered themselves revolutionaries of
sorts is beyond doubt. Heidegger, however, followed the path charted by
the proponents of the 'conservative revolution', believing in the 'spiritual
mission' of National Socialism, whose original potentiality and force were
to be 'gathered' (re-collected) by the comrade-like community of the university, those committed to the 'labour of the spirit'. The power this 'spiritual'
mission exerted over Heidegger was so strong that it still was in evidence in
the 1945 apology. There, Heidegger admitted that, in 1933, he was 'indeed
convinced that through the independent collaboration [*Mitarbeit*] of intellectuals [*die Geistigen*] many of the essential principles of the "National
Socialist Movement" could be deepened and transformed to enable the
movement to help overcome the chaotic state of Europe and the crisis of the
Western spirit [*Geist*]'.[7] As is clear from Heidegger's infamous 1933 rectorial address, 'The Self-Assertion of the German University', the undoing of
this crisis was to be achieved through the retrieval of the original meaning
of *Geist*, that is, through 'the determined (*knowing*) resolve to the essence
of Being'.[8] As such, 'spirit' was the expression of a more primordial mode of
techne, or knowing. Originally believing that National Socialism would set
an end to the 'crisis of the Western spirit', i.e. nihilism, Heidegger allegedly
gradually recognized that fascism itself was the political manifestation of
nihilism. As the 1945 apology sought to vindicate, his renunciation of the
rector position and his subsequent 'subversive' Nietzsche lectures expressed
his 'spiritual resistance' ('*geistiger Widerstand*')[9] to National Socialism. Yet,
in the final analysis, as Heidegger did not hesitate to admit, even at the
end of the war he still stood by the philosophical principles expounded in
the 1933 address. Attesting to the magnetic attraction National Socialism
exerted over the philosopher, this attempt at self-exculpation, just as much
as the 1966 *Spiegel* interview, still bore witness to the spectral presence
of the 'movement' in Heidegger's thought. Both documents corroborated
Herbert Marcuse's claim in a 1947–48 exchange with his former teacher
that Heidegger proved unwilling publicly to retract his own 1930s writings
or to denounce National Socialism's genocidal mission in unambiguous
terms. Faced with Marcuse's request that he explain his political choices
in the wake of the Holocaust, Heidegger continued to cling to National
Socialism, distancing himself from those, who, like Marcuse, 'judge the
beginning of the National Socialist movement from its end'.[10] Confronted
with Heidegger's belief that National Socialist ideology in its beginnings
promised 'a spiritual renewal of life in its entirety', Marcuse was shocked to

learn that the philosopher confused the 'liquidation of occidental *Dasein*' with its redemptive 'renewal'.[11] In essence, both the exchange with Marcuse and the 1945 apology showed Heidegger feeling 'betrayed' by National Socialism, unable as he had been to instrumentalize the 'movement' for his own philosophical ontology, that is, for the ontologization of politics.

Benjamin's revolutionary intervention followed a radically different course. Writing from the dialectical position of materialist cultural criticism, he designed revolutionary theses that were meant to prevent their possible exploitation by National Socialism and fascism. To do so, he appropriated the Marxist insight, defined in the *Communist Manifesto* and elsewhere, that the changed production relations and means of production had created a new historical subject and given rise to novel conditions for political agency. It was up to the potentially revolutionary masses to seize the new means of technological reproduction, which would help overcome the fascist aestheticization of politics. The revolutionary manifesto about art that Benjamin drafted did not just diagnose what was wrong with the fascist present; it called for the replacement of the old categories of artistic and bourgeois-individualistic production by means of an altered collective praxis based on technological reproduction. Pursuing the decline of the artwork's uniqueness and authenticity – its aura – Benjamin wholeheartedly welcomed the new media of technological 'reproducibility'. Film in particular emerged not just as a mass-produced medium but as the means *par excellence* for the very reproduction of the masses. In the filmic present, Benjamin believed, each individual in the collective possessed the 'human right' to be rendered on celluloid at least once in his or her lifetime. By contrast, more traditional aesthetic categories, such as 'mystery', 'creativity', 'genius' and 'eternal value' (*SW* 4:252), were prone to be instrumentalized by fascism in its quest to infuse politics with a misguided understanding of the cultic and cult-value. Framing his artwork essay with a prologue and epilogue dedicated to Marxism and fascism respectively, Benjamin grounded his argument in the famous chiasmic political imperative that has since come to define the stakes of political modernity: if fascism led to the aestheticization of politics, then communism was to politicize art. Clearly, art and politics likewise proved to be inextricably entwined in Heidegger's 'The Origin of the Work of Art'. For, in presenting the artwork as one possible manifestation of *aletheia*, or the truth of Being, Heidegger in the final analysis hoped to disclose the political mission that derived from this insight: the creation (not production) of art was the history-founding act of a people, very much on a par with the founding of a state or with the *poiesis* of philosophical leadership.

However, to calibrate the distinctions between Benjamin and Heidegger in this manner still means that one risks merely scanning the surface plane of their respective works. To venture beyond the immediate material surface one must disentangle two nodal points in their thought: aesthetics and technology. First, one must ask how both thinkers understood the relation that the work of art entertained to the field of aesthetics. Second, one needs to probe what kind of fate they ascribed to *Technik*. For good measure, it should be noted that the German term *Technik* is difficult to translate insofar as it can refer both to technique and to technology, a distinction that, if less important to Benjamin, is at the centre of Heidegger's demarcation of the original Greek word *techne* – as a form of 'knowing' (*Wissen*, not systematized knowledge) and access to Truth – from modern technology. Moreover, both Heidegger and Benjamin – if for dialectically opposed purposes – relied on the same theorist of technology: the jurist and essayist Ernst Jünger. As this chapter will argue, Jünger's quasi-mystical eulogies of trench warfare and the *Materialschlachten* of World War I left an indelible mark on the philosophies of Heidegger and Benjamin alike. As noted before, these apparent connections between both thinkers need to be supplemented by an analysis of the deep rift between their respective ethico-political convictions.

I *AISTHESIS*

It is no mere coincidence that both Heidegger and Benjamin dedicated their essays to the artwork rather than to aesthetics or aesthetic theory. The word 'artwork' (*Kunstwerk*) present in their titles indicates that both would attempt to overcome the history of 'aesthetics'. Moreover, both writers mediated their reversal of the aesthetic tradition through the same influential philosophical forebears: Hegel and Nietzsche.

As Heidegger observed in the 1936 Nietzsche lectures, the term 'aesthetics' itself originated in the eighteenth century, when it came to denote a new 'logic of sensuousness' (Baumgarten *et al.*), that is, the counterpart in the realm of feeling and the senses of what logic meant in the realm of thinking.[12] As such, the term signalled but one station in the long history of the decline of art. The erosion of art's 'knowing' relation to truth had already been diagnosed by Hegel, when in his lectures on aesthetics he declared the 'end of art' in modernity. To Heidegger, this history of decline had been prepared by the gradual forgetting and eventual obliteration of a more original Greek praxis of 'knowing' (*Wissen*). Yet, the German word *Wissen* was not to be confused with the more mundane meaning of 'knowledge'; rather, it served as the privileged translation of the original Greek word *techne*. This primordial know-how of Greek culture well preceded the modern era of 'representation' (*Vorstellen*), and the dispersal of knowing into discrete areas of knowledge (cogitation), whose division of labour was reified in Kant's division of the faculties and the three critiques (understanding, reason, judgement).[13] Thus, the aesthetic turn that would come to define modernity in fact expressed the hegemony of the Latin *subjectum*, resulting in an aestheticized culture prone to indulge in the fineries of subjective taste.[14] Perhaps Hegel was not quite off the mark when he claimed that, in modernity, art had been eclipsed by the dawning era of philosophy. Still, it was Nietzsche who fully fathomed that the crisis of aesthetics was the crisis of Western subjectivity. In the Nietzsche lectures, Heidegger addressed the philosopher's aphorisms on art, specifically those to be found in the unfinished *Will to Power*. Art here proved part of a staged countermovement, meant to halt the progressive advance of nihilism, sanctified in the phrase 'god is dead'. Nietzsche, so Heidegger argued, did not merely initiate a physiology of aesthetics – or an aesthetic physiology – whose negative (after-) image was the much maligned Wagner. Rather, Nietzsche's aphorisms on art produced a reversal, that is, a return to an 'ek-static' being in the proximity of what appeared at a distance, namely, Truth, or *aletheia*. In the light of the Nietzsche lecture course, the later epilogue ('*Nachwort*') about Hegel that Heidegger appended to his artwork essay appears as more than a marginal afterthought. For it shows Heidegger seeking to undo Hegel's dictum about the end of art by using it as a launching pad for the historical leap – *Sprung* – backward to art's forgotten origin, *Ursprung*. In mid-air, this jump backward into the past transfigured into a leap forward into the future. More than being just a dizzying backward-forward leap that was to be executed 'in theory', the leap in fact described the political destiny of the German people at the time of writing, the year 1935. Invoking the normative language of the imperative, Heidegger emphasized that such a leap was incumbent upon the German people if they were to seize their historical destiny.[15]

What is striking, upon closer scrutiny, is that Benjamin too relayed his artwork essay through Hegel's 'end of art' thesis and through Nietzsche's physiology of art. Once again, however, Benjamin had a notably different political agenda in mind. On the face of it, the opening sections of his essay merely seemed to trace a genealogy of the successive stages in Western conceptions of art. But as political theses, modelled on Marx's Feuerbach theses, they entailed a programmatic call for change and action, not just an exercise in interpretation. Indicating that the means of art production were to be altered by the new means of reproduction, Benjamin located the beginning of this reproductive process in Greek culture, namely in numismatics and the stamping of coins, then quickly moved on to the inventions of printing and etching in order to end with photography and film. In the process, the cult of the auratic art object had made way for a culture in which a fully 'transportable image' could finally be brought in proximity to the masses. Benjamin's real aim was to diagnose the pervasive modifications in the human perceptual apparatus wrought by the impact of technology. Especially the aesthetics of shock delivered by filmic montage and the critical interventions of cutting had forever altered human perception. As a result, the humanistic understanding of the relation between the producing subject and its products proved radically reversed, to the point where categories of perception and subjectivity were the effect of altered conditions in the means of technological production. It might at first appear that Benjamin just drew the logical conclusions of Nietzsche's prescient insight that aesthetics, *aisthesis* (perception), always already was 'physiological' in nature, inscribing its effects on the subject's body. Indeed, there can be no doubt that Benjamin sought to think through the dialectical relations between perception, body and aesthetics, already reflected in the very term *aisthesis*. But while Benjamin's method of analysis often was inspired by Nietzsche, he distanced himself from the latter's (Dionysian) aesthetics of ecstasy, much as did the mature Thomas Mann, whose *Mario and the Magician* described fanatical enthusiasm and difference-obliterating ecstasy as the elimination of the individual's critical faculty. Moreover, while in the 1920s Benjamin seemed wholly infatuated with the aesthetics of Surrealism, which propagated intoxication (*Rausch*) as a gateway to profane illumination or altered perception, in the 1930s he often would link such techniques of aesthetic rapture to a critique of 'anthropological nihilism'. Within the political parameters of Benjamin's technology essay, Nietzsche's aesthetics of ecstasy would have signalled the return of the cult value and ritual in the midst of the political realm.[16] Thus, not so much Nietzsche's physiological aesthetic as Freud's anchorage of psychoanalysis in the physiological and psychic scars of the traumatic shock formed the background of Benjamin's analysis. Freud had designed his theory of the nervous shock, trauma, and the repetition compulsion under the impact of shell shock and gas warfare, the horrific technological *Materialschlachten,* of World War I. In returning to Freud's trauma theory,[17] Benjamin dialectically transformed the technological shock into a revolutionary means of change. In the artwork essay, reproduction and repetition at the level of the body politic were seen no longer as symptoms of a collective neurosis or social pathology. In fact, Benjamin presented an analysis of shock very different from 'On Some Motifs in Baudelaire', which implicitly relied on Georg Simmel's early diagnosis of how urban shock and undigested sensory stimuli endangered the category of the individual, leading to a hardening of the shield of consciousness. 'The Work of Art in the Age of Technological Reproducibility', quite by contrast, charted how the media of shock produced altogether positive 'existential' modes of embodiment and corporeal 'habits'. Modernity's reproductive media and technological means yielded a new culture of distraction (*Zerstreuung*),[18] in which the fragmentation of a former aesthetic totality signalled the loss of human aura, that is, the waning of corporeal immediacy – its 'here and now' – cherished by the stage actor of yore. All signs were there, Benjamin observed, that such distraction had reached the level of habit formation. In the *Kino* palaces or movie theatres, whose inviting architectural constructions graced the metropolis, urban dwellers could find a mode of 'living' (*Wohnen*) and a new habitat, in which *Wohnen* (living) turned into *Gewohnheit* and *Gewöhnung* (habit) – a word play lost in the English translation (*GS* 1.2:505/*SW* 4:268). The formation of such altered collective habits did not just signal the points

of bodily inscription through which the ideological state apparatus reproduced itself; the latter point, it should be recalled, is one Althusser was to
make years later, when he offered a Pascalian reading of the metaleptic relation between kneeling, praying and believing. Rather, Benjamin welcomed
these revolutionary modes of production and perception, located at the level
of civil society, which forever transformed aesthetic and political modernity.
The new spatially marked 'absorption' or 'incorporation' of art, facilitated
by the film medium, as well as the concomitant construction of a new collective *habitat*, now enabled the spectator-masses to become true agents of
change. Art's absorption by the masses meant the end of the merely ocular
(spectatorial) relationship to 'auratic' art that Kant had justified in the third
Critique, where the disinterestedness of taste meant the timeless contemplation of the artwork from a respectable distance. Kant's aesthetic spectator
thus savoured a time of 'respite', a moment of standing outside the hustle of
(inauthentic) time. Schopenhauer made this aesthetic mode of 'distancing'
the linchpin of his *World as Will and Representation*, seeing in it the position of a will-less subject.[19] Opposing all such models of 'ascetic' aesthetic
contemplation, Benjamin opted for the tactile embodiment of de-auraticized
art in the body politic, hailing the mass's incorporation of art, facilitated
through the medium of architecture. The same utopian conception of
political renewal through architectural and urban transformation implicitly
guided his *Arcades Project*.

The politics of a new collective habitat and the praxis of dwelling that
Benjamin advanced in the technology essay and *The Arcades Project* were
considerably different from Heidegger's reflections on 'Man and Space',
the title of the 1951 conference in Darmstadt, where he delivered the
lecture 'Bauen Wohnen Denken'. Expressive of Heidegger's ontological turn,
this lecture read the practices of building, dwelling and thinking as the
putting-to-work, or manifestations, of a more authentic relation to Truth.[20]
Furthermore, where Benjamin hoped to describe the physiognomy of the
city dweller in the metropolitan arcades, Heidegger saluted a new paganism,
journeying to the Greek temple of Paestus, whose sacred ruins once were the
dwelling places of the gods. These differences emerge even more fully in the
radically opposed glosses Benjamin and Heidegger proposed of Hegel's end-
of-art thesis. In the final analysis, Heidegger hoped to undo the Hegelian
verdict, seeking to retrieve the indwelling of the absolute in the artwork. To
do so, the classical past needed to be actualized in defiance of the modernist
present, as Heidegger suggested in a remarkable philosophical reinterpretation of Winckelmann's classicist call that Germans imitate the Greeks to
become fully German.[21] By comparison, Benjamin pressed the implications of Hegel's philosophy of art to their logical limits, as he gauged the
changed physiognomy of the present. If the decay of the artwork's aura was
brought on by the technical reproducibility of the artwork, then this also
spelled the end of (Hegelian) art as '*das sinnliche Scheinen der Idee*' (the sen-

suous shining of the idea). In the technologically reproduced artwork, art's *Schein* (meaning both 'shining' and 'simulacrum') now appeared infinitely reproduced, calling into question the traditional hierarchical relationship between auratic original and defective mimetic copy. Welcoming the new relations of exchange, Benjamin reappropriated the Marxist category of 'exchange value', arguing that the masses' access to art first was made possible when original cult value made way for the artwork's exposition value. Clearly, the resulting condition did not spell historical decline, just as little as in *Origin of the German Mourning Play* the overtaking of the symbol by allegory had signified cultural decay. To explain the point, Benjamin, like Heidegger, returned to the Greeks, yet this time to declare the end of their philosophical system. In a compelling passage at the heart of the technology essay's second version, Benjamin hailed the demise of the old Greek value system, i.e. 'eternal value', a term to be added to cult value and exposition (or exchange) value (*GS* 5.1:361/*SW* 3:109). The artwork's perfection and perfectibility had been replaced by its 'correctibility', a new praxis exemplified by Chaplin's films, in which the techniques of cutting and montage allowed for a potentially infinite assembly and reassembly of the extant film stock. If Benjamin, like Heidegger, aimed to return to the ancient Greeks, then he did so only in an unconventional way: the analysis of the tactile impact of film on the masses amounted to the retrieval of the true meaning of the Greek word, *aisthesis*, or sense perception. True, at other moments in his intellectual deliberations, Benjamin often withdrew into the self-enclosure of melancholy, for example in the photography essay, where he lamented the disappearance of aura, whose fleeting presence occasionally shone forth from the photographed face, captured in old daguerreotypes. But such melancholy merely attested to the fact that he positioned himself at the threshold of modernity, seeking to think through the relation between its past, present, and future.

II　*TECHNE* OR TECHNOLOGY

Common accounts of the Heidegger–Benjamin relation assume that Benjamin readily accepted technological progress, especially the medium of film. Its particular mode of 'mediality' could easily be instrumentalized for left-wing political ends, as Brecht, Pudovkin and Eisenstein had demonstrated. In a similar vein, Heidegger usually is thought to have responded conservatively to modern (machine) technology. The latter view certainly is corroborated by the majority of his writings. In his 1929 *What is Metaphysics*, for example, Heidegger took on the dispersal of knowing (*Wissen*) in the modern sciences (*Wissenschaften*),[22] brought about through the proliferation of academic disciplines, or, what he considered to be the 'technical' organization of the university and its faculties. Along similar lines, the rectorial address posited that the renewal of the German university was to be achieved through the 'resolute' assumption of the spiritual task of 'knowing', a path from which modernity had strayed.[23] The numerous writings that Heidegger would consecrate to *Technik* in the 1950s vividly evoked the dangers of modern technology embodied in the *Gestell* (usually translated as 'enframing'). On the few occasions that he mentioned film or television, he summarily dismissed their supposed ability to bridge all distances, bringing 'the distant' or 'the foreign' nearer. The new media only increased the 'illusion' (*Schein* as semblance) of proximity, for humans only ever experienced authentic proximity in their nearness to things.[24] 'The Origin of the Work of Art' testified to this virtual absence of all modern media from Heidegger's thought. Although conceived at the height of European modernism, the lecture was devoted almost exclusively to Van Gogh's late nineteenth-century paintings of shoes and to Hölderlin's poetry. Following an argumentative line reminiscent of Hegel's classification of the arts, the lecture culminated in a celebration of poetic language, according to Heidegger the highest manifestation of art. Absent from the artwork essay, the modernist avant-garde appeared to be the indirect target of Heidegger's disquieting claim that the turn to 'primitivism' amounted to nothing more than a false start (*Anfang*), a misunderstanding of art's return to the origin (*Ursprung*). Certainly, the diatribe against the 'primitive' seems ominous, in the light of modernism's embrace of 'primitive art' and official Nazi policy, which branded both as 'degenerate art'.[25] All in all, Heidegger's artwork essay ostentatiously remained silent about the technological present, except for the philosophical examples it compiled – planes, radios, the sounds made by cars, such as the Mercedes – which were meant to disclose the thingness of things.[26] Yet, upon closer scrutiny these sets of observations about Benjamin and Heidegger's appraisal of modern technology once again need to be considerably refined and modified.

To start with Benjamin, it would be wrong to assume that he naively ignored the negative proliferation of the technological apparatus. Such an interpretation might seem warranted by the second version of his artwork essay, which welcomed the liberating, revolutionary accomplishments of the age of 'second technology', setting an end to the era of 'first technology'. Where the latter aimed at the complete instrumental mastery of nature (presumably in the interest of humanity's self-preservation), 'second technology' expressed humanity's ever-increasing playful distance from nature. Freeing humans from the 'drudgery [of work]' (*Arbeitsfron*) (*GS* 7.1: 360/*SW* 3:124, corr. trans.), second technology unleashed the beneficial elements of the human propensity to play (*Spiel* – a reference to Schiller's *Spieltrieb*). Exemplified by the old, auratic artwork, 'first technology' merely aimed to control nature by means of the category of *Schein* (shine, semblance, illusion). Still, the geopolitical dangers of a globalized (second) technology were all too apparent to Benjamin. In anticipation of what

Adorno and Horkheimer were to call instrumental reason in the *Dialectic of Enlightenment*, Benjamin's theses on history decried the exploitation of nature as matter, resource or source of energy, even in Marxist and social democratic accounts of human labour (*GS* 1.2:698–9/*SW* 4:393–4).[27] Such exploitation needed to be countered by means of the utopian socialist theories of Charles Fourier, who longed for a utopian merger with nature under the ethical lustre of a non-objectified moon and constellations of stars. As the epilogue to the technology essay clearly stated, the horrors of instrumental reason led to the aestheticization of politics and thus inexorably to war, in which technology staged its own 'slave rebellion'. Keeping the inequality of bourgeois 'property relations' intact, fascism retained its monopoly of technological (re)production, which it instrumentalized in the mass-orchestrated spectacles of globalized war. War turned the masses into mere matter, fodder for the automaton of the war machine. This fated confluence between aesthetics, violence, and war was exemplified particularly well by the Futurists' glorification of Italy's conquest of Ethiopia and by World War I, the first war to use poison gas. Clearly, second technology in its hybris went infinitely farther than intended, as humanity pursued its quest to expand the 'playing room' (*Spielraum*) of technology. In unprecedented manner, modernity witnessed the globalization of the 'space' of technology to the point where humans now interacted directly with the medium of technology in un-mediated fashion.

Benjamin's dialectical understanding of the relation between technology, humans, and nature is thrown into further relief in an unpublished fragment, one of the essay's 'paralipomena'. The fragment shows that Benjamin's genealogy of 'first' and 'second technology' was accompanied by a distinction between 'first' and 'second nature', reflecting different historical eras or world ages. This temporal model proved inspired by the concept of 'second nature', or the historical belatedness of modernity, which Hegel, Nietzsche, and Lukács had thematized in their respective philosophies (and whose allegorical version is to be found in Benjamin's *Origin of the German Mourning Play*). Noting that second nature – an 'originary supplement' of sorts – had always already existed and, in fact, 'given birth' to first nature, Benjamin presented fascism as the irrational longing to recreate 'first nature' in its blood-and-soil ideology.[28]

As for Heidegger: in the 1930s his stance towards inauthentic technology (*das Technische*) proved somewhat more ambiguous than his more widely known dismissive accounts might lead one to believe – at least, as we shall see, if one goes by a reference to National Socialism's *Technik* in the lecture course *Introduction to Metaphysics*. Before pursuing this connection, however, it is necessary to recapitulate the main elements of Heidegger's theory of technology. In the work of the 1930s, technology predominantly figured as the most recent manifestation of metaphysics, that is, as nihilism's 'will to will', which used all means possible to realize itself as its own end.

As such, modern technology attested to the obliteration of a more authentic Greek *techne*, whose essence was described particularly well in the central third section of the artwork essay, entitled 'Truth and Art'. Providing a philosophical genealogy (or etymology) of the term *techne*, Heidegger observed that the word originally signified neither a craft (*Handwerk*), nor art (*Kunstwerk*), and, least of all, 'the technical in our present-day sense'.[29] Rather, *techne* disclosed a mode of knowing, *Wissen*, a form of 'seeing' that was rooted in the Greek thought of *aletheia*, as the *Her-vor-bringen des Seienden* (*physis*, 'nature').[30] This primeval mode of 'seeing' was lost in the culture of the spectacle that had come to dominate Western modernity. At least, that was the argument that Heidegger set forth in another seminal lecture from the year 1935, 'The Age of the World Picture', when he related the inauguration of modern Western subjectivity to the Cartesian cogito and to a pernicious culture of representation (*repraesentatio*, *Vorstellen*). As the act through which the subject at once posited itself and a world of objects (*Gegenstände*), representational thinking transpired as an 'iconographic' turn, that is, as the hegemony of the image: the 'world image' (*Weltbild*). In many ways, Heidegger's own language philosophy sought to keep the oppressive burden of the image at bay. His deep 'iconophobia'[31] markedly separated his language philosophy from Benjamin's theory of the 'dialectical image', as well as from the latter's attempt to mediate between image and language – a project on which Benjamin embarked in his study of allegory (*The Origin of the German Mourning Play*).

Heidegger's critique of the 'thetic' act of representation (*Vor-stellen*) returned in his theory of the *Ge-Stell*, the monstrous technological construct that captured the essence of modernity. No text more so that 'The Question Concerning Technology' (1953) definitively described the all-pervasive presence of inauthentic technology in Western modes of thinking, building, and dwelling.[32] Here, Heidegger once and for all sought to delineate *Technik* (*techne*) from *das Technische*, the merely technological. The latter's essence consisted in a mode of negative collecting, encompassed by the *Ge-Stell*, through which reality and nature were subjected to far-reaching states of alienation. Insofar as it reduced nature to the lifeless collection of mere objects or to a 'standing reserve' (*Bestand*), modern technology engaged in the activity of *Bestellen* (ordering something to be delivered), which was far removed from the authentic act of creation: the *Herstellen* (*poiesis*) of poetry.[33] Implicitly using Greek *energeia* as a backdrop, Heidegger distinguished between authentic and inauthentic 'work', that is, between the artwork (*Kunstwerk*) and the power plant (*Kraftwerk*), or the potentially destructive proliferation of technology. Taking as his privileged example the Rhine river, he noted how the hydraulic plant had reduced the stream to being the mere deliverer of electrical energy, while Hölderlin's Rhine poem disclosed an original *techne*, a form of non-objectifying knowing or know-how that was essentially poetic.[34] '*Techne* belongs to the bringing-forth, to *poiesis*; it is something poetic'.[35] *Techne* here emerged in all its shining glory, as an act of disclosure (*Entbergen*), bringing humans into the proximity of Truth, *aletheia*. In keeping with the manifold, ambiguous nature of the Greek *aletheia*, however, the revelation (*Entbergung, Lichtung*)[36] of truth simultaneously came about through dissimulation or veiling (*Verbergung, Versagen, Verstellen*).[37] Modernity essentially engaged in an inauthentic mode of disclosure, set at a standstill in the fixedness of technology's construct (*Gestell*). As a defective technological construction, the *Gestell* expressed the Western subject's hybristic need for the activity of *Stellen* (literally 'positing'), enacted in its own 'self-positing' and in the positing of objects (*Gegenstand vs. thing*). Inauthentic technology could not be farther removed from the workings of the artwork, the *poiesis* (*Her-vor-bringen*) of truth. In many ways, 'The Question Concerning Technology' thus amplified the founding theses of the 1935 artwork essay.[38] Revising Plato's negative valuation of the arts and of poetry's relation to philosophy, Heidegger dismissed the erroneous belief that poetry (the essence of art) amounted to a mimetic 'lie' rather than to the setting-to-work of Truth.

'The Question Concerning Technology' is often cited as proof for the alleged affinities between Heidegger's critique of the destructive forces unleashed by modernity's inauthentic technology and the dialectic of instrumental reason uncovered by the representatives of the Frankfurt School. But the reservations expressed at the beginning of the present chapter that such comparisons jettison the incontrovertible differences in these movements' political platforms – philosophical ontology vs. Marxist practical history – also apply here. Moreover, one might wonder whether it makes sense to read Heidegger's 1935 artwork essay in an a-political vacuum, in neglect of the political frame within which it was originally drafted. For all Heidegger's claims that he sought to retrieve the original meaning of *techne*, it should not be forgotten that in the 1930s he considered National Socialism's political 'know-how' as one possible manifestation of Truth, indeed, as the realization of primordial *techne*. That politics – not just art, philosophy or religion as Hegel posited in his philosophy of art – could facilitate the actualization of *aletheia* was a claim Heidegger presented in the artwork essay. Among the various 'essential' ways in which truth could be put to work and in which humans could embody a more original *techne* were the artwork, sacrifice, philosophy (not 'mere' science, or *Wissenschaft*) and the act of founding a state ('*die staatgründende Tat*').[39] In fact, these various domains in some sense echoed Heidegger's 1933 rectorial address, which stated that labour service, military service and the 'service of knowing' (original *techne*) were '*equally original* [*gleichursprünglich*]'.[40] Perhaps one of the most damning assertions as to how *techne* was to be interpreted politically can be found in Heidegger's 1935 lecture course *Introduction to Metaphysics*, where he explicitly linked the term to Nazi ideology. Though the remark in question only takes the space of a few lines, it provides a glimpse of the linchpin that

held together Heidegger's philosophical and political views. Dismissing so-
called common misrepresentations of the philosophy of National Socialism,
Heidegger here defined the authentic 'inner truth and greatness of this
movement' as the 'encounter between [a] planetarily determined *Technik*
[*techne* or technology] and modern human beings'.[41] The connections that
Heidegger established between Nazi technology and *techne* can be thrown
into further relief, if one turns to the figure of Ernst Jünger.

As mentioned at the outset, Ernst Jünger's 1930 eulogy of 'total mobilization' had left an indelible impression on Benjamin and Heidegger alike, if
for very different reasons. Jünger's horrific essay sung the praises of World
War I, a historical event that he regarded to be far superior to the political
sea changes achieved by the French Revolution. The first global war once
and for all replaced a monarchical mode of 'partial mobilization', represented by the ancient warrior-soldier caste; thus, 'total mobilization' entailed
the global 'conversion of life into energy' and mobility. The outmoded
image of 'war as armed combat' was supplanted by 'the more extended
image of a gigantic labour process', affecting all sectors of society, including
'the modern armies of commerce and transport, foodstuffs, the manufacture
of armaments – the army of labour in general'. For Jünger such 'unlimited marshalling of potential energies, which [transformed] the warring
industrial countries into volcanic forces' presented 'the most striking sign
of the dawn of the age of labour [*Arbeitszeitalter*]'.[42] Total mobilization
amounted to 'an act which, as if through a single grasp of the control panel,
[conveyed] the extensively branched and densely veined power supply of
modern life towards the great current of martial energy'.[43] What Benjamin
most objected to were the so-called chthonic (thanatological) elements in
Jünger's theory of volcanic power, following which 'the emergence of the
great masses [contained] within itself a democracy of death'.[44] In Jünger's
glorification of global war, the well-aimed shot made way for deadly gas,
erasing the difference between civilian and combatant, reaching 'the child
in the cradle' – all the result of total mobilization.[45] The daily life in the
metropolis roused in Jünger not a defence of the endangered individual, to
be found in Simmel's 'The Metropolis and Mental Life', nor the dialectical
theory of Benjamin's *Arcades Project*. Instead, it triggered a 'pleasure-tinged
horror' as Jünger sensed that 'not a single atom is not in motion – that we
are profoundly inscribed in this raging process'.[46] The 'age of masses and
machines' turned all individuals into warrior-labourers.

Historical evidence suggests that both Benjamin and Heidegger almost
immediately responded to Jünger's 1930 call for 'total mobilization'. Indeed,
one might perhaps go so far as to claim that Jünger's text helped mould the
conceptual scaffolding of their respective artwork essays. In a 1930 book
review, titled 'Theories of German Fascism', Benjamin firmly denounced the
mysticism of (eternal) war and total mobilization, shamelessly on display in
Jünger's edited collection, *War and Warriors*. Noting how the genocidal use

of technology in gas warfare '[eliminated] the distinction between civilian and military personnel', Benjamin warned that this latest transformation of imperialist warfare was tantamount to the rule of 'eternal war'.[47] The book's nationalistic adulation of World War I and its mystical cult of war amounted to the 'uninhibited translation of the principles of *l'art pour l'art* to war itself' (*GS* 3:240/*SW* 2:314) – an observation that would claim centre stage in the technology essay. Technological destruction, having emancipated itself from strategic warfare, emerged as a pure end in itself. More so, Jünger's deeply metaphysical theory of total mobilization was the latest manifestation of German Idealism, which transformed nature (*physis*) on a global scale into a 'totally mobilized landscape' or the 'landscape of the front'. Turning soldiers, machinery, the struggling faces of the warriors on the front into 'the hieroglyphic sign of a strenuously advancing work of destruction', Jünger's destructive metaphysics of war projected the 'spiritual' principles of Idealism on to nature. Invoking language from his *Origin of the German Mourning Play*, Benjamin explained that Jünger's nihilistic ideology of death hinged on the corrupt use of both nature and technology:

> Etching the landscape with flaming banner and trenches, technology wanted to recreate the heroic features of German Idealism. It went astray. What it considered heroic were the features of Hippocrates, the features of death. Deeply imbued with its own depravity, technology gave shape to the apocalyptic face of nature and reduced nature to silence – even though this technology had the power to give nature its voice. War, in the metaphysical abstraction in which the new nationalism believes, is nothing other than the attempt to redeem, mystically and without mediation, the secret of nature, understood idealistically, through technology. This secret, however, can also be used and illuminated via a technology mediated by the human scheme of things. (*GS* 3:247/*SW* 2:319)[48]

Only the correct political use of technology, Benjamin suggested, could set an end to this eternal war, which, in truth, was the expression of a fascist class warfare. Technology would have to be freed from being a 'fetish of doom', so that it could become 'a key to happiness'. Not pacifism but the Marxist struggle, with its call for civil war, might end the metaphysical rule of death and eternal decline, so graphically exposed in Jünger's jubilant manifesto of war. To do so, Benjamin implied (not yet spelling it out, as he would in the later artwork essay), the masses would need to reclaim the technological means of production.

Heidegger's appropriation of Jünger at first seemed to take place outside the frame of the artwork essay, namely, in his collaborationist attempts to achieve the *Gleichschaltung* of the Nazi state at the level of the university. Thus, as his 1933 rectorial address documents, such 'Gleichschaltung' was to occur in the community of the 'workers of the spirit', those who know (*die Wissenden*), that is, those engaged in the *Wissensdienst*. This service to Germany's spiritual mission was to be shouldered by the German students, in addition to labour service (*Arbeitsdienst*) for the folkish community (*Volksgemeinschaft*), and military service (*Wehrdienst*).[49] In a 1945 attempt at self-exculpation, 'The Rectorate 1933/34: Facts and Thoughts', [50] Heidegger presented the rectorial address as an honest and harmless attempt to renew the plight of *Wissen* (authentic knowing vs. administered knowledge), no different from the philosophical project outlined in his 1929 *What is Metaphysics*. Through the marshalling of all possible forces (*Kräfte, energeia*), the 'movement' offered the opportunity to 'gather' and 'renew' the German people. His decision to assume the rector position, so Heidegger claimed, was motivated by his assessment of this historical possibility. Moreover, in Jünger's writings of the time he discerned an accurate diagnosis of the historical crisis and of the redemptive means for historical renewal. Recalling the circumstances that surrounded his assumption of the rectorship, Heidegger described the semi-secret meetings he orchestrated in the 1930s, whose sole purpose it was to discuss Jünger's 1930 essay 'Total Mobilization', a text that already 'announced [...] the basic features of [Jünger's] book *The Worker* [*Der Arbeiter*]'. With '[my] assistant Brock', Heidegger wrote, 'I discussed these writings in a small circle and attempted to show how they [expressed] an essential understanding of Nietzsche's metaphysics, insofar as the history and present of the Western world [were] seen and foreseen within the horizon of this metaphysics'. As such, Jünger allowed the group 'to think what was coming, that is to say, we attempted to face it in our confrontation with it'. In the winter of 1939/40, Heidegger 'once again discussed parts of Jünger's book *The Worker* with a circle of colleagues, [learning] that these ideas still seemed strange and disconcerting even then, until they were verified by "the facts"'. Jünger's 'idea of the rule and the figure of the worker' indicated 'the universal rule of the will to power within planetary history', expressed in Nietzsche's 'god is dead'. As Heidegger wished to suggest in 1945, this discussion of Jünger was merely meant to help overcome (*Überwinden*) modernity's metaphysics of the nihilistic 'will to power', through a return to the beginning (*Anfang*). 'Today', Heidegger concluded in 1945, 'everything is a part of this reality, whether it is called communism, or fascism, or world democracy'.[51] Apart from the sweeping gesture with which democracy and dictatorship were put on a par, this 1945 apology raised the question of how fact and interpretation relate to each other. Only if one accepts Heidegger's explanation can it be true that Jünger's writings merely served heuristic or diagnostic purposes. According to the logic of Heidegger's self-exculpation, the rectorial address and other pieces from the 1930s were earnest, well-intended attempts to reflect on the 'spirit' of the West (*Abendland*), taking place in the space where thinking was 'nurtured', namely, at the German university. To a certain extent, Derrida's *Of Spirit* followed this argument, insofar as he sought to separate Heidegger's rejection of the Nazis' biological race theories, those of Rosenberg and Baeumler, from his ill-fated belief in the movement's so-called 'spiritual mission'. Yet, this dualistic position, together with the standard account that Heidegger's philosophy radically rejected the planetary dimensions of modern technology, need to be revised and refined. As the reference to global (planetary) technology in *Introduction to Metaphysics* indicates, Heidegger did not wholeheartedly reject the Nazi orchestration of (war) technology, nor did he oppose Jünger's totallized (or global) militaristic mobilization.

A slippage of language in an anecdote, recounted by Heidegger's former friend, the philosopher Karl Jaspers, is revealing in that sense. Jaspers remembered how during a visit at his Heidelberg home in March of 1933, Heidegger, upon learning of Hitler's ascent to power, almost immediately took off for Freiburg, much earlier than planned, telling Jaspers: '*man muss sich einschalten*'.[52] This means literally, 'one must plug oneself in', and the phrase seemed to voice Heidegger's willingness to become a cog in Nazi techno-politics. Compounding matters more, the German expression *sich einschalten* also reverberates with the non-reflexive verb *einschalten*, which is used to denote the turning on of appliances, radios, and other techno-logical contraptions (which may explain why Jaspers needs to mention that Heidegger had just bought him a record of Gregorian church music, to which they had listened).

Naturally, the anecdote is just what it is: a brief moment in which the uncanny confluence of circumstances yields a momentary insight. For more tangible proof of Heidegger's political intentions, one needs to consider the evidence in the textual corpus of the 1930s. Only recently made publically available in volume 16 of the *Gesamtausgabe*, these writings repeatedly dem-onstrate that Heidegger condoned National Socialism's mobilization on a 'planetary' scale. Beholden to the matter-spirit model, exposed in Derrida's *Of Spirit*, Heidegger believed that the spiritual work-force of scholars at the university was a vital part of the more global mobilization of the 'move-ment' (*Bewegung, energeia*). This spiritual mission only could be actualized through the collusion of *techne* and *energeia*, whose original Greek meanings were to be realized in the political present. It is precisely at this juncture, then, that Jünger's theories proved fruitful, as they disclosed the expediency of the new technologies to the extent that 'total mobilization' generated the 'precise labour of a turbine fuelled with blood'.[53] What might have struck a sympathetic chord in Heidegger was Jünger's belief that such technological mobilization was rooted in a more originary existentialist process of decision-making, namely, the '*readiness* for mobilization'.[54] Belying Heidegger's later claims that the rectorial address merely criticized nihilism's 'will to power', the text rallied the student body, encouraging them to embrace the 'will to greatness' and 'will to essence' necessary for the preservation of 'earth-and-blood-like forces/energies' (*erd- und bluthafte Kräfte*).[55] In fact, the address proved riddled with the language of 'aesthetic' formation, shaping, collecting

(*Sammeln*) or the channelling of capable forces (*Kräfte*). Furthermore, the ambiguous word *Kraft* could evoke both 'energy' (*energeia*) and available human (work) forces, whose dispersion and distraction (*Zerstreuung*) needed to be averted by the 'movement'. But where the 1933 address consciously exploited the felicitous linguistic ambiguities of the German language, the 1945 attempt at apologetic self-exegesis proposed a reading that eliminated all possible militaristic innuendo.[56] As Heidegger claimed in 1945, all seemingly bellicose terms, including the students' *Wehrdienst* (military service), were merely to be understood in a philosophical, not a militaristic sense. Similarly, the blatant references to war (*Kampf*) in the rectorial address were simply translations of the Greek *polemos*, a word to be explained as spiritual or philosophical struggle (Heraklitus's fragment 53, *eris*).[57]

But does this strategic mode of self-exegesis truly make a difference or help to exculpate Heidegger's philosophy, freeing it from its entanglement in National Socialist politics? Not when Heidegger's 1930s writings are placed within the frame of Jünger's 'total mobilization'. The charge that Heidegger's 'spiritual mission' was far removed from biologistic or eliminationist Nazi propaganda loses all explanatory power once one situates Heidegger's philosophical project in the context of the 'division of labour' to which Jünger's theory of total mobilization subscribed. For implicit in this theory was the belief that the energies (*energeia*) of mobilization were to flow through the force fields of material labour just as much as they were to infuse the labour of the 'spirit'. Thus, against the backdrop of this division of labour, it is clear that the author of the rectorial address was 'plugged' into National Socialism's total mobilization at the 'spiritual' level. Once one adopts this contextualized reading of Heidegger's apology, it also becomes possible to see how the framework of this global ('planetary') mobilization, which embraced philosophical 'knowing' (original *techne*), linked the 1933 rectorial address to the 1935 artwork essay and the 1935 *Introduction to Metaphysics*. Leaping back to the Greek origin of *Wissensdienst*, the rectorial address found its centre of gravity in a Promethean adage, which gave voice to the original understanding of knowing (*Wissen*): *Techne d'anangkes asthenestera makro* ('But knowing is far less powerful than necessity'. 'Wissen ist aber weit unkräftiger denn Notwendigkeit.')[58] It was because of this 'creative impotence', Heidegger explained, that knowing was to 'develop its highest defiance'.[59] Usually misinterpreted as mere theory, Heidegger continued, Greek *techne* (knowing) in reality constituted the highest manifestation of *energeia*, or the *being-at-work of Truth*. Just like the artwork essay, the rectorial address thus proved centred in the quintessential concept of *Work* (*ergon*), or the being-at-work of Truth. When read together, these three texts make apparent that National Socialism's staging of global technology formed the complement of the 'spiritual' *techne* set to work in the artwork and philosophical questioning. Just as National Socialism mobilized the aestheticization of politics on a global historical plane, so Heidegger's philosophy provided the globally staged 'ontologization of politics'. Weary of the communicative (parliamentary) techniques of the democratic state, Heidegger welcomed the fated union of art and politics, both being acts of *poiesis*. As such, the rhetoric of (aesthetic) shaping, moulding or the bundling of available energies seemed to recall the horrific apocalyptic vision of the 'artists of violence' that Nietzsche had conjured up in his *Genealogy of Morals*, taking the strategic principles of Machiavelli's *The Prince* to their logical limit.

In the end, Jünger's framing model of 'total mobilization' allows one better to grasp the treacherous turn that the dialectic between aesthetics and politics assumed in Heidegger's thought. More than just the 'ontologization of aesthetics' or, conversely, the 'aestheticization of ontology' (Eagleton), one finds in Heidegger's work of the 1930s a treacherous 'aestheticization of politics'. This aesthetico-political construct really formed the scaffolding – the enframing (*Gestell*), to appropriate Heidegger's own terminology – underpinning his belief that the work of 'knowing' (spiritual labour) at the university and the being-at-work of Truth in the artwork were the manifestations of a more pervasive 'mobilization' of truth's 'energy'. The tightly interlocking elements of Heidegger's philosophical architectonics or aesthetico-political construct are such that they must cast doubt on any interpretation that neatly seeks to separate ontology, philosophy, or 'spiritual' labour, on the one hand, from the dirty business of strategic politics and technological warfare, on the other. Ultimately, Heidegger's writings from the 1930s, including the artwork essay, conjured up the horrific aesthetic programme against which Benjamin wrote his own artwork essay. Indeed, Benjamin did not just argue that the aestheticist production of art turned a blind eye to the violence of war; rather, the mobilization of war on a planetary scale in fact fulfilled an intrinsic aesthetic programme, which would culminate in humanity's spectacular and spectatorial staging of its own self-destruction – 'the artistic gratification of a sense perception altered by technology'. All too aware of the horrific potential of fascist politics, Benjamin rejected the separation of divine, auratic art from so-called base politics; for that delusion of separation, he implied, was in fact fascism's. Fascism's guiding slogan, as he stated in the final paragraph of the artwork essay, could best be captured in the Latin: '*Fiat ars, pereat mundus*' – 'Let there be art, let the world perish'. What made this assessment of aesthetics and politics so revealing is that Benjamin modelled it on a saying by Nietzsche, a philosopher whom he often criticized yet whose work he also mined for moments of insight. Turning to one of the more sober, perhaps introspective passages in Nietzsche's mature philosophy – *On the Genealogy of Morals* – Benjamin thus alluded to his critique of philosophy's 'ascetic' ideal. More often than not, Nietzsche had claimed, such philosophical asceticism merely hid more selfish interests from sight; in reality, the 'ascetic' ideal in sublimated fashion gave voice to the philosopher's 'boldest spirituality (*Geistigkeit*)' and to a concomitant 'impious wish': *'pereat mundus, fiat philosophia, fiat philosophus, fiam!...'.* 'Let the world perish, but let there be philosophy, the philosopher, me!'[60] When held against Heidegger's philosophical writings from the 1930s, these lines thus at once seem to provide a fitting frame for Heidegger's own 'boldest spirituality', that is, for his misguided 'spiritual mission'.

6

THE WORK OF ART IN THE AGE OF ONTOLOGICAL SPECULATION: WALTER BENJAMIN REVISITED

ARNE MELBERG

The work in question here is Benjamin's much-read treatise, 'The Work of Art in the Age of Mechanical Reproduction'. Is it still as pertinent now as it was when it was written in 1936 or when it was rediscovered in the 1960s? In order to answer this, I relate Benjamin's treatise to other efforts in aesthetical ontology from the 1930s: those by John Dewey, Martin Heidegger, and Jean-Paul Sartre. I will continue Benjamin's speculations on the fate of the work of art (and especially the literary work of art) during modernism: how does Benjamin relate to that *negative theology* that he finds in literary modernism? This is a negativity that I trace from Mallarmé up to Paul Celan (a movement of particular importance since Celan tried to leave Mallarmé behind). Finally I develop what will be identified as Benjamin's *pragmatics*: his search for alternatives to a negatively determined modernism in places as different as Naples and the cinema.

I THE ONTOLOGICAL IMPULSE AND THE LITERARY WORK OF ART

Europe in the 1930s was not only the time of popular fronts and fascism but actually also a period when aesthetical and literary ontology appeared to be a vital problem: now was the time to settle what art and what a work of art actually are. The relation between the political and the aesthetical dimensions was of course explicit for Walter Benjamin. It was a relation that triggered the success for the treatise 'The Work of Art in the Age of Mechanical Reproduction' when it had its belated breakthrough in the 1960s. It is a relation that inspires this revisit. In the meantime I have learnt that the relation between aesthetics and politics is at least implicit in those different and still stimulating proposals for an aesthetical and literary ontology that were suggested at about the same time. In particular, John Dewey's *Art as Experience* (1934), which pleads for the social importance of art, and especially modern European visual art. This occurs while he was developing what he calls a full *experience* in its optimal social *environment*. Martin Heidegger is another key figure. He completed the first version of *The Origin of the Work of Art* in 1935, in which he concluded that it is the work of art, and especially the poetical work, that constitutes truth and reality and thereby creates human history. Finally, Jean-Paul Sartre concluded in *L'Imaginaire* (1938) (in contrast to Heidegger) that the work of art has no direct relation to reality but becomes art by *negating* reality. (Ten years later, in *What is Literature?*, Sartre limits this negativity to 'poetry' and claims political intervention to be the task of 'prose'.)

These contemporary, but certainly very different texts, have an ontological impulse in common. (This goes for Dewey, too, in spite of his anti-metaphysical pragmatism.) Likewise, they share a mostly implicit belief in the political and social mission of art: art could be instrumental for democracy (Dewey) and could come to have an anti-fascist potential (Benjamin); it can create history (Heidegger) or become a refuge from historical reality and thereby a potential pocket of resistance (Sartre).

These ontological efforts could also be understood as a series of attempts to conceptualize literary and artistic *modernism*, which by this time had been at work for so long that it could be understood as epochal and therefore as a phenomenon in need of philosophy. Or is it perhaps only today that we can see modernism historically and discover the modernist inspiration behind the ontological efforts (as well as a modernist demand for ontology)? Such an inspiration is of course obvious for Dewey and Benjamin, since they relate actively to modernism, but I believe that modernism is in the background also for philosophically motivated ontologists like Heidegger and Sartre. Heidegger's prime examples are the early-nineteenth-century poet Hölderlin and the late-nineteenth-century painter van Gogh who had real importance for twentieth-century expressionism. While Sartre himself, while working on *L'Imaginaire*, contributes to modernism by writing the novel *The Nausea* (*La nausée*), where he insists on contingency and loss of meaning as the most important components of modern experience, i.e. exactly what was considered as constitutive for the reality of modernism.

What is art? And, above all: what is a work of art? A whole, complete, final and definite work of art? Heidegger and Benjamin, in particular, take an interest in this question and Heidegger relates the work of art to truth: 'That the work of art becomes a work is a way in which truth takes place'; 'Art is the truth that is put into work'.[1] For Benjamin it seems to be the other way around: the work of art is for him the historical category that is deconstructed by new technology and modern media. If Heidegger's work of art suggests, so to speak, a history that is not yet realized, while Benjamin's work of art already belongs to the past, they still have a kind of ideality in common. Heidegger's work of art has a shimmer of the future and I would think that the philosopher invests, in the work of art, some of those expectations for a decisive intervention in time that he cultivated ten years earlier, in *Sein und Zeit*. (Expectations that perhaps inspired his failed attempt, as a university Rector, to become the *Führer* of university politics.) Benjamin's work of art, on the other hand, is full of that nostalgia that he had a habit of investing in time past, staging his historical scenery in a way that was almost as dramatic as Heidegger's: both were inclined to view history as a series of fatal reversals, as revolutions. In the case of Benjamin, this apocalyptical imagination goes together with the famous messianism; in contrast, Heidegger's views on history, after the war, seem to level into fatalistic resignation. However, a closer look needs to be taken at what Benjamin's work of art actually is and why it already now – in 1936 – would be deteriorating.

In the first of the fifteen sections of Benjamin's treatise, he states that the work of art always could be reproduced but that technical-mechanical reproduction – which he exemplifies with lithography, graphics, photography, cinema, and the gramophone – is now so radically thorough, that it has 'captured a place of its own among the artistic processes [*Verfahrungsweisen*]'.[2] Reproduction is therefore no longer secondary in relation to an original and the unique originality of the work of art has simply ceased to exist.

Benjamin takes his examples from the aesthetics of visuality but also from the aural. But what about literature? It would seem that his thesis in this first section – that art has been infiltrated by the technology that around 1900 became the real productive force – is contradicted by literature, since literature for a long time has been produced and reproduced in printing. In another famous treatise written at about the same time, 'The Storyteller (*Der Erzähler*)', Benjamin proclaims the art of printing to be the historical caesura that once and for all separates real narration from modern forms, i.e. novels and journalism. And in the first section that I just quoted from this treatise on the work of art, he states that the 'enormous changes which printing, the mechanical reproduction of writing, has brought about in literature are well-known'. Nevertheless, the technology of reproduction does not influence the literary work of art fatally before 1900 and Benjamin does not try to explain this delay until section 10, where he touches the situation for the contemporary literary culture (*Schrifttum*) and makes a short comparison between the production of film and literature.

Benjamin now states that the technological infiltration has worked further in the art of film than in other arts – he continues his argument in section 11, where we learn that the cameraman 'penetrates deeply' into the 'web' of given reality (*dringt tief ins Gewebe der Gegebenheit ein*); film therefore breaks the controlling distance that was the presupposition of the traditional work of art. Earlier, in a note to section 4, Benjamin stated that technological reproduction is an 'external condition' to literature and painting while it is 'inherent [*unmittelbar begründet*] in the technique of film production'; the film has therefore eliminated the distinction between original and copy, and, as a consequence, levelled the relation between production and consumption. Now, in section 10, we are told that literature and indeed the whole literary culture is giving way to new technology so that the literary work of art is dissolved in the approach between writer and reader: around 1900 the reader of journals is activated into becoming the writer of 'letters to the editor' and today, in the Soviet Union, Benjamin claims to know that 'work itself is given a voice', making the literary expression an integrated part of working life and working capacity.

Benjamin seems naively optimistic here. That should not, however, restrict reflecting on the possible meanings of his statement: that the distance between writer and reader has diminished or perhaps even disappeared, thereby eliminating an important presupposition for regarding the literary work as a work. At first sight this seems manifestly wrong: the conventional view of modernism as it was established in the 1930s is that it emphasized the difference between avant-garde and popular culture, therefore also between writer and reader. Should perhaps Benjamin's diagnosis be understood in its utopian dimension, as an anticipation of something that could become possible? Perhaps the technological development of writing could confirm his expectations, since it now makes an electronic interaction between writer and reader quite possible. And, was perhaps such an interaction anticipated by some of the literary strategies of modernism? A clear example here would be Fernando Pessoa's *The Book of Disquiet*, written mainly around 1930 but published only in 1982. To call this book a work originating in a distinct writing-subject seems initially impossible because Pessoa makes one of his aliases responsible for the writing. More significantly, however, it is impossible because Pessoa left behind an amount of unsorted fragments and notes that only the editors have been able to arrange into a book: a work. Not surprisingly there exist different versions of *The Book of Disquiet*, with no possibility of deciding which one is the 'right' one. And why should not every reader be able to construct his own work out of the given material? In that respect, *The Book of Disquiet* is remarkably reminiscent of Benjamin's *Passagenwerk*, again an unsorted pile of fragments, notes and quotations that could be published in some kind of order only in 1982 ... Or, do perhaps these works – works? – only actualize older forms of cooperation between writer and reader, as when Dickens adjusted his instalments of *The Pickwick Papers* according to the reactions of his readers? Or, do they perhaps promise some unknown forms made electronically possible?

Perhaps Benjamin put his finger on some work-dissolving tendencies in literary modernism. The film is, however, his prime example and in section 9 he concludes that film has succeeded in nothing less than making art forsake its classical field: the 'beautiful semblance' (*Reich des schönen Scheins*). He is of course alluding to the very *Schein* that Hegel claimed to be the sensory (re)presentation of the idea and that Nietzsche embraced as the only accessible reality. But what does *Schein* mean when it comes to literature? To translate it, for example, into sonority or rhythm would be too narrow: such are relatively limited ingredients when it comes to constituting the phenomenon we call 'literature'. Perhaps literature could be identified instead as 'fiction'? Perhaps 'fiction' could be called the most important contribution to the *Schein* that makes up 'literature' and gives literature a relative autonomy?

In that case one must conclude that Benjamin's observation – that art finally has left the *schönen Schein* behind – is in conflict with our normal idea of the literary realities of the 1930s. Normally we think that modernism confirmed the autonomy of the literary work of art, while fictional literature drew a line between literature, biography and other forms of prose referring to identifiable reality. At the same time fiction won prestige and gained an unrivalled position in the literary field, not unlike its position in the best days of the Victorian novel. But should perhaps one try to read Benjamin's statement about the *schönen Schein* and, indirectly, about the decay of fiction, as analogous to the discussion above about the 'work', i.e. as an utopian ideality? As an anticipation of a situation that should be easier to identify today? It would, of course, be as far-fetched today as in the 1930s to hold that the arts have definitely left the realm of *der schöne Schein*, or that literature no longer could or should be related to fiction. On the other hand one could observe that the boundaries of fiction seem looser, in the sense that fiction no longer seems as important as it was for literature – at the same time as fictional devices are regularly used in visual media, including documentary films and news reports. At first sight this would indicate that Benjamin's diagnosis has been turned on its head: fiction and *Schein* have not lost ground at all; instead fiction has captured new ground. But perhaps a second view will adjust this perspective and rather reveal that fiction no longer constitutes literature and that *Schein*, just as Benjamin predicted, no longer coincides with art. We find fiction and *Schein* everywhere, meaning that there is no longer a line drawn around art and literature. If that is correct Benjamin's treatise has not lost any actual relevance, but could be read as a challenge for a new mapping of the field.

Benjamin's favoured term for discussing the *Schein* of art is of course the famous *aura*, coming up mainly in sections 2 to 5. After that the film is profiled as the prominent example of a non-auratic form of art. In section 4 Benjamin states that the aura of the work of art makes it into an object of ritual cult as a condition for its status as an autonomous work: 'the unique value of the "authentic" work of art has its basis in ritual'. In section 5 he continues his argument by stating that the art object of primordial times (*Urzeit*) had magic functions owing to the 'absolute emphasis on its cult value'. This magic was only gradually acknowledged as 'work of art' and has 'today' been replaced by 'exhibition value' giving the work of art 'entirely new functions'. The aesthetical function, depending on the *Schein* of art, will sooner or later lose its magic and will instead appear as 'incidental' (*beiläufig*).

Those formulations picked out from section 5 are actually staged as a dramatic history, condensed by Benjamin into one single sentence: from the ritual art of 'primordial times' through the time of the works of art, still based on cult, up to the art of today and pointing to the art of a future that will give art completely new functions that cannot be predicted (only that they are based on participation rather than cult). In order to emphasize that the artistic utopia has political dimensions Benjamin adds a note, where he refers to Brecht as making 'analogous reflections'. And Benjamin quotes Brecht: 'If the concept of "work of art" can no longer be applied to the thing that emerges once the work of art is transformed into a commodity, we have to eliminate this concept with cautious care but without fear.'

If we try to imagine literature in this drama it would appear, again at first sight, that Benjamin's history seems completely misleading. But might it perhaps be productive in its utopian dimension? That literature as an autonomous work of art would depend on a ritual context seems contrary to historical common sense. Rather by liberating itself from ritual, literature becomes the phenomenon that can be identified as literature. (This is generally thought to happen from the late Renaissance and onwards.) Literature hardly gains any 'autonomy' until Romanticism, if even then. Furthermore, the tendency to autonomy of the literary work of art seems to be strengthened with Modernism: in Benjamin's time works are created as never before. Proust's *A la recherche*, Joyce's *Ulysses* and Eliot's *Waste Land* could hardly be disconnected from the idea of a work of art. (It is different with some Benjaminian favourites like Kafka and Brecht: they operate in different ways on the boundaries of the literary work of art.)

The idea of a work of art had actually to wait for its modernist attacks until the late 1960s – the same 1960s that discovered Benjamin and gave Brecht a renaissance – with for instance Eco's *opera aperta* and Barthes's essay 'From Work to Text' (1971); only now were Brecht and Benjamin's optimistic views on the work as obsolete fully actualized. But still not in the way they would have imagined: for on the stage of aesthetics of the 1960s it was pictorial art, rather than literature and film, that attacked the Work; the clear examples here are conceptual art, 'fluxus', and the simulacra of pop-art. The literary avant-garde tried in their different ways to participate in these attacks. At the same time, independent film (in contrast to 'movies') was regarded as high-class art and the film-maker was celebrated as 'auteur'. Meanwhile movie-makers and TV-producers went back to Victorian novels (= 'real works') in order to find models for contemporary soaps ... everything in order to contradict Benjamin's prognosis! Also today it would seem premature to declare the work of art dead; instead one can find serious efforts to save the Work within aesthetical theory.[3] But perhaps Benjamin's diagnosis still has a kind of actuality in the sense that the Work today seems even more precarious than it could have been in the 1930s. It would be an exaggeration to give technology the full responsibility for a historical development that is quite as much due to institutional and ideological changes. Yet, it is difficult to avoid the impression that the idea of the work of art is not self-evident or functional when it comes to pictorial art and that the conditions of the literary work of art are changed when fiction is spreading over the traditional limits of literature.

When Heidegger explored the origin and essence of the work of art and proclaimed its potential as the creator of history – at the same time as Benjamin cancelled its future – he had the literary work in mind. He is of course stepping into van Gogh's famous shoes in order to establish his argument, but he still ends up by stating that the truth of being takes place by being *gedichtet*, that *all* art is essentially *Dichtung*, and that the linguistic work, 'poetry in a narrow sense', has a privileged place in the totality of arts.[4] It might seem as if Heidegger's work of art is to be found on another planet than is Benjamin's, but it can nevertheless be said that they have something in common. The difficulty in situating literature within Benjamin's technological fantasies – while literature makes the essence of Heidegger's art – has to do with the fact that the literary work of art *does not exist*. The literary work actually shows these thinkers as giving art what I have called an ideality. Heidegger asks himself: 'In what does art *exist*?' ('*Inwiefern* gibt es *die Kunst*?')[5] and his answer would be: it exists when it takes place. And who knows when it takes place? Benjamin's work of art has already taken place in a lost age of ritual and cult and the literary work is winding up. In strange ways it would seem that both thinkers point to the literary work as a *possibility* rather than a reality, therefore to the essence of the work of art as potential rather than actual.

The 1960s was the time for the 'open' work of art – or was it the creation of openings for art out of the work? – as well as for the rediscovery of Benjamin. Likewise for the thinker that more than anyone else aims to connect Benjamin's modernist impulse with Heidegger's ontological: namely, Maurice Blanchot, and especially those texts on the 'absence of the book', the subversion of the work and its not being put into work, its *désœuvrement*, he collected in the last part of *L'entretien infini* (1969). There, one can read that *désœuvrement* is the movement in the work that opens and surpasses the work. Like Benjamin, Blanchot regards the work of art as dissolved already by being completed, and like Heidegger he sees the work of art as not yet realized. And like both his precursors, he relates the dissolving realization of the work of art with dramatical historical caesurae. However, in contrast to both Benjamin and Heidegger, Blanchot understands the realizing dissolution as a consequence of its fundamental negativity; the ontological speculation of the 1930s seems, with Blanchot, to culminate in a negative theology on behalf of the work of art.

II   THE NEGATIVE IMPULSE

All modern efforts to determine the ontology of the literary work – the literary essence of literature – rest on some version of negativity: literature is not like all other linguistic communication, literature communicates *indirectly* rather than directly, literature *negates* reality in order to constitute a reality of its own, literature *kills* the real flower or the physical woman that is being named in a literary way (with an allusion to a famous figure of thought that Blanchot found in Mallarmé in his first large-scale determination of the essence of literature: 'Literature and the right to death', 1948). The negative characteristics of modern poetry are flourishing in the first chapter of Hugo Friedrich's *Die Struktur der modernen Lyrik* from 1956, where modern poetry is, for instance, 'abnormal', 'confusing', 'dissolving', 'incoherent', 'fragmentary', 'astigmatic', 'alienating'.

Also the closing off of literary expression into literary *work* follows this *via negativa*: the literary expression becomes the literary work by breaking relations to history, society, and originator. It is by negation or discontinuity that the literary work becomes an independent republic with a history of its own. This republic is the imaginary realm of pure literature or *fiction*, living by virtue of its negativity. Fiction is simply the literary way to disconnect from 'reality' in order to constitute a literary reality on its own. No doubt all these versions of negativity express a strong tradition in art, literature, and criticism. *So* strong, that it becomes tempting to forget the 'heteronomy' that infiltrates the 'autonomy' of modern art (according to the terms favoured by Adorno); or to disregard *fragmented* or even *positive* relations, i.e. a possible *continuity* between history, society, and artistic expression. However, negativity has certainly dominated the poetics of modernism, as it was settled in the 1950s not only by Hugo Friedrich but also in musical theory by Adorno, in the philosophy of literature by Blanchot, and in art criticism by Clement Greenberg. An important foreboding of the aesthetics of negativity was given by Sartre with the final chapter of *L'imaginaire* (1938), while Benjamin, in his treatise on the work of art, appears to use both negative and positive determinations.

In section 4 of the treatise Benjamin speculates on the dependence of ritual for the 'aura' of the authentic work of art and he includes 'the 19th Century idea of *l'art pour l'art*' in his argument. This 'doctrine' (*Lehre*) he explains as an attempt to activate an aesthetic cult as a reaction against 'the advent of the first truly revolutionary means of reproduction, photography' (and the art of printing has for the moment disappeared from Benjamin's aesthetical horizon). *L'art pour l'art* is a 'theology of art', according to Benjamin, and it has developed into a 'negative theology in the form of the idea of "pure" art, which not only denied any social function of art but also every relation to concrete subject-matter'. And in a parenthesis, Benjamin names Mallarmé as the first to have reached this position.

Furthermore, the first was to be the last: this is because it is in the era of Mallarmé that Benjamin finds the technological changes that finally disconnect the literary work from its 'aura' and therefore dissolve the work as work. The 'negative theology' of Mallarmé was, in other words, not only a realization of 'pure' art but also a contribution to its dissolution. Mallarmé was of course no last outpost in the history of the literary work of art, rather a pioneer for all those negative determinations that have characterized the aesthetics of modernism. Mallarmé is the starting-point for Hugo Friedrich's still unsurpassed history of modern poetry, as he is for Blanchot's attempt to conceive the work as realized in its *désœuvrement*.

When Sartre concludes *L'imaginaire* with a speculation on the ontology of the work of art he does not mention Mallarmé. But what Benjamin called a 'negative theology' (using a term that became current in the 1920s) would nevertheless be an apt characterization of Sartre's determination of our imaginative capacity as, exactly, negative. Sartre regards reality as a contingent flow of sensations and perceptions. 'Imagination' is the act whereby the subject handles the contingency of reality and tries to grasp the reality of things as figures, as finished shapes, as closed *works*. 'Thus the imaginative act is at once *constitutive, isolating* and *annihilating*.'[6] By imagination the subject 'constitutes' a new reality out of the ruins of real reality; for the new one is actually no reality at all, only a negation of the real one, a Nothing. In the act of imagination 'I grasp *nothing*, that is, I posit *nothingness*'. Negation is the very condition for the 'unreality' or nothingness created by imagination; therefore, also for the work of art, art being simply the aesthetically organized version of imagination. Sartre's strong emphasis on negation and nothingness, developed out of his reading of Hegel's *Phenomenology of Spirit*, seems like an overture to all the negative determinations that are characteristic of the aesthetics of modern art, at least in its theoretical versions. In practice – and today – the negativity of modernism would not appear quite as compelling; some would regard modernism as something of the past while others have started negotiations with the *positive* components of modernist tradition. Could perhaps Benjamin's more or less utopian speculation on the dissolution of the work of art be understood as such an early version of such attempts? Let me try such a possibility by making a detour via Paul Celan, who is most often regarded as a prime example of a consequently negative and even 'hermetic' modernist.

Would it be possible to read Celan (and not only Celan) as something else than a negatively determined modernist? Would it, for instance, be possible to read his poetry as a fragmentary contribution to a poetical diary? Or, as poetical letters to his own and our time? The fact is that Celan sent quite a few of his poems as letters (or as parts of letters) to contemporary addressees and that he (like, for instance, Sylvia Plath) dated his poems in the way one dates letters or entries to a diary (which is not always clear from his published works). One could perhaps say that his poetry becomes modern and 'hermetic' by our bracketing dates and context and reading it as modern poetry is normally read, i.e. as a negatively determined work of art. (I am not suggesting that reading his poetry as diary-entries or as letters would be unproblematic.) With a drastic simplification, it could still be argued that a negative and work-oriented reading makes Celan into a mumbling *prophet*, while the diary-reading makes him into a *witness* and his poetry into *testimony*. The terms 'witness' and 'prophet' are of course not incidental; they keep coming up in Celan's poetry. A prophet of sorts is met for instance in the Hölderlin-poem *Tübingen, Jänner* (from *Die Niemandsrose*) masquerading as a man of today with the 'light-beard of the patriarch' and trying prophetic talk: *er dürfte / nur lallen und lallen, immer-, immer- / zuzu* (which should be taken to mean that prophetic talk has now become meaningless). While the paradoxical situation of the witness is expressed with epigrammatic emphasis in the final lines of the poem *Aschenglorie* (from *Atemwende*): *Niemand / zeugt für den / Zeugen.* The witness is discreetly present in the poetical manifesto presented by Celan as *Der Meridian*. Celan here gives himself the task to 'think Mallarmé' in full consequence (*konsequent zu Ende denken*)[7] and he names negative categories like obscurity and disappearance as being important characteristics for modern poetry, with its 'strong inclination for falling silent'. But that cannot be all. Poems talk – *das Gedicht spricht ja!* – and always talk from a concrete origin, a time and a place: 'Perhaps one could say that every poem is inscribed with its "20th of January"?' (The 20th of January was a decisive date in the history of holocaust.) And the poem mumbles not only (prophetically) for itself about a Sartrean Nothingness but tries to speak on behalf of the Other: *in eines Anderen Sache zu sprechen.* The poem aims at a *meeting* with the Other in its poetical here and now. The essence of the poem is actually presence – *Gegenwart und Präsenz* – and the poem has, according to Celan, only this uniquely existing presence: *diese eine, einmalige, punktuelle Gegenwart.*

With these abstracts from Celan's poetological manifesto I want to draw attention to the fact that Celan's undeniable negativity – his pathos of falling silent – is compensated for by the *positivity* he claims for the poem as a *meeting* in full presence (or perhaps: in a utopian no-place). His positive categories – the presence of the poem, its call for a meeting – will of course not grant any happy and transparent poetical communication. The 'inclination for falling silent' interferes and makes his testimony stuttering and his expression fragmentary and stumbling, as if he witnessed something that could not be told or described. Perhaps one could read his poems as distinct reports from contemporary reality, reports that, however, incline to silence by leaving expressive gaps in the text of the poems. Still, one can glimpse in his poetry quite concrete events from his own history, which is not only his own but also the history of the Jews and perhaps more than that. As a poet he becomes therefore the not yet silent *Niemand*, who – after all! – gives evidence about those witnesses that have fallen silent. Simply, the point is, in this context, that the way we are used to reading Celan's poetry as typically modern – 'hermetic' – poetry interferes with the meeting that he is aiming at. If we instead conceive Celan's poetry as, for instance, notes from a diary or letters, we can glimpse, at least in fragments, what I have called a testimony: the language of the witness.

Benjamin mentions 'letters to the editor' and 'work reports' from the Soviet Union as not very convincing examples in his argument (in section 10 of the treatise) for the disappearing 'basic character' of the distance between writer and reader – a presupposition for the negatively determined work of art. If these examples can be excused as period-bound, then as Benjamin suggests they could be regarded as the *positive* openings of 'negative theology'. The letter and the testimonial report were after all my suggestions of alternative ways of reading and understanding Paul Celan's poetry. This should be understood as a claim not only about Celan, but about a certain poetic strategy within modernism. It can be concluded therefore that Benjamin was on his way to find alternative determinations to the versions of modernism that followed from the 'negative theology' predicted by Mallarmé. This negativity was later confirmed in the aesthetics of modernism but it was already breaking up in the practice of the modernists themselves.

III   THE PRAGMATIC IMPULSE

Benjamin is inclined to apocalyptic speculation and this, no doubt, contributed to his attraction in the 1960s to the 'new left'. At that time categorical answers were sought. The 'pure language', the 'absolute', and the catastrophically timely 'moment' were ideas that exerted an important fascination. Likewise, the proposition was that art could be changed, or perhaps already had changed, in a quite decisive way for itself and for the world. This propensity for large gestures is still very much alive among those theorists of media – Friedrich Kittler would be a prominent example – who today are developing ideas from Benjamin's treatise on the work of art. Central here is the contention that technological changes of media are instrumental for epochal changes of history. For my own part I have, on several revisits, grown more interested in Benjamin's capacity for attentive reading, his stylistic provocations, his interest in possibilities, his nostalgic resignation when facing the passing of time. Perhaps it is my own (or current) pragmatism that alerts me to his interest in the functions and contexts of art and aesthetic experience. Nowadays I like to fancy Benjamin in Paris in the 1930s as not very far from Pessoa's melancholy observer in Lisboa who is, according to *The Book of Disquiet*, diligently collecting observations, quotations, and formulations, a secret revolutionary restlessly abiding by the unexpected. Also Benjamin's treatise on the work of art appears to vacillate between the apocalyptic and the pragmatic: he expresses a strong expectation that decisive things are about to take place, or perhaps have already taken place, at the same time as he provides concrete and constructive observations on the technology, institutions, and functions of art.

Among the ontologists of the 1930s, Jean-Paul Sartre is probably the only one to lack pragmatic impulses; on the other hand he comes back, ten years later, to language as action in *Qu'est ce que la littérature*. Martin Heidegger's *Der Ursprung des Kunstwerkes* is of course dominated by the ontological impulse, as are his contemporary lectures on Hölderlin. Heidegger does not reflect on the institutions of art but when he is about to confirm the essence of art he cannot avoid its functions – after all, the work of art only exists when it takes place: when it functions. It is the other way around with John Dewey, who in *Art as Experience* derives the essence of art from its functional context. Dewey's basic thought – that only art will make it possible for humans to collect their flickering sensations, *transitory thrills*, into full *experience* – seems not far from Benjamin's predictions about the new experiences that are to be expected when the work of art becomes the result of intimate cooperation between producer and consumer. Benjamin may seem to say the opposite: 'experience has fallen in value', according to the first section of *Der Erzähler*, and in the treatise on the work of art he resolutely situates the art-experience in the past. That does not stop him, however, from expressing strong expectations for the new kinds of experience, which should emerge out of new functional contexts of art. Dewey imagined the modern and fully developed work of art as a decisive component in the interaction between man and his world, the work of art conditioning a valuable *environment*; Dewey becomes a kind of human ecologist treating art as a much too neglected condition of life. It is exactly this interaction between art and consumer that Benjamin explores in some of the most interesting parts of his treatise when he starts speculating on the possibilities of a new sensibility that could hide quite new experiences.

In section 15 Benjamin wants to scrutinize the received idea that the large audience, the 'crowd', wants 'distraction' (*Zerstreuung*). Whoever 'concentrates before a work of art is absorbed by it' (*Der vor dem Kunstwerk sich Sammelnde versenkt sich darein*); while the 'distracted' crowd absorbs the work of art (meaning that it is disseminated in the crowd). This is evident when it comes to buildings, according to Benjamin: 'Architecture has always represented the prototype of a work of art with a collective and distracted reception.' Nowadays this 'distracted' reception is developed through the film. Due to its 'shock effect' the film subdues the cultic value that is anyhow on the retreat in all forms of art; the film instead cultivates sensations that are both 'tactile' and 'optical', combining a 'discerning attitude' (*begutachtende Haltung*) with a distracted attention. 'The public is an examiner, although a distracted one.'

In section 14 Benjamin had argued that this new kind of reception (although 'always' having been related to architecture) had been prepared by surrealists and dadaists: facing the pictorial or literary work of the avant-garde, it is impossible to find the time for the 'concentration' (*Sammlung*) that was demanded by a traditional work. Instead, such works invited its audience to a 'vehement distraction' (*vehemente Ablenkung*) with the tactile qualities of a 'bullet'. The dadaistic shock was still wrapped up in a kind of morality, the avant-garde wanting to cause moral disturbance; the film has liberated itself and its audience from this morality while developing the tactile shock.

I have tried to summarize the argument in which Benjamin wants to combine his favourite term from his studies of Paris and Baudelaire – the shock, the 'bullet' – with the idea of distraction or dissemination as a decisive part of a new aesthetical sensibility. When Benjamin writes about Baudelaire, it is the sensations of the *flâneur* in the street that are based on shock; and the shock is regarded as constitutive for the modern and urban experience. Now, the shock moves forward in historical time: to the destruction, executed by avant-garde and film, of the traditional art reception, named 'concentration' (*Sammlung*) by Benjamin and associated to individual absorption in a kind of Kantian distance to immediate 'interest'. Now, the shock is characterized as a disseminated but still intensive distraction; the odd expression *vehemente Ablenkung* appears to be one of Benjamin's dialectical 'constellations', where he tries to freeze or concentrate conflicting movements in one expression.

What could it mean that something disseminates distraction while being triggered by a physical and mental shock? A *vehement* shock? Why is that 'symptomatic of profound changes in apperception', as Benjamin puts it in section 15: changes in perception, sensibility, and experience? And why is it the filmatic audience that takes the lead in this new sensibility? It seems difficult to answer such questions and still more difficult to localize Benjamin's versions of shock in an empirical reality; in that case the shock appears as far too simple a description of a complicated reality and as a narrow concept that hardly covers more than some part of the manifold experience to be found in the street as well as in the cinema. Instead one should judge the shock, and specially this 'distracted' shock with its *vehemente Ablenkung*, as if Benjamin is searching for alternatives to the position assigned to the art recipient in the classical and Kantian tradition. Here you were supposed to keep distance and control; Benjamin's modern consumer is instead affected by art, influenced, involved, changed, collectivized. Benjamin calls the classical position a concentrated *Sammlung*, the modern a distracted *Ablenkung*. An interaction between concentration and dissemination is actually going on in *all* reception of art, and Benjamin tries to accelerate this interaction by approaching the opposites to each other in paradoxical constellations like *vehemente Ablenkung*; likewise, with this final determination of the modern film audience as 'an examiner, although a distracted one'.

In expressions like these we can study how Benjamin puts himself together, concentrates, makes a *Sammlung*. Such is his style, his *prose*, to recall a term that Benjamin used in his early work on the art criticism of German Romanticism and called the 'idea of poetry': 'the notion of the idea of poetry as prose determines the whole art philosophy of Romanticism'.[8] Fifteen years later Benjamin not only had a more sober view of 'prose', but also had refined his own version of prose: to concentrate (*sammeln*) his distracted, contingent impressions of modern art and his experience of modern reality into paradoxical verbal constellations. Doing this he tried to give his readers the 'shock', that should dissolve received notions and leave room for something new. To concentrate what is contingently disseminated: that could actually work as a definition of modern prose!

Thus Benjamin's stylistic praxis could be regarded as a pragmatic version of modernist prose and as his effort to find an alternative to the 'negative theology' of the Mallarmé-tradition. But when he calls for this *vehemente Ablenkung* he moves beyond stylistics: in this constellation there is a glimpse of a 'dionysiac' fascination for a collectivity without subjects; 'dionysiac' in the Nietzschean sense, as an exstatic surpassing of individual identity. Benjamin seems to idealize the distracted dissemination of individuality at the expense of its *Sammlung*. Such fascination is recurrent and can be demonstrated for instance by the little essay 'Naples', which Benjamin wrote ten years earlier together with Asja Lacis (*GS* 4.1:305–16). The key words in this meditation on Naples are *porosity* and the *porous*. By this Benjamin/Lacis are aiming at the lack of definite borders between, for instance, everyday and holiday in Naples, or the tendency to dissolving borders between the old and the new, between finished and decayed buildings, or the theatrical interaction between building and action, or the non-existing border between private and public, sitting-room and alley. 'Porosity is the inexhaustible law of life in this city.' 'Porosity' means that the limits of the subject become flexible and contextually conditioned. In the Naples described by Benjamin/Lacis there are fleeting transformations between sitting-room, alley, café, and stage. There is no restricted zone for individual *Sammlung*; individuality is instead 'porously' disseminated in a dionysiac but urban setting.

Benjamin's 'porosity' from 1925 prefigures the *flâneur*-culture he was to localize in nineteenth-century Paris as well as the disseminated distraction he finds in the cinema of 1935 and associates with avant-garde expressions of art. Naples is of course described as a pre-modern precinct (and in that respect Benjamin joins a solid German tradition, as can be seen by comparing his essay to the enthusiastic description of picturesque Naples in Goethe's *Italienische Reise*). This is not necessarily one of Benjamin's many contradictions, but can instead be understood as a constant fascination with a 'dionysiac' dissolution of the subject. Benjamin in this way tries to diminish the distance between art and audience, a task that seemed to pay off, for instance, in the 'open' work of art, as it was understood in the 1960s. Benjamin's fascination could also be associated to the kind of collectivity, that was developed in the 1930s with fascistic pretexts. Benjamin's political aim with the treatise on the work of art was of course to give an alternative to fascism; still there are elements of his 'dionysiac' fascination that cannot be entirely separated from the collectivity that was a fact of his own time.

Perhaps such ideological associations could be avoided if we instead call Benjamin's recurrent fascination a pragmatic impulse in the sense that he makes individuality as well as art experience dependent on its functional context. The 'porosity' of Naples and the shock of Paris both contribute to the *vehemente Ablenkung* of the avant-garde paving the way for the distracted examiner whom Benjamin finds in the cinema. These examples have in common that context and function are decisive for the experience to be anticipated and for the individual to have an experience. Benjamin may seem to exclude experience as well as individuality and the traditional work of art from those contexts that he finds attractive in Naples and Paris; but he also anticipates new and unknown forms of aesthetical work and individual experience.

When Benjamin insists on the importance of technology and context it means that he modifies his ontological impulse as well as his apocalyptic tendencies; the ontology is pragmatically modified and apocalypse fades into a glimmer of possibilities. He may contribute to the 'negative theology' that transforms the aesthetical ontology of the 1930s, but he also goes beyond negativity on behalf of the new and yet unknown functions and possibilities of aesthetical activity. His version of the individual seems already completely disseminated, experience having fallen in value. But the disseminated individuals are open for new experience and the 'porosity' of their lives makes it possible for them to adapt, improvise, play, and experiment with their own boundaries. His works of art may be sentenced to the museal detention of lost aura; nevertheless aesthetical activity still adapts to new forms: the image is being copied, filmed, and spread in new ways. The literary work becomes letters, testimonies, documents – or perhaps the documents become literary? Benjamin's treatise on the work of art is *vehement* in its ontology and its apocalyptical view of history, but he also offers an *Ablenkung*, making it possible for thought to be distracted by the possibilities of the future.

7

THE MIMETIC BOND: BENJAMIN AND THE QUESTION OF TECHNOLOGY

FABRIZIO DESIDERI

(TRANS. JOSEPH FALSONE)

I THE TECHNOLOGICAL KNOT

Of all Benjamin's writings, his essay on 'The Work of Art in the Age of its Technological Reproducibility' is certainly the most quoted. At the same time, however, it is perhaps actually the least examined as far as its general philosophical implications are concerned. Numbered among these implications, without doubt, is the possibility of conceptualizing technology and the nexus of its relationship to human identity in a way that moves beyond the pathological oscillation between *misotechnia* and *filotechnia* afflicting much contemporary philosophical literature. On the one hand, a deeply catastrophic reading which sees in the present acceleration and transforming pervasiveness of technological development a threat to our future and an obscuring of human nature itself; on the other hand, an interpretation in a palingenetic key which detects in that same phenomenon the beginning of a new age, greatly expansive of human potentialities. Both these attitudes, whether arising from an anguished sense of alienation or moved by empathetic identification, lack that distance without which an understanding of technology in its essential boundaries is unthinkable. Distance here means the very possibility of measuring the extent to which such boundaries might lie within our own nature. To conceptualize technology entails examining our own identity; the significance (and the limit) of our ability to transcend the natural context. Technology bears witness, in fact, both to the bond which ties us indissolubly to that context as well as to the power, not so much to free ourselves, but rather to loosen the bond and tie it again with wisdom. With technology man ties a problematic knot, not only with the external natural world but also with his own nature. Precisely with the aim of analysing that knot, without presuming ingenuously to sever the thread of its original tragedy, we will reconsider Benjamin's celebrated essay in its entirety, at the very moment when it is enjoying renewed fortunes – at the very moment when Walter Benjamin's name encounters the present and he is invoked as the 'father of the internet'.

II   TECHNOLOGY AND POLITICS

One understands immediately why the nomadic inhabitants of the Net might hail Benjamin as one of their precursors. They choose Benjamin, far more than his friend Adorno; and Benjamin, rather than Heidegger. The first quite obvious motive lies in the type of relationship Benjamin's thought maintains with technology: not a 'fetish of doom' but rather 'a key to happiness', as Benjamin states in one of his most militant writings (a review of the anthology *Krieg und Krieger* edited by Ernst Jünger).[1] What is difficult to understand here is the measure of sobriety implied in this statement. By speaking thus, Benjamin in no way intends ingenuously to emphasize the thaumaturgic power of technological development.[2] His reflection arises rather from a criticism of the sacred bond which technology has formed with war. Benjamin intuits how this bond has its basis in the endurance of a magical relationship to nature, one which eliminates all distance in relation to nature. The sacralization of technology is nothing other than the complement of that which Benjamin will call, in his essay on the work of art, the 'aestheticizing of politics'. Set against both is the cipher of politicization, which is something more than and different to the redirecting of technology's instrumental character (of pure means) towards one aim rather than another. Against the theory of neutrality, Benjamin seems tacitly to set the theory of technology's constitutive ambiguity. Just as the Greek *pharmakon* is both poison and antidote at the same time, technology can signify either the destruction of human nature or its potentiation (and in the final instance, salvation). If in the earlier case it was the doctor's knowledge in relation to the patient's body which resolved the ambiguity, in the case of technology the discriminating element concerns the mode of relations between knowledge and the social body. The deciding factor in this case is the form assumed by that 'kingly art' which, for Plato, consists of politics: an art which does not share the specialization of other technologies (the internal logic of their development) but examines precisely the problem of governing the relationship between particular technologies and a common human destiny. If on the one hand the development intrinsic to technology has an almost natural rhythm which is in any case devoid of government, on the other hand the instance of government, which is proper to politics, cannot ignore the transformations of the human landscape produced by this plural rhythm of development.

It is therefore a question of reciprocally adapting the form of politics and the forms of technology. This implies harmonizing them in a relationship of dynamic correspondence: the opposite of a recourse to the mythical-aestheticizing arsenal as an apparatus for simplifying a problematic knot which involves both the detachment of the *polis* from the natural order and its necessary belonging to that same context. One could observe that, faced with this problem, Benjamin takes as his point of departure a genuinely Kantian assumption: the recognition of a permanent asymmetry between technological and moral progress. It is as if – observes Kant – humanity had two legs and proceeded swiftly with one while limping with the other.[3] If the concept of cumulativeness can seem problematic when applied to science, it appears much less so in relation to technology. Here, the difference between competing paradigms is a linear function of the effectiveness of pro-gressing. Technological innovation reveals itself to be an intimate quality of the autonomy of technology which, in each of its spheres and sectors, drives its own transformation (in a sort of blind, internal finalism) towards the 'automatism' of a second nature.[4] The technological paradigm *par excellence* becomes, in this way, that of the automaton: that which, in its essential contingency, contains within itself the origin of its own movement. In automatism, which assumes the form of a productive process characterized by the repeatability of procedures and the reproducibility of products, technology bends the spontaneous fortuitousness of becoming (*automaton* = chance) into a kind of natural necessity.[5] And this must be governed by that instance of liberty which contrasts politics as an intrinsically non-automatic art. Out of this arises its drama, exposed forever to the *facies destructiva* of the *quasi*-natural automatism of *techne*. Returning to Benjamin, his entire review of Jünger's anthology appears to be traversed by the problem of an *adaequatio* between human relationships and the always nonetheless imperfect automatism of technological progress; it appears traversed, in short, by the necessity of a political corrective. 'If this corrective fails,' Benjamin presciently observes (writing in 1930!), 'two million human bodies will indeed inevitably be chopped to pieces and chewed up by iron and gas' (*SW* 2:320–1).

III   ART AND TECHNOLOGY (HEIDEGGER AND ADORNO)

Soberly aware of its political drama, the manner in which Benjamin thinks about technology is never reductive or overemphatic. Overemphasis and reduction, after all, go hand in hand. Consider the case of Heidegger: here, technology can appear to be a fate which completes that of metaphysics, for the simple reason that technology is reduced to something other than itself. The essence of technology, Heidegger repeatedly declares in his well-known essay 'The Question Concerning Technology', is to be thought of as 'nothing technological'.[6] Identifying the modern essence of technology with a mode of ordering that disturbs nature in order to utilize it (with the imposition of a frame – the *Gestell* – which reduces nature to a 'standing-reserve'), Heidegger sets against this the meaning which echoes in the word's Greek origin. *Techne*, in its intimate connection to the dimension of knowledge (the *episteme*), indicates something much broader than a craft activity concerned principally with the production of means. Its producing shares with knowledge the capacity to unlock, to un-conceal, and it there-fore signifies above all the production-manifestation of truth, of *a-letheia*. For this reason, inasmuch as it is a 'mode of revealing', *techne* today concerns every productive dimension of making (even that dimension inherent to the sacred and to high art), and it belongs therefore to the sphere of *poiesis*. But this convergence of meaning between technological and poetic making in the pro-duction of truth holds only for that original state of unity in which art itself 'was called simply *techne*'.[7] The fate of modern technology is rather that of obscuring and masking the meaning of *poiesis* through its character of ordering. In this way, the work of art becomes the paradigm of the technological product, the model capable of illuminating the essence of the technological. The work of art can – as Heidegger maintains in his essay on 'The Origin of the Work of Art' – be explained *iuxta propria principia*. Even in the modern era, in other words, the essence of a work of art does not lie outside of itself: the origin of the work is nothing other than art itself. However, this privilege – to be understood as originating exclusively in itself – is not shared by technology. Technology's origin (and therefore, according to Heidegger's thinking, its very essence) is either brought back to a meta-physical attitude of thought or deduced from a *poietic* activity which makes the work of art a 'setting to work of the truth': the historicising opening of the strife between world and earth. In both cases, however, a diachronic divide also nonetheless subsists between the original meaning of technology and its present one.[8] Thus, the essence of technology is ultimately recognized in its original truth, either directly, in the history of Being (as a mode of its happening, of its becoming event and destiny) or in the opening character of the work of art (which exceeds the space of technology in that it contains its own origin, or is originating in the proper sense of the word: initial and instituting). In both these alternatives (between which Heidegger's thought oscillates indecisively) what always remains in shadow is, paradoxically, just that which is technological in technology and therefore, in the final analysis, technology itself.

A similar kind of overemphasis can be found in Adorno, even if there are significant shifts of accent. Technology, in Adorno's work, is a cipher of the administrated world: the agent of an objectivizing frenzy which progres-sively erodes the terrain of free subjectivity. The last remaining refuge in the face of this extreme form of the Hegelian objectivizing spirit is the negative dialectic which perception can set alight in great works of art: in works which, at the culmination of technical-compositional process and expressive will, exhibit the aporia of incompleteness and the enigma of what remains unexpressed. This gives rise to the substantial rejection from the sphere of great art of all those expressive-aesthetic forms where the technological element concerns not only the constructional principles immanent to the work, but also, and in a decisive manner, the very nature of their coming into being: that which Benjamin defines as their being essentially reproducible or, rather, reproducible from the beginning. It is as if, for Adorno, the situating of reproducibility at the origin of the artwork negated, almost *a priori*, the dimension of negative mimesis which constitutes the essentially constitutive tension of the relationship between art and nature.[9] While, as we shall see, it is exactly this nexus between the reproducible character of technological procedures and the mimetic attitude at the origin of artistic production that is one of the crucial points of Benjamin's essay.

The *novum* in the relationship between art and technology at the centre of Benjamin's analysis is the ultra-modern emergence of the principle of reproducibility. Focalizing this theme – in a progression symmetrically inverse to that of Heidegger – Benjamin projects the problem of the modern fate of the artwork against the political-conflictual background of technology. By involving the process of art-making at its innermost level, reproducibility reveals one of the essential characteristics of modern technology: that of welding innovation, communication, and reproduction together in a single process. The *opportunity* of technology, we might say, lies in characterizing its production in an eminently reproductive sense. The technological-reproductive instance here actually rivals the auto-*poiesis* of nature, directing its internal finalism to include even this feature in the automatic reiterability of its procedures. As a result, just where its 'conceptual' autonomy in the face of nature would appear to be greatest, technology – independently of the perfective or mimetic character of its products and even in the case of their perfect artificiality – attests to its mimetic bond with the auto-generative process of *physis*. Benjamin seemingly invites us to consider as much in his essay on the work of art. To understand how, it is worth retracing the essay's internal lines of development.

IV   TECHNOLOGICAL REPRODUCIBILITY AND THE DISENCHANTMENT OF ART

Works of art, Benjamin observes, have obviously always been reproducible in principle, but until now their reproducibility has functioned to safeguard their authenticity, maintaining the unique and unrepeatable character of their origin: the originality which makes them works of art in the modern sense of the term. What changes radically in the space of time which passes between the invention-diffusion of photography and that of film is precisely the idea of the work's authenticity: the idea of its originality. In this change, the work of art is, as it were, de-magicized, withdrawn from the state of primitive enchantment in which its cult value was prevalent. The disenchantment of art is brought about, in other words, by the enormous expansion of its 'exhibition value'. And it is exactly as a result of the absolute weight assumed by this value (by the pole of exhibition value at the expense of the ritual pole) that 'the work of art becomes a construct [*Gebilde*] with quite new functions. Among these, the one we are conscious of – the artistic function – may subsequently be seen as incidental' (*SW* 3:107).

It is only possible to define some of the features of this completely new construct which art, in Benjamin's eyes, is becoming, if we understand clearly what is meant at this point by the expansion of its exhibition function. The general sense of exhibiting is to render accessible, public; what is exhibited ceases to be secret (from this arises the theme of de-fascination, of disenchantment) but it does not for all this cease to be true. At work here is obviously what Adorno called Benjamin's 'illuminism' (ultimately interwoven, according to Adorno, with his mysticism) or if one wishes, the motif of 'profane illumination' formulated in the celebrated essay on Surrealism. What is profaned in this case is exactly the relationship between art and technology. There is a *pars destruens* of Benjamin's essay which runs wholly along this thematic thread: in the face of the perceptual disruption induced by the inherently reproducible work of art – reproducible, that is, at its own origin – to attempt to build an embankment out of the traditional categories of the philosophy of art, such as creativity, genius, contemplation, and the privileged character of aesthetic fruition (to name but a few), is to brandish a useless fetish. Here Benjamin does not in the least indulge in a mythologizing of art as the last refuge of authentic experience or of access to truth in opposition to the degraded character of everyday experience. For a simple reason, which can be inferred from his observations on the relationship between Dadaism and *réclame*: the traditional categories of the philosophy of art, in the modern profaning of the relationship between art and technology, become an object for the masses, just as works of art do. Hegelianly, it could be said, these categories realize themselves, they arrive at their unfolding conclusion. This is what Benjamin means when he notes how the distinction between author and public is beginning to lose its axiomatic character. If 'at any moment, the reader is ready to become an author' (*SW* 3:114), it is equally true that every distracted spectator can, and with good right, exercise the function of the critic. If 'the technological reproducibility of the artwork changes the relation of the masses to art' (*SW* 3:116), there is, implicated in this process, a progressive extension of the qualities of artistic genius to the common subject or – if you like – a progressive assimilation of aesthetic production to a banal and commonly accessible technological procedure. This is a phenomenon which Benjamin perhaps only glimpses, but which becomes more apparent than ever in the age of 'cyberspace'. To the technologization of nature, which, like a colossal artefact, creates the world we live in, it could be said that there corresponds a growing aestheticization of a world feigning the real immediacy of nature. It feigns what has become, in the land of technology, nothing more than a chimera – a view of immediate reality, and with it the possibility of astonishment, of perceiving its appearance as beautiful. Until, in short, there occurs the interpenetration of these two processes in the artificial production of immediate sensation which characterizes so-called 'virtual reality'.

V   ART AS PERFECTING *MIMESIS*

In the face of the overly lyrical glorifications of the virtual that are so popular today, Benjamin's reflection is still capable of acting as a salutary corrective. His diagnosis relating to the transformation of art in the age of its reproducibility does not entail its liquidation. It signifies rather a shifting of the problematic terrain of its actuality and function. This shift, which leads to a rethink of the very meaning of technology, can be summed up in a twofold formula. This involves, as far as the work of art in a narrow sense is concerned, a move from the sacred, *poietic* separateness of the work to the 'horizontal' criticality of the 'aesthetic experience'.[10] And, as far as technology is concerned in general, a move from the centrality of the idea of 'absolute production' to that of 'perfecting *mimesis*'. With this definition (*vollendende Mimesis*), Benjamin, in a note relating to his essay on the work of art, sums up the thesis according to which 'art is a suggested improvement on nature: an imitation [*Nachmachen*] whose most hidden depths are a demonstration [*Vormachen*]'.[11] In the ineradicable mimetic dimension of technology there is, then, that astuteness (and that trickery) which befit an activity born from 'knowing in advance'. Perhaps without intending it, in the play (which is not only linguistic) between *Nachmachen* and *Vormachen*, Benjamin recalls the originally Promethean character of technology. This is not, however, the aspect developed in the various drafts of the essay on the work of art and in the variants and notes which relate to it. The prevailing dimension is constituted rather by the grafting of the reflection's anthropological tenor on to an underlying Platonism which is never abandoned, not even in the late period of the formulation of the idea of the dialectical image. This leads Benjamin to insist on the productive (*poietic*) dimension of mimetic art, but also on the mimetic dimension which marks technology's productivity from the very beginning. Technology and art are in this way unitarily understood against the background of a mimetic relationship to nature. If there is a human faculty from which art in its broadest sense (as *techne*) springs, then it is, for Benjamin, to be identified in the mimetic rather than in the imaginative faculty. The 'primal phenomenon of all artistic activity', its very origin – we read in the second version of the essay on the work of art – lies in *mimesis* (*SW* 3:127 n.22). In this faculty and in the impulse which corresponds to it – as Benjamin had made clear in 'On the Mimetic Faculty' (1933) – what is in question is not only the ability to assimilate and to conform, but above all the ability to produce similarities.[12] If in the first case distance in relation to otherness is lessened to the point of identification-assimilation, the second case establishes a relationship with otherness, or rather, it produces the space of this relationship, the space in which one plays with alterity.[13] From this arises the polarity which dominates the mimetic attitude: on the one hand, semblance, on the other, play. Cult value and exhibition value are nothing but derivatives of this pair of concepts. Accordingly, what occurs in works of art with 'the withering of semblance and the decay of the aura' is nothing other than an enormous gain in *Spiel-Raum* (space for play) (*SW* 3:127 n.22).

It is here, perhaps, that Benjamin's analysis seems to be analytically less perspicacious. That is, at just the point where it is observed how in film 'the element of semblance has yielded its place to the element of play' (*SW* 3:127 n.22). It would be all too easy to observe that things do not, in reality, stand in these terms. Adorno had already brought to his friend's attention the fact that his analysis of the decay of the aura was lacking in dialectical development. In other words, there is a technological aura and therefore a survival and powerful resurgence of the element of semblance already visible in the pre-television and pre-information technology era on which Benjamin reflects (but, as we know, different historical-political necessities inspired the essay on the work of art: necessities that will find a theoretical formulation in Benjamin's philosophical testament, the thesis 'On the Concept of History'). In short, it is not only a question of film responding to the decay of the aura by factitiously constructing *personality* outside the studio. The claim of every contemporary person to being filmed already contradicts the thesis of a revitalization of the cult moment (the cult of the star) outside the work (rather than in the production of semblances of which it consists). If in making this observation Benjamin is referring to Vertov's *Three Songs of Lenin* or to Ivens's *Borinage*, one cannot help but think instead of Andy Warhol's well-known dictum.

VI   SEMBLANCE AS THE 'APORETIC ELEMENT' IN THE BEAUTIFUL

Certainly, it is not in the absence of an American experience that we can best grasp the true limit of Benjamin's essay. That limit lies instead in Benjamin's having so clearly set the idea of the aura against that of reproduction, almost as though it implied a kind of philosophy of art history. Much pleasure has been had by those critics of Benjamin[14] who highlight an ambiguous and wavering attitude towards the concept of aura: on the one hand, it appears in the essay as a sort of paradise lost of experience; on the other hand, nostalgia for this dimension of the past is criticized as a residual illusion. The reason for this oscillation (which Benjamin does not appear to resolve, even if one considers essays contemporary to the one on the work of art, such as 'The Storyteller') does not lie, however, so much in the notion of aura as rather in its identification with the idea of authenticity and uniqueness. It seems, on the basis of this identification, almost as though there had existed, at one time, an auratic art destined irremediably to disappear with the onset of the age of reproducibility. But this is quite a superficial reading of Benjamin's essay which ignores, if nothing else, its strategic collocation within the *Passagenwerk* project. Considered in this light, the shadow of a schema for a philosophy of history relating to the opposition between aura and technological reproduction fades into the middle ground, giving way to a reflection on the nature of experience and on the role which perception, memory, and reproduction play within experience. To understand how such a reflection might possibly develop, it will be helpful to recall a very important note contained in the essay 'On Some Motifs in Baudelaire'.

The note in question regards Baudelaire's *Correspondences* and consists of a meditation on the idea of the beautiful, which reconnects the threads of an argument developed many years earlier in an essay on Goethe's *Elective Affinities*. Benjamin is interested in demonstrating how an experience that tries to 'establish itself in crisis-proof form'[15] finds expression in Baudelaire's poetry. Such a form – he observes – can in the first instance only be sought in the sphere of the cult. When experience leaves this sphere it can only find refuge in the beautiful: 'in the beautiful, ritual value appears as the value of art'. Up to this point it seems we are not that far removed from the schema of a philosophy of history which underlies the framework of the essay on the work of art: first the cult (religion), then art as its surrogate (even if, it must be said, in the essay on the work of art the preponderance of cult value seems to indicate something closer to the artistic religion contemplated by Hegel in his *Phenomenology* rather than a pure and simple secularization of religious experience ...), and then a *tertium* yet to be defined, where the crisis of artistic reproduction runs parallel to a crisis in perception and, it follows, of experience itself. But it is in the actual development of the note that the most interesting innovations are to be found. The definition of the beautiful divides in two directions: in relation to history and in relation to nature. Both cases 'bring out the role of semblance' as 'the aporetic element in the beautiful'. As far as the historical dimension of the beautiful is concerned, Benjamin makes do with relatively few remarks: historically, the experience of the beautiful takes shape largely in response to the claim of a tradition which coalesces around a work – it is an '*ad plures ire*', an admiration of that which earlier generations have already admired.

We are dealing, in other words, with the passive dimension of the formation of taste as cultural conformity. It is one of the ways, in short, in which historical appearance is celebrated as aesthetic experience. The moment of discontinuity in the *habitus* of perception is instead attributed to the experience of the beautiful in relation to nature. What is in question here is not, obviously, a partition of the object (relating to the 'material' of the beautiful) so much as, to be precise, a formal distinction (relating to the quality of experience: to the character of immediacy and at the same time of critical potency inherent in a given act of perception).[16] In this case, what Kant would have called the 'beautiful in nature' presents itself as 'that which remains true to its essential nature only when veiled' (*SW* 4:352 n. 63).

What does Benjamin mean by this definition which he takes, citing himself, from his essay 'Goethe's *Elective Affinities*'? Among the many possibilities is, without doubt, the quality of *necessary semblance* which characterizes the beautiful, its purely relational character. Not an essence which conceals itself behind phenomena or (it is the same) which manifests itself in them, so much as something which unfolds itself in the pure perceptual relationship and which at the same time subtracts itself from any conceptual determination. In this relation both the maximum closeness to and maximum distance from what, for lack of a better expression, we call the object of experience (the beautiful 'thing') are celebrated. In Benjamin's words, what is 'beautiful' is 'the object of experience [*Erfahrung*] in the state of resemblance' (*SW* 4:352 n. 63). This is a state of being – or better, a state of never-having-been – from which we are remote. It is as though, in perceiving it, we remembered it. This is the reason why every experience of the beautiful is played out between the sensation of the never-before-seen and the familiar: between the tonality of pure beginning and that of recognition. In respect to this experience, the veiled quality of the beautiful already represents a reproductive instance: it is equivalent, in short, to the 'reproducing element of the work of art'. This is a statement of some importance. And Benjamin is very well aware of it: notice that he employs what is indeed a 'daring abbreviation'. With this brief observation Benjamin throws into some disorder the possibility of reading his essay on the work of art as marked by a diachronic contrast between a 'before' and an 'after' the artwork's technological reproducibility.

In the work of art as reproduction and *mimesis* – we read in the note contained in the essay on Baudelaire – consists rather the 'hermetic aspect of art'. If this is Benjamin's thesis on art and the beautiful, the *novitas* constituted by the age of technological reproducibility appears somewhat redimensioned. The tension between technological reproduction (in which, Benjamin reductively observes, the beautiful would not have 'any place at all') and the uniqueness-unrepeatability of the so-called 'traditional' work of art (that is, pre-technological) is a much less problematic tension than that between the mimetic-reproductive moment of the beautiful and the object (or rather the idea) which is always subtracted from it.

In bringing to light what art has always been, a variant of technology in general, the age of reproducibility provokes rather the question of why it is that in just this case (in the case of so-called fine art, or technology which contains within itself its own end) the mimetic-reproductive moment should prevail, instead of the purely productive and perfecting element of the other *technai*. Perhaps it is for the very reason that here it is a case of producing exactly that which cannot be reproduced. That which, in another daring abbreviation, we might call nature: that nature which we ourselves are and hence that character of anti-intentionality which always inheres to the form of experience as, for better or worse, that which we can do nothing other than remember. For this reason, the *techne* which aims at the beautiful is also called by Plato *techne mousikè*. Exactly to the extent that it is a *techne* inspired by the Muses, its (re)productive *mimesis* arises from the intimate solidarity between experience and memory. This is also the reason why its work is directed solely at perception, at *aisthesis*, but at a kind of perception which is paradoxically reflective and therefore capable of acting as the custodian of memory's gesture. In a word: perhaps what we find ourselves needing to think through in the age of the digital (re)production of the work of art is a crisis of memory resulting from a perceptual expansion.

For art, in the post-traumatic age in which we find ourselves living, in the age of a mass-anaesthetism, it is no longer a question of preparing (or still less, provoking) shock. The interiorizing and metabolizing of the shock principle has in a way undermined *a priori* the self-grounding of the work, rendering always more fragmented and mobile the relationship between its truth content and its own form; and, therefore, the very relationship between the 'messianic elements' of which the work's actuality consists and those 'retarding elements' in which perception is arrested.[17] Perhaps we are moving towards a more fluid notion (one tied more to perceptive immediacy) and at the same time an even more abstract notion (more cerebral) of the work and of beauty; in short: towards that more profane and at once more mystical conception of art glimpsed by Benjamin.

VII   *TECHNE POLITIKÈ*?

All this has, on the other hand, some inevitable consequences for the way we understand technology and its dramatic connection to politics. In the first place, technology, insofar as it is a 'second nature', also becomes more fluid, to the extent that it expands into an environment the dynamics of which are difficult to predict. This requires that we conceptualize technology in all the potency of its inherent abstraction. This has to be carried out to the point where the political problem relating to technological innovation's disturbing impact on social life will be one of governing not only the inevitable tension between society and nature in its immediate sense, but also the tension caused by the progressive artificialization of the environmental context of human life. Remembering that the principle of reproducibility which constitutes technology has a mimetic heart can deliver politics from the myth of its technologicist reduction (its levelling to the horizon of other technologies).

In the great retelling of the myth of Prometheus contained in Plato's *Protagoras, techne politikè* is not numbered among those arts which derive from the Promethean act. Politics, recalls Protagoras, is a supplementary gift from Zeus, who sends Hermes to distribute respect and justice among men. There is, then, in the art of politics an element of grace (or, if you like, a happy contingency) which eludes the dynamics of the transmission of knowledge and the teaching of skill typical of all technologies (of their intrinsic regularity). On the other hand, without this divine gift, men cannot 'band together' and 'secure their lives by founding cities'.[18] Protagoras has in mind here the threat of wild beasts and the necessity of learning the art of war, which is part of politics. But not even the demiurgical technologies, resources of basic human survival, are able to be preserved, to be stabilized and transmitted, without politics. The contingency which politics must govern is therefore – in the modern era primarily so – the reflected contingency, to the second power, of the social body, produced by the plurality of other *technai* and crossed by their reciprocal competition. The aporia towards which Socrates drives the sophist Protagoras, who is convinced that the knowledge from which political art is born is perfectly teachable to every citizen, lies in forcing him to admit that the art of politics presupposes an 'art of measurement' (*techne metretikè*) involving the discernment of excess and deficiency in relation to the good and the bad. This *techne*, which must always struggle with the *dynamis* of appearance (with the power of phenomenal actuality),[19] is what 'saves our life'.[20] It regards the meta-technological dimension of the *psyche*, where the becoming-one of Self-government coincides with the self-interrogating dimension of conscience.[21] For exactly this reason, it cannot be taught, cannot be transmitted: one can only learn it on one's own; so, in the final analysis, 'it is not an art'.[22] If *techne politikè* does hinge on this, then there is an unavoidable conflict between the intimately non-reproducible character of that which produces it (its essential gratuitousness) and the destiny-development of the technologies established in the Promethean act. This act – uniting technological knowledge (which Plato calls *entechnon sophia* in the *Protagoras*) in a single, necessary connection with the contingency of nature (the fire stolen from the gods) – can be called the gesture which founds the dominion of the artificial as the sole sphere in which human nature can develop itself and, even more simply, survive. On the other hand, this same dominion is itself devoid of government and it is therefore always exposed to the risk of an anarchic self-destructiveness. The circle of innovation, production, and diffusion which dictates its artificially evolutional rhythm drives it towards a necessary disproportion. It is essential, in this regard, to recall that at the origin of this productive *hybris* there is an instance of reproducibility in which human *techne* plays astutely with the generative power of nature. In this instance, technology confirms the contingency of its origin and, along with this, the fragility of the mimetic theft which embodies its significance. Only by remembering that, by remembering the necessarily disharmonious act with which man responds to his non-immediate adaptability to nature's rhythm, can *techne* preserve, in its deepest sense, the bond of distance separating man from nature but also from himself.

The measure of this double distance is already perceptible, in a manner not all that paradoxical, in the fact that the human being is not suited either to nature or to technology. This fact reinforces the meta-technological character of politics, insofar as it governs the plural and multifarious world of human passions, and reveals a highly vicious circle of reciprocal resolution between human identity and artifice. In this circle, a sense of technology perfectly forgetful of its mimetic origin (a technology as absolute production and therefore productive of its very own premises) would assert itself. That the possibility of a literally anarchic technology is implicit in the Promethean act is itself a part of its tragic character. It would not be so, however, if it did not also contain its own opposite: the possibility of transforming in a virtuous sense the circularity between artifice and nature as constitutive of the human essence.

Such a possibility, which certainly does not eradicate the primal tragedy (which is the very form of *techne*), is entrusted in the final instance to that opening of memory and of experience from which good politics can arise. Which also means containing *techne* itself within its internal limits. And this means thoroughly conceptualizing technology as *automaton*, or rather, the polemic unity between contingency and necessity, between innovation and reproducibility, between chance and destiny, between event and environment. Perhaps it is just this technological aspect of technology which has hitherto remained in the shadows. To illuminate it means to understand technology's essence as the pure mimetic artifice, at once both chance and law, in which it institutes itself. Even in the memory of its origin, the essence of technology is confirmed as something technological.

8

AURA, STILL

ROBERT KAUFMAN

I

How many heated debates last for 70 or 80 years – or more? Actually, lots of them, and even a shortlist of theological, cultural, and sociopolitical instances would take too long to enumerate here. The notion of historical acceleration might be invoked to suggest that such lengthy duration becomes increasingly rare in an ever more technologized, speeded-up modernity; but the idea of historical acceleration has itself been vigorously debated, not to mention that events on the ground during the last few decades, even when replayed at fastforward settings, offer evidence that old problems and struggles still have lifespans incommensurable with the admittedly supersonic newscycles that today report on them. Perhaps one realm where the great controversies *could* now logically be predicted to live very fast and die unprecedentedly young would be that which we tend to associate with art, aesthetics, criticism, and theory. Everybody knows that, at least since the dawn of modernism, art and theory have understood the need for constant, eye-catching change, on the model – if not as the ultimate example – of fashion. Postmodern dedication to recycling hardly seems to have eased that perceived pressure.

But contemporary reflection on modernism's aftermaths takes place in a context where modernism's original insurgency is now, depending on whose chronology we use, 90, 100, 120, maybe 140 years behind us. Meanwhile, postmodernism's initiatory salvos against canonical modernism now reach back – what, 30, 40, 50 years? – so far back that to more than one sharp undergraduate it seems to be, as with turtles, postmodernism all the way down. In that light, I would like to reconsider a now-70-year-old debate that presumably should have been long buried together with any straightfaced claims for modernism's living presence, much less its future. This is a debate that, against the apparent odds, continues going strong even as it has been transformed; the debate's ongoing character may tell us a bit about the continuing meanings of modernism, which was itself already mature (already 'late' by some influential accounts) when this specific controversy began.

At any rate, there really *has* been ceaseless dispute among artists, critics, and audiences, virtually since the day it began, about the effectiveness of Walter Benjamin's Marxian advocacy of those modern artistic experiments and forms that highlighted what he called 'technical reproducibility' (fatefully translated from German – initially into French – as 'mechanical reproduction'). Benjamin, of course, had been thinking in particular about the intentional or effective jettisoning of romanticism-identified notions concerning the *aura* created through the artist's imaginative labour, the trace-presence of something no longer literally, physically present but nonetheless still shimmering; Benjamin had likewise been thinking about abolition of the contiguous concept of *aesthetic autonomy.* The two had been brought together in the theory and practice of the romantic work of art, whose aura and autonomy were not only simultaneous but synonymous.

Whatever the merits of the positions initially and subsequently expressed in the debate, the last three decades have yielded a clear consensus that the real life of Benjamin's mechanical-reproduction theory has occurred during its posthumous celebration in postmodernism, precisely the period in which the culture of the copy, simulacrum, and reproduction has come to make modernism itself look romantically auratic. It therefore bears noting that some of the most challenging works of art and theory in late postmodernism have seemed to want to reassess – sometimes quite explicitly – the stakes of the original debate between Benjamin and his most important interlocutor, Theodor Adorno. In the first part of what follows, I will schematically rehearse the largely Adornian grounds on which these recent explorations have begun to make the surprising suggestion that new possibilities for a progressive, critical art and theory may depend on postmodernism being succeeded by more – by later – modernism. There are some clearly romantic entailments involved here, for the overarching issue has been Adorno's defence of a negatively approached aura (a negation raised now perhaps to the second or, really, to the third or fourth power), an aura whose critical value Adorno in effect deems to have survived Benjamin's proclamation of aura's supervention by technical-mechanical reproducibility. Adorno's effort of course builds on and subtly refunctions Benjamin's initial analysis of the loss of aura in modernity – an analysis Benjamin had happily stolen from German and British romanticism, not to mention the line of French poetics that begins with Baudelaire.

Our most familiar representations of the aura-debate have tended to cast it as a drama between, on the one hand, an elite, embattled, and hermetic commitment to a high modernist aesthetic that – for all its anti-romantic professions – stands as the inheritor of the transcendental impulse (this is the frequently presented picture of the Adornian position); and, on the other hand, a popular or populist engagement with the more immediate, evidently technical-mechanical situation – the modern experiential reality – of social labour (this is the Brechtian-Benjaminian position). There is no doubt about the intensity of the dispute. But even apart from considerations that commentators have raised about Benjamin's (and later Benjaminians') analyses of technical-mechanical reproduction itself – everything from the understanding of the filmic apparatus and its presumed shock effects, to the experience of sitting in the movie theatre, to the allegedly immediate, spell-breaking, critical response that cinema inculcates, to the actual character of the commercial cinema in Benjamin's time or ours – even apart from all those matters, it is worth asking whether the 'aura vs. mechanical reproduction' debate is to any degree accurately characterized when it is cast as a face-off between abstract aesthetic aether and concrete social labour.

That is, one may ratify or contest either side's vision of how art best instantiates social labour; yet precisely this *labour* is crucial to both sides in the controversy. Why? Because not just in Adorno, but at memorable moments in Benjamin as well, aura's trace-presence, its charged distance, its luminous and disturbing conjurations of otherness, had once registered – amongst other things – the potentials of a collective subject's labour power and agencies. Hence, in an ongoing duel with Brecht over Benjamin's aesthetic and critical soul, Adorno challenges not only what he sees as instrumentally productionist claims for the alleged inherently progressive character of an immediate embrace of mechanical reproduction; Adorno also holds fast to – and over the course of decades he develops much further and more explicitly – that nexus of aura and labour initially posited by Benjamin himself, and nowhere more so than in the domain of lyric poetry.[1]

Following Benjamin, Adorno consistently argues for the 'critical' nature of a modern aura whose point of departure he, like Benjamin, tends to locate in romantic lyric poetry. Adorno's rewriting of aura traces its criticality first from romanticism, and then from the later nineteenth century, on to modernism and after. In contradistinction to Benjamin's sometimes radically technologicalist stance, and especially in contrast to some of the most popular, post-1968 interpretations *of* Benjamin, Adorno asserts that German and British romanticism, French postromanticism, and then modernism itself are key stages in the development of an inevitably if complicatedly auratic artistic *experimentalism* dedicated to critical perception of 'the new' ('the new' here being understood ultimately as the not-yet-grasped features of the mode of production and, in fact, of all that is emergent in the social).

It is the dynamic character of auratic or autonomous art, Adorno contends, that enables critical thought (and the sociopolitical praxis it can generate) in the first place; the criticality that begins to emerge in auratic romantic art, Adorno insists, is indispensable rather than anathema to Marxian dialectics and other progressive or radically intended methodologies. Adorno therefore argues that those currents in twentieth-century art and criticism that emphatically celebrate an 'anti-aesthetic', and that one-sidedly indict or eschew auratic aesthetic autonomy in romantic or nineteenth or twentieth-century objects of study, thereby contribute – however unwittingly – to the destruction of genuinely critical response. In short, auratic art for Adorno stands not so much for bourgeois subjectivity and false consciousness as for the new critical possibilities made available by a kind of art and aesthetic experience that, precisely in its relentless dedication to the aesthetic, paradoxically winds up being *anti*-aesthetic*ist*.

Indeed, Adorno emphasizes that the concept of the *via negativa* auratic work of art – which since Benjamin has been stigmatized for enshrining a regime of 'aestheticization' – actually provides the basis for resistance to aestheticization. In play here is Adorno's key distinction (derived from his anti-essentialist, constructivist readings of Kantian aesthetics and modern poetics); this is a distinction precisely between the *aesthetic* and aesthetic*ization*.[2] Adorno contends that the aesthetic allows for the experimental development of a protocritical consciousness whose aesthetic play or felt spontaneity mimes social labour insofar as artistic making and aesthetic experience tend processively to discover aspects of the social that have been obscured by *status quo* conceptualizations of the latter; aestheticization, meanwhile, is for Adorno the proper name of an unreflective acquiescence to reification. The claim is that, despite the ways in which auratic art courts and sometimes falls into aestheticization, auratically invested artworks nonetheless make possible the exercise of those faculties whose development contributes invaluably to sociopolitical critique and praxis. The *intentional* abandonment of aura, Adorno believes, is what yields true (truly baleful) aestheticization (in the form of 'culture-industry' reifications designed to inculcate conformism rather than critical agency). The *intentional* abandonment of aura actually serves to efface and ratify, rather than to recognize, contest, or refunction, the phenomenon of reification. This occurs because the *intentional* abandonment of aura leads to a failure even to register negatively – through vexed attempts to create or access aura – the crucial modern phenomenon of aura's loss (or at least its apparent loss). What the *intentional* abandonment of aura then produces is not the critical objectivation of the reifying process, the bringing to light of the erasure of labour and the commodification of everyone and everything; what results instead is culture's straightforward, affirmational repetition of a consequently unchallenged reification.[3]

For Adorno and sometimes Benjamin, the effort negatively to register all this stands as a necessary attempt to gesture towards and reinvent aura in the very modernity that all too frequently appears to have banished it, that appears to have erased the sense of quasiphysical, quasicognitive, quasiexperiential otherness in art, an otherness that – to reiterate – is for Adorno fatefully linked to the social and its reality of, amongst other things, labour.[4] These last, moreover, are perhaps the original and ultimate objects of Adorno's simultaneous theorization of aura, 'second-reflection', and the *Ershütterung* or *shaking* of the subject in aesthetic experience. Adorno conceives *Ershütterung* as that which, by dint of aura's dynamic of charged distance, can break down the hardening of subjectivity – can break down through this *shaking*, in other words, 'the subject's petrification in his or her own subjectivity' and hence can allow the subject to 'catch … the slightest glimpse beyond that prison that it [the "I"] itself is', thus permitting 'the "I"', once 'shaken, to perceiv[e] its own limitedness and finitude' and so to experience the critical possibility of thinking otherness.[5] The schema is familiar to readers of *Dialectic of Enlightenment* and kindred Frankfurt texts: The baleful consequences of an instrumentalizing Enlightenment are to be addressed not by renunciation but by radical extension of Enlightenment; the problem of subjectivity is to be answered not by less but by more subjectivity, not by the existence of fewer but by the achievement of more subjectivities.

In our age of postmodernist celebration of endless technological reproduction – and just at a moment when a plethora of new translations and studies of both Benjamin and Adorno have appeared – there is cause to believe that Adorno's sustained modernist defence of the negatively auratic, (provisionally) autonomous work of modern art helps point towards a renewed vocation for auratic modernism today, and for those romantic (though not neoromantic) legacies in literature, art, and aesthetics that in complicated fashion underwrite modernist aura. Signs of such a development have again appeared in the various arts; even without broaching the phenomenon of the now-weirdly modernist status of so much work originally adjudged postmodern, one could cite the prominent examples, amongst many, many other instances, of the dances Trisha Brown has been making; the painting of well- and less-well-known artists, including Terry Winters, Sean Scully, Stanley Whitney, Dona Nelson, Richard Tuttle, Hanna Hannah, Marina Adams; significant aspects of the work of renowned poets like John Ashbery and Robert Creeley, as well as that of figures only beginning to receive the attention they have for some time deserved, ranging from – to mention only a few – Barbara Guest, Susan Howe, Michael Palmer, Robin Blaser, Nathaniel Mackey, Norma Cole, Mei-Mei Bersenbrugge, Laura Moriarty, Alfred Arteaga, and Marjorie Welish; the work of musicians located in various realms, from Dave Douglas, Gonzalo Rubalcaba and Charlie Haden, Maria Schneider, David Murray, Anthony Braxton, and Dave Holland, all the way over to – still, in their ongoing return aesthetic engagements – Pierre Boulez, Eliott Carter, and, really, far too many others even to mention.[6]

Though emerging from a landscape long presumed to be thoroughly postmodernized, the work of these artists has frequently reincarnated, in however different versions, one of the most charged practices discussed throughout the modernist-aura debate, a practice or mode that Benjamin and Adorno had placed at the heart of their respective analyses: *lyric abstraction*. And given that lyric poetry – not music, painting, or cinema – was the art form where Benjamin and Adorno could discover between them a fiercely shared dedication, it is perhaps appropriate that (with the possible exception of certain sectors of the music world, and the cinema of Jean-Luc Godard) the most germane recent reflections on the Benjaminian-Adornian articulations of the 'mechanical reproduction vs. aura' controversy have come in experimental lyric poetry. This is a development that has pushed beyond the expected matrix of today's German, French, and Italian poetry, expanding well into the *œuvres* of poets throughout Latin America, the US, and Canada. Here the fate of aura is again being tested in what Benjamin and Adorno had identified as being, at least since Baudelaire, the 'go-for-broke' arena of poetry's socioaesthetic experimentalism (the arena Benjamin and Adorno had indeed identified as the testing ground of poetry's very ability to continue affording critical perception of the new, its ability to help bring to light previously obscured aspects of the social). (For the traditions of poetics in which Benjamin and Adorno participate, modern lyric ambition stands as a, or even *the*, high-risk enterprise for literary art: The lyric poem must work coherently in and with the medium – language – that human beings use to articulate objective concepts, even while the lyric explores the most subjective, nonconceptual, and ephemeral phenomena, including aura itself. This theoretical or philosophical difficulty, concerning how simultaneously to think objectivity and subjectivity, also arises practically as lyric abstraction's great problem of form-construction: How to build a solid, convincing artistic structure out of something as evanescent as subjective song and how, in the bargain, to delineate or objectivate the impressively fluid contents of capitalist modernity?)[7]

Boiled down, the apparently Benjaminian and postmodernist argument has held that a critical poetics should be anti-lyric, anti-aesthetic, and committed to poetic methods ingeniously associated with technologically oriented reproduction, all in order to effect radical defamiliarization and the renewal of sociopolitical commitment. Meanwhile, playing careful variations on Benjamin's themes, Adorno argues that – at least since Baudelaire – the critical force of poetry depends precisely on the formal ability to make lyric itself critical (which is quite distinct from abolishing or getting beyond auratic lyric subjectivity and modern aesthetic autonomy). Preserving Benjamin's insights about how Baudelaire brilliantly makes lyric vocation confront the ostensible destruction of its own historical precondition – the kind of temporal-reflective *experience* apparently no longer possible, Baudelaire's poems seem to declare, in a radically commodified, high-speed, high-capitalist modernity – Adorno nonetheless effectively defends a lyric that begins by singing song's impossibility, but whose refusal of aura *tout court* would be the refusal of critique. In short, Adorno pushes on with the analysis set forth in Benjamin's 'On Some Motifs in Baudelaire', where a vexed discovery of lyric aura's power occurs precisely in the moment of marking aura's further dissipation and now-seeming impossibility.[8]

It would be useful to focus the rest of this chapter on the ways that contemporary experimental lyric reimagines this very process and, in that sense, keeps faith with aura. Yet it might prove at least as valuable to take a more unexpected step and make a literary-historical return to some of those Ur-moments and Ur-figures of lyric aura's seeming collapse in the face of modern technical reproduction – a return, in other words, to what retrospectively has been seen as a foundational or anticipatory moment for the modern–postmodern divide. Arguably, the acid test for the Adornian-modernist reading of aura's exponentially raised *via-negativa*-survival would be Brecht and Benjamin themselves. And it so happens that one of the least discussed episodes in the whole history of Left modernism and Critical Theory concerns Brecht's and Benjamin's intense re-encounter with – and finally, it would seem, their complexly modernist reinvention of – romantic lyric aura.

II

But in ways that turn out to involve far more than happy accident or coincidence, contemporary art itself seems to have been rediscovering – well in advance of criticism and theory – precisely these Brechtian-Benjaminian encounters with mechanical reproduction's presumed Other, lyric abstraction. Brief treatment of just one instance does more than help to inaugurate the retelling of the Brecht-Benjamin history in question; it actually illuminates and clarifies the stakes that will be involved in such historical recovery.

Consider for a moment the painter Stanley Whitney, now in his mid-fifties but known across three decades as a painter's painter. Whitney's work has been treated in analyses that emphasize his contributions to the continuance of Abstract Expressionism's formal experimentation with colour and line, with the drawing of geometric space and form by means of colour itself; and – alternately or in tandem with such formal concerns – Whitney's paintings have also been treated in terms that stress his commitments to thinking the Abstract Expressionist tradition together with African-American history and culture.[9] The relevant trajectory, as Whitney has often described it, includes the generative tension he experienced, as a young artist, between the stimulus of Clement Greenberg's enthusiasm about his paintings (during Greenberg's early 1970s visit to Whitney's New Haven studio) and an urgent attraction, felt at the same moment, to the work of the Black Arts Movement in general and the stance of Amiri Baraka in particular. Adamant through the years about working from an Abstract Expressionist matrix, Whitney has nonetheless undertaken a series of formal explorations that involve what he has consistently thought of as Black histories of colour, song, and rhythm in painting as well, of course, as the other arts. If Beauford Delaney, Alma Thomas, and Bob Thompson are only three of the more obvious precursors here, it is significant that Whitney likewise regards Mondrian in that light.[10]

Whitney has frequently collaborated with the poet Norma Cole. Cole is one of a number of contemporary poets whose work, though decidedly experimental, is adjacent to, rather than of, the avant-gardist writing generally described as 'language poetry'. The key difference revolves around the issue of lyric. For Cole, as for the poets mentioned earlier in this chapter, poetic experiment depends on, and is perhaps synonymous with, the stretching of lyric practice. A painter herself, Cole has been known not only for her poetry, but also for numerous translations, particularly from the French.[11] Indeed, the Baudelairean lyric counter-tradition forms a key strand in Cole's poetics, as do American lyric innovators of the post-World War II era (not least, the late Robert Duncan, to whom Cole was personally close; she has worked on several projects with Duncan's surviving life partner, the painter and collagist Jess).[12] 'Singularities: The Painting of Stanley Whitney', a text Cole wrote for one of Whitney's shows, begins to suggest profound affinities between painting and poetry in relation to the matter of lyric:

> The first circle recapitulates the ones to come. Each one will be different. Aphoristic dashes pin them down, at first from within, later from all possible directions. The elements can't all be moving at the same time. Where hesitation becomes rhythmic assertion, a dance steps into the recognizable system of moves called the physical lyric. In its transgression of its own system, each painting questions assumptions about generalization. The universe is composed of singularities.
>
> ... Critical focus manifests itself at every point. The painting is complete attention. Its every event is new and fresh and alert. Like a musician quoting a few bars of another song in his own song, the painter, at moments, makes tonal quotes: yes, thinking of Matisse here, remembering Bob Thompson's flat emblematic use of color here, articulating the Yoruban investigation of shape's numinosity, here.
>
> ... How do you begin something that has no apparent beginning? Like some poetry, like music, this painting unhooks color events from daily accountability in order to present configurations that offer experience belonging to painting, to looking at painting ...[13]

Exactly during this period of intense concentration on and writing about Whitney's paintings, Cole was completing and seeing into press a volume of poems entitled *My Bird Book*.[14] *My Bird Book* imagines its way through all sorts of birdsong and bird-flight, through the history of lyric's imagings of songful, reticent, and cacophonous birds; the volume meanwhile elaborates the sorts of constellations of colour, rhythm (felt, danced, seen), and melody that are so prominent in 'Singularities'. The epigraph to the volume's title-sequence enunciates the trajectory of those materials in a way that introduces *My Bird Book*'s compression of formal and social issues into charged birdsong, where both song and bird seem to rise as one:

Fly well, Kippie
Fly well, Kippie

(from *Songololo*)[15]

The cited *Songololo: Voices of Change* is Marianne Kaplan's unique documentary film of political and cultural resistance to South African apartheid on the eve – though the film's subjects and director did not know it was the eve – of Nelson Mandela's release from decades of imprisonment on Robben Island. In one of *Songololo*'s most remarkable scenes, the poet (and then-African-National-Congress activist) Mzwakhe Mbuli, accompanied by a group of Township jazz musicians with whom Mbuli is attending a memorial service for the saxophone and clarinet player Kippie Moeketsi ('he died a pauper/a victim of apartheid'), recites his elegy for Moeketsi:

… Like all birds do
Kippie did not forewarn us of
His intention to fly away
To the greatest giants of this world I say,
Fly well, Kippie,
Fly well, Morolong
The doors of your nest
Are wide open awaiting …

… the thought of your ministry
Will have an eternal home
In the hearts and the ears and the minds
In the thoughts and dreams

Fly back, through our dreams
Please, fly back through our thoughts
Please fly back during our manufacturing of
New sounds like you did,
Like you used to do

Fly well, Kippie
Fly well, Morolong[16]

The multiple lives and invocations of song and flight – Kippie Moeketsi's birdlike life of soaring song, gone now but recalled in the words, in the music, and in the attendings of Mbuli and the musicians and mourners (and later, the attendings of the film audience), and then re-chanted as the envoi of *My Bird Book* – of course constitute a series of attempts to meld song to memory and struggle. More precisely, these are linked and cumulative attempts to recognize and amplify thought's sung struggle *to remember*. It could no doubt be powerfully argued that in its original, immediate, clearly politicized context, such transcendentalism has nothing to do with the false consciousness so often imputed to literary and aesthetic schemes of transcendence. Mbuli, after all, has been hailed as an activist poet dedicated to modern development of oral traditions. It would be at the point of literariness or aesthetic self-consciousness – the replacement of the popular materials into more explicitly experimental refinements of form – that baleful aestheticization would kick in: lyric abstraction would formalize sociopolitical content into merely personal and/or merely formal expression; or so the argument usually goes. At least in the case at hand, however, the argument-from-context would be ignoring the evident intentions of the agents all along the chain: namely, their clear desire (proclaimed throughout *Songololo*) that their songs, poems, and stories be recirculated in as many modes and forums as possible. Compare the notion enacted in the disarmingly simple first line of 'Singularities', with its recursively rhythmic, sonic, and ideational chimings, which extend from the sentence's filiated beats to its linked *i*'s and *o*'s, its jointure of the geometrical and the historical: 'The first circle recapitulates the ones to come.'

In what might be *its* own go-for-broke move, *My Bird Book* resituates this debate about lyric, abstraction, artistic experiment, and the real.

'AFTER ARTHUR, or please let me be misunderstood'

What about the realism of lyric poetry?

B. Brecht

When will we go
    by ditch and by hill – slash and burn
have you found yet your sentence voiceless iris? There is
(what the poet says about flowers) a false accountability (what
someone says to the poet about flowers) someone is ordering
books burning bread space is mangled in the mistakes
doesn't involve *maniaque*[17]

The manic speed and demonic lyric skill that is here referenced belongs, certainly, to that child of Baudelaire named Rimbaud (the 'Arthur' of the poem's title), and the presented evilness of lyric beauty is at least in part its speeding-by-us, lack of straightforwardly referential, 'accountability'. Yet Arthur – or lyric poetry after Arthur – then turns out to be in dialogue, from the epigraph onwards, with none other than Brecht (for whom, incidentally, Rimbaud was always a crucial precursor). And as the poem continues, the need to be brilliantly, fashionably, *absolument moderne* interrogates, and is interrogated by, a partially Brechtian questioning of what the real *is* (what it is in itself, what it is insofar as it exits 'After' being taken up by 'Arthur', that is, by modern lyric):

p.s. dying as a sign as in I am
elaboration
by ditch and by hill
to lift with dehydrated fist
fit enough exactly like this
what model works
the coffin lid
without inflation
without exception
what model works responsible singing (may the farce be with
you) ropes in the brain what bounds intervention arises from
the safety boats
I want my freedom in safety! how to get what finds some
memory at the second remove

The vertiginous consideration of what is real for and in poetry – including the poem's registration of socially conventional phrases and ideas; the questions *what works?* and *what is work?* (re-sounded, as so much else in 'After Arthur', from *Une Saison en enfer*); the drunken-boat couplings of freedom and safety; the interanimations of Rimbaud's social poetics of homosexuality and a mid-to-late-1980s, barely dawning recognition or momentary postscriptum of AIDS' staggering toll ('p.s. dying as a sign as in I am/ … to lift with dehydrated fist') – comes to feel, as it sonically and ideationally makes precision and wildness identical, like *Verfremdungseffekt* itself, a clarity-in-estrangement as Brechtian as it is Rimbaudian.[18]

The appropriation and misquotation (in the poem's title) of Eric Burdon and The Animals' 1960s hit 'Don't Let Me Be Misunderstood' ('I'm just a soul whose intentions are good/Oh Lord, please don't let me be misunderstood') points towards a recognizably Brechtian way with materials that may or may not be genuinely popular in character, a confusion perhaps inherent in the materials' 'original' status as mechanical reproduction. ('After Arthur' only increases that generative confusion when, on the presumably Rimbaudian side of the ledger, it reroutes back into its own taut verse lines not only The Animals, but also the various prose-poem moments smuggled from *Une Saison en enfer*, with Rimbaud's virtousic ability to capture verse-tension for the prose-poem somehow honoured by being run in reverse-forward.) Cole's imagined Brecht-in-dialogue reveals a slyness redolent of the actual Brecht, always looking to incorporate the nonlyric materials while winking at the fact that something – something *lyric* – is thereby done to the materials, which are 'misunderstood' to the extent they are presumed to be exactly what they were before being taken up by a poet who, radical as he or she might be, nonetheless writes lyric. Yet that by no means implies that lyric or its contents have been levelled, have become inconsequential, or have been relegated merely to satire and parody:

> look at me turning into a *mother*
> tools, weapons, weather
> conversation on the rim
> quotes from people including myself
> on me more and more yours
> often stranded or familiar
> what's for us
> pink quartz interruption
> 'Shoot! Shoot at me!' when working social conventions
> until hell bottoms out but
> who would stir up furious firestorms
> but us and those we think of as kin?

The lines' pressure and controlled volatility, built as much from their calibrated beats as from their unexpected aural and thematic cross-chimings (as in *more yours* and *for us* and *firestorms*), seem inexorably to force a voicing of violence ('Shoot!') that's leagued with 'social conventions'. As the poem moves forward only to continue disclosing its own back-formation (notably including romantic lyric diction – in fact, Rimbaud's own modernization of romantic lyric diction, pulled now ever further ahead, with apostrophes directed in the first place to the question of labour and where, in an English phrasal context, it becomes ambiguous as to whether the lines apostrophize (as in 'O!') or just contract (as in 'top o' the morning' or 'I'm workin' o' it')), we learn that

> it's up to us romantic friends you'll like this
> we won't work o firetides!
>
> figures in the ground
> and the leaves turned down
> o seasons o castles a game in which the pieces don't move

and then, from this intense fusion of dance-song and grand lyric apostrophe that 'After Arthur' has whirled itself into, the poem in its last lines openly speaks its heretofore only implicit debate:

A.R. – Do I remember nature? myself?
– *no more words.*
I'm burying the dead in my gut.

B.B. – It's nonsense. You have to ignore
it. Depth doesn't get you anywhere
at all.[19]

Whether the poem's 'B.B.' (remember all those poems where Brecht calls himself 'poor B.B.'?) provisionally regards Rimbaudian experimental rethinkings of romantic and symbolist transcendence as 'nonsense', or, just as likely, regards naturalism's, *Lebensphilosophie*'s, or orthodox social realism's hosannas to content ('depth') as nonsense, remains ambiguous. And of course this ambiguity, though probably not of the canonically deconstructive variety, is the point.

For what Cole has here latched on to is that one of the great figures of twentieth-century artistic *engagement* had periodically identified lyric's porous and transformative – its abstracting, ambiguous – ways with its social materials as a necessary component of any worthy account of how art relates to social reality. But besides the imaginings, in 'After Arthur', of the ideational , not to mention formal (at the registers of rhythm, figure, syntax, tone, and diction) dance between Rimbaud and Brecht, the poem's epigraph and body speak volumes about a decades-long *theoretical* controversy. Along with literally thousands of other artists, critics, and students, Cole had initially encountered Brecht's question – 'What about the realism of lyric poetry?' – in the first paragraph of his anti-Lukács essay 'On the Formalistic Character of the Theory of Realism', widely available in English since the 1977 publication of *Aesthetics and Politics*. As it happened, in the midst of making her own poems, and in her ongoing relationship to Whitney's and others' painting, Cole had returned to Brecht's thinking about lyric, abstraction, and the real when she avidly – along with many fellow poets – read Kristin Ross's *The Emergence of Social Space: Rimbaud and the Paris Commune*, and saw Brecht's question suggestively quoted early in Ross's study.[20]

The *poesis* that 'After Arthur' achieves gives its readers to understand that Brecht's question is far more than a quip, and that for Brecht, lyric and its ostensibly problematic abstraction and expressivity are necessary rather than hostile to art's intercourse with reality. (This further explains why the poem's reanimation of Rimbaud is doubly framed and voiced by Brecht: initially by Brecht's own words and finally by 'Brecht's' posthumous *aperçu*. To be consciously After Arthur, the poem implies, is to hear and re-pose Brecht's Lyric – Brecht's Rimbaudian – Question.) Lyric, on this practical-theoretical view, experimentally commits its precision, emotion, musicality, and intellection to its social materials, attempting formally to realize its special versions of art's determinate indeterminacy, art's exact but capacious – and sociopolitically enabling – ambiguity. Yet one might hardly notice this stance on lyric emerging from the selection of Brecht essays offered in *Aesthetics and Politics*, or, for that matter, in most other anthologies that have intended to cover the Expressionism Debates. But Cole's hunch about the terrific force of Brecht's seemingly casual question about lyric – the hunch embedded in the quotation in 'After Arthur', reimagining, and enactment of the Brechtian Lyric Question – will turn out to be right on target vis-à-vis an unaccountably, or all too accountably ignored crux in literary and aesthetic history, to which we can now, finally, direct our attention.

III

In June 1938, Benjamin joins Brecht in Svendborg, Denmark, where the two exiles from Nazi Germany work together for several months, sharing ideas and manuscripts. Despite their differences of opinion with it, Adorno and Horkheimer had recently published Benjamin's 'The Work of Art in the Age of Mechanical Reproduction'. Meanwhile, for the previous two years, Benjamin and Brecht had both been associated with the German Popular Front, Communist-led 'anti-fascist literary journal' *Das Wort* (*The Word*), published in Moscow. Brecht served – quite often ambivalently – as one of the journal's principal editors.[21] For two years, the journal had run a series of translations (and articles on the contemporaneity) of the English romantic poet Percy Shelley; Benjamin and Brecht had followed these texts closely. In fact, as Benjamin and Brecht were entirely aware, *Das Wort* was following a long-standing tradition of Left German Shelleyanism that consciously traced itself back to Engels and Marx, and whose latter-day representatives included figures around Left German Expressionism and *Das Wort* itself, such as Alfred Wolfenstein and Walter and Gabriele Haenisch.

In July 1938, a month after Benjamin's arrival in Svendborg, Brecht writes and hands to Benjamin a group of essays intended for *Das Wort*; there is evidence that Brecht may have talked through the essays with Benjamin as he drafted them.[22] Some of these essays, which take issue with Lukácsian realism and defend the critical value of experimental art, have been quite familiar to Anglo-American readers since 1977, when they appeared in *Aesthetics and Politics*, and to German-reading audiences at least since the 1973 publication of *Die Expressionismusdebatte*. Brecht went ahead and submitted the essays to his coeditors at *Das Wort*, who declined to publish them.[23] But in addition to their fears about rocking the orthodox boat, the other editors of *Das Wort* may also have withheld publication of these Brecht essays in order to protect Brecht himself. If so, they had good reason; which is to say, the materials of our story get grimmer: A few months after *Das Wort* had published Walter Haenisch's January 1938 essay on Shelley, Haenisch became one amongst legions falsely accused, amid the general insanity in Moscow, of 'Trotskyite' and/or 'Social-Fascist' espionage. Haenisch was denounced and executed as a 'people's enemy'.[24]

One of these unpublished Brecht essays of July 1938 – which unfortunately is not included in either *Aesthetics and Politics* or in *Die Expressionismusdebatte*, and which has never appeared in translation – is 'Weite und Vielfalt der realistischen Schreibweise (Range and Diversity of the Realist Literary Mode)'.[25] The essay's central exhibit is Brecht's quotation, translation, and analysis of 25 stanzas from Shelley's *The Mask of Anarchy*. Two years earlier, *Das Wort* had published and commented on Alfred Wolfenstein's translation of 55 stanzas from Shelley's *Mask*. Brecht's translation aims for a crackling literalness that departs intriguingly from Wolfenstein's rendering of Shelley's poem.[26] (*The Mask of Anarchy* (1819) became one of Shelley's best-known responses to what was commonly known as Peterloo or the Manchester Massacre, an event in which armed cavalry attacked a huge but peaceful demonstration for parliamentary reform and workers' rights. Peterloo immediately achieved the iconic public, rallying-cry status that incidents like the 1960 Sharpeville Massacre in South Africa, and the Edmund Pettus Bridge attack on African-American civil rights marchers, would come to have for a later period. At all events, the modern British labour and parliamentary-reform movements both treat Peterloo as a foundational moment. For his part, Shelley fashioned the 91 quatrain-stanzas of the *Mask* in popular ballad mode. But, as commentators (including an approving Brecht) have remarked, Shelley also – inevitably – infused the poem with formal and stylistic elements more typical of his lyric practice.)[27] Brecht claims, as he begins his essay-translation, that 'the great revolutionary English poet P. B. *Shelley*' demonstrates how a vital fusion of aesthetic experiment, speculative imagination, and lyric song may lead to, rather than away from, critical mimesis of the real (the latter being virtually synonymous, throughout 'Weite und Vielfalt', with commitment).[28] Brecht's 'Weite und Vielfalt' thus develops the question only broached at the start of its companion-essay (the companion-essay that would later become widely available in German and in translation), 'On the Formalistic Character of the Theory of Realism': What about the realism of lyric poetry?

At the same time that he translates and analyses *The Mask of Anarchy* in 'Weite und Vielfalt', Brecht also translates nine stanzas from Shelley's anti-Wordsworthian satiric poem *Peter Bell the Third*, a translation which remains unpublished throughout Brecht's lifetime.[29] Brecht hands his *Mask* essay-translation and the *Peter Bell* translation to Benjamin; Benjamin copies out the *Peter Bell* stanzas, preserving them in the pages we know as the *Passagenwerk* or *The Arcades Project*.[30] Benjamin also quotes, and briefly comments on, Brecht's translation of *Peter Bell*'s famous 'Hell is a city much like London' stanza in 'The Paris of the Second Empire in Baudelaire' – an essay Benjamin happens to be in the middle of writing, and whose draft manuscript he gives to Brecht. Brecht reads that draft of 'The Paris of the Second Empire in Baudelaire' and copies out portions of it for the fragments *he is* writing on Baudelaire; Brecht meanwhile records his continued mulling over, and identification with, Shelley, and he likewise transcribes his energetically self-divided meditations upon Benjamin's comments about how aura animates an otherness that confronts both artist and audience.[31] The Brecht–Benjamin interchange, amounting almost to collaboration, is so intertwined that it is hard to tell the order of influence amongst these July and August 1938 writings. At any rate, a common set of subsequently canonized images and ideas – not least among them, an approach to lyric aura – appears in Brecht's Shelley essay, Benjamin's two most famous Baudelaire essays, and then Brecht's Baudelaire meditations and Brecht's later poetry.

Equally remarkable is an extended interpretive passage on Shelley and Baudelaire in Benjamin's *Passagenwerk*; based on Brecht's translation of the nine *Peter Bell* stanzas, it is clearly the fuller version of the super-compressed but much-better-known comparison of Shelley and the French poet that Benjamin offers in 'The Paris of the Second Empire in Baudelaire'. In the *Passagenwerk* entry entitled 'Zur Bilderflucht in der Allegorie' ('On Image-Flight in Allegory'), Benjamin more extensively develops the comparison of Shelley and Baudelaire. The remarks gesture towards a sense of how the two poets' divergent approaches to allegory chart the mode's modern fate in general:

> The incisive effect [in Shelley] depends ... on the fact that Shelley's *grasp* [*Griff*] of allegory makes itself felt. It is this grasp that is missing in Baudelaire. This grasp, which makes palpable the distance of the modern poet [Baudelaire] from allegory, is precisely what enables allegory [in Shelley] to incorporate into itself the most immediate realities ... Shelley rules over the allegory, Baudelaire is ruled by it.[32]

Benjamin says a good deal more, but his point is not to proclaim Shelley the greater poet. He implies instead that a turn in modernity and in the history of aura has apparently made Shelley's critical allegoresis unavailable to Baudelaire. Baudelaire finds himself too distanced from – from what? Benjamin's answer is that Baudelaire is too distant from auratic distance; and to be distant from auratic distance is to know an *immediacy* alternately so busy and blank that reflective experience seems unattainable. Auratic distance, to put it differently, provides the condition of possibility for the critical-reflective allegoresis Shelley can still undertake. The rest of Benjamin's analysis becomes virtually canonical for modern poetics and criticism: Baudelaire's intermittently critical triumph will be to make lyric poetry sing – severely and intensely – its own impossibility in the age of art's mechanical or technical reproducibility.[33]

While this is not the place for a full-scale treatment of the crisis of allegory in Baudelaire (or for Benjamin's ideas about the career of allegory in modern poetics thereafter), a few words are in order. *Allegory* is of course the contested term whose modern reprioritization over *symbol* stems in no small measure from Benjamin's 1928 study of the German play of lamentation, the *Trauerspiel*. For Benjamin, allegory's initial point of departure is that it represents the broken, ruptured truth of attempts at prematurely 'symbolic' reconciliation. Hence allegory signifies its own necessarily nonidentical – thus potentially critical and constructionist – character. Suffice to say here that the *Passagenwerk* section about Shelley, Baudelaire, and allegory is one of the key instances where Benjamin articulates his formal theory (of allegory's protocritical, constructionist nature) together with an historical instance of a lyric poet whom Benjamin, Brecht, and their circle definitely regard as progressive and committed: whom they regard, indeed, as *den grossen revolutionären englischen Dichter.*

Activated by Brecht and reconstellated by Benjamin, the 1938 matrix of Shelley, Baudelaire, and allegory generates two trajectories that currently concern us: towards the later art of Brecht himself, and towards the philo-sophical aesthetics of Adorno. Brecht, already having brooded over the poetic kindling, finds it reignited when, in his already strange Los Angeles exile, he belatedly learns (in 1941) of Benjamin's suicide at the Spanish border. The news contributes importantly to the devastating *Hollywoodelegien* and to texts bound chronologically, thematically, and formally to them. It has rarely been noticed that, among these texts, not only the poem 'Nachdenkend über die Hölle' ('Reflections on Hell') is indebted to the figure that that poem calls *'mein Bruder Shelley'*.[34] In fact, the larger groupings of related poems and drafts – which include three texts that explicitly treat Benjamin's suicide – are saturated with themes, directly translated quotations, paraphrases, and images from Shelley, all of them dealing in some way with aura.

Just as significant, in these poems, are Brecht's very complex treatments of tonal register, his stereoscopically introduced, mutually dissolving images, and a syntax of deceptive ease and elegance whose unreeling builds rather than releases tension.[35] All of which, Brecht signals time and again, come in no small part from that auratic, distant though animating source, Brecht's *'Bruder Shelley'*, who in Brecht's eyes had found interventionist commit-ment inseparable from auratic lyric impulse and formal aesthetic autonomy, not least in time of difficulty and loss. '*Wo ist Benjamin, der Kritiker?/ … Benjamin ist an der spanischen Grenze begraben./ … Ich fahre entlang den Bomberwerften von Los Angeles*' ('Where is Benjamin, the critic?/ … Benjamin is buried at the Spanish border./ … I drive along the bomber-hangars of Los Angeles').[36] It is not overshooting the mark to say that Brecht's almost too-terrible decision – to write wartime, Shelleyan elegy that could be taken for bitter satire, and vice versa – is a decision that should count as powerful, and intriguingly *late modernist* evidence for the acute readings that critics like James Chandler, Jeffrey Cox, and Steven Jones have offered of *Peter Bell the Third*'s historical originality: its relentless insistence on thinking modern lyric aura and negative, darkly satiric impulse together, and on thinking both in relation to modern poetry's ways of taking history's measure.[37] It seems barely necessary to add that Brecht's efforts in the face of Benjamin's death reinvent, via a just-beyond-reach *Shelleyan* lyric aura, exactly the critical possibility Benjamin had seen in Baudelaire as being, at most, only fitfully available (and available, in Baudelaire, virtually against itself, certainly less definitively, Benjamin had thought, than *in Shelley* and perhaps, Benjamin had conjectured, for what would be its historical endgame).

The overarching structure and phenomenology of Brecht's dark auratic poetry is not so different – after allowing for the enormity of further, ultimately inconceivable historical materials – from what Adorno will later treat as Paul Celan's necessarily stark apotheosis of this same Baudelairean counter-tradition in lyric.

> What Benjamin noted in Baudelaire, that his poetry is without aura, comes into its own in Celan's work ... The language of the lifeless becomes the last possible comfort for a death that is deprived of all meaning ... Celan's poems want to speak of the most extreme horror through silence. Their truth content itself becomes negative. They imitate a language beneath the helpless language of human beings, indeed beneath all organic language: It is that of the dead speaking of stones and stars.[38]

Adorno essentially rearticulates and extends Benjamin's earlier analysis: The lyric counter-tradition from Baudelaire to Beckett and Celan had always opposed official culture's 'culinary' version of aura, a version that whitewashed and abolished aesthetic aura's charged distance by promising instead to serve aura up immediately, by offering it in, and as, immediacy. Vis-à-vis *that* kind of aura, a 'critical' aura will appear – on first or maybe even fifth blush – as dissonance or, in the most extreme cases, as having no atmosphere, no aura, at all.

Brecht gives his Shelley-infused poems of shaken, bewildered, and bitterly enraged exile to Hanns Eisler, who works with the *Hollywoodelegien* and related texts of what will become the *Hollywoodliederbuch* and who then, one Los Angeles night in October 1942, sits down at the piano and premieres these impossible *Lieder* for an audience consisting of Brecht, Hans Winge, and Herbert Marcuse. Brecht only 'ups the ante' by then testily noting Eisler's distressing tendency, when Eisler 'speaks about, [though] not when he composes' the settings, to drop the elegies' significance down a rhetorical or formal-stylistic notch.[39] That is a fantastic micro-dispute to consider, because Eisler, far from undertaking a wholesale genre stripping or programmatic levelling of still-too-high and auratic elegiac verse, instead so virtuosically runs Schubertian and Schumannesque *Lieder*, French *chanson*, and Schönbergian twelve-tone composition in and out of one another, that it is hard to miss the settings' recognizably modernist tour de force of newly achieved form and voice. It is as if the (protopostmodern) levelling holistically occurs in what Brecht hears as Eisler's irritatingly interpretive-judgemental comments, so that the work itself can then move on to enact its real, critical desideratum: modernist virtuosity in the exploration, coordination, and imaginative synthesis of extremely diverse literary-musical materials and dauntingly various stylistic currents. Brecht acknowledges as much when he rather bluntly insists (against Eisler's alleged murmuring about the poems' mere occasionality or jottedness) on the *Hollywoodelegien*'s compressed monumentality and *gravitas*: 'these are full-scale poems' and 'in fact the compositions are probably really important as music too' ('*Dies sind volle Gedichte*' and '*in der Tat haben die Kompositionen wirkliche Bedeutung wahrscheinlich auch als Musik*').[40]

On the page and in Eisler's settings, the poems exert important influence, across at least three continents, on an increasingly late, still stubbornly persisting critical practice of modernist poetry and, to a lesser and even more temporally staggered degree, modernist music composition. Indeed, with their complicated reception-histories, the *Hollywoodelegien* and the poems immediately connected to them testify to the unexpectedly continued, vibrant existence *of* late modernism, well into the era commonly called postmodern (and in which modernism is of course regularly framed as canonical or reactionary object of critique).[41] The very fact of the elegies' modernist aesthetic and declaredly critical-romantic lineage, which for Brecht seems indissolubly linked to the poems' unblinking view of commitment's unpredictable paths in art and life, would appear substantially to reconfigure recent periodizations and style-characterizations of postmodernism and its much maligned antecedent.

That is, Brecht's late enterprise entails the nonparodic revivification of an ostensibly passé, auratic, lyric-aesthetic poetry, a revivification Brecht in part accomplishes by returning to and reforging the Shelleyan-Baudelairean imperative that lyric critically reimagine itself. Though not exactly hermetic, Brecht's negative-sideways, backward-forward path towards postauratic aura effectively tries to reidentify lyric vocation with – or as fuel for – Marx's old 'ruthless critique of everything existing', which in *its* turn casts a salutarily cold eye upon lyric's criticopolitical pretensions. Brecht's structuring of this fruitful and constitutive tension between aura and protopolitical critique amounts, astonishingly enough (since it is after all *Brecht* that we're talking about), to the reconjuration of something like a Left-Enlightenment, radically formal aesthetics from elegy ash. Recognition of such a project in his later poetry should begin to unsettle long-standard accounts of how Brecht (or Benjamin, for that matter) alternately models an exchange-value Left cynicism, and a mechanical-reproductionist, exhibition-value 'avant-gardist anti-aesthetic' (all of which, in solidarity with radically intended postmodernist art and theory, tend generally to oppose themselves to a more auratic modernism).[42]

The next logical step would be to guess that, insofar as Brecht had been pursuing what he had come to see as a consciously Shelleyan commitment to the critical-progressive potential of auratic lyric form, we could likewise infer Brecht's acceptance of the consequent result in the Shelleyan argument about such form: namely, that it can be taken from artists and works that are apolitical, that have become or perhaps always were downright conservative. The precise term for this problem is, in Shelley's vocabulary, *Wordsworth*.[43] But interestingly enough, we do not need to make the inference at all in Brecht's case, because Brecht goes directly there himself. In August 1940 – in the early aftermath of his and Benjamin's reencounter with Shelley and the question of aura, but before Benjamin's death and the poetry that Brecht begins to write thereafter – Brecht consciously bites the bullet, and he begins doing so during the Battle of Britain. Now in exile in Finland, and writing in his *Arbeitsjournal*, Brecht notes that he has found himself rereading Wordsworth and being 'moved to reflect [on] how varied the function of art is'; Brecht's reflection is prompted not just by Wordsworth's poetry in general, but by Wordsworth's most seemingly formal, apparently sociopolitically inconsequential, *lyricism*. And, as Brecht goes on to copy various Wordsworth passages into his notebook, he seems unable to resist observing that the Wordsworth volume before him happens to be a 1927 republication of the 1879 Wordsworth *Selected* that had been edited and introduced by that poet and critic of the barricades, Matthew Arnold.

At all events, though hardly dispositive regarding the renewed considerations of Brecht's support of or opposition to official Comintern and Party policy, it is worth remarking that this *Arbeitsjournal* entry about Wordsworth's poetics explicitly links Brecht's defence of the formal and experimental value of lyric aura to *anti-fascist* sentiment and activity. For Brecht specifically contrasts what, he hints, have been ill-judged Left indictments (of, for instance, the 'petit bourgeois' character of, and presumed audience for, Wordsworthian poetic 'idyll'), to what Brecht *now*, with some measure of self-directed irony, characterizes as the merely 'petit bourgeois' and lyric-Wordsworthian stances that have led English men and women rather courageously to resist Hitler (and a number of these Wordsworth-reading English 'petits bourgeois', Brecht takes pains somewhat wryly to record, had previously gone to Spain to fight Franco). The matter of Comintern- or Party-line arises because Brecht writes with evident sympathy for such 'petit bourgeois' poetics and politics at a moment when the Soviet Union and the Comintern had continued – in language Brecht previously had endorsed – to describe the British struggle against Nazi Germany as an inter-imperialist contest unworthy of solidarity from progressive forces. These reflections on the poetics and politics of Wordsworth's lyric aura finally lead Brecht to write out three complicated 'theses', as he calls them, about the 'danger[s]' of misunderstanding the values of poetry, artistic form, and aesthetic experience. The theses are inaugurated by a striking, well-nigh Adornian distinction – by a formulation, indeed, that reads as if its author had gone to sleep one night as Bert, only to awaken and write the next morning as Teddie: 'Art *is* an autonomous sphere, though by no means an autarchic one (*Die Kunst ist ein autonomer Bezirk, wenn auch unter keinen Umständen ein autarker)*'.[44]

Adorno characteristically gets back into the act by starting – or continuing – a fight. By letter, he complains to Benjamin about how bad Brecht's Shelley translations really are. Two funny things eventually happen, though; Adorno seems to change his mind, or at least, he warms to the way that Brecht had made the Shelley materials available to Benjamin's thinking about Baudelaire, commitment, allegory, and aura, which clearly come to affect Adorno's thinking and theory. In fact, in one of Adorno's most important statements on romantic and modern poetry's importance for modernist constructivism – the 1963 essay 'Parataxis: On Hölderlin's Late Lyric Poetry' – the entire Brecht-Benjamin rediscovery of Shelleyan aura is fantastically compressed and assimilated into Adorno's own analysis.[45] And just to stir up the pot some more, there are various indications that after the war, Brecht or some of those closest to him, may have come to share Adorno's doubts about the quality of Brecht's Shelley translations.[46] In that same postwar period, Adorno – while continuing to fight tooth and nail (and not always with complete cogency) against what he deemed to be Brecht's theoretical stances and Brecht's dramatizations of them in the theatre – accords ever more respect to Brecht's poetry, going so far as to designate Brecht and García Lorca as the only twentieth-century European poets whose auratic lyric power could hold its own in terms of aesthetic importance against the more hermetic, more evidently *symboliste* and surrealist poets of the Baudelaire-Mallarmé-Rimbaud tradition whom Adorno tended to favour.[47] Suffice to say that it would take more pages than I have already used to outline the rest of the story of how the poetic matrices and the question of aura at issue among Brecht, Benjamin, and Adorno shape the manner in which Adorno will go on to understand poetry's role in contributing to a potentially critical modern aesthetic.[48]

IV

What are the elements that combine to make particular versions of lyric critical, rather than just official or 'culinary'? In terms of the different historical moments at issue in this chapter – those of Shelley, Baudelaire, the modernist years of Brecht and the Frankfurt School, and then our own period – what contexts, and artistic practices, distinguish the critical from the institutional? The question demands an essay or two in its own right, but a few points can be suggested. First, it would probably be misguided to imagine that some method or set of criteria could produce a definitive answer. There was, after all, good reason in each of the moments treated above to believe that what might have begun as a critically auratic practice had eventually lost its animating sense of aura's loss, so to speak; hence the rediscovery, in each case, of critical auratic distance (through an experimental willingness to understand and approach aura negatively, even if that would seem to require radically turning away from whatever had lately been trading under aura's sign). The pages of the earliest issues of a journal like *October* provide powerful testimony about how and why certain institutional histories and artistic practices could coalesce to make lyric abstraction seem as official as official could get, however much one might object to the notion that the underlying problem was lyric abstraction *per se*.

Such a scenario – of an inevitable back-and-forth between lyric abstraction and the contestation of it – certainly accounts for significant portions of modern and postmodern literary, artistic, and critical history. Whether grasped in relation to some overarching conceptual-historical telos, or simply as a spiralling binary structure that operates only formally (without any predetermined content or logical endpoint), the pattern is recognizably Hegelian. But that recognition provides one among several clues that, for all its undeniable power, such an analysis of when, how, and why lyric periodically becomes critical seems to miss something crucial about the ways that Benjamin, Brecht, and Adorno (and the contemporary artists mentioned in this chapter) approach lyric aura. One way to begin trying to understand this would be to remember how aura's crisis comes to be so important for Benjamin's (and – through Benjamin's influence – for Adorno's) theory and practice of the *constellation* and *force-field* (*Kraftfeld*). These latter are often and rightly understood as an intellectual attempt nondeterministically to locate and dynamically connect elements (historical, socioeconomic, cultural) that are not initially given as relational, but that, when animated – constellated – into conjunction create or reveal a signifying force-field. That force-field for its part illuminates the larger social reality whose elements have been brought together in affinity and tension (rather than in a falsely integrative totalization) to make the constructivist force-field itself visible.[49]

What seems to have escaped attention in much recent commentary is how profoundly *un*Hegelian in form and content, how opposed to pregiven, back-and-forth schemes of thesis-and-antithesis, are the ambitions and engagements of the constellation and force-field. (That opposition makes perfect sense; Benjamin has correctly been described as possessing scarcely a Hegelian bone in his body.) In a manner that begins in his early work – and that reappears so powerfully in 'On Some Motifs in Baudelaire' and the 'On the Concept of History', and that informs virtually every page of the *Passagenwerk* – Benjamin resists the idea of approaching historical analysis from the standpoint of a (Hegelian) conceptualism that always has trouble allowing that which has not yet been conceptualized (that which is historically emergent and hence the basis for the *new* concept) to emerge. This is to say that Benjamin's most characteristic impulses are based in, or based in attempts to radicalize, the critical force of Kantian reflective aesthetic experience and judgement.[50] The immediate sources for Benjamin's exploration of the constellation and force-field of course include Nietzsche, Emerson, and astronomical discourse. But perhaps the key factor that makes Nietzsche's and Emerson's thought so congenial to Benjamin is the idea, developed out of Kant (by Nietzsche, Emerson, and many others), that there exists a noninstrumental yet precise, coherent, nonarbitrary mode of thought – the aesthetic – that contributes formally towards, and that imaginatively reinvigorates, conceptual knowledge, while itself foregoing substantive conceptuality and the modes and logic of argumentation and discursivity.

In the relevant Kantian framework, 'reflective aesthetic judgement', paradoxically synonymous with estrangement and defamiliarization, operates as the felt-as-necessary (but notoriously difficult to account for) 'bridge' between nature and freedom, cognition and morality, theoretical and practical reason, fact and value. In short, the aesthetic bridges objective-conceptual knowledge (or the objective world to which such knowledge corresponds) and the subjective human capacity for a critical agency that would be more than arbitrary in relation *to* objective knowledge of existing reality. (Here I can only assert something that deserves full elaboration elsewhere: Contrary to so much of contemporary Marxian and Marxian-inflected theory's 'anti-aestheticist' hostility to aesthetic experience and aesthetic judgement, Marx himself intentionally marshals the aproetic but by no means paralysing structure of Kantian reflective aesthetic judgement precisely for the 'theory of *praxis*' announced in his *Theses on Feuerbach*.) The key idea is that aesthetic thought-experience, while feeling itself to be cast in or aiming for conceptual thought, is not yet substantively-objectively conceptual. In proceeding via the *feeling* that it is objective (that it is keyed to judgements that could be universally shared), aesthetic thought-experience maintains the form – but only the form – of conceptual thought. The inherently experimental exercise of that formal capacity can produce, to paraphrase Kant, a wealth of thought-emotion that cannot be reduced to any determinate, presently existing concept, and that thus can create the materials with which to construct new concepts and the sociopolitical dispensations that would correspond to them.[51]

All of which helps clue us in to another level of the constellation's and the force-field's significance. Benjamin, to be sure, employs the constellation and force-field to *grasp* the crisis of the apparent loss of aura (especially or ultimately the crisis of *lyric* aura: hardly surprising, given lyric's canonical place in the history of art, aesthetics, and poetics, and in Benjamin's own thought). But at some point, the Benjaminian constellation and force-field rightly become understood as inseparable *from* lyric aura. That's another way of saying that the Baudelairean-Benjaminian crisis of lyric aura (the crisis of the availability, in capitalist modernity, of the sort of reflective experience that in its turn makes possible a noninstrumental yet nonabritrary, potentially emancipatory capacity for constructing new conceptual-objective knowledge) is really the crisis-question of whether, and how, critical thought and agency are still possible. Critical lyric is a 'go-for-broke' articulation, in the language of art and aesthetics (and, especially, poetry) of the condition of possibility for a more-than-subjectively-arbitrary thought that is nonetheless not bound by the rule of existing concepts and the argumentation proper to them. This is exactly what is at stake when Benjamin – and, following him, Adorno – enunciates the constellation and force-field. In the celebrated phrasing of the 'On the Concept of History' (which is, amongst other things, Benjamin's updating of Marx's aesthetically theorized rejection, in the *Theses on Feuerbach*, of Left-materialist determinism), the constellative act blasts the *Jetztzeit* (the now-time, the present that emerges beyond the picture offered by society's currently ruling concepts) out of the continuum of history, out of the seeming continuum presented by reigning concepts.[52]

Lest one still imagine that lyric and the constellation/force-field merely parallel one another, Benjamin repeatedly indicates (in language Adorno will constantly echo and ratify) that the constellation and force-field themselves partake fundamentally of aesthetic theory and artistic practice. This profoundly aesthetic dimension becomes palpable when one considers Benjamin's often-stated specification of what, within criticism, constellative form requires, of how and why it creates or brings into view a force-field: In writing that seeks to present constellative critical thought, each sentence should strive to point back – formally and substantively – to a constantly moving centre from which that sentence has all along radiated. That is no small task; and if Benjamin's ideal of an in-motion writing that structurally fuses imagination, precision, and formal-stylistic tork seems to demand the impossible, that is probably because Benjamin develops the notion and practice largely through his formidable engagements with the formidable artists of the Baudelairean lyric counter-tradition. (The Benjaminian mandate further requires that the critic not aestheticize criticism, that he or she not write criticism as if it were lyric poetry, not write as if the links between these modes could be used to declare them by fiat identical or interchangeable. Criticism's relationship to lyric's constellative form is thus best grasped as aesthetic, not aestheticist: The kinship stems from the overlapping but distinct relationships that both criticism and art maintain to *mimesis*, to a mode of thought-representation that does not in the first instance operate via conceptuality and argumentation but through an experience of affinity and difference – although criticism finally must work to enunciate, in the language not of *mimesis* but of conceptuality, the contributions *towards* conceptuality that art, that *mimesis*, has nondiscursively offered.)

Such an analysis allows us freshly to see that Benjamin's constellation/force-field stands as one of the great modernist, constructivist reimaginings of that familiar old lyric-aesthetic friend whom it thereby radically reinvents (not least by way of a properly modernist parataxis that restages romantic articulations of parts and wholes): organic form. In Adorno's more musically based vocabulary, such constructivist reimagining or genuine carrying forward of organic form appears, in advanced modernity, as the simultaneously dissociative and structural principle of dissonant composition. On this view, constellative form simply *is* the theory-practice of the critical-progressive, self-consciously modern artwork. If in an earlier, romantic era, organic form attempts to realize a critical dynamism through explicit involvement with lyric risk, so constructivist form's greatest challenge, its go-for-broke game in later modernity, involves the effort to constellate, and – however covertly or implicitly, however sideways-slanted the renderings, however inclusive of ostensibly nonlyric or antilyric materials and methods – the effort to approach lyric aura.[53]

In this expanded sense, lyric aura is not simply an important phenomenon that must critically and historically be accounted for, the effect of a style or mode inevitably subject to being neutralized once officially approved, and thus bound to be contested in its own turn. While such contestation necessarily occurs, and while the back-and-forth account obviously has much to commend it, it is also the case – at least for Benjamin, Brecht, Adorno, and the contemporary artists mentioned above – that critical lyric is tuned to the very possibility of historically, reflectively accounting for *anything*. That is, lyric aura signifies, or is keyed to, the possibility of an act of understanding that proceeds in a more than merely instrumental, *and* in a more than merely arbitrary, manner; in short, it proceeds in a manner directed towards meeting at least the minimal requirements for critical agency. That's why the apparent loss of lyric aura (it might again be helpful to speak in terms of the apparent distance *from* the aesthetic distance already comprehended by lyric aura, of the seeming disappearance or collapse *of* the charged distance that lyric aura already signifies) is such a crisis for the figures at issue throughout this chapter, who all consequently conceive the reimagining or reinventing of lyric aura as an ongoing commitment to the possibility of *constellating*, to the possibility of constructing constellative form.

As Adorno insists in his numerous elaborations of Benjamin's 'On Some Motifs in Baudelaire', the modern inability to hear lyric music – not only lyric's obvious modernist-constructivst dissonances, but also, inside or alongside the latter, the survivals of lyric melodiousness and mellifluousness – is the inability to hear art stretching towards critique. When the rejection of a warmed-over, too-easy, programmatic transcendentalism results in the essential abandonment of lyric aura – when the governing interpretive yardstick adopts, in order to stigmatize lyric aura itself, precisely the least-realized creations or readings of lyric's emphatically nonempirical, nonrepresentationalist 'I' (the 'I' actually best understood as a construction-towards-aura that seeks, via necessary fictions, negatively to allow subjects provisionally to transcend their own empirical experiences and consider other subjects and objects) – then the consequent result all too often is the effective abandonment of art's ability to stimulate critical agency.[54]

V

Would it not be possible to substitute, for such extensive *explication des textes Frankfurtiens et Brechtiens*, something quick and more easily communicable? That Brecht, Benjamin, and Adorno *did* all hurl invectives at the culinary might make the latter appear a promising, negative shorthand that could replace all this dense literary-aesthetic history and theory; too promising. For not only would it be dicey to assume that there will always be a ready-to-hand method for distinguishing between the critical and the culinary; it also would be problematic to believe that Brecht, Benjamin, and Adorno were themselves always able to do so. (Their own subsequent ironic or ambiguous institutional status is hardly irrelevant to the question of making such neat distinctions.) Indeed, in their different and sometimes unexpected ways, each proved himself salutarily suspicious of correctly progressive, Left, or oppositional definitions of what should or should not count as critical or auratic. And interestingly enough, this is one of those areas where despite themselves Brecht and Adorno may share more between them then either does with Benjamin. For Benjamin can be fairly relentless in his denunciations of the culinary; Brecht and Adorno generally match him, and yet are at points far more given to notice, or to wonder about, the moment where genuine, desirable and desire-filled sensuous experience – rather than certifiably trivial taste-testing – just might be at issue. That odd configuration of Brecht and Adorno on this question of abstraction, lyric aura, and taste might yield important new materials for, of all things, the provocative rethinking of Abstract Expressionism opened up by T. J. Clark a few years ago.[55]

In any case, there is good evidence that full awareness of the significant confluence or overlap between them would have driven Brecht and Adorno mad. But that might itself constitute the best evidence for the reality of such a confluence, and for its value as a place from which to start thinking about the modernisms that may already be succeeding our late postmodernism. The enticing (if fragile, provisional, *constellative*) possibility of a Brechtian-Adornian (and a Brechtian-Celanian, Brechtian-Beckettian) convergence in art and theory can by no means tell the whole story about contemporary indications that modernism may still have a present, let alone a future. On the other hand, it is no small thing to realize that in the eyes of Brecht, Benjamin, and Adorno (the very figures who in the Left tradition are so frequently said to have helped set the stage for the collapse of aesthetic distance) there really was – and there really was intended to have been – aura, still.

9

WALTER BENJAMIN AND THE TECTONIC UNCONSCIOUS

DETLEF MERTINS

The writings of Walter Benjamin include appropriations and transformations of modernist architectural history and theory that offer an opportunity to broaden the interpretation of how the relationship between the 'unconscious' and technologically aided 'optics' is figured in his commentaries on cultural modernity. This chapter focuses on three moments in his writings, each of which touches on this topic in a different way: first, on Benjamin's reading of Carl Bötticher's theory of architectural tectonics as a theory of history in which the unconscious serves as a generative and productive source that challenges the existing matrix of representation; secondly, on Benjamin's transformation of Sigfried Giedion's presentation of iron structures into optical instruments for glimpsing a space interwoven with unconsciousness, a new world of space the image of which had seemingly been captured by photography; and thirdly, on Benjamin's suggestion that the mimetic faculty continues to play within representation, history and technology to produce similarities between the human and the non-human. In each instance, Benjamin reworked the dynamic dualism of nineteenth-century architectural tectonics – (self)representation seeking reconciliation with alterity – into a dialectic. In so doing, he set the cause of revolution (of a modernity yet to come) against metaphysical and utopian claims, progressive and regressive alike.

I TECHNICAL FORMS

In the opening segment of his well-known exposé for *The Arcades Project* of 1935 – 'Paris, Capital of the Nineteenth Century' – Benjamin referred to the architect and historian Carl Bötticher, and he was not flattering (*GS* 5.1:45–59/*AP*, pp. 3–13). He associated Bötticher with what he elsewhere referred to as the nineteenth century's deficient reception of industrial technology, that is, the problematic production of images in which the old persists and intermingles with the new. He called these 'wish images' in which 'the collective seeks both to overcome and to transfigure the immaturity of the social product and the inadequacies in the social system of production'. Benjamin explained that, Janus-like, such wish-fulfilling images (which is how Freud had characterized dreams) tended to direct the visual imagination 'back upon the primal past', thus linking their power of prophecy (for that which is to follow appears first in the images of dreams) to 'elements of primal history – that is, to elements of a classless society'. Intimations of a classless society, achieved in the collective unconscious, mingle with the new to produce 'the utopia that has left its traces in a thousand of configurations of life, from enduring edifices to passing fashions'. Benjamin offered Charles Fourier's utopian vision of a community housed in a phalanstery as such an image that combines promise and problematics. He considered its architecture a 'reactionary metamorphosis' of the arcades into 'the colorful idyll of Biedermeier' inserted into the austere, formal world of the Empire.

For Benjamin, it was the destiny of the working masses to realize the non-instrumental potentiality of industry and yet the latent physiognomy of technical forms remained constrained under the rule of the bourgeoisie, just as the workers were themselves. Concurring with Max Weber's analysis of how Enlightenment rationality had 'disenchanted' the world, he nevertheless recognized that modernity was not yet free of myth. Things produced as commodities under the conditions of alienated labour were enveloped by false mythologies, as evident in advertisements, fashion and architecture. 'Capitalism', he noted in *The Arcades Project*, 'is a natural phenomenon with which a new dream-sleep came over Europe, and in it, a reactivation of mythic powers' (K 1a, 8). These myths, which Georg Lukács had drawn attention to as being characteristic of the class consciousness of the bourgeoisie, gave the world of reified commodities the appearance and status of 'nature' – a second nature that occluded the original as it exploited it.[1] To awaken from the nightmare of capitalist phantasmagoria, to dissolve mythology into the space of history was Benjamin's principal aim for *The Arcades Project*, which he thought of – in terms similar to the work of dreams and dream analysis – as his *Passagenarbeit*, or work of passage. In Jeffrey Mehlman's apt formulation, 'Benjamin's work on the phantasmagoric glass and iron arcades of Paris constituted a devastating enactment of the messianic dream of plunging into evil, albeit to defeat it from within'.[2] Benjamin's reading of modern architecture and photography during the late 1920s in Germany (*neues Bauen* and *neue Optik*), like his reading of their histories, was informed by these problematics of dream-consciousness – the resistance posed by the old for passage across the threshold of modernity into an undistorted and fully revolutionary state of redemption.

Having noted in the exposé that the emergence of construction in iron was critical for the appearance of the skylit and gaslit Parisian arcades during the fashion boom around 1820, Benjamin referred to Bötticher's conviction that the art forms of the new system of iron construction must follow the formal principle of the Hellenic mode. As Mitchell Schwarzer has shown,

Bötticher's tectonic theory centred on the hermeneutic problem of architectural ornamentation or (self)representation seeking to interpret the raw ontological moment in which artifice is created out of unformed matter, drawing new and unassimilated appearance into the already given system of architectural representation.[3] Benjamin went on to describe the Empire style, which conformed to Bötticher's prescription, as being the equivalent in architecture to 'revolutionary terrorism' in politics, for which 'the State is an end in itself'. Invoking a kind of functionalism against the politics of historicism, which served to legitimate the present by reiterating the forms of the past, he wrote:

> Just as Napoleon failed to understand the functional nature of the state as an instrument of domination by the bourgeois class, so the architects of his time equally little realized the functional nature of iron, with which the constructive principle begins its domination of architecture. These architects design supports resembling Pompeian columns, and factories that imitate residential-houses, just as later the first railroad stations will be modelled on chalets. (*GS* 5.1:46/*AP*, p. 4)

That Benjamin sided with the engineer against the architect is clear from the first part of the exposé, in which he suggested that engineering had a revolutionary role to play, not only for architecture but for society. Having already introduced this theme in his essay 'Surrealism' of 1929, and again, more radically, in 'Erfahrung und Armut' ('Experience and Poverty') of 1933 (*GS*, 2.1:213–19/*SW* 2:731–5), Benjamin returned to it at the end of the exposé. There he took up what he called the surrealists' gaze across 'the ruination of the bourgeoisie' and observed:

> The development of the forces of production shattered the wish symbols of the previous century, even before the monuments representing them had collapsed. In the nineteenth century this development worked to emancipate the forms of construction from art, just as in the sixteenth century the sciences freed themselves from philosophy. A start is made with architecture as engineered construction. (*GS* 5.1:161–2/*AP*, p. 13)

By linking 'artistic' architecture to the phantasmagoria of bourgeois capitalism, while at the same time linking 'engineering' architecture to social revolution, Benjamin radicalized and politicized the conflict between engineering and architecture that had marked the nineteenth century. He drew it into the overarching dialectical struggle between the classes and the new and old.

In this context, Benjamin's reading of Bötticher's tribute of 1846 to Karl Friedrich Schinkel takes on a rather strategic significance for the dialectical theory of architecture that may be glimpsed between the lines of his writings.

It was, of course, in this text – 'The Principles of the Hellenic and Germanic Ways of Building with Regard to Their Application to Our Present Way of Building'[4] – that Bötticher had extended his theory of tectonics to the matter of iron. Having previously analysed the two great historical styles – the trabeated Hellenic system and the vaulted Germanic-Gothic – he turned to speculate on the architecture of the future, the new architecture that so many in the nineteenth century longed for so intensely. In the notes of *The Arcades Project*, Benjamin assembled the following excerpts:

> Another art will emerge from the womb of time and will take on a life of its own: an art in which a different structural principle will sound a more ringing keynote than the other two ... A new and so far unknown system of covering (which will of course bring in its train a new world of art-forms) can appear only with the adoption of an unknown material, or rather a material that so far has not been used as a guiding principle ... Such a material is iron, whose use for these purposes began in our century. Further testing and greater knowledge of its structural properties will ensure that iron will become the basis for the covering system of the future and that structurally it will in times to come be as superior to the Hellenic and medieval systems as the arcuated medieval system was to the monolithic trabeated system of antiquity ... The structural principle is thus to be adopted from the arcuated system and transformed into a new and hitherto unknown system; for the art-forms of the new system, on the other hand, the formative principle of the Hellenic style must be adopted. (F1,1)[5]

For Bötticher, the new iron architecture had a double origin – structure pursuing a 'new and hitherto unknown system', while art assimilated the new with the old principles of antique form. In his earlier writings, Bötticher had introduced the twin notions of *Kernform* and *Kunstform* (technical form and art form) precisely to account for what he took to be the necessary relationship between material origins and idealized re-presentations of material properties and structuring forces in Hellenic and Gothic architecture. This relationship was central to his understanding of architectural style *per se*, as an integrated system of production and symbolization. He conceived of unmediated material and structural self-expression on the one hand, and interpretative self-representation through ornament on the other, as mutually mediating and hence indivisible. In transposing this historical schema into the future, into his speculations about the physiognomy of a new iron architecture, he clearly hoped to promote the emergence of an equally integrative architectonic system for the new epoch.

Yet in positing the split between nature and culture as a condition of modernity, Bötticher inscribed into his tectonic theory an unending struggle to maintain their mutuality over the process of historical development. If in linking 'technical form' and 'art form' to the opposition between Germanic and Hellenic styles Bötticher had hoped to draw on the integrative strength of his dualism to forge a new and higher architecture through *stylistic* synthesis, his strategy may have had the opposite effect. It merely confirmed the split that was becoming increasingly apparent and freed the impulse for a new structural principle from the obligation to represent itself through the mediation of old tectonic systems.

Benjamin's brief commentary on these passages reveals that he took Bötticher's notion of a double origin as a sign of conflict rather than the complementary relationship that Bötticher had intended. Subtly reworking Bötticher's dualism, Benjamin noted that his history demonstrated the '*dialectical* deduction of iron construction' (F1,1, emphasis added). In so doing, Benjamin was informed by Alfred Gotthold Meyer's prior reworking of tectonic theory in his posthumously published *Eisenbauten* (*Iron Constructions*) of 1907.[6] Benjamin held Meyer's book in the highest esteem calling it a 'prototype of materialist historiography' (*GS* 3:170). He singled it out in 1929 as one of four books that had 'remained alive', the others being Alois Riegl's *Late Roman Art Industry* (1901), Franz Rosenzweig's *The Star of Redemption* (1921), and Georg Lukács's *History of Class Consciousness* (1923). In his book, Meyer had been critical of the Berlin tectonic school inaugurated by Schinkel, for its insistence that traditional forms and principles of architectonic expression, developed for stone and wood, be used to assimilate iron construction into the art of architecture. Instead, Meyer adopted engineering as the vital and dynamic basis of a new architecture that would grant to technical forms the potential of a new self-generated beauty. Where Bötticher found, in 1846, that the various efforts to shake off the shackles of the past had not yet achieved persuasively original art forms *or* structural systems, Meyer spoke of the Eiffel Tower of 1889 in terms of a 'new beauty, the beauty of steely sharpness' and the expression of a new tempo of tectonic vitality. While Bötticher argued that 'the acceptance and continuation of tradition, not its negation, is historically the only correct course for art ... leading it toward the destined emergence from tradition to a newborn, original, and unique style', Meyer's later more *sachlich* and anti-representational approach to the relation between art and iron technology was distinguished by his refusal of any wilful symbolization. Instead he favoured the supposed immediacy of material properties, calculations, purposes and modes of production. He conceived of beauty as the immanent expression not only of the material but of the society that produced it. Where Bötticher feared what remained outside the system of order, Meyer embraced the rush and terror of the technological sublime.[7]

While rejecting Bötticher's prescription for contemporary architecture, Meyer and Benjamin both reiterated aspects of the theory of history that underpins his tectonics, in which material and structural innovations are seen to emerge from a mysterious source – 'the womb of time' – to play a leading role in the formation of a new system. For Bötticher, a new structural system specific to a new material was to be born out of the old in the same way that a distinctive and integral Roman vaulted architecture had emerged out of the Hellenic through a process of hybridization, mutation, and rationalization. Botticher employed metaphors of birth, metamorphosis and 'unconscious urges' (p. 155) and suggested that 'any generation destined to create a new style ... [will] need to start the process of formal creation from the beginning'. Meyer, too, was interested in the unknowable source of new architectures, but located such new beginnings on the drawing board of rational engineering calculations and structural diagrams. In the case of iron construction, the drawing board of rational engineering calculations and structural diagrams constituted such a new beginning, with the path to formal self-realization moving from elementary to complex and from part to whole. In 'Experience and Poverty', Benjamin likewise mobilized the blank rationality of the engineer's drawing board as a groundless ground for a new (proletarian) society, for starting again at the beginning, albeit within the phantasmagoria. In the exposé, he referred to construction as the 'subconscious of the nineteenth-century', taking the phrase not from Meyer but from the young architectural historian Sigfried Giedion, whose book of 1928, *Building in France: Building in Iron – Building in Ferro-Concrete*,[8] Benjamin admired almost as much as Meyer's.[9]

Conflating metaphors of organic growth and subconscious impulses, Giedion held that the new forms of iron construction, and the new forms of life (mass society) that emerged with them, began as kernels struggling within the old to gradually assume their own identity. His story of the historical passage of iron construction follows a morphological evolution – from the simple iron roof frame of the Théatre Français of 1786 to the full realization of iron's potential in the vast spans and gracefully engineered arcs of the Palais des Machines of 1889. This natural progression was, in his portrayal, hindered by the persistence of tradition amongst architects, until the twentieth century, when they finally took up the task of bringing what had emerged in the dark subconscious of industrial labour into the clarity of a self-conscious architectural system, distinguished by a new kind of spatial experience.

Benjamin's quotation of Giedion's thesis about construction as the subconscious of the epoch may be considered in relation to a pair of images that Giedion used graphically to present what he took to be the line of development from the glass façade of an exhibition hall of 1848 to the curtain wall of Walter Gropius's Bauhaus at Dessau of 1925–1926 – the technical form 'finally' purified, refined, and self-reflexive. But it should also be read in conjunction with Benjamin's commentary on it: 'Shouldn't one rather', he suggested, 'substitute (for the subconscious): "the role of the bodily processes", on which "artistic" architecture would then lie like dreams supported by the scaffolding of physiological processes?' (O°,8). In reworking

Giedion's dualism into a dialectic between physiological processes and phantasmagoric dreams, Benjamin pointed to the immanence of truth within the expression of bodily labours and the physiognomy of historical events. This immanence, however, remained impeded by bourgeois controls, albeit less in the technical realm (unworthy of bourgeois attention) than in the artistic.

The architecture of emerging mass society could, then, be seen as beginning not only in the corrupt form of the bourgeois arcades but also in the less deficient forms of utilitarian structures – engineered bridges, train stations, grain silos, exhibition halls, and, of course, the factory, the nascent home of workers and engineers. 'It is', Benjamin wrote, invoking Bötticher's terms, 'the peculiar property of technical forms (as opposed to artistic forms) that their progress and their success are proportionate to the transparency of their social content. (Whence glass architecture)' (N4,6). Even in the technical realm, Benjamin treated this transparency as mediated – historically, materially and perceptually. With respect to the artistic realm, he suggested: 'One can formulate the problem of form for the new art in this way: When and how will the form-worlds of the mechanical, in film, in the building of machines, in the new physics, etc. rise up without our help and overwhelm us, make us aware of that which is natural about it?' (K3a,2). When and how, in other words, would construction – pursuing its own inherent logic of purification, working within but against the system of production, working within but against the object riddled with error – bring about the ruination of bourgeois culture and society, and do so without overt politics, but rather through a collective physiological labour that had the character of a constantly renewed originary upsurge?

II   OPTICAL INSTRUMENTS

By considering tectonics within the problematics of representation, Benjamin was able to both clarify and radicalize the terms of the tectonic discourse, while functionalist architects and historians of his generation merely eschewed representation, confident of their capacity to step beyond it and materialize the elemental primitiveness of utopia in the here and now of white prismatic volumes, curtain walls, and cantilevered slabs. For Benjamin, the process of physiognomic immanence freeing itself from distorting mediations was not only incomplete but could not, in fact, be fulfilled by humanity alone. In seeking to conjoin radical messianic Judaism and revolutionary historical materialism, he considered such redemption contingent on suprahuman intervention. The hope and even excitement that Benjamin revealed in describing the arcades, exhibitions and panoramas of the nineteenth century as residues of a dream world (L1, 3) at the beginning of the bourgeois epoch came from a conviction that in them it was possible to glimpse the true face of prehistory, which remained opaque in the artifacts of his own time, that is at the beginning of the next epoch ushered in by the proletariat. 'For us,' he noted, 'the enticing and threatening face of prehistory becomes clear in the beginnings of technology ... in that which lies closer to our time, it has not yet revealed itself' (K,2a,1).

Benjamin's historicized theory of technological productivity in the field of architecture underscores the significance of metaphors of passage for his theory of history. At the same time, it sets up another constellation of metaphors concerning a new optics – the expansion of vision made possible by modern technologies including iron structures that provided unprecedented views of the city, glimpses perhaps of the 'enticing and threatening face of prehistory' (K 2a, 1) yet to come. As is well-known, Benjamin's 'artwork' essay of 1935–1939 introduced the idea that an equivalent analytical practice had emerged in the realm of the visual to psychoanalysis in the realm of the psyche. Sigmund Freud's *Psychopathology of Everyday Life*,[10] Benjamin observed, had 'isolated and made analysable things which had previously floated unnoticed on the broad stream of perception. A similar deepening of apperception throughout the entire spectrum of optical – and now also auditory – impressions has been accomplished by film' (*SW* 4:256). The technique that Benjamin singled out to exemplify how 'through the camera ... we first discover the optical unconscious, just as we discover the instinctual unconscious through psychoanalysis ' (*SW* 4:266) was the close-up – the blow-up, the enlargement, the cropped image, the fragment. 'With the close-up', he observed, 'space expands' (*SW* 4:256). Moreover, the

> enlargement [of a snap-shot] not merely clarifies what we see indistinctly 'in any case', but brings to light entirely new structures of matter ... Clearly, it is another nature which speaks to the camera as compared to the eye. 'Other' above all in the sense that a space interwoven with human consciousness gives way to a space interwoven with the unconscious. (*SW* 4:266)[11]

Such a space interwoven with unconsciousness was palpable for Benjamin, who consistently located the unconscious in the material world itself, not outside, behind, above or below it, but within – as he did the 'truth content' of the work of art and 'traces' of prehistory. In his first essay on surrealism, 'Traumkitsch' ('Dream Kitsch') of 1925, he distinguished the analytics of the surrealists from those of Freud precisely for tracking down 'the traces not so much of the soul as of things' (*GS* 2.2:621–2). For Benjamin, truth was hidden from casual observation, but resided in traces within the welter of base material. He considered it the task of criticism, like the task of history, to make fragments of truth visible and dominant. Regardless of medium, he considered criticism an activity of stripping its objects bare, mortifying them, dragging the truth content of what is depicted in the image out before it, not as 'an unveiling that destroys the mystery but a revelation that does it justice' (*GS* 1.1:211/*OT,* p. 31). Thus the negativity and destructiveness of criticism opens up a moment of revelation, which in turn opens the future potentiality of the object. This notion of potentiality was related to Benjamin's proposition that phenomena have a natural history, that their nature lies in the full and concentrated scope of that history – in their pre-history as well as their present state. The idea that this natural history could be fulfilled may be understood within Benjamin's thought as approaching his hope for redemption from yet another perspective.

In the 'artwork' essay, Benjamin was concerned with the problem of the work of art in the modern industrial epoch, distinguished not only by mechanical reproducibility but by phantasmagoria and commodity fetishism. In this context, Benjamin's concern for the intermingling of old and new focused on the perpetuation, into the era of capitalism, of the old phenomenon of aura, which he defined as a uniqueness that, in earlier times dominated by ritual, had enveloped the work of art as 'the unique appari-tion of a distance, however near it [the object] may be' (*SW* 4:255). During the nineteenth century, the phenomenon of aura had become an agent of bourgeois mythology working to maintain dominance over the masses. Without such constraint, he suggested, the class consciousness of the masses would tend to destroy aura as a function of a desire 'to "get closer" to things spatially and humanly' (*SW* 4:255). The photographic image enabled them to get hold of an object at close range, prying it (in its objectivity) from its auratic encasement. Elsewhere, he wrote of other tactics for achieving similar ends: proceeding eccentrically and by leaps to rip things out of context in order to highlight the seemingly inconsequential details of larger structures ignored by the dominant class; and inventing a *historiographic telescope* capable of seeing through the phantasmagoric fog – a haptic-optic instrument for bringing the tangible, tactile concreteness of things closer to view.[12]

Just as psychoanalysis treats dream images as rebuses or picture puzzles whose manifest content must be deciphered, so Benjamin discovered in the photographic close-up a technique for reading latent content *within* the manifest, for seeing hidden significance *within* the surface. But what was it that he hoped to see? Perhaps justice with respect to the past; repressions and oppressions worked through; the object or event released to fulfil its myste-rious potentiality; the enticing and threatening face of prehistory.[13] And how might this have appeared? In his 'Surrealism' essay of 1929, he suggested that 'we penetrate mystery only to the degree that we recognize it in the everyday world, by virtue of a dialectical optic that perceives the everyday as impenetrable, the impenetrable as everyday' (*SW* 2:216). Perhaps these were the affects of the close-up that he had in mind when, in a well-known passage of the 'artwork' essay, he wrote that the moment of the close-up bursts open the prison-world of the everyday metropolis, the milieu of the proletariat – the bars and city streets, offices and furnished rooms, railroad stations and factories that 'seemed to close relentlessly around us ... so that now we can set off calmly on journeys of adventure among its far-flung debris' (*SW* 4:265/*GS* 1.2:499–500).

Benjamin left several concrete clues to the kind of (impenetrable) images that he associated with such adventurous travelling. Twice in the notes of *The Arcades Project*, he recorded his interest in Giedion's photographs of the Pont Transbordeur in *Buildings in France*. His letter to Giedion, a few weeks following the publication of the 'surrealism' essay, reveals the strong affinity that he felt for Giedion's historiography – his admiration for what he called Giedion's 'radical knowledge'. In *The Arcades Project*, he wrote that 'just as Giedion teaches us we can read the basic features of today's architecture out of buildings of the 1850s, so would we read today's life, today's forms out of the life and the apparently secondary, forgotten forms of that era' (N1,11). Familiar with the discourse of the new optics (led in the late 1920s by Giedion's friend Lázsló Moholy-Nagy), Benjamin took this ability to read the future in the past as contingent on a new technologically mediated vision. Implicitly, he affiliated this with the tactics developed by the surrealists to produce profane illuminations, glimpses of a sur-reality within the banal experiences of everyday life – within, for instance, the extraordinary iron and glass structures of nineteenth-century Paris. One of Benjamin's notes begins by citing Giedion's 'encounter' with the 'fundamental aesthetic experience of today's building' in the

> windswept stairwells of the Eiffel Tower, and even more in the steel supports of the Pont Transbordeur ... [where] things flow through the thin net of iron spanning the air – ships, sea, houses, masts, landscape, harbour. Lose their definition: swirl into one another as we climb downward, simultaneously commingling.

He then went on to note that the 'glorious views of the cities [which] the new iron structures afforded were initially the exclusive privilege of the workers and engineers' (N1a,1). Elsewhere he continued: 'For who else but the engineers and proletariat climbed these steps, which alone at that time provided an opportunity to recognise the decisive, new spatial feeling of these iron constructions' (F3,5).[14]

While similar structures had been built in Rouen, Nantes, and Bordeaux, it was the swaying, hovering and dizzying Pont Transbordeur, built by the engineer Ferdinand Arnodin in 1905 across the industrial harbour of Marseilles, that assumed special significance among the avant-garde. Giedion observed how this 'balcony springing into space' – photographed by Moholy-Nagy, Germaine Krull, Herbert Bayer, Man Ray, and others – had entered the unconscious of modern architecture in Germany.[15] In his words, 'The "new architecture" has unconsciously used these projecting "balconies" again and again. Why? Because there exists the need to live in buildings that strive to overcome the old sense of equilibrium that was based only on fortress-like incarceration.'[16] Giedion had even featured the astonishingly delicate yet bold 'transporter', built to carry a small ferry across the harbour without interfering with the boats, on the cover of *Building in France*. His photographs, as well as his words, treat its spatial and optical affects (like those of the earlier Eiffel Tower) as paradigmatic of the emerging epoch. Of course, Meyer had already taken exciting images of technology, such as the bridge over the Firth of Forth, as demonstrating that 'the power of [iron] speaks to us and in us in every great train station and exhibition hall, in front of every great iron bridge and in the fast-paced modern metropolis' (Meyer, *Eisenbauten*). Giedion, too, mobilized a rhetoric that echoed the aesthetics of the sublime, but not as aesthetics. Invoking dematerialization, spatial extension, shadowless light, and air as a constitutive material, he revelled in the fluid and gravity-free interweaving of subject and object and in the unsettling movement, formlessness, and metamorphosis engendered by the pulse of life in iron structures. Both Meyer and Giedion eschewed bourgeois aesthetic categories, and instead treated these new spatial experiences as the structural conditions of the emerging era. For them, technology's transformation of buildings into fleshless open bodies of skeletal transparency, like its transformation of the nature of vision with microscopes, telescopes, aerial photography, and X-rays, marked the emergence of new modes of perception, cognition, and experience specific to the emerging era.

Hovering weightlessly and breathlessly above the harbour of Marseilles, Giedion's 'iron balcony' served to reframe and shatter the familiar, harsh world of the industrial metropolis, providing Benjamin with a graphic image of the 'threshold' of awakening from the false dream-consciousness of the bourgeoisie. It is telling that Benjamin focused on photographs by Giedion that were quite distinct from his dizzying and destabilizing images of the Eiffel Tower, which Giedion had described as the first instance of the montage principle and exemplary of the tendency of the new structures to open themselves to all kinds of possibilities, to blur the boundaries of their autonomy in favour of relationships and interpenetrations in which the subject is united with the object in the creative process of space-forming. Instead, by selecting abstracted, fragmented close-up views of the harbour's edge taken from the top of the structure and through its open framework, Benjamin effectively distinguished between two moments in Giedion's thinking: one Benjamin identified as 'radical knowledge' serving historical self-consciousness and justice; the other, enthusiastically proclaiming that a new immediacy had already arrived under the sign of a vitalist, technologically mediated transparency in which 'there is only one great, indivisible space in which relationships and interweaving rule instead of fixed borders'. Benjamin focused, not on images of the great iron structures themselves, but on the unprecedented views of the city that they afforded. Among Giedion's photographs, only the ones singled out by Benjamin treated the view as mediated, and only in them was the unacknowledged misery of working-class life both revealed and simultaneously transformed into the site of revelation, just as they had been in Moholy-Nagy's constructivist film *Marseille, Vieux Port* of 1929.[17]

While Benjamin admired the rationalized technical forms of these montage structures (he too referred to the Eiffel Tower as the first instance of montage), he focused on their role as viewing instruments. Their web-like structures provided opportunities to crop, cut, reframe, and abstract the familiar. Like the lens of a camera, they could reveal hidden secrets and provide glimpses of the estranged within the city of representation, 'the tiny spark of contingency, of the here and now, with which reality has (so to speak) seared the subject' (*SW* 2:510). Benjamin called these views glorious, for they released something of a magnificent potentiality locked within the reality of alienation and exploitation. With Giedion's camera and the power of the close-up to expand space and reveal secrets, Benjamin collapsed Bötticher's tectonic dualism, transforming the hermeneutics of origins into an immanence within representation whose visibility in the present was, however, contingent on technology's most powerful instruments of optical analysis. To open the object riddled with error, Benjamin mobilized a dialectical optics that 'further insight into the necessities governing our lives ... on the other hand, it manages to assure us of a vast and unsuspected field of action [*Spielraum*]' (*SW* 4: 265).

III   MAGICAL SIMILARITIES

The effects attributed by Benjamin to the Pont Transbordeur bear a striking resemblance to his treatment of photographs by David Octavius Hill, Karl Dauthendey, and Karl Blossfeldt in his essay 'Little History of Photography' of 1931 (*SW* 2:507–30/*GS* 2.1:368–85). The fact that a portion of this is repeated verbatim in the section of the 'Artwork' essay that deals with the power of close-ups to explode the experience of the metropolis invites a reading of Giedion's photographs in terms parallel to Benjamin's reading of these other images. In this way, a third reformulation of the tectonic problematic may be inferred from his writings.

In his essay on photography, Benjamin suggested that, in contrast to painting, with photography 'we encounter something new and strange' (*SW*: 2:510). His interest was captured, to begin with, by one of the numerous calotypes that Hill had made of fishwives, fishermen, and children in Newhaven, Scotland between 1843 and 1847. Unlike the precision and fidelity of the more expensive daguerreotypes, the soft orange-brown and sepia calotypes, with their diffuseness and transparency, were considered by some the most engaging and truly artistic medium, and came to be admired for their power to evoke personality, to find the presence below the surface, to probe behind appearances. Referring to Hill's portrait of Mrs. Elizabeth Hall, Benjamin observed:

> in Hill's Newhaven fishwife, her eyes cast down in such indolent, seductive modesty, there remains something that goes beyond testimony to the photographer's art, something that cannot be silenced, that fills you with an unruly desire to know what her name was, the woman who was alive there, who even now is still real and will never consent to be wholly absorbed into 'art'. 'And I ask: How did the beauty of that hair, those eyes, beguile our forebears? How did that mouth kiss, to which desire curls up senseless as smoke without fire?' (*SW* 2:510)

To underscore his concern for the immediacy of lived experience, as captured by the photographer in a tense relationship with his own artful idealizations, Benjamin turned briefly to a picture by Karl Dauthendey, a German post-mortem photographer of the late nineteenth century living in Moscow at the time the photograph was taken. Benjamin's description invokes an image of Dauthendey himself, together with the woman he was engaged to, lying in the bedroom of his home, shortly after the birth of her sixth child. Her arteries were severed and her gaze absorbed in 'an ominous distance'. The silent violence of this image is both shocking in relation to Hill's and revealing of the unconscious realm that Benjamin saw opened up by the new optics. With these photographs already in mind, Benjamin then continued:

> Immerse yourself in such a picture long enough and you will realize to what extent opposites touch, here too: the most precise technology can give its products a magical value, such as a painted picture can never again have for us. No matter how artful the photographer, no matter how carefully posed his subject, the beholder feels an irresistible urge to search such a picture for the tiny spark of contingency, of the here and now, with which reality has (so to speak) seared the subject, to find the inconspicuous spot where in the immediacy of that long-forgotten moment the future subsists so eloquently that we, looking back, may rediscover it. *For it is another nature that speaks to the camera than to the eye: 'other' in the sense that a space interwoven with human consciousness gives way to a space interwoven with the unconscious ... It is through photography that we first discover the existence of this optical unconscious, just as we discover the instinctual unconscious through psychoanalysis.* Details of structure, cellular tissue, with which technology and medicine are normally concerned – all this is, in its origins, more native to the camera than the atmospheric landscape or the soulful portrait. Yet at the same time photography reveals in this material the physiognomic aspects, image worlds, which dwell in the smallest things – meaningful yet covert enough to find a

hiding place in waking dreams, but which, enlarged and capable of for-mulation, make the difference between technology and magic visible as a thoroughly historical variable. (*SW* 2:510–12)[18]

Adding yet a third image to this constellation, Benjamin turned to the 'astonishing' plant photographs of Professor Karl Blossfeldt, designer and teacher at the United States Schools of Free and Applied Art in Berlin. The images appeared in Blossfeldt's book of 1928, *Art Forms of Nature*,[19] together with an introduction by the gallerist Karl Nierendorf, whose thoughts share certain affinities with Benjamin's own – thoughts on the 'unity of the creative will in nature and art' (p. vi); their respective embodiment of a profound sublime secret; 'joining the two poles of the Past and the Future' (p. iii); how the modern techniques of photography and film as well as microscopes and astronomical observatories 'bring us into closer touch with Nature than was ever possible before, and with the aid of scientific appli-ances we obtain glimpses into worlds which hitherto had been hidden from our senses'.[20]

Paraphrasing Nierendorf, Benjamin wrote that Blossfeldt's uncanny pho-tographs

> reveal the forms of ancient columns in horse willow, a bishop's crosier in the ostrich fern, totem poles in tenfold enlargements of chestnut and maple shoots, and gothic tracery in the fuller's thistle. Hill's subjects, too, were probably not far from the truth when they described 'the phenom-enon of photography' as still being 'a great and mysterious experience' – even if, for them, this was no more than the consciousness of 'standing before a device which in the briefest time could capture the visible envi-ronment that seemed as real and alive as nature itself'. (*SW* 2:512)

At the risk of reduction, condensing Benjamin's eloquently woven thoughts may help to register more emphatically the link between these various ideas: that the most precise technology can give its products a magical value; that the photographic enlargement can reveal a secret within the physiognomic surface of things; that that secret is visible in a tiny spark of contingency with which reality has seared the subject, in inconspicuous spots where in the immediacy of that long-forgotten moment the future subsists so elo-quently that we, looking back, may recognize it; and that we may recognize it as another nature, one interwoven with unconsciousness. All of this makes possible a great and mysterious experience, an experience of the natural within the human and the human within the natural; an experience whereby the difference between technology and magic is seen to be strictly historical, implying not only their commonality, but also a future potentiality.

That magic – the correspondence between the natural and human – has a history and that this was subsumed into the history of technology was most explicitly treated by Benjamin through the concept of similarity in his essays 'Doctrine of the Similar' and 'On the Mimetic Faculty', both of 1933.[21] There he described how humanity's special gift for seeing and producing similarities between the human and non-human has a history that is both phylogenetic and ontogenetic – that is, a history within the species that parallels its history within the life of each of its members. In other words, this faculty changes over the course of historical development as it does over the life of each person. Just as 'children's play is everywhere permeated by mimetic modes of behaviour ... the child plays at being not only a shopkeeper or teacher but also a windmill and a train' (*SW* 2:694), so in other essays Benjamin characterized the proletariat as the new-born children of the emerging industrial age, whose games always try to begin again at the beginning.[22] While it appears that the mimetic faculty has decayed over time, that 'the perceptual world [*Merkwelt*] of modern human beings seems to contain far fewer of those magical correspondences than did that of the ancients or even that of primitive peoples' (*SW* 2:695), Benjamin suggested that this faculty has, rather, been transformed into a *non*-sensuous similarity, now borne exclusively by language. 'This bearer is the semiotic element [of language]. Thus, the nexus of meaning of words or sentences is the bearer through which, like a flash, similarity appears' (*SW* 2:722).

But Benjamin's apparent exclusion of the sensuous here needs to be qualified by the dependence of language on the sensuous media of speech and script, just as flames rely on substances that burn. Notwithstanding his emphasis on modern semiotic language, Benjamin also treated modern technologies of mechanical production and reproduction – photography and film, glass and iron – as bearers of correspondences between the human and the non-human. Benjamin's concept of similarity concerned the effects of things as much as their attributes. As technical forms that had been reduced to the limit of their objectification, these media (like the sober technical language that Benjamin admired in Bertolt Brecht and Paul Scheerbart) held the special potential of not only materializing similarity in their elemental form, but bringing the similarity hidden in other things into momentary visibility. They were instruments capable of producing glimpses, which the snap of the shutter, the dynamite of the tenth-of-a-second, was able to rip from the flesh of history and preserve (*SW* 2:696–8).

Believing that every epoch dreams its successor, Benjamin was especially attentive to utopian schemes. One of his earliest versions of *The Arcades Project* was even named after an image by the French humorist J. J. Grandville, from his 1843 satire of modernist utopias, *Another World*.[23] In his précis of 1928–1929 'The Ring of Saturn or Something about Iron Construction', Benjamin suggested that a small cosmic vignette by Grandville might demonstrate, in the form of a grotesque, the infinite opportunities that the nineteenth century saw opened up with construction in iron. Focusing on the adventures of a small goblin trying to find his way around in space, Grandville's story was accompanied by an etching that depicts an iron bridge with gas lanterns springing from planet to planet in an indefinite perspective, an unending passage into the infinite depths of space. The 333,000th pillar, we are told, rests on Saturn, where the goblin sees that the ring of this planet is nothing but an iron balcony on which the inhabitants of the planet take the evening air. Preceding Bötticher's text on iron by two years, and the Crystal Palace by nine, the bridge and balcony are remarkably modern and free of historical stylization. Later, in the exposé of 1935, Benjamin still included this image in the section on 'Grandville, or the World Exhibitions', calling it a 'graphic utopia'.

To be able to commune with the cosmos, to link the past and future, to produce similarities between representation and alterity without restriction – such could be the opportunities of technology and industrialization pursued rationally to their ultimate potential beyond the exploitation of nature under capitalism. But let us remember that this image of absolute unity and openness was a satire of utopians like Fourier and the Saint Simonians, that Benjamin admired the caricatures of Karl Kraus for 'creeping into those he impersonates in order to annihilate them'[24] and that he concluded his tribute to the utopian fantasist Paul Scheerbart, written in the final months of his life, by recalling that 'art is not the forum of utopia ... Of that greater (some)thing – the fulfilment of Utopia – one cannot speak, only bear witness'.[25]

10

AURA, FACE, PHOTOGRAPHY: RE-READING BENJAMIN TODAY

DIARMUID COSTELLO

I INTRODUCTION

Walter Benjamin's essay 'The Work of Art in the Age of its Technological Reproducibility' has been familiar to Anglophone art theory since the early 1980s, when it was used by a generation of critics, many of them associated with the journal *October*, for one of two purposes: either to underwrite various photographic and lens-based art practices that had emerged in the late 1970s, or to retrieve the work of avant-garde movements such as Surrealism and Dada from their marginalization by modernist theory – or both. This fact alone tells us one thing; that in the context of art theory, Benjamin's work on photography, like his work more generally, was first received as a resource for theorizing postmodernism in art, and read accordingly.[1] This chapter takes this reception history seriously enough to suggest that it has distorted the way in which Benjamin's work – notably the category of 'aura' – is generally understood within art theory. Typically, this has led to its reductive application to localized debates about the respective values of photography and painting, debates in which Benjamin's work is routinely invoked to valorize the radicality of the former over the conservatism of the latter. Not surprisingly, this narrow focus is accompanied by a tendency to miss the breadth of what was at stake for Benjamin himself – namely, the waning of a *general* category of experience – and the ethical repercussions of this transformation. By now, postmodern theory has congealed into just the sort of critical orthodoxy that originally motivated its own critique of modernism, and its claims are ripe for critical scrutiny in turn. Against the dominant reception of Benjamin within postmodern art theory, then, I want to do four things in this chapter.

First, I want to retrieve the richness of Benjamin's early paper, 'Little History of Photography' (1931), from the programmatic uses to which its claims are put in the later, but better known, essay on technical reproducibility (1936). The idea of 'aura' originates in the earlier paper, in the context of a discussion of the qualities of early portrait photography – a fact I take to be significant. The later paper takes over his original definition of it verbatim, but employs it to critique the 'cult value' of pre-industrial art more generally. Against this more polemical use to which Benjamin puts the idea of aura in the later paper, a use to which art theorists have deferred, I shall argue that 'Little History of Photography' is both more sensitive to the detail of specific photographic images, and more cognizant of the importance of artistic agency in actualizing the *conflicting* possibilities afforded by new technologies. Second, I intend to bring out the complexity of Benjamin's attitude to the social and cultural changes he characterizes in terms of the 'withering' of aura, by relating the claims of the artwork essay to his later use of the term, notably in 'On Some Motifs in Baudelaire' (1939). Re-situating the idea of aura in this broader context brings out two kinds of tension in Benjamin's conception of aura – a tension in his attitude towards it, and a conflict in his characterizations of it. It reveals, for example, that Benjamin both celebrates *and* mourns the liquidation of the aura, rather than just affirming it, and that he equivocates between what I will call a 'specific' (photographic) and a 'general' (experiential) conception of what aura is.[2] Given the degree of complexity of Benjamin's own conception of aura, my third aim is to contest the reductive use to which Benjamin's artwork essay has been put within art theory, where the notion of aura tends to be detached from this wider context, disguising the magnitude of what is at stake for Benjamin himself. For Benjamin, the fundamental issue is *not* that an 'aura' may be predicated of some objects (paintings) but not others (photographs), but that a fundamental category of experience, memory and perception permeating human possibilities of encountering the world, other persons and works of art more generally is in the process of fading away.[3] That something so basic as the structure of experience might be changing, under the pressure of new technologies, represents for Benjamin both an opportunity and a threat. My fourth aim, in making this case, is to bring out the ethical undertow of Benjamin's remarks on aura. This is especially apparent in the Baudelaire essay, where Benjamin characterizes auratic experience as what we undergo when we feel an object of perception return our gaze; that is, what we feel once we credit an object of perception – be it a person, a photograph, or a work of art – with the ability to *look back* at us. This more ethical dimension of aura, and the consequent repercussions of its demise, serves to recast Benjamin's earlier remarks about the 'magical quality' of early portrait photography – the sitters of which conveyed the uncanny impression of seeing their viewers in turn – in a new light, and puts pressure on his apparent celebration of its destruction.

The chapter is structured as follows: I begin by taking Douglas Crimp's use of Benjamin's texts as indicative of art world appropriations of Benjamin in the early 1980s. Despite it being one of the more philosophically cogent uses of the artwork essay to underwrite contemporaneous photographic art,

I will show that Crimp's reading distorts Benjamin in several key respects. With that in place I turn back to trace the genealogy of Benjamin's notion of aura across three key texts in the 1930s, beginning with his earliest remarks about it in 'Little History of Photography'. Here I focus on the close connection between Benjamin's early remarks about aura and portraiture, and I draw attention to a problem in Benjamin's argument when he attributes aura directly to reality as opposed to its representation in early portrait photography. When I turn to Benjamin's subsequent generalization of aura in the paper on technical reproducibility, I suggest that it makes clear that aura pertains to the *subject* rather than the *object* of perception, namely, to a particular modality of experience on the part of a perceiving subject. I call this the experience of 'aesthetic transcendence', and I take it to represent Benjamin's mature conception of aura. The rest of the chapter is given over to my own re-interpretation of such transcendence, as flagging up a more general ethical dimension of experience. To bring this out I focus on two clues in Benjamin's account of film, and I suggest that these ethical overtones of aura inevitably impact on Benjamin's attitude towards its 'withering', making it far more conflicted than its presentation in art theory tends to acknowledge. Here I turn to Benjamin's later essay on Baudelaire; in particular, I use it to reconsider his earlier remarks about the human face serving as the 'ultimate retrenchment' of aura. It is at this point that the specific (photographic or technological) and the general (ethical or experiential) dimensions of Benjamin's concept begin to pull in conflicting directions. In conclusion, I turn to the portraits of Thomas Ruff and Rineke Dijkstra. Although Ruff and Dijkstra clearly present two very different ways of dealing with the face in contemporary photographic art, I argue, in the light of my ethical reconstruction of aura that, in spite of those differences, indeed precisely because of them, their work points to the ethical significance of works of art *per se*.

II   THE RECEPTION OF BENJAMIN'S TEXT IN RECENT ART THEORY

The reception of Benjamin's work on photography and reproductive technology in first generation postmodern art theory during the late 1970s and early 1980s was over-determined in (at least) two respects. The key art world determinant was the simultaneous emergence of two antithetical artistic sensibilities: the 'neo-expressionist' painting promoted in blockbuster shows such as *Zeitgeist* on the one hand, and the appropriation-based 'pictures' photography brought together in the show of the same name on the other. That these movements were perceived as being antithetical is nicely captured in Hal Foster's contemporaneous theorization of a 'postmodernism of reaction' (read painting) vs. a 'postmodernism of resistance' (read photography).[4]

From the vantage point of this way of parsing postmodernism, technologically mediated lens-based art was perceived as a critique of the values on which the resurgence of painting relied (namely: creativity, spontaneity, originality, authenticity, self-expression, subjectivity and craft skill). That is, values regarded as politically reactionary by a generation of theorists simultaneously working through the post-structuralist critique of authorship then being canonized by the American academy.[5] As a result, Benjamin's critique of the 'cult value' of traditional art forms – art forms that photography was taken to have dispatched – was read through both the resurgence of figurative painting and post-structuralist critiques of the author-function, now transposed into the domain of art.[6]

Among the original participants in this debate Douglas Crimp stands out as having made the most philosophically cogent use of Benjamin to underwrite a distinctively postmodern, appropriationist, photographic practice. This is the body of work and accompanying theory that has come to be known simply as *Pictures* after the show of the same name curated by Crimp himself at New York's Artists Space in 1977.[7] What makes Crimp's recourse to Benjamin more sophisticated than most art world appeals to Benjamin of the time is the fact that Crimp recognizes that, for Benjamin, aura is not a predicate attaching to one category of artwork (i.e. paintings) at the expense of another (i.e. photographs), but rather picks out a quality held in common – or not at all – by art in general at any given moment in history:

> the aura is not an ontological category as employed by Benjamin but rather a historical one. It is not something a handmade work has that a mechanically made work does not have. In Benjamin's view, certain photographs have an aura, whereas even a painting by Rembrandt loses its aura in the age of mechanical reproduction. The withering away of the aura, the dissociation of the work from the fabric of tradition, is an *inevitable* outcome of mechanical reproduction.[8]

But despite recognizing that aura is a property of art in general – or not at all – at any given historical moment, Crimp fails to pursue this thought to its conclusion; namely, that aura is not a predicate pertaining in the last analysis to *objects of* perception – be they works of art, things or other persons – at all, even though the grammar of propositions in which the term appears may lead us to believe this. Rather, it pertains to the *structure* of perception itself, i.e. to a particular way of perceiving the world that the slow optics of early photographic equipment both embodied and objectified. Aura is best understood as a predicate pertaining to the subject rather than the object of perception; it describes how that subject is capable of encountering its objects, whatever they may be – namely, auratically or otherwise. Once the *capacity* to perceive 'auratically' wanes then, evidently, nothing will exhibit an aura any longer; this is to say that aura is a quality that not only requires a subject for its perception, but a specific, historically circumscribed, mode of perception on the part of that subject. But what finally makes Crimp's use of Benjamin typical of early postmodern art theory is not only that he fails to draw this conclusion, but that he perceives Benjamin, rather undialectically, as an unqualified champion of this transformation of perception:

> Although it may at first seem that Benjamin lamented the loss of the aura, the contrary is in fact true. Reproduction's 'social significance, particularly in its positive form, is inconceivable', he wrote, 'without its destructive, cathartic aspect, its liquidation of the traditional value of the cultural heritage'.[9]

I am not suggesting that Benjamin does not say what Crimp has him say, but rather that what Benjamin means when he says what he says cannot be understood if read through the essays on photography and art alone. Crimp arrives at the conclusion he does because he takes Benjamin to be talking about artworks in general rather than, more broadly, the nature of perception – or even experience – in general. As such, his interpretation suffers from the general tendency in art theory to read Benjamin's writing on art and photography in isolation. Thus, while Crimp may be right, in a qualified sense, to say that aura is an historical category, he is wrong to claim both that its atrophy is an *inevitable* consequence of technological advance, and that this is simply cause for celebration (at least for Benjamin). On the first of these points Crimp is, it has to be said, being faithful to a tendency in Benjamin himself (even if, in Benjamin's less determinist moments, he is willing to grant that how a technology is *used* is crucial to its implications).[10] But on the second he is simplifying to the point of misrepresentation, by abstracting from Benjamin's more ambivalent remarks on the decline of aura. While on the question of whether aura is an 'historical' category, it would be more accurate, I think, to say that it is a 'structural' category pertaining to a *form* of perceptual experience that is itself subject to transformation over time.

Nonetheless, Crimp's Benjamin is as good as first-generation appropriations of his work in Anglophone art theory get. Despite this it remains one-dimensional. And given that this is the kind of reading from which I want to retrieve the original texts, I now turn to Benjamin's own writing. In doing so, my interpretation will be driven by the following interrelated questions: How does the notion of aura first arise for Benjamin? What does he mean by it? What does he say about its destruction? What is at stake in this destruction? And what is Benjamin's attitude to what he describes? With this in place, I will focus on the significance of the face in Benjamin's argument.

III   THE FATE OF AURA: BENJAMIN ON EARLY PORTRAIT PHOTOGRAPHY, ATGET AND SANDER

Benjamin invokes 'aura' for the first time in 'Little History of Photography', while trying to account for the exceptional quality of portrait photography in the decades prior to its industrialization. He singles out the portraits of David Octavius Hill, among others, claiming that in his work 'the most precise technology [could] give its products a magical value, such as a painted picture can never again have for us' (*SW* 2:510). Benjamin attributes this quality to what, half a century later, Barthes would call the photograph's 'punctum': 'the tiny spark of contingency, of the here and now, with which reality has (so to speak) seared the subject' (*SW* 2:510).[11] More generally, he attributes the high aesthetic achievement of early portrait photography in the 1840s and 1850s to the fact that many of its first practitioners, like Hill, originally trained as painters, and as a result brought an artisanal commitment to the craft of their subsequent practice as photographers. But it was not only the practitioners of photography who stood out in its pre-industrial phase: of their sitters Benjamin says: '[t]here was an aura about them, a medium that lent fullness and security to their gaze even as it penetrated that medium' (*SW* 2:515–16). As Crimp notes, Benjamin attributes this emphatic quality to a fleeting confluence of social and technical factors; on the one hand the technical ascendancy of the photographer, and on the other the social and political ascendancy of his subjects:

> every client was confronted, in the person of the photographer, with a technician of the latest school; whereas the photographer was confronted, in the person of every client, with a member of a rising class equipped with an aura that had seeped into the very folds of the man's frock coat or floppy cravat. For that aura was by no means a mere product of a primitive camera. Rather, in that early period subject and technique were as exactly congruent as they became incongruent in the period of decline that immediately followed. (*SW* 2:517)

The decline Benjamin has in mind occurred during the period in which technical advances in photography, notably faster optics, dispelled this aura from the print at the same time as it was banished from reality by the 'deepening degeneration of the imperialist bourgeoisie' (*SW* 2:517). The poor light-sensitivity of early photographic plates had made long exposure times necessary, requiring 'the subject to focus his life in the moment rather than hurrying on past it'. 'During the considerable period of the exposure', Benjamin observes, 'the subject (as it were) grew into the picture, in the sharpest contrast with appearances in a snapshot' (*SW* 2:514).[12] But once faster optics became available this was no longer necessary, to the detriment of the 'magical' quality exhibited by early photography. Despite this, Benjamin is at pains to forestall the conclusion that the aura of early photography was 'the mere product of a primitive camera' (*SW* 2:517). Nonetheless, as regards the claim that is supposed to establish this fact – namely, that the bourgeois sitters of early photography 'came equipped with an aura' that was 'banished from reality' by the increasing degeneracy of their class at the very moment faster optics eliminated it from the print – Benjamin fails to provide an argument to support it. It remains at the level of assertion: to constitute an argument, Benjamin would need to marshal independent evidence for predicating an aura to the *subjects* of early portraiture in the first place. Given that his only basis for doing so is the changing appearance of the photographs themselves, he cannot claim to know anything about the way a world *unmediated* by its photographic depiction may have appeared without begging the question. In the absence of further argument, or corroboration independent of the photographs themselves, Benjamin's claims about the aura of what is depicted, as opposed to the aura of its depiction, raise the worry that he is simply projecting the characteristics of early photographs back onto what they depict. When, evidently, one cannot infer that a person possesses an aura from the fact that their depiction does.

But setting these reservations about Benjamin's claims concerning the subjects – as opposed to their portraits – to one side, what made a period of technical advance at the same time one of artistic decline, for Benjamin, was the fact that photographers themselves responded regressively to technological progress; they sought to simulate the atmospheric qualities of early photographic portraiture by aping the effects of painting. If the first generation of photographers' initial training as painters was painting's gift to photography, the artfully posed studio portrait and the retouched negative, Benjamin quips, were 'the bad painter's revenge on photography' (*SW* 2:515). From this Benjamin concludes that 'what is again and again decisive for photography is the photographer's attitude to his techniques' (*SW* 2:517). The insight of this remark, which can be generalized across the arts, is sadly lacking from his own treatment of the *intrinsic* social and political significance of film as a medium in the later essay on technical reproducibility.[13] Nonetheless, it is because he recognizes, at least here, that the practitioner's *attitude* to their medium is a decisive determinant on what they are able to accomplish within it, that Benjamin champions Eugène Atget. Atget, according to Benjamin, was the first photographer to break the pretence that afflicted photography once it sought to imitate painting: 'He was the first to disinfect the stifling atmosphere of conventional portrait photography in the age of decline. He cleanses this atmosphere – indeed, he dispels it altogether: he initiates the emancipation of object from aura, which is the most signal achievement of the latest school of photography' (*SW* 2:518). Atget, Benjamin claims, 'looked for what was unremarked, forgotten, cast adrift'; his pictures 'suck the aura out of reality like water from a sinking ship' (*SW* 2:518). Benjamin attributes this achievement to the emptiness of his images or, more accurately, to their *absence of people*: 'almost all these pictures are empty … They are not lonely, merely without mood; the city in these pictures looks cleared out, like a lodging that has not yet found a new tenant' (*SW* 2:519). Atget's images of empty courtyards and terraces, architectural details and shop-windows, are pictures of a city bereft of its inhabitants – akin, one might say, to a body bereft of consciousness – a *vacant* city, the very antithesis of the depiction of subjective interiority that is the preserve of portraiture, traditionally construed. Benjamin's remarks tie the rout of aura to the emptiness of Atget's street scenes, to their absence of people and, hence, to their distance from portraiture, and thereby imply that the presence of aura has a special relation to the depiction of persons.

In fact, Benjamin ties aura, more specifically still, to a particular *way* of depicting persons, as becomes clear when he turns to the work of August Sander, the other broadly contemporary photographer singled out in 'Little History'. In Sander's case, the meaning of Benjamin's alignment of anti-portraiture with the rout of aura and, by implication, of aura with portraiture, is thrown into even sharper relief, as Sander's project to document the social strata of German society consists of *nothing but* images of people. Despite this, Benjamin aligns his work with that of Atget, so far as aura is concerned. Benjamin was responding to *The Face of our Time*, a book of 60 images published in 1929, and suppressed by the Nazis in 1933, that previewed a project that was intended to run to 45 folios of twelve prints. Not surprisingly, given the terms in which he champions Atget, Benjamin claims that Sander's images of *people* are anything but *portraits*, conventionally construed: 'August Sander has compiled a series of faces that is in no way inferior to the tremendous physiognomic gallery mounted by an Eisenstein or a Pudovkin, and he has done it from a scientific viewpoint' (*SW* 2:520). For Benjamin, the salient artistic and political feature of this gallery of faces is precisely that they are *not* portraits. This is what these images share with the way people appear in the Russian films Benjamin admires – people who Benjamin claims had 'no use for their photographs', allowing 'the human face [to appear] on film with new and immeasurable significance' (*SW* 2:519–20). Opposing Sander's photographs to the conventions of commercial portraiture, Benjamin emphasizes Sander's scientific and ethnographic ambition, his intention to impartially commit to record the entire range of social types, an encyclopedia of social roles or functions rather than an album of persons. The aim of such work, for Benjamin, is to objectively document its historical moment. Benjamin cites Döblin approvingly: 'Just as there is comparative anatomy, which helps us to understand the nature and history of organs, so this photographer is doing comparative photography, adopting a scientific standpoint superior to the photographer of detail' (*SW* 2:520). What Atget and Sander share, then, is a documentary ambition to record the physiognomy of their historical moment, by training their cameras on a city and a people respectively. For Benjamin, it is this intention, and the attitude towards the photographic medium that this intention expresses, rather than that medium *per se*, that makes the work of both anti-auratic. This suffices to point up the fallacy of attributing *intrinsic* progressive value to any medium in virtue of its constitution, mechanical or otherwise, in abstraction from how it is *used* by a given artistic agent – as was typically the case when Benjamin's work was harnessed to the cause of photography vs. painting in early postmodern theory, and was also the case in Benjamin's own account of film. What remains unclear is what Benjamin actually *means* by 'aura'.

IV 'A STRANGE WEAVE OF SPACE AND TIME': BENJAMIN'S DEFINITION OF 'AURA'

The closest Benjamin comes to defining 'aura' is a curious analogy he offers mid-way through his discussion of Atget's empty street scenes. Here he pauses to reflect explicitly on its meaning for the first time. Benjamin uses the same analogy again, five years later, in the 'Work of Art' essay (*SW* 4:255). The terms in which it is framed are instructive:

> What is aura, actually? A strange weave of space and time: the unique appearance or semblance of distance, no matter how close the object may be. While resting on a summer's noon, to trace a range of mountains on the horizon, or a branch which casts its shadow on the observer, until the moment or the hour become part of their appearance – this is what it means to breathe the aura of those mountains, that branch. (*SW* 2:518–19)[14]

What is immediately striking about this analogy is, as Benjamin acknowledges when he uses it again in the later essay, that it seeks to illuminate the aura of an historical, cultural artifact – the photographic print – by reference to that of a natural object. Indeed the image Benjamin conjures is nothing if not a traditional, even Romantic, one of the aesthetic appreciation of nature. And given that this kind of experience is what Benjamin will go on, famously, to proclaim is 'withering' in a mass society, the Romantic provenance seems highly appropriate; for what could be more alien to modern urban existence than the leisure to pause on a summer afternoon to immerse oneself in a distant vista? Nonetheless, the terms in which this analogy between natural and artistic aura is cast repay close attention. The notion of a 'strange weave of space and time' is clearly framed in such a way as to invoke the Kantian forms of intuition, the structuring, or formal, constraints on our sensory intuition of the world for Kant.[15] This is significant because it demonstrates that the real object of Benjamin's interest is the structure of experience, i.e. the underlying *form* to which all experience must conform in order to be experience at all – as opposed to the *content* of any particular experience. And the fact that Benjamin calls the kind of experience he is interested in a 'strange weave', a 'unique appearance or semblance of distance, no matter how close the object may be' suggests that the structure of this particular species of spatio-temporal experience is of a different order altogether to that of our everyday intuition of the world. On the temporal axis it suggests a kind of reverie in which time expands, in which one is contemplatively immersed in – or absorbed by – the object of one's perception; and on the spatial axis it suggests a distance distinct from that of mere measure, that is, a distance – or rather 'appearance of a distance' – *preserved in the face of proximity.* This is a 'strange weave' indeed: an immersion in the experience of an object that retains its distance despite that immersion, and in so doing transcends it. Without wishing to sound obscure, this can be best described as the experience *that* there is something about an object that transcends our experience of it, an opacity internal to our experience of the object itself. What distinguishes this order of experience from more transparent, everyday, experience is that its structure – the 'strange weave of time and space' – makes this opacity palpable, and thereby affords a moment of transcendence within the immanent horizon of our experience itself. This is not as obscure as it may at first appear; for on this reading of Benjamin, 'aura' turns out to be his term for what is more generally called aesthetic experience, that is, a mode of experience that is typically described as transcending our everyday ways of engaging with the world. In the 'Work of Art' essay, Benjamin ties 'aura', the name he gives this unique kind of experience, back to art's origins in magic and ritual, and appends the following footnote:

> The definition of the aura as the 'unique apparition of a distance, however near it may be', represents nothing more than a formulation of the cult value of the work of art in categories of spatiotemporal perception. Distance is the opposite of nearness. The *essentially* distant object is the unapproachable one. Inapproachability is, indeed, a primary quality of the cult image; true to its nature, the cult image remains 'distant, however close it may be'. (*SW* 4:272, n.11, emphasis in the original)

This is the equation of 'aura' – or aesthetic immersion in a transcendent object – with the atavistic remnants of magic and cultic experience still buried in our relation to art in a disenchanted world for which the 'Work of Art' essay is famous. It is this aspect of the essay that has tended to be taken at face value by art theorists looking to enlist Benjamin's work as a theoretical underpinning for lens-based art, or as a way to critique work in more traditional media.[16] But detaching Benjamin's remarks on the cultic origins of art from his more general claims about the changing structure of experience is what leads to the more superficial and reductive interpretations of Benjamin in the art world. And this despite the fact that both here, and in his earlier 'Little History', Benjamin conceives the atrophy of this supposedly 'cultic' way of relating to the world in more general terms, terms he ties to the characteristic spatio-temporal horizons of mass experience. For it is the typical *forms* of mass experience, Benjamin argues, that are intrinsically hostile to the preservation of aura:

> the social basis of the aura's present decay ... rests on two circumstances, both linked to the increasing significance of the masses in contemporary life. Namely: *the desire of the present-day masses to 'get closer' to things spatially and humanly, and their equally passionate concern for overcoming each thing's uniqueness by assimilating it as a reproduction* ... The stripping of the veil from the object, the destruction of the aura, is the signature of a perception whose 'sense for sameness in the world' has so increased that, by means of reproduction, it extracts sameness even from what is unique. (*SW* 4:255–6)[17]

The process of mutual adaptation between the new urban masses and the texture of life in the modern city that the dominance of this form of perception engenders is the context for Benjamin's discussion of 'aura' in the later essay. What is significant about the masses in this regard is the way in which their forms of interaction with the city foreclose earlier – more auratic – modalities of experience. That is, modes of experience that prized particularity and difference over sameness, and distance over closeness. Modern cities as experienced by the masses are hostile to such experience, both spatially and temporally. On the temporal axis, the typical experiences of life in the industrial city – being jostled by the crowd, traversing busy streets, repetitive work on automated production lines, clock-time – amount, for Benjamin, to a series of miniature shocks that fracture temporal duration into a series of discrete moments lacking narrative coherence.[18] While, on the spatial axis, the need to take hold of all manner of goods quickly and easily, and to make the one available to the many, Benjamin implies, breeds an intolerance of distance and uniqueness, exacerbated by the culture of cheap copies that the new reproductive technologies make possible. Taken as a whole, the transformation of experience this entails rules out in advance the possibility of that 'strange weave of space and time' and, with it, contemplative immersion in a transcendent object required for the maintenance of auratic experience:

> One might encompass the eliminated element within the concept of the aura, and go on to say: what withers in the age of technological reproducibility of the work of art is the latter's aura. The process is symptomatic; its significance extends far beyond the realm of art. *It might be stated as a general formula that the technology of reproduction detaches the reproduced object from the sphere of tradition.* (*SW* 4:254)

In the 'Work of Art' essay, as Crimp argues, Benjamin celebrates such destruction, seeing it as the final emancipation of the work of art from its 'parasitical dependence on ritual', the 'location of its original use-value'; hence its liberation for other ends.[19] This is what Howard Caygill refers to as Benjamin's 'active nihilism', his affirmation of technology's cathartic destruction of the cultural heritage as a way of opening up new possibilities for art, possibilities free of the atavistic commitments still buried in more auratic modes of relating to art.[20] For Benjamin this is no small matter, since this destruction of the cultural heritage entails a 'tremendous shattering of tradition' that undermines a culture's ability to transmit its collective store of historical experience. Just as the accumulation of experience at an individual level requires the capacity to embed present experience in a broader seam of past experience, thereby giving it density and weight, so the accumulation of experience at a collective level requires that a culture preserve some means of transmitting its store of experience through its artifacts. Once these artifacts are detached – reproductively – from their original spatio-temporal contexts and the historical testimony sedimented therein, whatever cannot be easily reproduced is no longer transmitted. Benjamin himself is far more circumspect about these consequences of the destruction of aura – not least since they fly in the face of his own idea of substantive experience in 'Some Motifs in Baudelaire' – than many of his commentators.[21] Benjamin's account of experience in the strong sense requires that present experience be embedded in past experience at both an individual and a collective level; that is, it requires just what is lost when an artwork, person, or event is stripped of its presence through reproduction. This more elegiac aspect of Benjamin's thought is the flipside of the 'liquidationist' dimension routinely singled out by art theorists. For this Benjamin, once experience is reduced to a sequence of punctual moments bereft of underlying narrative coherence, the subject loses the ability to engage with its objects auratically; similarly, once culture is consumed by means of its reproductions, the historical testimony once lodged in the unique spatio-temporal presence of the artifacts reproduced falls away.

THE ETHICS OF AESTHETIC EXPERIENCE: TWO CLUES TO WHAT IS AT STAKE IN THE WITHERING OF AURA

In the 'Work of Art' essay film serves as the fulcrum for the mutual adjustment between the masses and urban life to which Benjamin attributes the 'withering' of aura. Film, for Benjamin, is a ballistic art that assails its spectators with a series of shocks they then have to parry. The jump-cuts and montage of avant-garde Russian film, Benjamin argues, constitute a ballistic 'training' in urban living, a schooling for the 'human sensorium' in shock, the pervasive experience of modern urban life:

Film is the art form corresponding to the increased threat to life that faces people today. Humanity's need to expose itself to shock effects represents an adaptation to the dangers threatening it. Film corresponds to profound changes in the apparatus of apperception – changes that are experienced on the scale of private existence by each passerby in the big-city traffic, and on a historical scale by every present-day citizen. (*SW* 4:281, n.42)

The political significance of film as a medium is that it teaches the masses to master such experience and thereby bring their life in the city, which otherwise threatens to overwhelm them, under control. This is the use-value of film, and it is political. The nature of film, as Benjamin construes it, is clearly inimical to auratic experience. The tactility of its shock effects brooks no distance; it forecloses the possibility of auratic immersion by refusing to let its audience be: whereas 'painting invites the viewer to contemplation [in such a way that] before it he can give himself up to his associations', Benjamin observes, '[b]efore a film image, he cannot do so. No sooner has he seen it than it has already changed. It cannot be fixed on … This constitutes the shock effect of the film which, like all shocks, seeks to induce heightened attention' (*SW* 4:267). Of course, one can take issue with Benjamin's claims about film, as many have done since Adorno, on the basis of the absorptive spectacle of Hollywood film.[22] But this is less easily said of the Russian avant-garde films (e.g. Sergei Eisenstein and Diego Vertov) that Benjamin has in mind. Yet this in itself shows the fallacy of attributing *intrinsic* political significance to an artistic medium or technology in abstraction from *how it is used* by an artistic agent. In this respect Benjamin's account of film lacks the subtlety of his earlier account of photography as an artistic medium, despite being derived from it.

Benjamin's account of film as an art form that both responds to, and shapes in turn, the transformation of experience brought about by urban existence has been discussed at length in the literature, and I do not wish to dwell on it here. Rather, I want to bring out what it suggests is at stake in Benjamin's view of auratic experience more generally. I shall broach this by way of two clues that operate just below the surface of Benjamin's own claims in his discussions of the cinematographer and the film actor. The first is his analysis of the different relations a cinematographer and a painter have to what they depict. To bring this out Benjamin draws an analogy to the different relations a surgeon and a magician have to their clients: 'Magician is to surgeon as painter is to cinematographer. The painter maintains in his work a natural distance from reality, the cinematographer penetrates deeply into its tissue' (*SW* 4:263). The terms in which Benjamin discusses what is at stake in the degree of 'distance' that the two activities tolerate suggests an *ethical* dimension to auratic experience for the first time. Where the magician heals the sick by laying on hands, thereby respecting their patients' bodily integrity, the surgeon – like the cinematographer – cuts into it:

The magician maintains the natural distance between himself and the person treated; more precisely, he reduces it slightly by laying on his hands, but increases it greatly by his authority. The surgeon does exactly the reverse; he greatly diminishes the distance from the patient by penetrating the patient's body, and increases it only slightly by the caution with which his hand moves among the organs. In short, unlike the magician (traces of whom are still found in the medical practitioner), the surgeon *abstains* at the decisive moment *from confronting his patient person to person.* (*SW* 4:263, my italics)[23]

What this image flags up is the ethical significance of aura, its relation to respect – here figured as respect for bodily integrity or, more generally, as an ability to relate to others *as others*. The surgeon has to cross this boundary in order to operate. At that moment he ceases to relate to the patient as a person (an end), and begins to relate to him as a body, i.e. as a medical problem to be solved. By this, I do not mean to suggest that advances in modern medicine are unethical; I simply mean to draw out what I take to be at stake in this analogy for Benjamin, given the context of his surrounding remarks on aura. Looked at in this light, these remarks suggest that an auratic relation to a work of art carries an implicit ethical charge or, more strongly, that this relation might serve as a model for thinking about the ethical dimension of experience more generally. Artworks, as Adorno remarks, 'open their eyes'.[24] At their most compelling, works of art *look back* at us, appearing to exhibit a subjectivity of their own, a subjectivity capable of putting us in question. Now, if this is what is disappearing as a result of the transformations in the structure of experience that Benjamin is tracking in terms of the withering of aura, then what is disappearing is not only our ability to appreciate the aura of a Rembrandt painting in the age of technical reproducibility, as Crimp suggests, but our capacity to perceive or respect the uniqueness, difference or distance of *any* object of experience whatsoever – including that of other persons. If aura names a general category of experience that is fading as a consequence of the transformations of our experience of space and time brought about by technological modernity, then it must be the very *possibility* of experiencing – let alone respecting – difference or particularity that is ultimately at stake.

The second clue to what is at issue in the demise of aura – one that functions as a companion image to that or the surgeon/cinematographer versus the magician/painter – is provided by Benjamin's comparison of the screen and stage actors' relations to their respective audiences. Film substitutes an image for the real presence of the actor in the space and time of the theatre. Unlike the actor on stage who, Benjamin claims, can adjust their performance in response to its reception by their audience, the film actor's image is dead; unlike the embodied actor, it cannot be said to 'look back'. Moreover, unlike that of the stage actor, the film actor's role unfolds through a series 'takes' only brought together subsequently in the edit suite; as a result it lacks the narrative coherence, on the plain of the actor's own experience, of an equivalent role on stage. Moreover, this replacement of a living unified presence by a dead fragmented one is mirrored in the reception of the actors' respective performances. Rather than taking place before a living audience, the film actor's performance takes place before the dead eye of the camera – with which, Benjamin claims, its audience is encouraged to identify – an eye that is dead because it sees, but *without returning the gaze.*[25] Like the surgeon, the film audience no longer encounters the object of its perception 'man to man', that is, as a person. 'For the first time', Benjamin observes, 'the human being [in this case the actor] must operate with his whole living person, yet forgoing its aura. For aura is tied to his presence in the here and the now. There is no facsimile of the aura' (*SW* 4:260). What fades in the transition from auratic living presence in the theatre to reproductive presence in film, then, is the last trace of an intersubjective relation between actor and audience. That is, the last trace of this as a relation *between persons.*

V   *ERLEBNIS* VS. *ERFAHRUNG*: BENJAMIN'S ATTITUDE TO THE 'WITHERING' OF AURATIC EXPERIENCE

Not surprisingly, the magnitude of what is at stake, ethically, in the decay of auratic experience, has consequences for Benjamin's attitude towards what he describes. It makes his attitude far more conflicted than it is frequently represented as being. This applies to his philosophical commentators as much as it does to his reception by art theorists. Rather than simply welcoming the rout of the aura, as Howard Caygill and Rodolphe Gasché maintain, I shall argue, in concert with Susan Buck-Morss and John McCole, that Benjamin's attitude is marked not so much by ambivalence as by a double-edged response. He welcomes *and* mourns its passing simultaneously; his remarks about aura manifest both a 'liquidationist' and an 'elegiac' undertow, and which is prominent depends on what dimension of aura as a general category of experience is under discussion.[26] This is particularly noticeable in 'On Some Motifs in Baudelaire' (1939), when Benjamin discusses memory and experience in more general terms than in the earlier essays on art. What he says here – both about the antithetical relation between shock and authentic experience, and about the significance of feeling one's gaze returned by an object of perception – retrospectively recasts his earlier positive remarks about film as a ballistic training in shock, and his pejorative remarks about the cultic uses of photography, in a far more ambivalent light.

'On Some Motifs in Baudelaire' is a complex essay, and I shall not attempt to summarize it here; rather, I shall focus on how it takes up the themes of shock and the gaze from his earlier writings and, in so doing, reformats some of his earlier claims. Central to this essay is the distinction Benjamin makes, while discussing Baudelaire, between two varieties of experience, marked by the words *Erlebnis* and *Erfahrung.* The former is experience conceived in the minimal sense of merely living through, or enduring, the present moment; the latter is a more substantive, thicker conception of experience. Only the latter has density to distinguish us as individuals, while embedding us – as individuals – in a wider field of shared understanding: 'Where there is experience [*Erfahrung*] in the strict sense of the word, certain contents of the individual past combine in the memory with material of the collective past' (*SW* 4:316). Despite this, Benjamin maintains that the weaker, more impoverished form of experience, in which events remain confined to the hour in which they occurred, has become the dominant schema for modern experience. This is a product of the pervasive experience of shock in modernity; it is the form of experience that results when existence is reduced to a series of shocks to be parried by a consciousness functioning essentially as a defensive shield. A shock that is 'parried by consciousness', Benjamin claims, drawing on Freud, gives the 'incident that occasions it the character of an isolated experience [*Erlebnis*], in the strict sense' (*SW* 4:318). It drains it of affect, thereby consigning it to the moment of its occurrence:

> The greater the shock factor in particular impressions, the more vigilant consciousness has to be in screening stimuli; the more efficiently it does so, the less these impressions enter experience [*Erfahrung*], and the more they correspond to the concept of isolated experience [*Erlebnis*]. Perhaps the special achievement of shock defence is the way it assigns an incident a precise point in time in consciousness at the cost of the integrity of the incident's contents. This would be a peak achievement of the intellect; it would turn the incident into an isolated experience [*Erlebnis*]. (*SW* 4:319)

When this becomes the dominant form of experience, the present is increasingly cut adrift from the past, because it is no longer *assimilated* to past experiences. As a result, the collective store of past experience is no longer transmitted, along with present experience, to the future. For Benjamin, then, the ongoing transmission of tradition is only possible where there is experience in the full sense; that is, the accumulation of a largely unconscious repository of shared understanding. But by fixing events in consciousness, shock prevents their assimilation to this unconscious repository. Benjamin is following Freud in claiming that consciously registering an event and that event leaving a memory trace are antithetical in the same system; that only what bypasses our conscious defences and thereby leaves a memory trace amounts to experience in the full sense, experience that has been embedded in a store of unreflective past experience: '[O]nly what has not been experienced explicitly and consciously, what has not happened to the subject as an isolated experience [*Erlebnis*], can become a component of *mémoire involontaire*' (*SW* 4: 317).[27] What has been lived through, by contrast, leaves no trace: what we are conscious of (*Erlebnis*) and what we experience (*Erfahrung*) are antithetical, because what has been registered in consciousness has been parried, drained of affect, leaving no trace.[28] On this view, once shock experience just *is* experience in general, substantive experience becomes a thing of the past. But what is most striking about Benjamin's analysis of shock as the schema for impoverished experience in the present context is the way in which it retrospectively recasts his earlier celebration of film – *with which it is entirely consistent* – in a much less positive light. For on this account, the ballistic training film provides in mastering shock must contribute directly to the atrophy of substantive experience. This, then, is the underside of the 'shattering of tradition' that takes place when objects, events, memories and experiences lose their aura. It is the cost of the 'present crisis and renewal of humanity', and it makes Benjamin's attitude to the withering of aura more conflicted than is generally acknowledged (*SW* 4:254).

VI   ENCOUNTERING OTHERS AS OTHERS: AURA, FACE, PHOTOGRAPHY

These tensions in Benjamin's account of aura, and his attitude towards its passing, become most acute when he turns to its implications for our capacity to encounter one another as others. This is where the specific and the general dimensions of the category cross. By the 'specific', I mean those aspects that derive from, and pertain specifically to, the history of portrait photography in which the idea first arises; by the 'general', I mean the more global remarks about the structure of experience that Benjamin raises off the back of that account over the following decade, culminating in the essay on Baudelaire. I want to suggest that, in the last analysis, these pull in conflicting directions; that what might be thought salutary at the specific level (the erosion of a cultic relation to early photography, if that is what it is, as an instance of the ongoing disenchantment of the world) is impossible to regard in the same light when looked at from the more general perspective (as the capacity to perceive, and hence respect, difference and particularity *per se*, as the ability to respond to others as others). These two axes of the concept intersect most clearly in the experience of portraits in which the sitter's gaze anticipates and returns that of its viewer. That photographic images of the face have a privileged relation to the experience of aura was apparent in the earlier essays: in the implied link between aura and a particular way of representing persons suggested by Benjamin's anti-auratic verdict on work of *both* Atget and Sander in the 'Little History' essay; and in the 'Work of Art' essay's equation of a particular use of portraiture with the residue of an earlier, more cultic, relation to art:

cult value does not give way without resistance. It falls back to a last retrenchment: the human countenance. It is no accident that the portrait is central to early photography. In the cult of remembrance of dead or absent loved ones, the cult value of the image finds its last refuge. In the fleeting expression of a human face, the aura beckons from early photographs for the last time. This is what gives them their melancholy and incomparable beauty. (*SW* 4:258)

But the Baudelaire essay provides, for the first time, a transparent rationale for this connection of aura and face by attributing it to the unique ability of the face to *look back*, returning the gaze. This was implicit in the earlier texts – for example, in the claim that what gave early photography its 'magical quality' was the impression that its subjects could see their viewers in turn[29] – but the Baudelaire essay makes this explicit. And, as with the examples of the cinematographer and actor, what is at stake here is the relation between aura and intersubjectivity; specifically, a formal rather than substantive notion of intersubjectivity that turns, minimally, on the ability of another subject, in other regards just another phenomenal object *within* my world, to return my gaze as a subject, that is, as an agency or intelligence or point of view *onto* that world, and hence from outside it. For the subject to feel itself held in the gaze of another in this way functions structurally as another instance of that 'strange weave of space and time' discussed earlier with reference to works of art; it opens a moment of transcendence within the immanent horizon of consciousness.[30] Like the experience (*Erfahrung*) that bypasses consciousness despite leaving a memory trace, the gaze of the other comes to me from within my world (consciousness), despite being a point of view onto that world from outside it, and hence transcending it. In this respect the face of the other functions as the limit of my world; it puts the sovereignty of my own subjectivity in question. The face is a prophylactic against solipsism. This is apparent, in the Baudelaire essay, when Benjamin ties the 'fullest experience' of aura back to the experience of another returning one's gaze. As the opportunities for encountering others in this way decrease, through the increasing use of reproductive technologies, so too do our opportunities to encounter one another as persons:

What was inevitably felt to be inhuman – one might even say deadly – in daguerreotypy was the (prolonged) looking into the camera, since the camera records our likeness without returning our gaze. *Inherent in the gaze however is the expectation that it will be returned by that on which it is bestowed. Where this expectation is met ... there is an experience* [Erfahrung] *of the aura in all its fullness* ... Experience of the aura thus arises from the fact that a response characteristic of human relationships is transposed to the relationship between humans and the inanimate or natural objects. The person we look at, or who feels he is being looked at, looks at us in turn. *To experience the aura of an object we look at means to invest it with the ability to look at us in return.* (*SW* 4:338, my italics)

That photography records but does not see, and hence does not return the gaze, is for Benjamin photography's constitutive contribution to the demise of aura, in virtue of its mechanical nature. Given this, Benjamin implies, responding to photography auratically is a category mistake of sorts, the animistic transposition of a relation between humans to a relation between persons and inanimate objects. For this reason, its rout is to be welcomed as part and parcel of the disenchantment of the world. But this is where the tension between the general and the specific in Benjamin's various characterizations of aura becomes acute: for what might seem salutary, viewed in terms of disenchanting our relation to photography taken in isolation, seems much more problematic, if viewed in terms of Benjamin's more general characterizations of aura as a place-holder for emphatic experience *per se*, that is, a category of experience applicable not only to our relation to the *depiction* of persons in photography, but to our ability to experience *personhood* as such. In so far as aura picks out an experiential possibility – the ability to the appreciate distance and uniqueness, hence the capacity to respond to the particularity of others as others – that is waning, what may appear from the more restricted viewpoint as a salutary purge of atavistic residues in secular practices, appears from the more general perspective as the reduction of everything in the world – other persons included – to the status of mere objects. And celebrating such a reduction, particularly at the historical moment in which Benjamin was writing, is tantamount to celebrating barbarism.

VII THE FACE IN CONTEMPORARY PHOTOGRAPHY: RINEKE DIJKSTRA AND THOMAS RUFF

In conclusion, I want to say something about how the reading of aura proposed in this chapter might impact on our perception of more recent photographic portraiture. I shall do so by way of some brief remarks about the work of Rineke Dijkstra and Thomas Ruff, two contemporary European photographers who persistently record the face in their work, albeit in very different ways. And I want to suggest that, initial appearances not withstanding, their work partakes of a deeper continuity that serves to bring out the underlying connection between our experience of other persons, the depiction of other persons, and works of art more generally. To give some idea of the generality of what I take to be at stake: if my claim, which I shall do no more than set out speculatively here, is granted in principle, then it should apply to any serious body of art in any medium, visual or otherwise.

The orthodox view of Dijkstra and Ruff runs something like this. Dijkstra's work turns on the formation of an empathetic relation with her subjects. This is evidenced by series that document the same individuals over extended periods in their lives, and by her preference for a particular kind of inward, non-exhibitionist, personality (with which she claims to identify), and which tends to be accompanied by a certain awkwardness before the camera.[31] This is especially apparent in the series that brought her international recognition, recording adolescents of various nationalities on beaches, where their semi-exposed bodies seems to exacerbate their innate adolescent awkwardness and self-consciousness, which Dijkstra then further exacerbates by not instructing her subjects in how to compose themselves, despite the concentration her way of working demands of them. All this, particularly the awkward self-possession, is made apparent in the portraits themselves. Ruff's work, by contrast, has no truck with such time-honoured homilies concerning the expression of subjective interiority in portraiture. Schooled in the Becher's rigorous tradition of objectively and systematically documenting the *appearance* of the world, without laying claim to any deeper truth or insight, Ruff's work may be read as a hard-nosed rebuttal of the belief that photographs are capable of communicating anything about their sitters' psyche or soul. This is most evident in the series of large-format straight-to-camera passport-photograph-style portraits that brought Ruff to international attention. These works, initially of the artist's friends and acquaintances, and consistently of subjects from his own generation, are characterized by a large-format, straight-to-camera, closed-cropped, no-nonsense directness (and it is striking how the few images that depart from this format fail aesthetically). Throughout, the work makes a virtue of a neutral, detached observation, and the serial way of working, in concert with the similar ages of the subjects, tends to homogenize differences and downplay individuality. On this account, Ruff would be a kind of latter-day Sander, documenting a generation rather than engaging in portraiture as that activity is traditionally understood, and thereby refusing the comforts of engaging with others that Dijkstra's work seems to hold out. Such other, largely presentational, similarities as there are between their work (large format, colour, high production values, and so on) serves only to make these more fundamental differences in attitude and intention more apparent.

This is the orthodox view: it sees Dijkstra and Ruff as occupying polarized artistic positions. I do not disagree with this view, so far as it goes, it just does not go very far. Here, then, is what I want to say: what the work of both artists shares above and beyond such differences, indeed precisely *in virtue* of such differences, is a distinctive – i.e. unwavering, uncompromised, coherent – viewpoint onto the world. The work of both is marked by a *particular* artistic vision; each is stamped with an immediately recognizable set of priorities and assumptions about what is salient in the world. (Of course, an adequate account of either's work, but particularly Ruff's, who works in a variety of non-portrait series besides, would have to say much more, but what I have said should suffice for my purposes here.) Thus, it is not the *sitters* who look back at us from the work of either Ruff or Dijkstra in the last analysis but, rather, the *artists* themselves. What we see when we look at their work, indeed, what we see (what we experience) when we look at, or otherwise engage with, any substantial body of art, photographic or otherwise, representational or abstract, visual, verbal, or aural, is the manifestation of such a distinctive point of view onto the world. This, after all, is a large part of why we *value* the work of one artist over another. That is, because we respond, or find ourselves called to respond, to the point of view onto the world opened by one artist's work rather than that opened by another's. In this respect it has much in common with why we value other persons. Analogously to what we see when we see another person looking back at us, what we encounter in a work of art is a point of view onto the world or, more strongly, the opening of a competing world that potentially challenges that which we take ourselves to inhabit. This is hardly a novel claim: but what it suggests is that we respond to works of art and, *a fortiori*, artists' œuvres taken as a whole, in much the same way that we respond to other persons' actions taken as a whole – that is, their lives, and how they live them, taken as a totality – as cohering in particular ways, ways redolent of particular commitments, beliefs, and priorities. Artworks, like other persons in this regard, express particular viewpoints onto the world. In virtue of the fact that works of art are made by persons, they do not just show things; they also manifest particular attitudes *towards* or *about* what they show. Like my earlier account of the face, which was in this respect just a cipher for others *per se*, works of art are marked by a two-fold ontology: they are at once both inside and outside my world. Like persons, in virtue of possessing a point of view onto what they present, works of art transcend their material substrate: they are at once both things in my world, and subjective viewpoints upon it from outside it. In this respect, artworks, like persons, *look back*, and thereby make a claim on us. This is trivially true of photographs that depict the human face, but it is true in a far deeper sense of works of art and other persons *per se*. And it remains true of our relation to art and other persons, for just so long as we retain the capacity to respond to difference and particularity. In this respect our relation to works of art functions, structurally, as a place-holder for our relation to other persons. Artworks are the face of the other. Aura marks this spot.

BENJAMIN ON ART AND REPRODUCIBILITY: THE CASE OF MUSIC

RAJEEV S. PATKE

Nothing more was needed than a piece of pliable cardboard bent to the shape of a funnel, on the narrower orifice of which was stuck a piece of impermeable paper of the kind used to bottle fruit. This provided a vibrating membrane, in the midst of which was stuck a bristle from a coarse clothes brush at right angles to its surface. With these few things one part of the mysterious machine was made, receiver and reproducer were complete. It now only remained to construct the receiving cylinder ... When someone spoke or sang into the funnel, the needle in the parchment transferred the sound waves to the receptive surface of the roll slowly turning beneath it, and then, when the moving needle was made to retrace its path ... the sound which had been ours came back to us tremblingly, haltingly from the paper funnel, uncertain, infinitely soft and hesitating and fading out altogether in places.

(Rainer Maria Rilke, 'Primal Sound', 1919)[1]

I A PLEA FOR MUSIC

Rilke's childhood experiment invokes the primal aura of sound through the paradox of its repeatability. It underscores the perpetuation of sound as inscription, while revealing technology in the guise of a mirror that reverses technique. Production and reproduction are grounded in separate realms of materiality that constitute the limit conditions in which specific forms of transmissibility produce signs as sound and language. Rilke anticipates Benjamin's intimation that 'now the mirror image has become detachable from the person mirrored, and is transportable' (*SW* 4:261). The preoccupations that led Benjamin in the 1930s to his theses on the relation of technology to art also prepared the way for his description of the decline of storytelling after the advent of the book. The artwork essay, through its several versions, aspires to a general application that is belied by its focus on cinema and the visual arts, though it fulfils in exemplary fashion Benjamin's consistent ambition for criticism 'to liberate the future from its deformations in the present' (*SW* 1:38).[2] Its references to music are confined to glances at the development of recording technology around 1900 (*SW* 3:102), the separation of audience from music in the gramophone record (*SW* 3:103, *SW* 4:254), the Dadaist use of 'an enchanting fabric of sound' as missile (*SW* 3:267; *SW* 4:119), the profusion of trash in the music industry (*SW* 4:278, n.29), and Leonardo da Vinci's disparagement of music as less lasting than painting (*SW* 4:279, n.33). As in Heidegger's essay on 'The Origin of the Work of Art' of the same period, 'the thing-character of the work' retains the sense of an object with a tangible body and a unique afterlife in space and time.[3] The elision of music leaves the imprint of its absence as a trace which retains the kind of faith that led Adorno to the belief that 'Benjamin's concept of aura ... may touch on the music-like quality of *all* art' (*B*, p. 7). This chapter explores the scope for a wider application of Benjamin's ideas by examining the effect of reproducibility on music and extending the reference to include music beyond Europe.

Benjamin's letters indicate the programmatic nature of the artwork essay in their recognition that technological reproducibility created possibilities that had differing implications for socialist and fascist orientations to art.[4] In October 1935, he wrote to his friend Werner Kraft:

> I am busy pointing my telescope through the bloody mist at a mirage of the nineteenth century that I am attempting to reproduce based on the characteristics it will manifest in a future state of the world, liberated from magic. I must first build this telescope myself and, in making this effort, I am the first to have discovered some fundamental principles of materialistic art theory. (*C*, p. 516)

It is a curious aspect of the contingency bracketing this aim that neither of the two friends who tugged from opposite sides over Benjamin's unresolved elective affinities found satisfaction in his treatment of a materialist theory of art. Adorno niggled away at the worry that the desire to oppose Fascism in art led Benjamin to betray the dialectical nature of the antithesis between the auratic and the mass-produced artwork. He complained for over 30 years that Benjamin ignored the degree to which external developments in technology were not as germane to art as the need to develop internal techniques that would sustain distance and autonomy in the teeth of the culture industry.[5] More laconically, Brecht underlined the tension between idealism and materialism that haunts Benjamin's aura:

> Benjamin is here. ... he says: when you feel a gaze directed to you, even behind your back, you return it (!). The expectation that what you look at

looks back at you, provides the aura, the latter is supposed to be in decay in recent times, together with the cultic ... It is mysticism in a posture opposed to mysticism. It is in such a form that the materialist concept of history is adopted! It is rather ghastly.[6]

Brecht's characteristic response, as noted by Benjamin, was to cut the Gordian knot: in the age of mass reproducibility, the artwork might be rescued in its function even if the concept might have to be eliminated, along with its past associations (*SW* 4:274, n.16).

II   BENJAMIN AND MUSIC

There is sufficient evidence to suggest that music was not close to Benjamin's interests.[7] When he is mindful of its contemporary plight, as in 'The Author as Producer' (1934), it is subsumed in a general antithesis between external developments in technological means of reproduction and the internal failure of the arts to evolve new modes of production to resist or shape the power of the reproduction process. He quotes with approval the view of Hans Eisler that 'an ever-increasing process of rationalization' is likely to render the phonograph record and the sound film into canned commodities, unless the artist as producer learns to resist the economic mobilization of technology for mass consumption by trying to renew from within 'the world as it is' (*SW* 2:775). Eisler was to collaborate a decade later with Adorno on *Composing for Films*, a text which repeats with heavy sarcasm the fear that the criterion 'of reaching the consumer as effectively as possible' might even give us the 'Moonlight' Sonata 'sung by a choir and played by a supposedly mystical orchestra'.[8] Benjamin shared Adorno's anxiety, but his hope for an artistic technique that might resist the rationalizing power of technology turned to photomontage, as subsidized by Brecht's Epic Theatre. Benjamin believed that the 'superimposed element' of the *gestus* had the power to disrupt 'the context in which it is inserted' (*SW* 2:778), an enthusiasm that left Adorno unimpressed. In *Aesthetic Theory*, he repeatedly expresses doubts about the adequacy of photomontage, reiterating the view that 'Technical forces of production have no value in themselves' (p. 247). In the 1930s, he preferred to develop from Benjamin the dialectical relation inherent to *Technik* as technique and industrial process.

The motif that most impressed Adorno came in the form of a relatively brief but suggestive allusion to music in the context of the relation between allegory and Trauerspiel in *The Origin of German Tragic Drama*. In 'the musical philosophy of the romantic writers, who have an elective affinity with the baroque', music symbolizes a myth of origin for the relation between creativity and language. As invoked in the poetry of pastoral plays, and exemplified in recitative and opera, it represents the primeval condition of humanity with what Johann Wilhelm Ritter referred to as 'unsurpassed purity, power and innocence'. The belief that word and script or speech and writing are at source one subsidizes the notions that all creativity is a form of language, such that 'every image is only a form of writing ... only a signature, only the monogram of essence, not the essence itself in a mask' (*OT*, pp. 213–14). Benjamin treats the claim that all the arts derive from the unity of thought and language as concluding the 'virtual romantic theory of allegory' on a question whose answer would

> have to bring oral and written language together, by whatever means possible, which can only mean identifying them dialectically as thesis and antithesis; to secure for music, the antithetical mediating link, and the last remaining universal language since the tower of Babel, its rightful central position as antithesis; and it would have to investigate how written language grows out of music and not directly from the sounds of the spoken word. (*OT*, p. 214)

A decade later, Adorno acknowledged the influence of this motif in a letter of 17 December 1934:

> I would also like especially to count your remarks about music, and about the gramophone and photography, as further evidence of our agreement – in a few weeks you should hopefully be receiving something which I wrote about a year ago concerning the nature phonographic records, a piece which takes a specific passage in your book on Baroque drama as its point of departure and simultaneously employs the category of ambiguous and alienated thinghood in almost exactly the sense in which I now see you are construing it in the piece on Kafka; and above all the same is true of your remarks on beauty and hopelessness. (*CC*, p. 67)

Ironically, Benjamin's self-effacing reply reiterated his sense of music as a 'field otherwise remote' from his own (*CC*, p. 119; *C*, p. 517), though as late as 1940 he recapitulates the romantic thesis, citing Vico as a source (*SW* 4:364). Reading Adorno on jazz in 1936, he was willing to recognize an analogy between syncopation in jazz and his own preoccupation with 'shock effects' in film (*CC*, p. 144). However, two years later, he qualified this recognition:

> The subject matter of your work touches upon my own in those parts which relate certain characteristics of the contemporary acoustic perception of jazz to the optical perception of film as I have described it ... [but] I do not mean to suggest that acoustic and optical perception are equally susceptible to revolutionary transformation. (*CC*, p. 295; *C*, p. 619)

He is – perhaps intentionally – ambiguous about whether he was reluctant to extend the analogy between his approach to film and Adorno's approach to jazz, or whether he perceived film to possess a greater potential for revolution than music, and therefore found music less germane to his art theory, a point Adorno was willing to concede (*C*, p. 590). Adorno went on to promote another analogy between their views during this period, by claiming that Benjamin's treatment of developments in Impressionist and Abstract painting as a reaction to the rise of photography was parallel to his account of the relation between twelve-tone music and the rise of the gramophone record. Michael Chanan has remarked aptly of this claim: 'In this equation, the abandonment of tonality equals the abandonment of representation and atonality equals abstraction. Historical justification for this reading is ambiguous.'[9]

The last years of the correspondence between Benjamin and Adorno bring up a handful of significant encounters that link Benjamin's concept of aura to Adorno's work on music. In a letter of 18 March 1936, Adorno expresses unease about Benjamin's concept of aura, claiming that the idea of aesthetic autonomy is dialectical, and 'compounds within itself the magical element with the sign of freedom' (*C*, p. 128). The issue at stake is the recognition that if 'the auratic element of the work of art is in decline', that is 'not merely on account of its technical reproducibility', but because 'the autonomy of the work of art, and therefore its material form, is not identical with the magical element in it' (*C*, p. 129). A letter of 9 December 1938 avers that Benjamin's 'analysis of the psychological types engendered by industry' complements and strengthens the argument of his own essay on regression in listening (*C*, p. 590). A letter of 29 February 1940 returns to Benjamin's treatment of aura in relation to Baudelaire, to ask: 'Is not the aura invariably a trace of a forgotten human moment in the thing, and is it not directly connected, precisely by virtue of this forgetting, with what you call "experience"?' The issue centred around Adorno's unease at the idealism he declared latent in Benjamin's desire to 'retain this trace', 'in those things which have now become alien' (*C*, p. 322). Adorno preferred to enlist the notion of aura to refract the hermetic element in art, which he believed would reinforce aesthetic autonomy in its resistance to ideology. Meanwhile, Benjamin in the artwork essay had moved on from the nostalgia he attached ambivalently to his thesis of the decline of aura in the 'Little History of Photography' (1931). Aura shimmers like a chameleon through Benjamin's writings.[10] Note 15 in the third version (SW 4:273–4) rejects idealism because, he claims, it conceives beauty as always undivided. The revision expands Note 9 from the second version (SW 3:124) by quoting from Hegel's Lectures on Aesthetics to the effect that artistic reception has moved, or oscillated, between the artwork as an object of veneration and reflection. The third version of the artwork essay inflects aura to signify a category of 'spatiotemporal perception' (SW 4:272, n.11), a kind of hallucination or illusion of the 'unapproachable' that persists regardless of its material proximity. We might describe its significance here in terms of a Bakhtinian chronotope of cult value that has its retrospective being in the realm of 'beautiful semblance' (SW 4:261),11 which the second version had described as the affect associated with a first technology (SW 3:127, n.22). According to Benjamin, technological reproducibility marks the twentieth century as the age of a second technology, which, by definition, involves the 'shrivelling of the aura' (SW 4:261).

Criticism was not always a one-way street between the two. In 1938, Adorno's chapters on Wagner induced Benjamin to put aside some of his Mandarin courtesy and relish the irony of using music to make a telling point against Adorno's attempt at a 'salvation' of Wagner, while remaining committed to the view that the progressive elements in his music were mixed with the regressive. Benjamin points out that the logic of the position requires a kind of writing that would 'have to exhibit a particular affinity with musical form itself', since 'Salvation is a cyclical form, polemic a progressive one' (*CC*, p. 259). He goes on to regret that Adorno has compromised those elements in his music theory which link opera with consolation, resistance, and happiness, while intent on reifying the motif of eternity as a form of phantasmagoria. Alban Berg, and 'his indescribably proud modesty',[12] was to provide a more congenial common ground between them.[13] Benjamin particularly liked the description penned by Adorno under the bizarre yet apt pseudonym Hektor Rottweiler: 'He has undercut the negativity of the world with the hopelessness of his fantasy' (*C*, p. 523).[14] Many years after Benjamin's death, Adorno was to draw attention to a different resemblance, that between Webern and Benjamin.[15]

Adorno continued to draw upon ideas from Benjamin in his later work on music, as when he treats Beethoven as a musician who does not invent, but instead, discovers his music. This 'revokes the *a priori* untruth of music's voice, of its being music at all, the immanent movement of the concept as an *unfolding* truth'.[16] The composer is thus 'the stenographer of the objectified composition ... in Benjamin's phrase, "the clerk recording his own inner life"'.[17] Adorno's preference for finding over making, and for music before its sound, is not far from the abstract idea of a primal language as invoked in Benjamin's early essay 'On Language as Such and on the Language of Man' (1916), which implies that music could be treated as a kind of paradisiac language that performance and notation render, in their different terms, as translation.

Meanwhile, the Romantic myth of a unified origin for the arts, a history of the degeneration of that unity into the antithesis between speech and writing, and an association of music with writing rather than speech, have remained open questions for discourse on music after Benjamin. The idea of art as a form of primal language can be assimilated to the kind of view developed by Derrida, which views writing 'before it is linked to incision, engraving, drawing, or the letter' as referring to 'the instituted trace, as the possibility common to all systems of signification'.[18] *Of Grammatology* takes up Rousseau's version of the antithesis between the voice of speech and the voice of song to address the question of origin and separation that preoccupied Rousseau, and concludes its deconstructive reading with the view that 'Degeneration as separation, severing of voice and song, has always already begun … The history of music is parallel to the history of language, its evil is in essence graphic.'[19] Derrida's reading of Rousseau's valorization of the primacy of speech over writing, melody over harmony, and the association of music with voice rather than sound, suggests that 'there is no origin at which the supplementation Rousseau hopes to avoid is not already inscribed'.[20] Traditions that prioritize the oral aspects of music over the graphic might be expected to endorse belief in the primacy of sound over sign, but, as the Indian musicologist Ashok Ranade remarks, 'even the Vedic tradition essentially consisted of oral transmission of the written material'.[21] This reinforces the view stressed by Alastair Williams, that 'even improvisation contains the articulatory features characteristic of musical notation'.[22]

III   EXTRAPOLATIONS FROM THE ARTWORK ESSAY

Benjamin's artwork essay devotes considerable attention to film, and the displacement of aura brought about by the disembodied dissemination of the actor among the masses. 'Reflections on Radio' (c.1931) calls such displacement a form of 'barbarism' (*SW* 2:544). The situation of the actor in the film studio corresponds to that of the musician in the recording studio in terms of 'the fundamental separation between practitioners and the public' (*SW* 2:543). That makes it possible to extrapolate several of Benjamin's ideas from film and radio to recorded music, using both the second and third versions of the artwork essay as a kind of palimpsest.

The most vital difference stressed by Benjamin is that between the natural and the artificial mode of production: the latter involves a breaking up of the integrity and wholeness of the interaction in which the producer and recipient share the same space and time. The process of production is determined by technological intervention. In the studio, the principle of 'selection before an apparatus' (*SW* 4:277, n.27) and the principle of the second-take prevail in the service of the illusion of infinite perfectibility. Music-making is mediated through the apparatus of recording, turning the performer into someone who produces only or primarily for the sake of reproduction, whereas, in a natural environment, the performer 'measures himself against tasks set by nature, not by equipment' (*SW* 3:111). In the studio, the time of production is broken up: the coherence, sequence, and integrity of production as performance are subjugated to the need to produce a simulacrum that will resemble performance. The studio-edited performance is thus an illusion 'of the second degree' (*SW* 4:263). Natural performance-conditions are violated in order to produce their semblance. Ironically, when 'live' performances are recorded, either with or without the knowledge of the producer, the end-product often fails to match the finish of the sound in a recording perfected under studio conditions. Artifice thus provides a better illusion of actualization than natural performance, especially with music whose production coincides with its reproductive mode, as in the case of rock music.[23] The sense of an aura perverted, or renaturalized, are both outcomes of the curious situation in which audiences value their participation in the 'mediatized' reproduction even more than their presence at the scene of production.[24]

When sound in the studio is produced and modified under circumstances that make performance artificial (*SW* 3:111), and production submits directly to the reproductive process, 'the human being is placed in a position where he must operate with his whole living person, while forgoing its aura', and the studio makes '*productive use of the human being's self-alienation*' (*SW* 3:112–13; *SW* 4:260). The producer may have no audience beyond the technicians present at the recording; alternatively, the producer may be supplied with a small studio audience. In the latter case, any member of this artificial audience functions as recipient not for his/her own sake, or in his/her own person, but as token for the type, in order to simulate the semblance of presence in the studio's construction of an illusory context for production. Such an audience suffers from the additional disadvantage that Benjamin identifies in respect of the film audience: a tendency for individuals who constitute a mass to react in ways that end up regulating one another (*SW* 3:116), thus compromising the freedom of individual response.

When the artifice of such production is made reproducible through recording, it is translated into the materiality of a medium (such as tape or computer data) and then retranslated into the commodities of reproduction. As commodity, music becomes the means through which the consumer becomes the collector, who 'takes up the struggle against dispersion' (H4a,1), and the fetishist, 'who, through possession of the artwork, shares in its cultic power' (*SW* 4:272, n.12). Sound perceived as music through human conventions is rendered in the very different terms of sound as perceived through the conventions of acoustical physics, in a disjunction that has a visual parallel: 'it is another nature which speaks to the camera as compared to the eye' (*SW* 4:266). The difference between the two is disguised when we consider that as technology advances, the sound as produced and the sound as reproduced become less and less distinguishable in humanly affective terms, making it all the more important to recognize the radical difference between them, which Friedrich Kittler stresses in an instructive comparison:

> Overtones are frequencies, that is, vibrations per second. And the grooves of Edison's phonograph recorded nothing but vibrations. Intervals and

chords, by contrast, were ratios, that is, fractions made up of integers. The length of a string (especially on a monochord) was subdivided, and the fractions, to which Pythagoras gave the proud name *logoi*, resulted in octaves, fifths, fourths, and so on. Such was the logic upon which was founded everything that, in Old Europe, went by the name of music ... In frequency curves, the simple proportions of Pythagorean music turn into irrational, that is, logarithmic, functions. Conversely, overtones series – which in frequency curves are simple integral multiples of vibrations and determining elements of each sound – soon explode the diatonic music system. This is the depth of the gulf separating Old European alphabetism from mathematical-physical notation.[25]

The separation of the performer from a natural audience denies him or her 'the opportunity ... to adjust to the audience during performance', and 'This permits the audience to take the position of a critic, without experiencing any personal contact' with the producer (*SW* 4:259–60). In 'the here and now' (*SW* 3:103, *SW* 4:253) of natural production, the time of the music has primacy. Producer and recipient are both bound to its continuity and integrity. The 'cult of the audience' (*SW* 3:113) controls the market forces that affect the economy of the studio and what it reproduces. This may be described as the external control over production by the masses: 'Those who are not visible, not present while he executes his performance, are precisely the ones who will control it' (*SW* 3:113). The technologically equipped audience exercises a corresponding internal power over the reproduction. In playback mode, the time of the performance becomes secondary. The recipient has mastery over the music, and can pause, rewind, skip, and generally play fast and loose with the music and its temporal continuity. The continuity of the artwork as recording is thus subject to the whim of the recipient. The listening condition for music is no longer time, but its simulation. Music as objectified in a commodity can recreate the illusion of any segment of primary time within its secondariness. As objectification, it functions as a prosthetic meant to compensate for, or deflect from the human lack of control over the relentless linearity of time. It can appear to cheat time by repeating it in a stylized form. This can be said to resolve the antitheses Benjamin sets up in the artwork essay to the advantage of the first category: between distraction and contemplative immersion, between distraction and concentration (*SW* 3:119; *SW* 4:267), and between play and semblance (*SW* 3:127). The archetype of 'being alone with one's God' (*SW* 4:281, n.40) is displaced by being alone with one's commodity, 'the Blue Flower in the land of technology' (*SW* 4:263).

Finally, the economic rationalization enforced by technological reproducibility feeds the hunger-to-expand on the creation of commodities, which leads to an ever-increasing profusion of producers and consumers, in excess of their natural proportions in society. Benjamin makes the point through Aldous Huxley's *Beyond the Mexique Bay* (1934):

> artistic talent is very rare ... the proportion of trash in the total artistic output is greater now than at any other period ... The gramophone and the radio have created an audience of hearers who consume an amount of hearing-matter that has increased out of all proportion to the increase of the population and the consequent natural increase of talented musicians. (*SW* 4:278, n.29)

Such are the implications that account for why, even if the reproduction 'may leave the artwork's other properties untouched', Benjamin feels that they 'devalue the here and now of the artwork' (*SW* 3:103), and revise 'Humanity's need to expose itself to shock effects' through a revision of 'the apparatus of apperception' (*SW* 4:281, n.42).

IV MUSIC, TECHNOLOGY, ADORNO

Benjamin offers few direct and sustained engagements with music. Therefore, a second way of eliciting a wider application from his ideas is to approach them obliquely through the effect and recoil they produce in Adorno, who was impressed and disquieted by them in almost equal measure, from the 1920s to 30 years after Benjamin's death. Adorno's engagement with the practice and theory of music is marked by a sustained commitment to aesthetic autonomy, a predilection towards an idea of Modernism based on an admiration for the Second Viennese School of composers, and a marked antipathy for Stravinsky and jazz. It is also marked by a caustic pessimism about the culture industry which can sometimes become self-stultifying. An early essay, 'The Curves of the Needle' (1928), is marred by a conviction that the female voice on record, unaccompanied by the female body, sounds 'needy and incomplete'.[26] This prejudice can be placed in an ironic light by transposing the testimony of the earliest recording-engineers who found, in India, that many male vocalists taught themselves to sing at a higher pitch, because that made a more cutting impact, literally and metaphorically, on the 78rpm record as a medium for music.[27] The 1928 essay also makes a literal attempt to apply Benjamin's idea of aura as the semblance of distance to the record as art object. Distracted by the poor quality of early recordings, Adorno claims that in the music emanating from the *Schallplatte* (as from the bourgeois photographs that Benjamin would cite in 1931 in his 'Little History of Photography') 'the subtlety of colour and the authenticity of vocal sound decline as if the singer were being distanced more and more from the apparatus'.[28] In 'The Form of the Phonograph Record' (1934), Adorno provides a more convincing application of Benjamin's notion of art as inscription to the technology of the gramophone, in which 'through the curves of the needle on the phonograph record, music approaches decisively its true character as writing'.[29] Benjamin had been preoccupied with an elective affinity between the Romantic and Baroque symbolization of music. Adorno gives the 'priestly hieroglyph script' of the musical artwork the characteristic slant of a persuasion wary of the culture industry and its exploitative 'message of capital'.[30]

His 1938 essay 'On the Fetish-Character in Music and the Regression of Listening' is energetically pessimist about the mutation of the listener-as-subject into the 'acquiescent purchaser' of 'standardized musical goods' mesmerized by a 'collective compulsion'. A letter of 9 December 1938 declares affinities between his interest in acoustic phenomena and Benjamin's interest in optical phenomena (*C*, p. 590), a claim partly endorsed by Benjamin, though he was unprepared to do the same with Adorno on jazz (*C*, pp. 326, 629). He reported being struck by Adorno's closing remarks on Mahler's ability to integrate fragments of regressive materials into a music that 'stood athwart the concept of musical progress', representing a form of resistance to regressive listening that had been 'seismographically recorded forty years before it permeated society'.[31] Adorno sets up a dialectic between the ascetic and the aesthetic impulses that valorizes dissonance as a metonymy for the subject's freedom from banality, and alienation as the proof of resistance to the reduction of music into a sign of the alienation brought about by consumerism. This has a parallel in Benjamin's attachment to the shock effect of art as a means of inducing a 'heightened consciousness' (*SW* 4:267). The relation between technology and technique is treated negatively: Adorno will have none of the cult of beautiful voices and master violins. Music, he claims, has become the pretext for a commerce that reifies it into commodity in an economy of *ersatz* substitution that converts use-value into exchange-value. Music turns to fetish; the listener, manipulated by the machinery of distribution and advertising, regresses; the musical event turns into a social ritual; aura degenerates into illusion; and the performer gets reinstated in a falsely auratic light.[32] In subsequent discussions, aura is interpreted to represent that which 'makes art-works a closed structure of meaning – the aura that seals them from the degradation of reality, their fastidious refinement … [which] carries the privilege of *noli me tangere* into its innermost sanctum'.[33] More recently, Eva Geulen has developed the implications of aura away from this idea of the hermetic, along the lines of something perceived in the aftermath of its evanescence. This is a nuance made explicit in Benjamin's fourth note to the third version: 'a medieval picture of the Madonna at the time it was created could not yet be said to be "authentic". It became "authentic" only during the succeeding centuries' (*SW* 4:271).[34]

Adorno distinguishes between the function of time in and outside music. Each may be irreversible, but the two differ in a crucial respect, even before technological reproducibility steps in to make musical time repeatable:

'music can never wrest itself from the invariant of time', but 'once this invariant is an object of reflection it becomes an element of composition and no longer an a priori' (*Aesthetic Theory*, p. 23). The key element is the ability of musical form to assimilate itself to time while assimilating time into its structuring of sound. Far more poignantly and sublimely than the plastic arts, music lives and dies in time. Duration and its lapse are intrinsic to the significance we attach to its existence. Wallace Stevens wrote in 'Sunday Morning': 'Death is the mother of beauty'.[35] Benjamin underlines the Baroque aspect of the same paradox in his reminder that in death 'the body too comes properly into its own' (*OT*, p. 217). Adorno concurs, adding the insight that for music to be free of the desire for duration, it must 'internalize its own transience in sympathy with the ephemeral life', lest technological reproducibility give music an intimation of 'the emerging omnipotence of the permanence of art' (*Aesthetic Theory*, pp. 27–8).

Adorno's usefulness reaches a limit when it comes to music that is performed without the primacy of a score. In a loose sense, all such traditions can be described as improvisational, although improvisation in jazz is closer to Indian than to Western classical music. In improvisational traditions, individual performance relates to, and stems from, a pattern or idea of music loosely governed by a set of techniques and assumptions about musical form that constitute a genre for that practice. Individual performance in such traditions bears an unusual relation to repetition. Each performance is unique, but bespeaks a tradition through the genre whose conventions it uses, in order to create an auditory experience that is at once both new and old. Each performance relates to other performances of the 'same' music as non-identical iteration. The idea of performance thus engages with originality through repetition, but revises the conventional idea of repetition from the recurrence of the same to the idea of alternatives, versions, or collaterals that refer to contingent actualizations of form and genre but not to an original *ur*-version. Andrew Benjamin's development of the implications of repetition, in the essays collected in *Present Hope* (1997), helps to transpose the idea of 'iterative reworking' from Walter Benjamin to improvisational music in general:

> The process of reworking re-presents the given in such a way that other possibilities that are in some way already inscribed within, and thus which are brought with it, are able as a consequence of that work – and thus also as constitutive of that work – to be revealed.[36]

Such a notion of repetition valorizes the present tense of music – its 'dialectics at a standstill' (*AP*, pp. 911–12, 917) – as its true and only being, a predicate of – without being a prediction from – the abstract conception whose perpetual renewal and reproducibility it ensures by resisting closure, so that no performance is ever the last word. Performance thus celebrates its own incompleteness as a sign of hope 'linked to a form of finitude rather than being a mere counter-measure to the complete', opening again and again 'the possibility of a repetition taking place again for the first time'.[37]

V THE VIRTUAL AND THE ACTUAL

The difference music makes to any attempt to theorize art may be approached in the recognition enjoined by Adorno in 1938: 'music represents at once the immediate manifestation of impulse and the locus of its taming';[38] 'The unique nature of music, to be not an image standing *for* reality, but a reality *sui generis*':[39]

> an art that, more than all the others, seems to have its *esse* in its *percipi* and to enjoy little existence of its own beyond the moment of hearing it. On the other hand, it is precisely the tenuousness of musical object-hood, this more thoroughgoing passage of the artistic object into the sense organ itself ... that suddenly seems to put a different face on the old subject-object problem, without 'solving' it by violence, abandoning it as false or metaphysical crux, or projecting a mirage of reconciliation or spurious atonement between the poles.[40]

Music requires the idea of the artwork to resist an ontology derived from the visual and plastic arts. Above all, as noted by Sam Weber, it requires a clarification of the relation between real and virtual.[41] Deleuze recommends a pairing in which the virtual is antithetical to the actual, and the possible is antithetical to the real.

> The virtual is opposed not to the real but to the actual. *The virtual is fully real in so far as it is virtual.* Exactly what Proust said of states of resonance must be said of the virtual: 'Real without being actual, ideal without being abstract'; and symbolic without being fictional. [42]

When music is added to the compound idea of the artwork, the notion of an aura that recedes or decays as the artwork recedes in time or gets duplicated begins to look less worrying. During the 1930s, Benjamin expresses an anxiety about the damage sustained by art through reproducibility that stems from the habit of treating the artwork as an object whose technological reproduction entails, in Pierre Lévy's words:

> a change of identity, a displacement of the centre of ontological gravity of the object considered. Rather than being defined principally through its actuality (a solution), the entity now finds its essential consistency within a problematic field. The virtualization of a given entity consists in deter-

mining the general question to which it responds, in mutating the entity in the direction of this question and redefining the initial actuality as the response to a specific question.[43]

Lévy's notion of the artwork as the response to a question corresponds to the approach adopted by Benjamin's early essay on Hölderlin (1914–15), in which the task or the *a priori* facing the poet is defined as a question (the poetized, *das Gedichtete*) to which the poem is the answer (*SW* 1:20). According to Lacoue-Labarthe, the question functions like a prerequisite that 'signals, in both Heidegger and Benjamin toward the essence (or the Idea) of poetry'.[44] Benjamin's orientation to poetry in 1915 is more suited than his preoccupation with photography in 1931 or his concern with cinema in 1935 to reconcile the virtual-as-real aspect of the artwork with its mode of existence as an entity with a unique history in space and time. The earlier essay permits the recognition that an artwork is a realization of the possible while also representing an interpenetration of the virtual and the actual. In the case of music, and especially in traditions based on improvisation that cannot be relegated to a first technology of the past, the fear that the reproduction devalues 'the here and now' becomes little more than a fetish of origin.

  The claim for an original event from which all copies derive applies in a literal way to the performance recorded in a studio for the purposes of mass dissemination. The notion applies to the score and its performance in a different way. As with Beethoven, so also in his discussion of Mahler, Adorno resists the conflation of conception and execution, claiming: 'Mahler's music is never disfigured by the knowing experience of the interpreter'.[45] Music is conceived as an idea whose production might be damaged by performance, which is already its re-production. His alternative: 'To compose music in such a way that the performance cannot destroy it, and so virtually to abolish performance'.[46] Adorno's concept of music as preceding, and almost indifferent or resistant to, performance is not very far from the kind of phenomenon illustrated by Roger Scruton with reference to Bach's music: '*The Well-Tempered Clavier* on a piano, or a harpsichord, by a quartet of brass or woodwind, or by the Swingler Singers are all performances of *The Well-Tempered Clavier*'.[47]

  Adorno remarked: 'Each work, insofar as it is intended for many, is already its own reproduction' (*Aesthetic Theory*, p. 33). Applied to the case of a composer who performs his own music, we could say that the first performance does not diminish the 'here and now' of later performances. Neither the score nor the first performance can claim greater authenticity than any of the composer's other performances. Later, when the score or a recording of the composer as performer serves as the model for later performers, perhaps on instruments dissimilar to the ones used by the composer, their music-making might lack the authenticity of the composer's performances, but lack of authenticity would not prevent recognition of the possibility that their execution or interpretation might sound more 'authoritative' than the composer's. The second version of the artwork essay claims: 'The authenticity of a thing is the quintessence of all that is transmissible in it from its origin on, ranging from its physical duration to the historical testimony relating to it' (*SW* 3:103). And the fourth note to the third version qualifies: 'Precisely because authenticity is not reproducible, the intensive penetration of certain (technological) processes of reproduction was instrumental in differentiating and gradating authenticity' (*SW* 4:271). If Benjamin's theses are to apply to a notion of art that includes music, his recognition that authenticity occupies a gradient in relation to the reproductive technology has to be made to correspond with the possibility that music's peculiar mode of multiple existence – as virtuality, performance, and score – permits a separation of authority from authenticity. Authenticity in a narrow sense might be attached to 'the here and now', but music permits this to be actualized on a gradient, in repetitions that do not aspire to, or need to aspire to, a first idea of an origin or an original. Indeed, to be present in a church where Bach might be improvising on the organ, or sit in the front row as Beethoven plunges into the keyboard, might possess a magical sense of an aura that abides, however momentarily, instead of the romanticism of one that is perceived in the moment of its going. However, if the music is to be parted from its composer, and granted its autonomy, then the magic of attending a first performance cannot entirely clear itself of the stigma of reifying music as its performance and fetishizing the chronotope of composer in performance.

Music as the virtually actual and the renewably repetitive enables a mitigation of the alternately tragic and revolutionary sentiments with which Benjamin endows aura in 'Little History of Photography'. If we think of the artwork in terms of a painting or a building, the technologically reproduced copy refers back to the original as to the actual. If we think of the artwork in terms of music, then the performance actualizes what is virtual, with the Deleuzean proviso that 'the virtual must be defined as strictly a part of the real object – as though the object had one part of itself in the virtual into which it plunged as though into an objective dimension'.[48] Music that begins its life in a medium other than sound, as in a score, can be said to have a possible existence that awaits realization. When performed, the realization of the score as an acoustic entity can be said to actualize what we then infer as its virtual existence. The music in intentional terms, when written as the score, has its being as potentiality; in its affective condition, when contemplated as a whole, it has its being as virtuality; in renditional terms, when performed, it has its being as interpretation or version. In improvisational music, the realization of the possible is also at the same time an actualization of the virtual.[49]

Benjamin's notion of origin places the artwork in the context of ritual and magic. The history of artworks points to an origin prior to its aestheticization, as when music forms part of the communal life or religion of a people, which Benjamin calls first technology. The crucial difference between first and second technology is that the older modes are participative and communal, whereas music as an aesthetic entity splits the musical event more thoroughly between performance and reception. In Benjamin's terms, it splits semblance from play (*SW* 3:127). We might add that the former finds a function for music outside the music-making, while the latter finds an end in the contemplation that constitutes aesthetic pleasure. The activity of the latter is rendered passive to all other performative aspects of the music-making beyond its reception (and valorization). One might well say that this constitutes, already, a separation from or displacement of origin, in which music as art is already its own re-production. This is no mere transposition of cult value into exhibition value, since in being received as art, participative commonalty is transposed into a culture of reproduction and reception that splits performer from the audience.

The decline of aura begins at the origin, with performance becoming art. In the reproduction, the performer and the listener are both alienated from the chronotope of performance.[50] Such distance obtains equally in the reproduction of music and the plastic arts. However, what happens between copy and original in the plastic arts differs from what happens with music and its reproduction. In the visual or plastic arts, the copy cannot bespeak or embody the unique material history of the original, nor its rootedness in tradition, which contributes to its authority and aura. In the case of music, the notion of a unique history cannot really apply to the score or script as material object. Since music comes into being in time as performance, to treat authority or authenticity as attached to its physical objectification would mean little more than making a fetish of the score. Even the event of recording (especially if it is in the studio), would not have the authority of an original painting or piece of sculpture, since the production takes place for the sake of reproduction. Ironically, the artifice of a studio recording more fully approximates to the ideal for the reception of music, as exemplified in the recording career of a musician such as Glenn Gould.

In summary terms, music is not a thing; its origin is virtual; its authenticity does not depend on objectification; the historical testimony relating to it does not expire with its cessation in time, it hibernates as potentiality; and its transmissibility is not diminished by copies; on the contrary, it requires iterability. In the case of Western music, these copies generally take the form of scores; in improvisational traditions, the copies resided in the chain of memories that transmit such music down through the generations, and since the twentieth century, this option has been open to supplementation and correction by recordings.

VI   MUSIC, INDIA, TECHNOLOGY

India provides fertile ground for an analysis of the interaction between technology and music. There are several reasons for this. Recording technology came to India almost immediately after its industrialization in the West. Its influence on the relation of music to society was immediate and massive. India has a long oral tradition of art music based on narrow systems of patronage and transmission. The radical changes brought to the production, transmission, and reception of music by the recording industry reinforced other changes under way during the early decades of the twentieth century. These had the collective effect of moving India towards a modern practice of music that many musicians still regard with mixed feelings. These changes offer confirmation for some of Benjamin's views on the damage sustained by art through reproducibility. However, they also provide evidence for a resilience and resourcefulness to the interaction between tradition and technology that could not have been anticipated from Benjamin's perspective in the 1930s. The third version of the artwork essays invokes 'Humanity's need to expose itself to shock effects' as representing 'an adaptation to the dangers threatening it' (*SW* 4:281, n.42). The Indian context provides a detailed demonstration of what is entailed in a culture adapting to a second technology that acts as 'a system in which the mastering of elementary social forces is a precondition for playing with natural forces' (*SW* 3:124). Daniel Neuman, one of the earliest social historians of music to apply Benjamin to the Indian context, identifies a concern with authenticity and tradition as the chief 'problem for Hindustani music today'.[51] Gerry Farrell devotes a whole chapter of *Indian Music and the West* to developing the implications of the fact that India was 'the Asian vanguard of a massive commercial enterprise which was already well established in America and Europe, a business concerned with cornering lucrative, untapped markets'.[52]

   The classical or art music of North India needs be distinguished from participative and communal forms such as folk and devotional music.[53] The latter can be described, in terms of the second version of the artwork essay, as part of the cultural practice of a first technology, of the sort that makes 'the maximum possible use of human beings' (*SW* 3:107). From Benjamin's perspective, the productions of a first technology belonged to the European past. In India, this technology coexists in the here and now, cheek by jowl with art music. The latter may be differentiated from the Western musical tradition in terms of five features: First, the Indian musical tradition foregrounds melody and rhythm, at the expense of harmony. Second, it is primarily an oral tradition, in which transmission has functioned largely without a system of notation comparable to the Western score.[54] The perspective adopted by Benjamin in 'The Storyteller' toward the role of memory in the traditional story applies exactly to the role of musical structure and its transmission through memory in Indian music. Like the traditional story, music 'does not expend itself. It preserves and concentrates its energy and is capable of releasing it even after a long time' (*SW* 3:148), and memory 'creates the chain of tradition which transmits an event from generation to generation' (*SW* 3:154). In this tradition, reproducibility is internalized as virtuality, and in that form, it remains indispensable to the transmissibility of music, even if individual musicians have been known to develop their own personal shorthand as guides to performance or as archives of lyrics, while pedagogic practice began to modernize itself under the impact of musicologists like V. N. Bhatkhande (1860–1936) and the evangelical pedagogy of V. D. Paluskar (1872–1931).[55]

Third, Indian art music does not provide an equivalent to the Western institution of individual authorship: a musical structure is generally not composed by any single individual or group, instead, it is inherited as part of a continuous oral tradition (although individuals might set lyrics of their choice to specific melodies, and the occasional performer might compose a 'new' melodic hybrid). Fourth, it collapses or dissolves the Western distinction between composition and performance, between composer and performer, and hence between music as idea and performance as interpretation. It constitutes a form of citation that alludes to a pattern, and then proceeds to actualize that pattern, in a way that refers back to the pattern and can be compared with, but not superseded by, other actualizations. The performer is, in one part, also the composer, although the performance owes its form to a convention, and draws upon a received repertoire of musical elements, techniques, and effects that are part of a tradition peopled by a large, loose, and nameless assemblage of previous performances and performers, transmitted and assimilated through ear and mouth. Fifth, the notion of pitch in Indian music is relational rather than absolute, 'there is no absolute or fixed pitch for the tones' of India music.[56] A tentative sixth distinction can be suggested briefly here in terms of the thoroughly syncretic nature of Indian music, in which the classical element derives and differentiates itself from, while constantly returning to, its partial ancestry in folk traditions. It shows a similar complicity between the sacred and the profane, and a full sense of the play of erotic pleasure compounded with the act of performance, in which music, as vibration (*nāda*), echoes and repeats the primal act of creation as reproducibility.[57]

The voice and instrument rely for transmission on auditory memory, and accept all the lapses and distortions to which such transmission is prone. The given or *a priori* element for the classical system is a set of melodic paradigms called *rāgas*. Each *rāgas* constitutes a pattern of melodic ascent and decent, along with distinctive musical phrases. When performed, it is set to a rhythmic pattern which adopts one or more of three tempi. The *rāga* is a structure of melodic and rhythmic potentialities, which leaves the realization of the music to improvisation within a framework in which, as Bonnie Wade points out, 'flexibility and latitude for creative imagination are prime elements'.[58] The exact structure, the proportion between constituent parts, and the duration of each musical event remain an open-ended interaction between freedom and determinacy. Such music can be said to exist, when not performed, as an incipience latent between the abstract notion of an oral tradition and in the musician's potential for music-making. Transposing Benjamin, one could say, a *rāga* is 'an idea that could be called an ideal, because it refers not to the immanent form of the problem but to the transcendent content of its solution' (*SW* 1:218); and transposing Adorno, one might call *rāga* 'the yet to be in works, their utopic trace' (*Aesthetic Theory*, p. 172). In a literal sense, such music does not exist when not performed; whereas a symphony, an opera, or a play exists, even when not being performed, in the materiality of score and libretto, so that 'the primacy of the text over its performance' renders the score as 'indeed the thing itself' (*Aesthetic Theory*, p. 100). Contrariwise, the mode of existence of the Indian artwork has a natural affinity with the startling but apt comparison between music and fireworks made by Benjamin's (and Dora's) friend, Ernest Schoen, who was a student of Debussy: 'the unsurpassable noblesse of fireworks ... [is] the only art that aspires not to duration but only to glow for an instant and fade away' (*Aesthetic Theory*, p. 28).[59]

Next, a condensed account of the salient features of the recording industry in India will indicate the appropriateness of using it as a test case for the extension of Benjamin's ideas. The Gramophone Company was founded in London in 1898, under licence from Emile Berliner, the inventor of the gramophone. The machine parts were manufactured in the US, assembled in London, the material recorded globally *in situ*, and the discs manufactured first in Hanover and later from other locations.[60] The first Indians were recorded in London the following year, in 1899, and the first recordings in India took place in 1902. The motive was not ethnomusicology, but the intention of creating a market close to where the material resources were available: 75 percent of the shellac from which the physical substance of gramophone records was manufactured came from India.[61] In the first decade of the twentieth century, the Gramophone Company sent three major recording expeditions to India. By 1910, the Indian market boasted 75 different recording companies, with European and local labels in competition with the Gramophone Company for a share of the market.[62] The discographer Michael Kinnear reports: 'by mid 1908, it is estimated that there was upwards of 10,000 different recordings of the various styles of Indian music on the market'.[63] The Gramophone Company's earnings for 1910–1913 show an average sale of almost half a million records and over 6000 machines per year, with a revenue that doubled in six years from the initial take of more than 700,000 rupees in 1905.[64] The first Indian pressings were issued from Calcutta in 1908, and in 2000, commemorating 100 years of recording technology, Suresh Chandvankar (the secretary of The Society of Indian Record Collectors) estimated that the total number of gramophone records issued in India would amount to about half a million, each with 500 to a few hundred thousand copies.[65] This massive industry saw the implementation of a whole range of developments in recording technology through the century, from the acoustic/mechanical (1877–1925), the electrical (c.1926), the magnetic (c.1940), to the optical (c.1960).[66]

Technik as recording technology forced *Technik* as structured sound to reconfigure its textural and structural elements. Music could no longer repose in the brevity of performance and the porosity of human memory: musicians became self-conscious. The record gave music a new form of citability, it transformed music-making into a form of evidence, like Atget's photographs of deserted Paris streets, which Benjamin describes as a crime scene (*SW* 2:527; *SW* 3:108; *SW* 4:258). In the record, the peopled landscape of musicians performing before an audience was cleared for a reproductive process conducted before a mechanical apparatus (*SW* 3:108). The record as physical object of value reduced the spontaneity of performance even as it invited the consumer to succumb to 'the putrid magic of its own commodity character' (*SW* 3:113). Increasing sophistication of the reproductive process seduced musicians to the cosmetic treatment of sound for its own sake, distracting them with what Adorno, in a phrase of Eduard Steuermann, calls 'the barbarism of perfection'.[67] The cult of beautiful sound also produced in consumers a musical equivalent to the phenomenon described by Benjamin with reference to film audiences: 'psychic immunization' (*SW* 3:118).[68] Reproducibility also led Indian musicians to selectivity: the temptation to record a small selection of their repertoire for the masses, and to reserve the more abstruse or cherished part for smaller, more discerning, or more paying audiences. Recordings split music not only from the chronotope of natural music-making, but from the traditional associations of *rāgas* with specific times of day, seasons, and to traditional archetypes of experience, mood, and sentiment. The exigencies of the recording studio put aside such orthodoxies. Performances recorded regardless of their traditional correspondences encouraged listeners to do the same, providing a specific example of the potential damage sustained by tradition.[69]

The technology of reproduction forced a series of fixed time limits on the duration of musical recordings: around 3–4 minutes for the 10-inch/12-inch 78rpm disc, increasing with the EP and LP record formats to over 5 and 45 minutes respectively, and then to over 72 minutes with the audio compact disc. Each increase in the limit of the recording format made it possible for the musician to develop a more ambitious musical structure, although, to begin with, the improvisatory nature of Indian music had to fit its tendency toward indefinite expansion and repetition within a Procrustean limit. This led to an ongoing dialectic between freedom and control, and between the limit as challenge and opportunity. Not every musician was able to profit from the expansion. Ironically, as the duration of the recording medium increased, Indian music was given back its traditional liberty with time, although the intervening experience with briefer durations no longer permitted a safe return to the dilatory modes of the pre-technological era. Music-making submitted to the most severe form of miniaturization in the 78rpm format: performers responded by condensing and re-proportioning the constituents of the *rāga* structure. Technological limitation was converted by the more resourceful musicians into an aesthetic opportunity, illustrating the kind of dialectic Adorno invokes for the West in the 1930s. For example, the female vocalist Zohrabai Agrewali (c.1868–1913) became a model for later musicians in the selection and presentation of three-minute performances, often creating a 'beautiful semblance' of sustained duration and relaxed pace.[70] One might apply to the best vocalism in the 78rpm format what Adorno said, in an oddly ambivalent compliment, of Webern and Benjamin, that they were 'like letters received from a kingdom of dwarfs, in miniature format, which always looked as if they had been reduced from something of vast dimensions'.[71]

The miniaturization of music in its 78rpm format neatly underlines the ironic and dialectical relation between technology and tradition. In 'Music and Technique', Adorno notes a specific consequence to the ongoing historical dialectic between changes in techniques of performance and changes in the technology underlying the manufacture of musical instruments:

> advances in mechanical reproduction that make it possible to fix music, like the plastic arts, independently of ephemeral performances with their arbitrary features, bring reproduction decisively closer to production ... If works become their own reproductions, the time when reproductions will become the works cannot be all that far way.[72]

He argued that when the tension in such a relation slackened, technological reproducibility led to a desiccation of forms. In the context of Indian music, Gerry Farrell claims, with a mixture of plausibility and overstatement, that 'the music on early recordings is as much a creation of Western technology as a representation of traditional music genres'.[73] The vocalists fared better than the instrumentalists under the duress of extreme compression, and what Adorno would have called 'the memorability of disconnected parts'.[74] Farrell claims that it also encouraged artists 'to give greater weight to the composed, or fixed, parts of the performance, at the expense of the more developmental forms of improvisation'.[75] Neuman concedes much less to the damaging effect of technology, and notes the widely shared belief that 'the old masters squeezed the essence of a *rāga* into three minutes, and what we hear are perfect miniatures of *rāgas*'.[76]

In sociological terms, the musicians' access to a wide and faceless public loosened the hold of the widespread prejudice that had associated music and dance in India with the decadent culture of the courtesan and her patrons.[77] The musician's capacity to shape audiences was availed by the most successful of early Indian vocalists, Gauhar Jan of Calcutta (1873–1930) and Jankibai of Allahabad (1880–1934). The scale of the public recognition and monetary remuneration they accomplished was rarely matched by even the most successful male vocalists.[78] In Benjaminian terms, music broke free from cult value, enabling the artist to reach the masses in a widened transmission of exhibition value. This did not generally lead to an uncritical cult of the performer, as Benjamin had feared in the context of Fascism. In India, it offered some relief to female musicians from the traditional stigmatization of their profession. However, the delinking of performer from reproduction also abetted the delinking of music-teacher from pupil. This has had a double-edged result. The record gives access to repeated listening, which can be put to pedagogical use in learning techniques independent of teachers, notation, or the strict control of tutelage characteristic of the orthodox tradition, in which the transmission of techniques and styles was confined within a patriarchal *gharānā* (household) system.[79] A musician as father-teacher might transmit different elements of the tradition he had imbibed, and only to his progeny and disciples, fitting the teaching to the potential he discerned in each pupil. 'They are extremely possessive pf their traditions', notes the musicologist Bonnie Wade.[80] Records enabled a break from this system and its power to nominate and regulate authenticity. Contrariwise, the democratization of access to musical materials brought about by technological reproducibility was bought at the price of subverting the cohesion built over generations by the exclusivity principle operative in the *gharānā* tradition, which was responsible for the highly individuated styles of each musical genealogy. The response to this development has been divided among musicians: traditionalists lament the dilution of individuated styles by the eclecticism that radio and records facilitate, while modernists celebrate freedom from the stranglehold of the *gharānā* system, enjoining younger musicians to celebrate hybridity and the death of hermeticism.

The power of the gramophone record was aided after the middle of the twentieth century by radio. The economic status of the average professional musician came to depend more on this humble but reliable source of patronage than on the uncertain earnings of record sales. In India, the sale of recorded music, and its broadcast by radio, did not have the effect Michael Chanan reports for the West in the 1920s and 1930s: 'a general reduction in public musical performance'.[81] In his essay on 'Theatre and Radio' (1932), Benjamin, who had considerable experience with radio broadcasting, describes the two institutions locked in competition, with radio the likely victor because of its capacity to use a more advanced technology to reach wider masses (*SW* 2:583–6). The Indian evidence suggests that this supposed conflict between 'live' performance and radio or records can resolve itself in a symbiotic relation: the reproducibility of music through radio, record, and cassette made Indian audiences *more* – not less – receptive to 'live' performance, although it has not transcended Huxley's scepticism (*SW*

4:278, n. 29): good musicians remain as rare as before, and listeners do not often match enthusiasm or purchasing power with discrimination or discernment in their approach to music. However, on balance, it is possible to claim that music *has* prospered; not just economically, but in terms of transmissibility, awareness, and a more democratic system of patronage.[82] From the perspective of the consumer, the gramophone record was affordable only for the section of the population Benjamin called the 'compact mass' (*SW* 3:129). The 'proletarian' mass has had to wait upon the advent of the relatively low-cost cassette before becoming capable of making a commodity out of music from the 1960s. In terms of the culture industry, the fate and fortune of art music in India has depended on, and been marginalized by, the vastly greater economic success and mass appeal of film music.

The impact of technology on tradition has produced mixed results rather than a simple confirmation of Benjamin's predictions and apprehensions. The materiality of the recording (tape, CD, DVD) both captures and distorts the value attributed to tradition. Music survives the brief duration of its making through an archive of frozen and repeatedly revivable sound whose mode of existence as an impress on inert matter remains separated from the human origins it replicates. However, the recording medium does more to music than ensure its mere repeatability: it also enables an awareness of tradition to be preserved and exemplified. In a tradition whose transmissibility is fraught by memorial decay and a general tendency to imprecision, hyperbole, and falsification, recordings provide precise materials with which to educate the ear of performers and audiences. The access to musical evidence cuts both ways: if models of interpretative excellence are objectified, such performances get raised to the pedestal of what Neuman calls 'archetypal' status,[83] exercising a normative and constraining effect on the scope for future improvisation. It also facilitates the kind of withdrawal from the 'live' audience to the second-take option emblematized for the twentieth century in the studio career of Glenn Gould.[84]

Both features can be illustrated by adding the latest medium – the Internet – to the medley of technologies that have interacted with music, and with one another, through the course of the twentieth century. As a single example of what has a vast and yet-to-be-fully-tapped potential, one can examine the radio lectures on Indian music made accessible by Patrick Moutal, Professor of Indian Music at the Conservatoire National Superieur de Musique in Paris, on his website.[85] If we consider his two-part lecture on the *rāga Darbāri Kānadā* ('the *rāga* for kings, and the king of *rāgas*'), it can be noted that he provides free access to a survey of all the major vocal and instrumental expositions that have survived through the twentieth century through the medium of recorded sound. Such an archive accomplishes several functions: it provides the bases for an informed reception, and a more cultured performance practice; although, as previously noted, such access bypasses the need for admission into any specific *gharānā*. Thus, technological reproducibility abets human reproducibility while it transforms performance practices: tradition is not only preserved, but the conditions for its survival and continuance are modified and shaped towards a set of canonical directions. The changes enforced and enabled by technology mix gain with loss as functions of change. In this context, if authenticity is to be retained as a notion of value divested of the cultic and the occult, it has to be treated as in continual metamorphosis. Neuman probably overstates his case in claiming that 'it is equally admissible to say the aura can be transferred from presence in a live performance to preservation in a recorded one'.[86] Nevertheless, the case of Indian music clearly intimates that there is no future for aura in nostalgia.

THE WORK OF ART IN THE AGE OF ITS ELECTRONIC MUTABILITY

KRZYSZTOF ZIAREK

I

From October twentieth, 1995, Seiko MIKAMI has been showing her work 'Molecular Clinic 1.0' at ArtLab, in Tokyo. This is a work in which participants manipulate the atoms of a virtual spider that lives in the ArtLab server. The theme of this exhibition is 'molecular structures', and is a reference to the molecular biological paradigm that any biological liquid or solid can be artificially reconstructed through altering the molecular strings which compose it … The sum of interventions naturally affects the spider's living environment in unpredictable ways. In this context of unlimited transferability, innumerable combinations are possible, all woven together by the heartbeat of the computer's clock.

The final result is a reflection of the collision, division, etc. of each individual information environment; their access terminal, their access domain, which atomic program they possess and the resultant molecular combination. The supplementary effects or effectiveness of each individual cell's health is something that no one can predict. This project is both a test of bioinformatic processes, and a look at the unpredictable nature of both biology and virtuality. The very process of exhibiting this first on the Internet is part of the artwork itself. The differences between users' experiences, prejudices and preferences, parameters are all part of this art work.[1]

The manipulable, mutating spider created by Seiko Mikami weaves a web of new relations defining the work of art today, a nexus of interactions in which art and technology, manipulation, and creation, appear to merge and thus underscore art's essentially technical nature. Art in the information age appears to identify itself increasingly in terms of its advanced technical character, displaying the complex techno-informational underpinnings of both form and content. This is why the problem which arises in the context of works like Mikami's spider, re-posing the question of the disappearing autonomy of the aesthetic sphere, concerns the specificity of artworks today, their possible difference from technology and from the patterns of manipulation intrinsic to the operations of power. Is the spider to be seen in terms of mutation and manipulation, or perhaps as questioning the increasingly elusive difference between them? And which aspects of the project – the project defined in terms of computer programming, bioinformatics, virtuality, and interactivity – render it into a work of art rather than a piece of sophisticated technology, which gives the participants the experience of virtual and vicarious control over molecular structures? Is the unpredictability inherent in the virtual dimension of the work, and underscored in the above description, the defining characteristic of artworks today, at the time when art, responding to the recent developments in contemporary, heavily technicized, social praxis, becomes capable of virtual existence and decides to emphasize mutability as the mode of its being? Never before has unscripted participation, or the interaction of the work's 'audience' (or perhaps better, its co-makers?), been inscribed to such an extent into the work's modality of existence. One can not only see the spider or track its evolution by periodically checking the link to its website, but repeatedly interact with it and affect its development, becoming in effect part of the work's creative process. And by its virtual existence in cyberspace, the artwork opens new dimensions of interactive temporality, which blur the boundaries between reception and creativity. Above all, what seems idiomatic about such an artwork is the preeminence of its temporal unfolding, of its changing, future-oriented existence, over all the other aspects of the work. The work's technological, artistic, and informational facets become mutable inscriptions in a temporally fluid, interactively shaped modality of its being. And it is this modality of the artwork's existence that becomes its 'substance': transformational, interactive 'effects' that delineate the work's artistic dimension. Yet this new status is made possible by a thorough saturation of the work's time-space with informational technology. At the basis of the creative interactions and virtual mutations gathered into the work is the new technical ease with which various aspects of being become available to us as information and as such become subject to unprecedented manipulation. The artwork thus appears to walk a thin line between becoming part of the technics of manipulation and maintaining a sense of its distinctive force as art. This proximity between growing manipulative power and the force of artistic work marks the present course of art.

II

The recurring preoccupation of 'The Work of Art in the Age of Its Technical Reproducibility' is the changing function of art with regard to the growing influence of technology on everyday life as well as on artistic production. On the one hand, these new functions of art, as Benjamin suggests, tend to introduce an unprecedented danger of aestheticizing experience, but, on the other, they also can, by dispelling the auratic existence of artworks, render them political in novel and radical ways. The migration of reproducibility in film into the very constitution of the work alters art's role from the object of aesthetic experience to, at its extreme, a machine-like device for the reproduction of the possibility of collective mobilization. As it examines these emergent transformations in art's social and political character, Benjamin's essay points to an even more radical reinterpretation of art made necessary by the impact of new technologies on artistic processes: beyond metamorphosing functions of artworks, modern capital and its evolving production technologies seem to be precipitating a deeper shift in the very nature of art. The epigraph from Valéry's *Pièces sur l'art* unmistakably points the third version of the essay in this direction: 'We must expect great innovations to transform the entire technique of the arts, thereby affecting artistic invention itself and perhaps even bringing about an amazing change in our very notion of art' (*SW* 4:251). Yet Benjamin's text is most cryptic precisely on this point. While it shows and documents modifications in perception, aesthetic experience, and the social function of art made manifest by the development of the film industry, it interrupts its reflection with the enigmatic statement about politicizing art. This closing remark appears to tie the emerging change in the very notion of art to the problem of its politicization. However, while Benjamin takes a good deal of care to explain the social and technological conditions behind what he calls the aestheticization of experience, and points to the glorification of war in Marinetti's writings as a contemporary example of how such an aestheticization operates, the statement about the counter-movement to aestheticization opens onto silence. One way to 'read' this silence would be to suggest that Benjamin is not quite sure how to think this alternative 'politicization', given that it is barely nascent and not quite yet articulated. The final remark of the essay, that 'Communism replies [to the fascist aestheticizing of politics] by politicizing art' (*SW* 4:270), distinctively points to art's role in communism, but if one follows this link, it folds back into the problematic of the aestheticization of experience: communism reduces art to ideology and propaganda, and even at its best, it produces an elaborate doublet of the technicization and aestheticization of being, which makes possible an engineering of experience as a fusion into totality that is at once aesthetic and technological. In short, the communist idea of art could be seen as the production of a new techno-aesthetic of existence.

This is why I would suggest that this final sentence of 'The Work of Art in the Age of Its Technical Reproducibility' should be read with reference to the avant-garde and its radical aesthetics. Clearly, this is the case with Surrealism, as another essay by Benjamin indicates, but also with Dadaism, and, yes, Futurism, especially Russian but also Italian Futurism, certainly in the years before the World War I, when the radically novel Futurist 'performances' and artworks erupted on the European cultural scene precisely in the name of contesting aesthetics and 'politicizing' art, and succeeded in galvanizing diverse avant-garde movements before Italian Futurism made a political alliance with Fascism, even if its revolutionary early aesthetic could not be quite made to align itself in a similar way. To unfold the implications of the possible change in the notion of art suggested by Benjamin's essay, one needs to read the references to the avant-garde in terms of a radical de-aestheticizing of art. As I indicate elsewhere,[2] this de-aestheticization does not simply mean stripping art of the 'patina' of the beautiful but involves a more 'revolutionary' disinvestment of art from aesthetics, that is, a divorce from the very idea that art is constituted primarily as an aesthetic object of experience. This attempt to produce art non-aesthetically, or, speaking in historical terms, to make art 'after aesthetics', forms indeed the core of the avant-garde's 'revolution'. The attack on the institutions of art, and even on the very notion of art as an institution, is a corollary of this broader move to shed the aesthetic construction of art. As an alternative to the aestheticization of experience, politicization in the context of the avant-garde means undoing the aesthetic framing of art and opening up anew the question of art's 'essence'. This undermining of the aesthetic as the discourse *of* and *about* art, perhaps best manifested in Dadaism, particularly in Duchamp's works and readymades, is the strongest signal that what Valéry sees as the possibility of a decisive change in the notion of art is indeed at work in the avant-garde. In short, the avant-garde rejects not art but the aesthetic concept of art, with its corollary social and cultural functions and institutions. This disavowal does not mean that art becomes immediately political, that the political importance of its themes, content, or even new forms, becomes transparent or easy to evaluate. Rather, what is called for is a rethinking of the very way in which art can be political, on the order of Adorno's formulation in *Aesthetic Theory*, which claims that it is form understood as the inscription and reconfiguration of social antagonisms that makes it possible for art to be socially critical.[3] This 'form' is not simply differentiated from content or themes, but, instead, must be seen as tracing itself upon both the formal and the material aspects of art, making both the work's content and its formal organization the scene of the reinscription, and thus of the critique, of social praxis.

III

When Benjamin wrote 'The Work of Art in the Age of Its Technical Reproducibility', he captured the historical moment and its effects on the changing character of art in terms of three ascendant and interrelated features: the disappearance of the aura, the inscription of reproducibility into the structure of the artwork, and the politicization of collective experience. At the time that Benjamin remarked on the dissipation of the auratic character of art through reproducibility, there had already been another pronounced tendency in avant-garde art, one not only responding to the loss of the aura but in fact violently disavowing any remnants of the auratic status of art. It is precisely in terms of shock effect and the dissipation of the aura that Benjamin evokes Dadaism in his essay: 'What they achieved by such means was a ruthless annihilation of the aura in every object they produced, which they branded as a reproduction through the very means of production … Dadaistic manifestations actually guaranteed a quite vehement distraction by making works of art the centre of scandal' (*SW* 4:266–7). Both Dadaism and Futurism parody and undo the remnants of art's aura, but also note that the reproducibility and technicity characteristic of modern experience elicit a different resonance from art: it is not just the case that art no longer exists as an auratic object, but that, in a more radical gesture, it emphatically disclaims the status of an object. For the avant-garde, art in the age of technical reproducibility resonates as an event, which, foregrounding art's dynamic and transformative character of a work, calls into question the understanding of artworks as aesthetic objects. Futurist or Dadaist 'art events' become important precisely to the extent to which they begin to disclose art *as* an event, displacing the emphasis from art's object-character to its event-character. It is of course necessary not to forget that Benjamin ties Marinetti's Futurism with the growing problem of the aestheticization of experience, but just as important is the recognition that Futurism, before its name, if not its early aesthetics, becomes hijacked by Marinetti's ideological and political commitments, is responsible for the sudden eruption on the scene of European culture of the phenomenon of art as event.

In the aftermath of Futurism, as much Russian as Italian, a significant difference emerges between art's existence as a created object and its working as an event, a distinction that operates beyond the aesthetic categorizations of form and content. The implications of this shift of emphasis from object to event go beyond the effect precipitated by the technological evacuation of art's aura, for they call into question the aesthetic categorization of art, that is, the understanding of art in terms of aesthetic experience and its corollary terms such as judgement, form/content, subject/object, affect, taste, etc. To Benjamin's trenchant diagnosis of the aestheticization of experience and its dangerous political implications, we need to add a different sense of aestheticization, not of experience but of art itself, to arrive at a more complex picture of what transpires in the avant-garde. The idea of art as event emerging in Futurist and Dadaist performances calls into question not only the aestheticization of experience but also the traditional aesthetic idea of art, forcing us to rethink art beyond aesthetics.[4] This is the manner in which Futurism, Dada, and their aftermath reformulate the Hegelian idea of the end of art: what ends is not art but aesthetics, that is, the governing optics through which art is seen as an object of subjective aesthetic experience and as a cultural commodity. Emerging in the Dadaist aftermath is art as event, that is, art which is de-aestheticized, enlivened, and transformed through the casting off of the artwork's aesthetic conceptualization and its corollary inscriptions in social practice.

Because art as event exceeds and calls into question the constitution of art as an aesthetic object, the event is neither aestheticized nor politicized, certainly not in the sense of becoming a vehicle or means for political or ideological critique. It can perhaps be thought of as political because its complicated, non-linear temporality undoes the logic of presence and absence and the metaphysics of subjectivity on which political commitments and ideologies, as well as communities and collective identities or mobilizations are based. Art as event becomes of political importance precisely by virtue of critiquing, as Adorno would say, the very terms on which social praxis operates.[5] Being both more and less than praxis, art calls into question the narrow sense of praxis, and thus of politics, which operate in terms of domination. As Adorno puts it, for art, action understood within the parameters of social praxis is 'a cryptogram of domination'.[6] Therefore the primary question emerging from modern(ist) art is not the aestheticization of experience but, in Adorno's view, the critique of domination, or better, of machination and manipulative power, which serve as the template for action and praxis. For Adorno, art is emphatically not an alternative site for political critique, for a kind of politics by other means, or an extension (either as representation or as amplification) of social antagonisms or political arguments coursing through the fabric of society. Art is 'political' to the extent that, as event, it undermines the practices of power and domination, which serve as the blueprint for politics and action.

IV

When in the aftermath of aesthetics art manifests itself as, in essence, an event, the issue of art's proximity to and difference from technology begins to occupy centre stage in reflection on art. Film serves so well as the template for Benjamin's rethinking of the function of twentieth-century art not only because reproducibility appears in film as the very medium of art's existence but also because such reproducibility discloses the fact that technology has come to operate at, or perhaps even *as*, the very nerve centre of art. In other words, technology is not just a means for artistic exploration, a source of new materials and techniques, which serve artists in expanding and revising the horizons of artistic production. Rather, reproducibility discloses art as *techne*, as technical in its essence, and, consequently, as one instantiation among many of the prevalent technicization of being characteristic of (post)modernity. As Valéry suggested, technology not only changes the functions of art but also brings about mutations in the very concept of art, modifications that increasingly disclose art as primarily a matter of technology. When aesthetics stops being the dominant optics of art, technology begins to assert more and more its claim on artistic production. In Heidegger's essays on art, technology, and language, there is a sense that with the end of aesthetics, what appears as a new opening for art is the possibility of its non-aesthetic function.[7] The corollary of this possibility, however, is the fusion of art and technology, where the disclosure of art's essentially technical character would constitute the contemporary version of the Hegelian death of art. The ambivalence of this historical moment manifests itself in the fact that the instant of art's 'liberation' from the strictures of its aesthetic formation coincides with the possible disappearance of art's distinctiveness and its progressive merger with technology. This eventuality is often read in the context of the avant-garde as the end of the separation between art and everyday life. While this diagnosis is not false, what animates this possibility of the coalescence of art and technology is the increasing technicization of being and relations characteristic of modernity. Thus what is called into question in the avant-garde is not only the separation of art from social praxis but also the distinctiveness of artworks from technology.

Film exists as, in principle, its own reproducibility, that is, as the possibility of its own reproduction in different contexts, locations, and times. This facility of reproducibility is not just a means of diffusion but reflects the new mode of existence associated with film, namely, the idea that the 'essence' of film lies not simply in its new aesthetic dimension but in reproducibility as the new principle of how art works. Underneath its aesthetic appearance, modern art works technically, not aesthetically: it works primarily in the medium of its reproducibility, not through its aesthetic features. The interactive Web art, which has quickly developed from its recent nascence to more sophisticated computer programs/works, appears to feed on the same idea that attracted Benjamin's attention to film: the technological basis of the existence of the work. From 'rudimentary' Web-based works in which one turns lights on and off in order to interact with them, to more complicated projects like Mikami's spider or Kac's 'Genesis', in which the Internet 'interactors' actively participate in shaping and modulating the evolution of either virtual artistic creations/programs or real techno-artistic environments, Web art seems to operate on the principle of virtual availability for interaction/intervention. When one turns on the light and induces mutation in the bacteria with the 'artist's gene' in Kac's 'Genesis',[8] one brings into being a possibility inscribed in the very principle of the work. A work like 'Genesis' operates as an open-ended array of possibilities of mutation, whose existence is brought into being through an elaborate, pre-programmed, though also unpredictable and, at least in some sense, unscripted, interaction of the willing participants in it.

Whichever perspective one adopts in discussions of Web art, what seems not to be in question is the technological medium/principle of the existence of such works. For instance, in Kac's notorious 'Green Fluorescent Protein Bunny' project, art appears to fully merge with science and technology. The 'artwork', the 'Green Fluorescent Protein Bunny', is a product of genetic technology, which, transplanting the fluorescence gene into a rabbit, arrives at the creation of a transgenic animal. While Kac claims that the work of transgenic art is the bunny together with the ethical and aesthetic discussions it has been generating, one can imagine a situation in which a similar product of genetic science also generates a comparable wave of debates, without claiming to be a work of art. Is then the difference between art and technology one of the type/scope of discussions it provokes or questions it raises? Kac's own work, especially the 'Genesis' project, seems to indicate otherwise. In 'Genesis', science is used quite ironically to produce an 'artist's gene', whose mutating effects in the bacteria appear to foreground and call into question precisely the very principle on which science and technology operate: computation, machination, and manipulative power. The question which 'Genesis' raises reaches beyond both the problematic of the ethics of genetic experimentation and the idea of interactivity which underlies much of today's Internet artistic innovations. It points at the heart of the contemporary dilemma of art: is art primarily *techne*, that is, a form of technological manipulation of different materials (from solid materials like wood or marble, to electronic data, virtual environments, and genetic codes), or is art to be differentiated from technology? And how, in what terms, are we to think this difference?

In 'The Question Concerning Technology', Heidegger hints at the possibility of a critical distinction between two types of *techne*: one, which operates in terms of producing, rendering available, and processing, could be called a technical *techne*, and the other, a *poietic techne*.[9] It is this second type of *techne*, the *poietic techne*, which Heidegger associates with art, and, in other contexts, with the idea of letting be and releasement from manipulative power. Echoing Adorno, one could say that, if the technical *techne* operates on the principle of manipulation and domination, then the *poietic techne* is a way of manipulating artistic materials in a manner that undoes power and manipulation. The distinction between technology and art would then lie in the manner of their *techne*, or, differently put, in the way in which they are technical. Technology, including the different technologies which contemporary art employs, is, in its essence, predicated on the idea of manipulation. In the information age, this principle implies that everything is determined in terms of its availability as information: what exists is seen as translatable into information, and thus as intrinsically predisposed to being stored, manipulated, and processed as data. Art, by contrast, uses the same techniques to base its existence in the technological world but shapes them differently, specifically in a way that undoes the manipulative momentum of power. Kac's 'Genesis' can be seen precisely as a work of art that instantiates this dilemma: it not only foregrounds this question and presents it for reflection but, in fact, stages it. To put it differently, Kac's work exists as this dilemma, enacting precisely the scission between art and technology. What makes 'Genesis' a work of art, beyond the consideration of traditional aesthetic trappings, is precisely this capacity to show what, in Adorno's terms, might be called the narrow untruth of the technological praxis as manipulative power over being understood as information. Art coincides with technology when it limits itself to participating in the overall manipulative practice of contemporary technology. It then serves as an element in the globalizing exercise of power, which operates increasingly in terms of the availability of what is as information. Kac's 'Genesis', whose 'artist's gene' is constructed as a translation into a sequence of amino acids of the Biblical phrase about man's dominion over existence, ironically demonstrates the narrowness of the conception of being predicated on power and manipulation. It thus marks a vital space of difference between technical manipulation at the basis of the culture of information and the artistic 'production' which manipulates in a way that aims at undoing manipulative power. This distinction between technical and *poietic* manipulation is a critical difference in a preeminent sense: it is the site of 'crisis', of a scission and a decision between the technical and the *poietic* character of art. This largely unperceived 'crisis' of contemporary art marks precisely the space of such differentiation and decision. What keeps art alive today is, in this perspective, its capacity to stage this crisis, that is, to keep the scission between *poietic* and technical *techne* in play.

V

It is symptomatic that Benjamin chose film as the focus and the engine of his argument, a 'crossover' genre between mass culture and art, between entertainment production and art creation. For it is film that instantiates the difficulty of maintaining the difference between high and low art, between popular culture and artistic endeavours, perhaps illustrating the progressive dissolution of art into the ever-multiplying products of mass culture and entertainment industry, which constitutes a distinctive mark of twentieth-century society. Film is the medium of the convergence, and perhaps of a still valid differentiation, between art, mass culture, and technology. It is possible, therefore, to argue that film is a decisive locus for thinking art in the twentieth century, in just this sense that at play in film are the questions of art's specificity and its difference from entertainment products, on the one hand, and of art's relation to technology, on the other. These two questions remain the key parameters for the problematic of art's 'death' (or, looking at the issue from another side, art's continuing life, perhaps even its possible revitalization?) in the contemporary world. Since entertainment products increasingly involve the most advanced technologies, from information and the Internet to telematics and virtual reality, and since their entertainment value becomes entwined with the novelty of the cutting-edge technology employed in their development and operation, the problem of popular culture and its growing appeal appears to be intrinsically related to the intensifying influence of technology on contemporary experience. Without utterly simplifying the issue, one could say that the question of entertainment is progressively coextensive with the problem of technology, and even more so in the sense that, while technology is indispensable to entertainment and its diffusion, the growth of entertainment seems predicated upon the disappearance of technology *as* a question.

The more technology becomes ingrown and structurally determinant of entertainment and its industries, the more it vanishes from view as a problem, as a question worthy of inquiry; instead, it is taken as a given, whose influence upon contemporary life is widely acknowledged but, at the same time, remains largely unreflected. Of course, there are always questions of better, more advanced, and more lucrative technologies, even questions of their beneficial and/or detrimental effect on society and environment, debated from such diverse points of view as good business and profitability, on the one hand, and ethics and global development, on the other. Yet, what such questions do not inquire about, and what, one has the impression, they often prevent one from raising, is the issue of the technicization of today's reality. Beyond 'good and evil' (of technology), there is the question of the technicization of being, the problem that being increasingly unfolds as information and becomes constituted into the terms of power and manipulation. Sophisticated contemporary means of manipulating information from digital imagery to genetic codes are symptoms of the technicization of being in its macro and micro dimensions, from global phenomena and the world-wide reach of tele-informational industries to the sense that being increasingly manifests itself as manipulable information. This manner of inquiry constitutes perhaps one of the ways in which one could ask today about a possible difference between art and entertainment: while entertainment feeds from and back into technology, using its latest achievement to raise its potential appeal and market value, art, immersed in new technologies as much as entertainment, if not more in some cases, still asks the question of technology, or better, the question of the technicization of being. Entertainment, because of its technological hype, keeps us playing the game of technology, drawing us more and more into it to divert attention from the question of technicization; art, by contrast, makes technicization into the very question of its existence. For art to be dead would mean today to be like entertainment. Not because entertainment is 'bad', 'low', or 'popular', though it often might be all of the above, but because entertainment evades the question of the technicization of modern being. It lives off it but in a way that seems to render that very question irrelevant. And if art is alive in the twenty-first century, it is precisely to the extent to which it is capable, often by employing the latest technologies, as in the Net or transgenic art, of rasing technology as a question, perhaps as *the* question, which allows it to keep open the problem of the technicization of being.

VI

Benjamin's principal question concerned the change in the notion of art in view of its technical reproducibility. It was reproducibility, most visible in Benjamin's day in film, that transformed art's reception as well as the impact artworks had on the audience, cementing what began with photography as the displacement of cult value by exhibition value.[10] Under those conditions, art no longer worked primarily in terms of subjective, aesthetic experience but acquired new parameters of reception: collectivity and 'distracted' mobilization. 'The greatly increased mass of participants has produced a change in the mode of participation ... A person who concentrates before a work of art is absorbed by it ... By contrast, the distracted masses absorb the work of art in themselves' (*SW* 4:267–8). For Benjamin, film viewers do not exist as individual subjects as much as they come to constitute a temporary collective, which, finding itself in a state of distraction and absent-minded-ness, lays itself open to aesthetic/political manipulation. The absent-minded absorption of the work of art becomes a habitual reaction, in which the solu-tions provided by art get translated into the reactions of mobilized masses:

> The sort of distraction that is provided by art represents a covert measure of the extent to which it has become possible to perform new tasks of apperception. Since, moreover, individuals are tempted to avoid such tasks, art will tackle the most difficult and the most important tasks where it is able to mobilize the masses. It does so currently in the film. (*SW* 4:268–9)

Art thus appears to achieve unprecedented effects on its audience, mobi-lizing and triggering reactions on the level of bodily enervations through which, relying on the audience's absent-mindedness, artworks are able, as Benjamin implies, to almost literally 'embody' their own solutions in the public's reactions. Absorbing the work of art, the audience in its habitual dis-traction begins to enact the solution presented in the work. Obviously, a lot depends in this context on the kind of 'solutions' the work presents and the goals towards which it is able to mobilize its audience. We should remember here that Horkheimer and Adorno's analysis of the culture industry is just around the corner.

With contemporary Web or Net art, art's relation to its audience finds itself determined by a novel situation, which might be described in a word as interactivity. The idea of participating in the mutation of bacteria or in the virtual 'genetic' evolution of a Web-based spider program introduces a new configuration of the relation between artworks and their 'audience' just in this sense that it becomes increasingly hard to describe the experience of art's audience as either passive or active. In fact, it seems inappropriate to speak in this case of an audience, and more fitting to describe the partici- pants in such works as interactors. While it is true that in such situations one's participation is circumscribed by the conditions of the art's existence and the programming possibilities inherent in the work, the actual course of the work's development cannot be predicted or scripted. In a sense, all the possibilities in which a work like Mikami's spider might evolve appear to be circumscribed by the capacities of the program which constitutes the work's virtual existence. Thus, it could be said that all the possible evolutions of the spider exist as potentially programmed into its mode of operation. Yet the network of interactions that develops during the existence of such works on the Web, the people who come into contact with the work and choose to either participate in it, to observe it, or not to bother with it at all, creates a strange map of electronic connections and interactions, ones that might be traced and charted, but which, more importantly, exist as literal inscriptions in the evolution of the spider.

This virtual network of interactions and its 'genetic' map reflect an impor- tant change in the mode of existence evidenced by Web art. Such works are no longer just reproducible; they exist as virtual, and as such, remain intrin- sically open to temporal interactions and interventions. If Benjamin chose to describe the then new phenomenon of film in terms of reproducibility and collective absorption, contemporary Web-based art would have to be charac- terized through features such as mutability and interactivity. The electronic existence of Web artworks renders them accessible for interaction at any and all times, and from virtually all possible locations, granting, of course, the accessibility of computer technology and Internet connection. Ontologically speaking, the work's electronic and virtual existence is marked not only by possibly global accessibility but also by intrinsic mutability: such work is not only intrinsically open to change through interaction but its very existence and success are predicated on the 'audience'-influenced mutation.

This idea of mutability and interaction, of importing into the work of art the element of a real happening, hearkens back to the days of the prominence of happenings and even to their 'prehistory' in Futurist and Dadaist perfor- mances. One could ask whether this emphasis on the 'live' – unscripted, unpredictable, temporal, and open-ended – character of the artwork's exis- tence, which is much in evidence in twentieth-century art, might be seen as in part a reaction to the reverberations of Hegel's dictum about the death of art. Clearly there is a marked anxiousness in twentieth-century art about art's loss of contact with reality, which reflects the apprehension that art

appears to be in its funereal phase. The need to make art live, to emphasize its happening and to literally inscribe temporality and unpredictability
characteristic of life into the artwork's structure, has certainly to do with the
historical conditions of art's existence in the epoch of its presumed death.
At the same time, this pull towards happening seems equally to reflect the
growing perception that the increasingly technicized existence is robbing
experience and being of their qualities of temporal unfolding: temporality
becomes a matter of calculation and manipulation, much like other forms
of information, and art responds to this situation with increased emphasis
on the temporal, 'live' dimensions of existence. Art as a live event, as a happening, a mutation, or an interaction, becomes a marker of the sense that
art as 'mere' representation is dead: it is not enough to reflect on experience,
albeit critically, and it is instead necessary to stage art as the instantiation of
the very unfolding of experience. This deliberately temporalized unfolding
of experience in art seems to address precisely the prevalent foreshortening
of being into information, which, no longer characterized by the rhythm of
its unfolding and temporality, becomes instead circumscribed in terms of
availability for storage and processing.

We arrive here again at the notion of the event as the mode of art's existence in the aftermath of the death of aesthetics. In other words, though one
can read modern and avant-garde art in terms of a certain death anxiety,[11]
it would be more correct to see this phenomenon as a celebration of the
newly disclosed character of art as event, which comes to the fore precisely
as a result of the dismantling of the traditional aesthetic forms of art. The
preoccupation of twentieth-century art with art as a live 'event' has to do
precisely with the reconfiguration of the artwork as an event, and of the constant tension between the object and the event dimensions of the artwork,
which characterizes post-aesthetic art. Thus the anxiety over art's possible
demise, which has continued to be with us for the past couple of centuries,
and became quite palpable in aestheticisim and modernism, coexists in the
twentieth century with a different response: a celebration of the emergence
of art as event, so characteristic of the work of Dadaism, Stein, Khlebnikov,
or Białoszewski, to name here just a few examples.

In many respects, recent Web works like the spider and 'Genesis' function
as events, since they are intrinsically futural in their character, open to their
own virtualities. Art's character of an event marks with its specific force also
the reception/interaction that such works inscribe into their very mode of
existence. One could speak of the traces of the interactive event that exist
inscribed in the 'final' form of the evolving spider or in the bacteria environment, but the interactive participation of the 'audience' in such a work scripts
a new and different mode of response to art. What is important about such
interactivity in the context of Benjamin's concern with collective response
to new art forms, is that its format alters the optics of the aura, collectivity,
and absorption. For the collective which Benjamin has in mind when

writing about film exists as a largely passive audience, ready for becoming mobilized by the work of art into undertaking a task or enacting a solution. The interactors of Web art participate in the work on different terms, without knowing other participants or ever becoming synchronized with them in a kind of an artistic space-time continuum. Instead they inscribe themselves into a fluid and futural matrix of interactions and mutations which resembles not an artistic object but an art event, in the sense elaborated above. This event undercuts the linear sense of temporality on which collective mobilizations rely. What such an event enacts is precisely the irreducibiliy of art, and of the temporality instantiated in it, to the models of subjectivity, identity, and collectivity based on the notions of synchrony, fusion, totality, presence, etc. The new aspect introduced by Web-based art is the possibility of interaction at the same time from multiple and different locations. The fact that Web artworks are often characterized by intrinsic mutability implies furthermore that the interactive collective which develops through participation in the work over the time of its duration comes into being as, in principle, open-ended and changeable. In fact, it is this temporal dimension of transformation which decisively marks the net of interactions arising as a response to and a reshaping of the work. The participants in the work form a web of interactions constituted as temporal and futural in its structure, interventions which do not assume or produce any collective identity but become instead gathered into an open-ended and metamorphosing nexus. The collective here would have to be thought without direct reference to identity: while one influences the mutation of the art project, one does not inscribe one's presence or identity into it.

The collective, though this word appears to be no longer appropriate in this context, becomes reformulated away from the notions of identity and synchronized action/attitude, and gets turned towards a new sense of relating configured as unpredictable, futural, and event-like. One peculiarity of the event, when thought in the context of Benjamin's remarks about the change introduced in reception by film – from absorption *into* the work of art to the absorption *of* it by the audience – is that the event is not about absorption: it neither absorbs nor becomes absorbed, but, rather, transforms through interaction the parameters of praxis, i.e. the modality of relations which configure the social. Thought in this way, the event might be precisely a way to (re)think the revolutionary praxis to which Benjamin alludes at the end of 'Surrealism': a 'bodily collective innervation' acting as a revolutionary discharge through which reality transcends itself (*SW* 2:217–18). The futural direction, the moment of transformation, and the sense of interaction seem to be all in play there.

In the interactive Web art, one's inscription in the artwork is marked by its time and by the location from which it comes; it thus remains singular and specific, without, however, claiming a particularity for it. What begins to emerge through the phenomenon of interactivity and its virtual horizon is a different sense of relationality, of a kind of an inter-being, which operates somewhere between the particular and the universal, the individual and the collective. What changes in such an interaction is that its mode of being no longer has a site, either the individual or the collective, but instead unfolds as a between, as an event of relating. This mode of relationality would not be then characterized as manipulation or mobilization but instead as inter-action. This is why such participation in the work is neither passive nor active, neither assertive nor dismissive of one's identity, but instead evolves a different mode of relation: what I have elsewhere called the middle voice of letting be.[12] Another way of looking at this issue would be to say that identity here becomes a matter of the event at the interstices between the individual and the collective. It taps into the very scission, the between from which individuality and collectivity emerge and assert themselves in their continuing interplay. Within this between one is neither an individual nor a member of a collective but comes to be marked and transformed by the futural dynamic of the unfolding event. The work of art in the age of its electronic mutability prompts us to rethink the notion of collectivity in terms of such an interactive, changing, and futural event. It is within the horizon of such an event that one would have to think the 'politics' of the artwork after aesthetics.

VII

The work of art exists today in the age of informatics and globalization. Information is not only the currency of the contemporary world but, more importantly, appears to determine the essence of modern being. If being in modernity is technological, today this technological determination finds itself in the phase of information, which is characterized by the global availability of what is, whether objects, beings, occurrences, or experiences, as information. Any and everything appears intrinsically convertible into information, rendered available as data, and disclosed as predisposed to being stored, manipulated, and (re)programmable. From genetics to global data banks, being manifests itself today as information and comes to be constituted in terms of a certain technicity, by which I mean here the avail-ability and manipulability of being as information. Does art today respond to the same 'informational' demand? How can art be thought in the context of globality?

In the present circumstances, global seems to mean primarily intercon-nection and openness to difference. Considered in this perspective, the work of art in the age of globalization appears to be characterized crucially in terms of being interactive, open to multiple and unexpected modifications, and defined in its electronic and virtual existence by an intrinsic mutability. Such a work of art is not only structurally open to the possibility of different interpretations and reproduction in varying contexts, that is, to existence defined in terms of its own reproducibility, but becomes characterized above all by mutability. Perhaps this mutability, literally like the mutating genetic code of Mikami's virtual spider or the genetic changes induced by the artist's gene in Kac's 'Genesis', discloses another emergent layer of the artwork, described as intrinsically mutable. Such artwork is not just reproducible in different circumstances but mutates and evolves, while remaining the 'same'. One could argue that works of art have always had a degree of mutability inscribed in their mode of existence, which allows them to persist as works through historical and social changes. What is different about contemporary art is that it literalizes this transformative ability: it is no longer the matter of changing contexts or capacity for multiple interpretations, but of a different ontological structure of the artwork: in short, of a different mode of essentially interactive and transformative existence. This emergent 'mutating' character of the artwork in the epoch of its electronic existence underscores the fact that, historically, it is art's character as event that comes into focus when the aesthetic formation of art is called into question. In this sense, what we are witnessing today in art's development is still the legacy of the avant-garde. Producing art outside of the aesthetic parameters, the avant-garde engages with technology, and not just with technological products and processes, but, more broadly, with the technicization of experience. What emerges from this encounter is the *poietic* force of the event, counterposed to the false novelty of technological products and to the progressing efficacy of rendering different aspects of being into available resource.

For Benjamin, the crucial distinction in understanding the changes in art's function was the one between manipulation of the audience and politicization. In the epoch of globalization, which seems to operate on the principle of shifting multiple and global interlinking, the question of art (and technology) might be posed in terms of the mode of relation instantiated in artworks: relations of power and manipulation, reflective of the world structured on the principle of domination, to recall Adorno, or relations that, as in Kac's 'Genesis', undermine the idea of dominion. In other words, it is not just the question of the artwork being open to difference but also of how this openness is figured, or, in other words, of the modality of relating instantiated by the work. What depends on this difference in the mode of relations, i.e. on the distinction between the *poietic* and the technic/manipulative relations enacted in the artwork, is the form assumed by present globalizing tendencies, together with the mode of relating/linking at work in them. As an event, the work of art releases force relations from their inscription within the manipulative operations of power. Relations in the artwork have a different momentum than power, and as such call into question the very constitution of forces and relations into forms of power. If globalization manifests itself in the increased macro- and micro-manipulative scope and intensity of power, then the specificity of the artwork in the age of globalization comes from how it re-disposes relations through the *poietic* force of its event, giving them a different amplitude. Rather than being measured in terms of availability and information, relations in the artwork are given a non-manipulative momentum, and allowed to keep open the space of emancipation from power.[13] Revealing themselves as a mode of *techne*, artworks remind us of the difference in the vectors of *techne* between power and releasement from power; they 'mobilize' by desisting from and demobilizing power. If this tendency in art begins to manifest itself with its idiomatic force in the early avant-garde 'events', it continues to gather importance with the increasing technicization of being in the age of information. Becoming more and more involved with and dependent upon technology, contemporary artworks often come close to completely identi-fying themselves with technological manipulation, only to remind us, even if infrequently, of their 'critical' difference, that is, of the crisis and scission between *techne* and *poiesis*. Artworks enact this scission and configure it as an event, whose futural momentum evacuates power. The mutability which comes into the foreground in recent art can be seen as underscoring precisely a transformation in the power momentum of relations. One could say that in the artwork power 'mutates', and comes to desist from its own manipula-tive and productionist drive, thereby becoming non-power, a silent mark of art's event. It is perhaps as such a mutation in power that art's politicization needs to be thought today.

13

REHEARSING REVOLUTION AND LIFE: THE EMBODIMENT OF BENJAMIN'S ARTWORK ESSAY AT THE END OF THE AGE OF MECHANICAL REPRODUCTION

SAUL OSTROW

Being a critic involved in the practical application of theory, my interest in 'The Work of Art in the Age [Epoch] of its Technical Reproducibility' (1935–36) is pragmatic.[1] Its articulation of culture as a network in which each component respectively influences the identity and the economies of the other, supplies me with a model by which to focus and rethink the relationship between the aesthetics and cultural politics of our times. Consequently, by employing Benjamin's perspective we may be able to evaluate the various discourses and practices that have come to circumscribe our thinking about art and the role that aesthetics and culture play in today's cultural and political arena.

The chronicle that from a US point of view complies in principle with Benjamin's 'artwork' essay envisions technological change as both the cause and the effect of a process by which artists came to resist, submit, or adapt themselves to the influences of reproduction. Often formalist in nature, this view begins with art's secular turn during the early nineteenth century and then closely tracks the development of Modernism. Its primary focus is the emergence of Romanticism's 'art for art sake' philosophy, which sought to wrest art's legitimacy from the authority of state and church. This early expression of the bourgeois ideal of individualism transformed art conceptually as well as performatively into an apparently autonomous practice, now only subject to changes of taste, style, and fashion. Having attained self-determinacy in thought, artists were required to establish the essential terms of art as a discipline in practice.

Abandoning the claim that they portrayed moral and universal truth, the early Modernists privileged formalist and aesthetic innovation as the means to articulate a materialist vision that would verify art's intrinsic values.

Although art came to be understood as an expression of the artist's 'self' in the world, this pursuit resulted in what appeared to be art's disengagement from social and political concerns and its retreat into esoteric and idealist aspirations. Although this withdrawal was perceived as a form of aesthetic resistance to the old order, it generated on the part of artists who believed that art was a tool capable of forming social and political consciousness, an aggressive anti-aesthetic, anti-art mode of expression. In the 1960s, in the closing days of Formalism, Benjamin emerges as the prophet of art's re-politicization and reintegration into the realm of the social. The problem of course is that for Benjamin this is achieved at the expense of art's aura. Consequently, for liberals and the Left, the loss of aura was just another example of how technology and capital had undermined the humanist foundation upon which art's relevance and value rested. The best part of this situation is that this paradox was an articulation and an irresistible consequence of the very change and progress that Modernism had fetishized.

It is important that we recognize that the process that Benjamin is responding to in the 1930s actually began in the mid-nineteenth century when paintings, sculptures, and prints that appealed to the taste of the newly emergent petit bourgeoisie came to be mass-produced. This state of affairs, depicted in Gustav Flaubert's *Sentimental Education*, combined with the staid and conservative views of the academy, threatened art's vitality if not its very existence. The response to the conflict between art's traditional identity and the changing social environment of the late nineteenth century resulted in a revolt against the conventions of art itself. The emergent coterie of artists that would come to make up the schools of Realism, Impressionism, and Post-Impressionism having been exposed to photography, mass-produced lithographic images, and non-Western cultures, set out to move beyond dogmatic adherence to the rules of perspective, classic aesthetics, and the craft criteria established by the 'grand' tradition of the Academy. In place of traditional values and practices of the Academy, the new Modern artists of the mid-nineteenth century accentuated colour, flatness, and painterly process, as well as in terms of subject matter embracing all that was identified with the modern. Overstepping the bounds of convention, their rejection of the stylization and idealism of Neo-Classicism and the virtuosity and reverie of Romanticism represented the new generation's particular mixture of humanitarianism and materialist realism. They instead focused on images that represented the alterations that were taking place in 'everyday life' due to the industrial revolution and the bourgeoisie's ideology of individualism, entrepreneurship, and leisure.

In the context of the changes in social fashions and lifestyle that accompanied the industrial revolution and the rise of the bourgeoisie, artists came to understand that the new materialist aesthetic of immediacy, scientific objectivity, and realism that they promoted had political implications. They and their work were an expression of the rise of the bourgeoisie as a class and a culture. By emphasizing the characteristic formalist qualities that bound them to tradition, while rejecting the conventions of such modes of artistic production, these artists' challenge to the old aristocratic culture also came to expose the deeper subjective and objective contradictions of the new social reality of modern society in ways that the moralizing genre painting of the previous generations had not. The manifestation of this predicament was the rejection of the new art by the bourgeoisie in favour of the art of the now deposed aristocracy that would now play a role in their legitimization.

The collapse of the Academy's moribund commitment to outmoded values and standards resulted in the cultural triumph of the nineteenth-century avant-garde and its eventual institutionalization. The frustration induced by the bourgeoisie's adaptability contributed to ever-increasing nihilist challenges to the traditional conception of the role of art and artist. The values and standards of the bourgeoisie rather than the conventions of art became their target. The early-twentieth-century vanguard's project of negation self-consciously sought to test the essential qualities of the means and modes of cultural expression and to expand them both formally and conceptually. This process of negation and inclusion came to be the means by which culturally to resist the influence of middle-class taste, and the inevitability implied by the bourgeoisie's newly formulated vision of historical determinism and essentialism.

As succeeding generations of artists set about proving that there was nothing essential about traditional forms of artistic production, it not only became possible to stylistically expand upon these to give expression to the iconography of modern life, but also allowed for works of art to contain actual bits and pieces of the real world. This move towards using the real as a means of expression became the foundation for the most important innovation of twentieth-century art, the development of collage by Max Ernst, Pablo Picasso, and George Braque. Collage led to photomontage, while the Dadaists, in particular Kurt Schwitters, extended this process to produce assemblages of found objects and everyday detritus. His *Merzbau* constituted an environment that could be inhabited, and with it art ceased to be an object. The inherent rejection of traditional materials and crafts contributed to the development of the vision of an art that would materially transform the everyday, given expression by the Russian Constructivists' and the Bauhaus' embrace of industrial processes and a functionalist aesthetic. In this, they were following the logic employed by Marcel Duchamp when he designated mass-produced objects and images as art works.

This 'lowering of standards', in which everything potentially had aesthetic value, seemed to imperil the cultural field itself. Cutting up colour paper, photographs, old prints, wallpaper, and other printed materials, or having sculptures and paintings industrially fabricated, obviously does not require the same types of skills that a naturalistic rendering of an apple with condensation on its skin does. The reaction to art's transformation into an indifferent though perhaps idiosyncratic thing led other artists to attempt to recuperate the strategy of the nineteenth-century avant-garde, which had sought to preserve art formally and aesthetically. Although committed to expressing materialist or transcendent philosophies, these artists emphasized art's phenomenological content, just as the Impressionists had at the dawn of Modernism, by seeking refuge in the inherent qualities of their processes and materials. By entrenching self-expression in art's traditional media the artists sought to sustain art's aura by producing that which could not be produced by any other means. This tendency over the course of the modernist enterprise both restricted and advanced art's engagement with its own absorption into the logic of standardization and reproducibility.

In the 1930s, faced with an onslaught of commercially marketed kitsch and a vanguard committed to abandoning art, Clement Greenberg, in his essay 'Avant Garde and Kitsch' (1939), takes up Benjamin's theme of technology's effect on art. Though expressing what appears to be a Marxist view, Greenberg's orientation is wholly different from that of Benjamin's artwork essay in that he finds no redeemable qualities in the possibility of the new media that holds out such potential in Benjamin's eyes. Given the politics of the moment, Greenberg considers it preferable to preserve the integrity of traditional art – to hold the bourgeoisie to their own ideals – rather than to transform art into a new entity. Greenberg believed that focusing on the artwork's material qualities and intrinsic values of form as content, rather than emphasizing meaning, constituted an act of resistance to Capital's debasement of culture and its abandonment of its highest ideals.

In the context of Greenberg's formalist hypothesis of the 1930s and 1940s, the Abstract Expressionist artists of the early 1950s appeared to him as the only force capable of maintaining art's aura (presence), and of warding off the challenges of a debased mass culture and the anti-art aesthetics of the post-war avant-garde. Greenberg viewed the latter as being foolishly committed to novelty and to the demise of art's traditional value. Not only did the Abstract Expressionist artists represent to him a genuine struggle for a personal truth in the face of depression and war, but they also demonstrated a renewed moral dimension. Thus ironically, while Abstract Expressionism's aesthetic (and rhetorical) insistence on presence was oriented towards preserving art's aura, and resisting the effects of reproduction, its message of individualism and heroic struggle came to be turned into an image that could and would be reproduced and parodied by mass culture. In the face of this seeming crisis Greenberg came to view the reductivism, emotional restraint, and formalism of such artists as Helen Frankenthaler, Kenneth Noland, Frank Stella, Morris Louis, and Jules Olitski, and the sculptor Anthony Caro, as the true heirs of the Abstract Expressionist artists. Dubbing these painters' style 'post-Painterly Abstraction', Greenberg promoted them as being capable of sustaining art's undefined though renewable sense of quality in the face of its continued debasement.

For Greenberg, and for the circle of young critics that he had attracted to him in the 1960s, which included Michael Fried and Rosalind Krauss, the adaptation of the logic and conditions of mass production to art was anti-humanist, and therefore antithetical to their notion that the work of art was a source of an embodied experience that could provoke self-consciousness, rather than being merely an intellectual exercise. To those younger artists who were sensitive to the prohibitive nature of their critical rhetoric, and to the obstacles that the success of Abstract Expressionism seemed to impose, such difficulties were compounded by their experience of a mass culture augmented by glossy magazines, billboards, Technicolor movies, and the new medium of television, all trying to sell a mass-produced lifestyle. This cultural environment left them feeling that they would have to find new means by which to make art a more inclusive mode of expression so that it might compete by appropriating aspects of mass culture. To these artists, all that seemed retrievable in the wake of Abstract Expressionism's success was an aspiration fuelled by frustration, disillusionment, and a desire to be contemporary. These motivations coalesced into an anti-aesthetic, anti-art, anti-subjective attitude intent on embracing art in its de-sublimated state. Consequently, by the late 1950s, a split had formed between those who continued to work in traditional modes and those who turned to collage, assemblage, and new materials.[2]

Voicing their self-evident dissatisfaction with the inability of traditional art to offer up an alternative to the image world of mass production, the new vanguard repressed the codes and practices that had come to represent a modernist vision of intentionality and self-expression. They instead gave expression to the post-War era's sense of distance, banality, and standardization. For instance, Robert Rauschenberg and Jasper Johns, by literary and literal means, each in his own way articulated the split between art's form and content by exposing that as an image a painting is always already a reproduction, and yet as an object it is a thing-in-the-world. If these two artists are exemplary of the conflicted nature of modern art's 'self' as it is rooted in the opposition between abstract and figural, Frank Stella, within his series of systemic paintings, asserts art's objecthood by actualizing the relationship between image and concept as being that of depicted shape and its supporting form.

Antithetical to the Abstract Expressionist artists' commitment to spontaneity and individualism, Stella's logical and workman-like approach to painting reordered both the image and the practice of the artist. Self-consciously, Stella's early production mimics that of the assembly-line of automobile production, as does his tendency to re-design his work every two or three years.[3] Within the rationalizing tendencies of 1960s culture, Stella's work straddles the fence between Formalism and Minimalism in that his literalization of painting's inherent structural and aesthetic qualities also function as a reminder to his audience that the world of artifice (commodity), rather than human exchange, has become the source of their conceptual and aesthetic pleasures. In this context Andy Warhol is the exemplary model of an artist who, iconically and performatively, explicitly acknowledges reproduction and mass culture as the primary condition that art must address. Casting himself in the role of celebrity, idiot savant, and a citizen of the demimonde, Warhol's work not only is a depiction of the consequences of a culture being submerged by the spectacle of mass culture and reproduction, but also offers up an aesthetics of resistance by being neither high nor low, but a hybrid of the best of both. Warhol's use of socially loaded imagery is a recasting of the modernist idea of the vanguardist in rebellion against the cultural status quo, which in this context is an aesthetic rooted in an indifference to the popular culture.

As Benjamin had come to recognize, art that knows no original cannot be degraded by the means of reproduction, for nothing of the experience of it, or its identity, is lost, and as such Warhol's multiple images know no original that is not already a reproduction. The differences that exist between them are of colour and the chance occurrence of the medium, which results from the silkscreen process by which they are made. Beyond this, their similarities and dissimilarities are indistinguishable – interchangeable in their blatant banality, and only subject to taste. These imperfections constitute a *fractura* that along with various compositional strategies breaks the illusionary nature of his imagery. This in turn disrupts the cycle of enticement and deferred satisfaction induced by the imagery he uses. In this way, we can see a parallel between Warhol's adaptation of silkscreen to painting, and Picasso's use of collage to sustain painting's effect as a viable form of representation and experience. Likewise, Jackson Pollock's appeal to process and chance played a similar role in discarding the tradition-laden baggage of painting, and for similar reasons. Each of these artists within their work articulates an aspect of the complex discourse network that defined the practices and claims of a cultural environment that was increasingly defined by the technologies of reproduction and distribution.

Despite the often optimistic visions of the political nature of Pop and Minimalism as they emerged from the formalist field of Abstract Expressionism, these practices though capable of exposing art's culpability and its emerging commodity nature, did little more than articulate and confirm that the conditions that had haunted and endangered traditional art's capacity for nearly 100 years were growing stronger. Consequently, in the hopes of escaping what seemed to be art's inevitable fate as commodity, artists declared that its object nature was expendable. Refuge was sought in the idea that art was nothing more than a concept and in search of a mode of presentation. From this proposition the practices of conceptual art emerged. This history of art which ends in art as idea, though represented as a chronicle of resistance, actually records art as it is moved into line with industrial models of production and thought.[4] The result is that Modernism is brought to its end just as the age of mechanical reproduction itself is being replaced by the 'information age' ushered in by developments in electronics and the technologies of communication.

The birth of the Postmodern era was correspondingly characterized by a modernist nihilism committed to turning art history into a catalogue of ready-made styles that could be indiscriminately exploited (appropriated) and used to question the final Modernist myth: originality. Yet for all the diversity of recycled forms, styles, and aesthetics that circulated in this period (the 1980s–90s), art continued to be optimistically preserved as an immutable idea regardless of its institutionally moribund and compromised state as commodity and fetish. Much of this work, though it sought to reconnect culture to its political base, in form and content continued to echo the same essentialist and immutable discourses that Modernism had once set about to dismantle. When all was said and done, these works not only allowed themselves to be art, but also insisted upon it. As such, the resulting appropriation and adaptation of mass media imagery and norms, or historical styles in the name of critique, were no more or less illuminating, informative, significant, or insightful about our lived experience than the TV commercials we watch daily. The result of this history is that the preservation of art as an immutable idea regardless of its form is a conceptual problem, which continues to tie us to Capitalism's cultural ideologies.

In effect, Postmodernism's new reality is insignificantly different than the old Modernism, because Postmodernism 'new' model quickly reified into an essentialist discourse of universals, whose principles of difference, diversity, and multiplicity come to be nothing more than a new taxonomy. For all of its self-consciousness, Postmodernism continues to be incapable of offering up alternatives to the very cultural conditions that it was to invalidate or make transparent. Instead of alleviating our sense of alienation and hopelessness by creating new and imagined possibilities with which to explore and intervene in our existence, as Benjamin had hoped for, we were offered a comforting confirmation of our vulnerability to manipulation, and reminders of our victimization. So regardless of rhetoric or intention, seemingly art can never play its political role in the transformation of society, but will always serve the status quo. In this context, Benjamin's artwork text comes to be little more than a pessimistic prediction of the phantasmagoria of manipulation and false-consciousness that awaits us, leaving us to ask whether this fate is inescapable.

Other histories and other outcomes are possible. While what I have presented so far accounts empirically for the influence of the mechanical on mainstream art of the twentieth century, I do not believe that this is the only story to be told, for it does not truly address Benjamin's analysis of technology's effects on culture and art, nor the messianic role he envisions for it. In its recapitulation of art's modernist history, it does little more than repeat the positivist view that the resistance to technology's erosion of art's aura is cause, and art's changing modes of expression is effect. This vision of technological determinism sets aside Benjamin's critical belief that technology will give us access to the unconscious contingencies of our lives, and create a forever-mutable present under terms other than those of Capital. Adding fluidity and transformation to this equation requires that we construct a more complex history for the art of the period of mechanical reproduction. A more radical history, which does not make the pursuit of maintaining art's aura (and humanism) central, given that the true nature of the power of technology and consumerism now make themselves apparent.

For Benjamin, our ability to realize the full potential of the means that we have made and continue to make available to sustain thought and expression is always already incomplete. In other words, the fetter that Capital imposes on the productive forces is our tendency to think of the new in old terms – seeking within the new the fulfilment of past promises. In part this project persists because we are still brought up on the myth of art's social relevance, yet do not comprehend that cultural change is dependent on the vision of the humanist project of transformation and emancipation through self-consciousness rather than short-term political considerations of morality and conscience. Consequently, we must note that Benjamin's cautionary tale is equally focused on conceptual and material conditions, and that the subject of the artwork essay is as much a description of the instrumental thought that orders culture, as it is of art's historical condition. If art's circumstance can be thought of as being analogous to that of society as a whole, then collectively and individually we can understand how Benjamin's political aesthetic is part of a process of transformation by which we, not art alone, are to become something other than what we have learned to think of ourselves as. Reciprocally, if an aura needs to exist in this era, it can not be something related to the past, but has to be something related to our present future.

If we look at the present, we can, with a little distance, recognize that in acknowledging the end of Modernism, we desire to rewrite history by including those practices that momentarily remain unabsorbed. Our goal seems to be to appropriate them into a process by which art may continue by learning the lessons that they offer up. But, rushing to correct past mistakes and annex the world of alterity, we fail to recognize that in so doing these practices come to be transformed into their other – that is, into the means of making art, rather than that of resisting art. If these practices we now set about to redeem have an ability to supply us with models capable of revising our society's values and standards, and of giving us access to aesthetic and conceptual models capable of empowering us, this is not to be achieved by adapting them to make art, but by moving beyond them. The fact is these practices that we now wish to make exemplary were premised on the idea that they would never be fixed. By ignoring this fact, we demonstrate that we still have little or no understanding of what effect such recuperation might have due to our investment in our institutional conception of art and culture revealing itself as ever-unchanging. Even Greenberg willingly admitted that good or bad, it was all art.

What went unaccounted for in the history with which I began this chapter, though very much a part of that history, are those 'artists' that performatively put art at risk. Included among the Futurists, Dadaists, and Surrealists were artists whose projects were neither meant to sustain, preserve, attack, nor challenge art, because for them art had already been transformed into a general form of cultural expression, and all that stood in the way of the recognition of this fact were those artists who could not free themselves from the appeal of the concept and institutions of art. Under the slogan of 'art into life', they promoted dissolving the division between the two. So while a genealogy of art forms, as they move from painting and sculpture to collage and then through the readymade to concept, can be established easily enough, those who sought to re-order and transform perception within the context of social and political life are given only anec-dotal importance. These artists (if we can even call them by that name), in turn came to be marginalized, not because what they did was not signifi-cant but because the record of their activities, which is anecdotal in nature, could not be reconciled with our continuing belief in the spiritual and moral nature of art. With this in mind, the path I am about to take you down leads to such peripheral entities as Allan Kaprow, the father of Happenings, who today is being given significant attention as a reprised history of post-War Modernism is being written.

In 1957, Kaprow decided to surrender himself to the 'worldly'. Extending the logic of collage and assemblage, he produced mixed media environ-ments that consisted of discarded bits and pieces of the real world, and then produced non-theatrical performances that he called 'happenings'. Both practices were informed by ideas of chance and change, the temporal and the variable. By calling our attention to the source of the 'junk', and the commonplace events that ordered our lives, Kaprow found he could produce an uncanny effect that gave expression to the disintegration and tastelessness of everyday life. In choreographing these events, Kaprow cel-ebrated the commonplace and human activity without fixing them formally or aesthetically – his happenings left no residue other than some arbitrary documentation and narratives supplied by onlookers or participants.

Given his interest in events rather than objects, Kaprow's work mirrors that of the artists who were organized under the name Fluxus by George Macuinas in the early 1960s. Interestingly, what all these artists have in common is a connection with John Cage's influential view that music, dance, and art could be made from anything. In this regard, Cage encour-aged artists not only to accept chance, but also to recognize it as a creative and essential element of art-making. These artists had developed a brand of non-art/anti-art that emphasized the use of scores, performance, and multiplicity – that often could be realized by anyone. Although the popularity and novelty of such art and its accompanying attitude has been relatively long-lived, these artists are represented as nothing more than neo-Dadaist. Despite their common interest in producing works that demanded physical engagement as well as conceptual interaction between the artist and viewer, what separates Kaprow from Fluxus is that Fluxus intends that their own endeavours will ennoble the illogical or overlooked by transforming it into art. Interestingly, Cage's views also had a significant effect on Robert Rauschenberg who knew Cage from Black Mountain College, and then through Rauschenberg, Jasper Johns, and Cy Twombly, these ideas influenced the various artists who came to be identified with Pop, Minimalism, and Conceptual Art.

This simple revision of the standard formalist history to include the likes of Kaprow, Fluxus, and Cage is little more than a 'tar baby'. Its anti-formalism represents not an alternative but a supplement to the reading I began with. While much of the work produced by these artists is non-media-specific, and has both fracture and change built into it – they now take on essentialist qualities rather than retaining their state of relativity. In the early 1970s, in a series of articles,[5] Kaprow recognizes this farce when he denounces anti-art because he believes it has just become another way to make what he refers to as art-art. Having no fear of the power of technology to mediate and transform our experience of the world, he proposed that the world as a place is more interesting due to technology than to what artists continue to make. As such, he envisions the un-artist that engages the commonplace, and is indifferent to the institutions of art, yet accepts it as one context within which to circulate their ideas or information about their activities. Here again, the residual logics of Modernist negation and positivism that infest our thinking make such accounts acceptable. Inversely, it makes it difficult for us to evaluate how the strategies of post-War Modernism (1946–1974) might be understood in the context of Benjamin's view of mechanical reproduction in some other manner. Neither account is without merit, in that both can be understood as representing forms of resistance in the absence of social revolution: that of sustaining aura as an effective counter to the anaesthetization of everyday life that Benjamin equated with the monumentalizing romanticism of Fascism, and that of generating new modes of expression to replace and undermine the authority of older ones. However, is this enough?

I will now attempt to construct another genealogy; one built on a closer reading of Benjamin's text rather than on art history. By drawing a parallel between Benjamin's views and conditions in the 1960s at the end of the age of mechanical production, this account will try to take into consideration the nature of how the present transforms its past. While such an account may not help us to understand the indeterminacy, reflexivity, and inconclusive nature of the continuity upon which our own present has come to be formed, it might confirm Benjamin's relevance and perhaps prescience. Our goal is to understand how ideological engagement comes to be manifested in and through a political aesthetic rather than mere protest or resistance. This requires that we travel the line of thought embedded in Benjamin's essay, from its inception in the 1930s to its culmination in the 1960s when the age of mechanical reproduction was coming to its end.

To begin with, we must acknowledge that our cultural sphere, and the politics that circumscribe it, has been subject to consistent change since the industrial revolution, otherwise we will misperceive our situation as only quantitatively different than that of Benjamin's in 1930s Germany. Today, with the substantial relocation of the political to the realm of culture, the conflict between Fascism and Socialism of Benjamin's day bears little resemblance to our own struggle against the hegemony of instrumental thought. Our struggle against Capital today is characterized by the antagonism of imagination and creativity vs. standardization and sublimation. At present, the commodification of our diverse desires, and the corresponding sense of disempowerment, leaves us voluntarily vulnerable to manipulation, domination, and exploitation. This represents the greatest threat to liberal democracy, and has replaced the threat of openly repressive systems of government, with the potential to curtail our liberties in the broadest sense.

The emergence of Walter Benjamin, and the Frankfurt School thinkers with whom he is identified, was concurrent with the transition from Marxism to liberalism on the Left, and the transition from existentialism to structuralism in the post-War period as a dominant framework with which to theorize art's political and social function in the context of mass culture. 'The Work of Art in the Age of Mechanical Reproduction' (as the artwork essay was first titled in English), though written between 1935 and 1937, was not available in English until the early 1960s, when it immediately came to be used to explain art's vulnerability to the terrifying and de-humanizing vision of the loss of aura by the very technological means we had come to celebrate. Liberals and intellectuals perceived artists as their natural allies in the struggle for individual autonomy, freedom of expression, and licence – because the history of Modernism appeared to be that of a consistent struggle to create the present in a progressive and individualistic manner, against those conservative forces for whom modern culture represented the degeneration of human ideals and values. Therefore, as an interpretative tool, Benjamin's entry into the canon of theoretical works at once valorized both the ongoing desire for an art of spiritual and aesthetic value and the contradictory anti-aesthetic tendency that were being championed by the last vanguardists of high modernism in the name of resistance and cultural revolution. These iconoclastic and nihilist cultural tendencies were understood not only as serving as a counter-weight to the type of conformity subscribed to by both Left and Right, but also as a model of real freedom and self-determination.

At that time, for the sake of relevancy, critics and theorists focused on the concepts of aura and political aesthetics to tie past to present. The liberal appeal of the eternal message of repressive power became the de-historicized product, which allowed for a vernacular application of Benjamin's views to Vietnam-War-era politics. This resulted in an emphasis on the idea that art in the age of mass culture could reconnect socially by offering up a message of analysis and social protest in itself, rather than in conjunction with the as yet unrealized aesthetic models of freedom and mutable experience. While we obviously must apply what tends to be thought of as the two most salient points of the artwork essay – the loss of art's aura due to its reproducibility, and Fascism's aetheticization of the political – we cannot do so in a manner which canonizes the vision of the social and cultural politics of the 1930s as they came to be applied to the 1960s, when Benjamin's essay came to be popularly addressed.

Benjamin does not propose that the age of reproducibility naturally ushers in a progressive political culture of aesthetics and awareness, nor does he propose that the redemption of what has apparently been made obsolete is part of that agenda. Art's political nature is available to both the Left and the Right for it is not necessarily a means of liberation, but simply a tool. What mechanical reproduction has done is to give the masses access to an open-ended exegesis on the patterns of variation and change, and in return the consciousness of the masses has been made accessible. It is this admixture that constitutes art's political forms, practices, and content, and it is for this reason that Benjamin locates the difference between Right and Left within their respective aesthetic. As with Baudelaire's observations in 'Painter of Modern Life' on how photography, lithography, and the emergence of public life had a distinctive effect on modern life and art, Benjamin likewise advances a view intent on updating technology's impacts upon the public spheres of culture and politics. Benjamin orientates this analysis within the hypothesis that Capitalism always already constitutes a fetter on the means of production, and as such restricts both society's and culture's ability to develop freely. As such, reproduction contributes to the potential for the development of a culture whose form and content is empowering – that is, political in the strictest sense of that word. Yet under Capital this possibility is first deformed and then exploited to other ends.

All too often, discussions of these points tend to separate the political, cultural, and psychological aspects, which Benjamin seeks to bind together into a discourse network. More than iconically (in terms of subject matter), for Benjamin this network inseparably affects not only the practice of art performatively (by revising the role and conception of art and artist), and structurally (the forms it may take and the means by which it circulates), but also its reception (aesthetically). Consequently, Benjamin sees the age of reproduction not in iconic, but in performative and aesthetic terms whose conditions are temporal rather than constant. This is the reason that

Benjamin, rather than bemoaning the loss of aura, would have us instead consider our dependency on it, as well as on the desires and expectations that are bound to the work of art, which come to restrict it formally as well as socially.

The psychological, cultural, and political conditions that arise from the diminishing and denigration of direct experience, and the repression of aesthetic modes of expression, are the principal focus of Benjamin's discussion of the loss of aura through the proliferation of copies (or replicas without originals). The sense of loss of self, which gives rise to a mass psychology typified by extreme alienation of self that results from the capitalist mode of production, is reinforced by the state of distraction. Induced by mass culture, this leaves people open and defenceless against emotional and psychological manipulation. No longer having a sense of themselves, they seek reaffirmation external to their own existence through the fetishization of some larger entity – in Benjamin's era Fascism, or the Party's promise of a place in history, or in our day and age an abstract notion of freedom and individuality affirmed by the promise of access to goods and services.

In his formulation of the political nature of an art that can at first counter this trend and then go on to be a supplement to our sense of self, Benjamin envisions Communism as putting us on the road to such individual and collective self-realization by freeing technology's productive potential. It is in this context that Benjamin differentiates between the notion of a political aesthetic that counters the aestheticized politics of Fascism, which, by moving the viewer ever further away from the object of their experience, manipulates them emotionally by creating the illusion of an immutable past, and an inevitable future at the cost of the present. For Benjamin this loss of the present, of the immediacy of presence, constitutes not only a significant impediment to mass culture's ability to be even useful in the struggle for liberation, but also constitutes our vulnerability to control. As long as the means of production and culture remains centralized in the hands of the forces of reaction, its only function is that of control and manipulation. Yet despite his anti-Capitalist, anti-Fascist, pro-Communist rhetoric, Benjamin, try as he may, never produces a prescriptive, self-enclosed vision, nor one that denies the possibility of transformation of both society and art. At best he offers us a vision of the work of art transformed into something that offers up access to the ever-changing present of the unconscious that is subject to ideology and the flux of material conditions and social forces.

The transformation of art from a cult object into a form that reflects the mutability of life constitutes for Benjamin the politicization of the work of art, for it reduces rather than increases distance between the viewer and the object of their desire. These spatial relations are a crucial metaphor for Benjamin, and the effect of changes in these spatial relations on consciousness and perception are what take the place of aura. Yet often when reading about the artwork essay we are supplied with a vernacular, left-liberal, humanist interpretation that envisions the term 'political' as denoting the social, and aura comes to be nostalgically associated with the spiritual – the loss of which is represented as yet another example of Capital's baseness. This substitution makes political engagement and the preservation of aura a priority, and leads away from a discussion of what might constitute the type of political aesthetic that Benjamin foresees. Susan Buck-Morse[6] suggests this would be one of presence and embodiment that gives us access to the 'optical unconscious' – that state that opens us to the possibilities of change not only in time but also in the moment. It is the realization of such fluidity that Benjamin sees when he embraces the potential that technology offers in terms not only of the transformation of art's form, content, and tradition, but also of our experience of it and us.

For Benjamin, the aesthetic response, which while being entangled with feelings must also be conscious and as such thoughtful, produces an awareness of the self in relation to its object. Feelings in this sense are not the opposite of rationality (or intellectuality), but are at one with it. For Benjamin the aesthetic response is like any other physiological response except that in this case it occurs within the discourse network of art. Here emotions are differentiated from feelings, and are posited as a force of intellect that fuels and motivates the individual rather than inducing a withdrawn and subjective state.[7] Consequently, rather than an act of immersion in which one's individual response and awareness of self becomes submerged, a political aesthetic is one that plunges one into a state of consciousness or a state of selflessness that is no longer vulnerable to being programmed because the subject and its object occupy the same time/space. This aesthetic, which distinguishes emotions (non-conscious responses) from feelings (conscious responses), offers up an alternative to a techno-aesthetic premised on unwillingly being acted upon rather than being engaged in one's experience. In this, Benjamin imagines an art capable of stimulating a self-awareness of the desirability of self-preservation and self-realization, rather than merely evocation of pleasure, fear, etc.

By connecting aesthetic issues to the categorically social one of consciousness and self, Benjamin in the artwork essay records his own consciousness of culture's changing role in the political process. As such, we can interpret his vision of mass media at the end of the 1930s as being comparable to how industrialization was perceived in the early part of the nineteenth century, and how we have come to embrace the notion of technology in our own. His optimistic vision of a political culture made possible by reproduction parallels the early-nineteenth-century liberal dream of universal emancipation from need premised on large-scale industrial production's potential to produce enough material goods to satisfy the needs of all – while reducing the need for labour time. The failure to realize liberation from want through the democratization of production was in part a consequence of a failure on the part of the workers and middle classes to recognize that technology alone is not enough to change the content of our self-conception and social relations for the better.

In his critique of mass media and culture's potential under Capital, Benjamin echoes Marx's analysis that it was a residual feudal consciousness that had come to order mass production, creating a fetter on the realization of its true potential, both materially and socially. Subsequently, in recognizing that the dismantling of art's cultish forms in the long term creates a psychological state that contributes to the cause of liberation, Benjamin identifies that under Capital the reciprocal simulation of aura, which is expected by the consumers of mass culture, hampers art's transformation into a tool of liberation. As such, under Capital everything that is desirable is turned into its dysfunctional other. Under the terms of capitalism, reproduction (technology/mass media) is used to fix its own message of the immutability of the moment, which is circulated as marketable commodities meant to appeal to the broadest possible audience.

The contradiction between the ideal (potential), and what is desirable market-wise is the foundation of the industries of mass culture and advertising's ever-increasing saturation of the cultural environment, which simultaneously provides individuated as well as common experiences. The effect of the constant dissemination of bourgeois values embedded in the seemingly neutral space of leisure time and personal consumption, has transformed subjectivity itself into an object of aesthetic experience. In these moment feelings and thoughts are reconstructed, producing a simulated self, which in turn is experienced and affirmed as mutable in terms of its wants, but as essential in terms of its content. This manifestation of an essential selfness presents itself as an 'as if' metaphor in which the self is regarded 'as if it' were an object, and 'as if it' were an autonomous subject. This leaves us with a vision of ourselves in which consciousness and the moment-to-moment restatement of self comes to be illusionistically self-determined. The irony is that the selflessness that is achieved via consumerism and mass media, though characterized by mutable perspectives under the conditions of late Capital, rather than being a source of empowerment becomes a tool of social control by setting the form and content of freedom against one another.

The illusion of having control at least over our self in a world that we increasingly feel helpless within, transforms the sense of egolessness, which was envisioned as a means by which we would liberate ourselves from the machination of instrumental reason and logic, into an impediment to our acting in our own collective interest. This sense of alienation is enforced by mass media's ability to create an environment within which our fantasies are projected back on to the world, qualitatively turning reality into a spectacle in which what is imagined and what may be actualized become undifferentiated and unobtainable. The experimental filmmaker Guy Debord, who was the principal theorist for the Situationiste International (SI), under the heading of a critique of the society of the spectacle, proposes that the promise of joyous disembodiment in which we no longer have to be our 'selves', rather than leading to new-found freedoms, results in the realization that under Capital we are made prisoners of our own isolation and self-absorbed desires.

Most of us today, consciously, or unconsciously, suspect that everything, from our lifestyle choices to new products and services, is little more than a façade that barely conceals the new corporate bourgeoisie's drive for hegemony over our lives. It is no wonder that conspiracy theories concerning all aspects of government and business emerge alongside the enthusiastic promotion of computers, CD-ROM, interactive games and TV – we are promised that instantaneous communication is the key to the decommodifying of all cultural formations, which will eventually guarantee our freedom. Here again, is the conflicted message, or the old carrot and stick, for what our new mass culture of digital technologies does is to take us out of, rather than put us into, unmediated contact with one another. Isolation, SI proposed, is the real content of the form of selflessness that afflicts our society.

Paradoxically, what plays an important role in the development of these conditions is the late-nineteenth-century transformation of the Enlightenment view that imagination + fantasy was the devil's playground, because the natural order of things came to be inverted and scrambled in these realms. Through modern science and psychoanalytic theory this vision of imagination has come to be reassigned a rational function. The psychoanalytic theories of Sigmund Freud, for instance, advanced this cause by giving the imagination a significant role in our construction of reality, individually and socially. For Freud the objective world was only the raw materiality from which we constructed our reality of subjective reasoning and interpretation. Freud's view gave rise to the more conventional notion that on the personal level the authentic vs. ersatz could not be distinguished because no 'objective criteria' outside of consensus, or convention, can determine the true worth of such differentiations – in other words the real is what we think it is and we are what we think. This concept of subjectivity's role in the construction of reality is employed in support of the bourgeois ideological representation of individuality, freedom, and will, though again what these have come to be stands in contradistinction to what may be realizable, if it were not for the economic terms of capital.

Again we arrive at collage, though this time we are required to consider it both literally and metaphorically given that Modernism's operable model of reality and its accompanying subjectivity is that of assemblage. It is this correspondence that made collage the single most important formal, conceptual, and technological innovation of the twentieth century – for it not only allows the artist to rehearse their work before committing to a final state, but by means of the fracture of the disparate sources of its elements and processes announces this to the viewer. Consequently, those artists intent on recuperating a sense of self, or negating the experiences of banality, alienation, and the negativity that Capitalism's increased hegemony had inflected, politically and culturally, upon all aspects of daily life, found themselves simultaneously maintaining and disassembling the essentialist vision of art, or compensating for it by making work with explicit social content that presumes the essential power of art as a means of communication and affirmation. The result of this strategy is that the conflicted nature of the artwork in the modern world is made literal, while the inability of reproduction to replicate the work in all of its material aspects is made visible. Inversely, traditional art, by suppressing the processes by which it comes to fruition when reproduced, only makes the internal conditions of the artwork inaccessible to the viewer, leaving the viewer with the notion that the work of art and its dematerialized image are one and the same.

The illusion of continuity – the denial of fragmentation's consequences – are made explicit in the artwork essay with Benjamin's observations on how the embodied performance of the actor (artist) comes to exist in a constant state of deferral as it comes to be replaced by an assemblage of rehearsed (practised) moments pieced together. What are therefore viewed are the assembled fragments, which form a gestalt that becomes an acceptable substitute for the live performance previously consisting of diverse factors and qualities. Such an illusion is sustained by denying the audience any reminder of the qualitative difference between the cinematic and live performance. Yet, while assemblages of discreet moments are without aura, the culture industry turns aura into a fetishistic quality that it associates with any new product. The performance is then instilled with and validated by a continued appeal to the aura, be it that of the actor, the performance, the director, or the cinematic work itself. Reciprocity between the effect of the camera/apparatus and the process of montage on the actor's performance, as Benjamin observes, fails to materialize, and the audience is made to assume the viewpoint of the camera. In this instance the processes of montage and assembly are represented as functional, and are made to disappear. Consequently, montage, the editing and the assembly of bits and pieces of images and events, while appearing to be inherently functional, is determined by aesthetic decisions. We find in the practice of montage a parallel to the condition of the work of our subjectivity, which comes to be a mere construct of disenchanted images, signifiers, shorn of aura or experience, which pieced together in turn re-enforces the sense of selflessness and disembodiment that capital has found a more useful tool of control than direct force.

The erosion of a sense of authenticity and the denigration of direct experience that concerned Benjamin in the 1930s, by the mid-1950s against the backdrop of Cold War politics imperilled modernism's utopian vision of the future. The critiques developed by Henri Lefebvre and Raymond Williams of commercialism, and the cultural regimentation and standardization of everyday life under Capital, represented Western Society as having given itself over to the hegemony of a fixed ideology of hierarchy and duality. While these critiques abandoned classical Marxist cultural theory, and attempted to account for the qualitative changes that were taking place within Capitalism itself, the American conservative theorist Daniel Bell was claiming that functionally the notion of ideology had ended.[8] What now filled its place were the conflicted misconceptions that split society along cultural and social conditions, rather than those of economic class.

By the 1960s, the views of the Left and Right coalesced into concerns for the social dynamics of identity politics, family values, and multicultur-alism. The struggles for 'self-determination' in the context of gender and race consequently came to be perceived not as a supplement to class struggle but as a political goal in and of themselves. Effectively, these struggles for self-realization and empowerment redefined politics, relocating social struggles from the economic sphere to the cultural by making individual liberty and freedom of choice overriding ideological issues and the aesthetic object of everyday life. Being under siege by anti-Communists, the liberal Left embraced this agenda, making the cultural sphere the last bastion of their resistance to the viral spread of ideological and political repression. Consequently, culture appeared to be the most powerful weapon that the Left had in the battle for 'men's' minds.

The SI, founded in 1957, was a somewhat marginal, rag-tag, ad hoc assemblage of self-proclaimed revolutionaries, intellectuals and avant-garde artists sporting Surrealist, Marxist, Maoist, and Frankfurt School beliefs, who held the unique view that Capital as an institution and a system had co-opted not only its opposition (Soviet State Capitalism), but also the very desires that that opposition represented – that of self-realization and progress. In this scenario Capitalism and the bureaucratic state (Soviet Socialism) need no longer be openly repressive to maintain political, social, and economic dominance, but merely play their role of 'Other' to maintain their respective power. Even conservative reaction to liberal cultural policies was a charade, another means by which to create and maintain the illusion that through the power of individual (individuated) freedom of expression, and cultural 'democracy', access to power could be achieved. Based on this analysis SI postulated that the bourgeoisie had successfully shifted the site of political struggle from the economic to the cultural sphere. This had been achieved via mass media's repetition of reified concepts, which took the idealized forms of freedom, individuality, subjectivity, progress, etc. and turned them into their simulacra. Even under the terms of near total domi-nation, the hegemonic drive of Capital, SI reasoned, continuously seeks out reasons to apply technology to those territories of human activity that either had previously eluded their colonization or had been liberated and therefore required re-colonization.

Employing public forms such as communication technologies to infiltrate and re-organize the private sphere in the name of convenience and profit, Capital uses the market-place to offer up its own inventory of simulated and commodified experiences for sale, encoded in such oxymorons as 'authentic' real imitation wood grain. This in turn is reinforced by means of assurances that such representations are symbols of the 'realer world' of our desires. It is by these means that liberal cultural policies supply the populace with a sphere of relative autonomy, and self-determination came to be associated with consumerism. The market-place and the distractions offered by the culture industry supply the middle classes with access to goods and services that contribute to their sense of social status, while promising yet withholding such access to others.

Under the cultural conditions of consumer society, any real ability to determine social and economic policy ends. This led SI to believe that the main contradiction they could exploit was the incongruity between the political and cultural spheres that such a policy produces. Given that Capital is not homogeneous in its stages of development, and that contradictions exist between capitalist states, as well as between national and international capital, the task that SI faced was to expose these conditions by deed, that is, by the creation of situations, 'a dialectical organization of partial and transitory realities' that would supply a model of authentic freedom, while at the same time exposing the repressive nature of the state that fosters the Society of the Spectacle.

Amidst their own factional struggles and organizational splits and purges, SI's membership set about formulating a programme by means of intervention and recuperation that would escalate the battle against the positivism and instrumentality of bourgeois thought within the cultural sphere. Their intent was to transform art, which for them had already ceased to exist, into a true political weapon, rather than merely a tool for propaganda. Just as they rejected the opposition between the Soviet Union and the West, SI declared their independence from the task of preserving the traditional culture and its vision of the artist, while appropriating these to their own ends.

SI saw their principal task was to produce forms of cultural intervention that were temporal in nature, mutable, and constituting what might be considered a serious form of play capable of resisting co-optation, while exposing the anaesthetized politics of the societal spectacle of capital.

Every situation, as consciously constructed as can be, contains its own negation and moves inevitably toward its own reversal. In the conduct of an individual life, a situationist action is not based on the abstract idea of rationalist progress, but on the practice of arranging the environment that conditions us. Whoever constructs situations, to apply a statement by Marx, 'by bringing his movements to bear on external nature and transforming it ... transforms his own nature at the same time'.[9]

What SI proposed was an aesthetic position capable of countering the instrumental logic of capital and consumer culture, which orders both production and society. The functionalist nature of Capital cannot tolerate the drift, the happening, the dematerialized object, or what might be considered non-directed play, because it can neither control nor commodify it. Being the product of acts that know no rules and have no standardized form, such play subjects art and culture to an endless series of transformations that come to constitute a model of the unregulated economy of freedom and power that is necessary for individual and collective liberation. By resisting the impulse to preserve art, or for that matter be acknowledged as artist, SI found that they could produce situations that were direction-less, productless and self-satisfying, capable of interrupting convention and routine.

At the same time that SI was plotting social and cultural revolution, Allan Kaprow, without the stated intention of being politically provocative, also employed the notion of purposeful play to structure his 'happenings'. Confronting art's ever-increasing state of reproducibility, and the art-making strategy of the anti-artist, he sought to produce that which could not be represented, or reduced to mere image, because the work took place in time and left no residue.[10] Perhaps most importantly it existed performatively. In developing his ideas, Kaprow was responding in part to what had become of the action painting in which we are told that the painting is merely the residue of the creative act which is really the act of its making – in other words, the un-retrievable act of creation is the art, and it is within this lived experience that aura resides.[11] In the case of an artist like Pollock this act was carried out in the privacy of his studio, until he performed it for the photographer Hans Namuth, who turned it into a series of dramatic pictures and a movie, documenting and fixing not only the process but the art-act of the artist. The photographs and film objectified what had up to that minute been a totally subjective and unconscious act of self-absorption, and turned it into a rehearsal for all future paintings, not only by this artist but by those who would follow his example. Rather than preserve the aura of the object or that of the author, Kaprow on the contrary produced happenings that exist as an assemblage of simultaneous moments that could be neither documented nor represented in its entirety. 'If we admit that work that "succeeds" on some days fails on other days, we may seem to disregard the enduring and stable and place an emphasis upon the fragile and impermanent.'[12] By discarding the notion of media specificity, and that of the art object, and focusing on the event and experience, Kaprow transforms the everyday into an endless array of unmediated experiences.

While SI's 'situations' were conceived of as a form of direct political action, intervention, and propaganda, Kaprow's Happenings created what might have been thought of as being exemplary alternatives to the instrumental logic that had come to order our everyday actions by producing exaggerated situations in which his audience could act out their own freedom. 'We can clearly see that the development of our task presupposes a revolution that has yet to take place, and that any research is restricted by the contradiction of the present.'[13] Consequently, SI found a way to rehearse Revolution, while Allan Kaprow found a way to rehearse Life. They did this by offering their audiences/collaborators an embodied sense of time, duration, and process. Despite the differing perspectives of SI, Kaprow, and other individuals and groups that held what are still thought of today as marginal positions, a culture that was temporal in nature and diverse in form was modelled. Ironically, marginal and fringe-like political groups such as YIPPIES, Provos, and the Diggers, as well as other elements of the international hippie and youth culture which had taken up the slogan of freeing the imagination, transformed these practices not only into forms of direct action and protest but also into alternative lifestyles. Comparably, the fracture of experimental music, film, and theatre of the period appears to also correspond to the general criteria of the political aesthetic that Benjamin envisioned as being capable of confronting us daily and of countering Capital's aura, which results from its capacity to arrest time by fixing itself in a forever-unchanging and immutable present.

If the view that the process of co-opting and commodifying all aspects of daily life, social as well as cultural, has, since the late 1950s and early 1960s, been completed, seemingly goes against what might be taken as common sense, its extremeness does not lie in its claim that there is nothing outside the sales pitch of the market-place. We all recognize that today the ideals of availability, mobility, and convenience are offered to us openly as a panacea for the ongoing crisis that circumscribes the promise that our lives will in time be better. The radicality of this proposition actually lies in its demand that we question the vision of our 'self', which these promises of cultural self-realization appeal to in terms of our analogue dependencies. To do otherwise leaves us reactive, occupying a fixed position, in which the future, rather than being an opportunity to formulate an alternative vision based on new contingencies, is never anything more than the deferred past. If Benjamin, Debord, and Kaprow have any importance to us, it is because they tell us something about this condition.

If we are to accept Benjamin's analysis of technology's effects, and the conditions these bring forth, what is needed – always and already – is a multiplicity of strategies and tactics, capable of negotiating new goals marked by the contradictions of their own coming into being. On that note, I leave the subject of the embodiment of Benjamin's artwork essay in the heyday of the 1960s, and will not advance beyond that period in discussing their relevance to contemporary culture except for the brief comments that have already been made about the Postmodern. This is not because I believe the project Benjamin committed himself to is no longer resonant, nor that Kaprow and SI's views are not applicable, but the opposite. However, while the examples of SI and Kaprow supply models for the political aesthetic of the 1960s and

1970s, they do not point the way to what should now be done. The fact that these instances represent what but not how points to another theme that is central to my understanding of the artwork essay – that of recuperation.

If Benjamin's historical and cultural economy, as represented in the artwork essay, requires that we acknowledge that Capital and the habits of thought it propagates – though now qualitatively different from those of the 1930s – continue to be a fetter on the project of our liberation, this also requires us to acknowledge that institutional thought achieves this by closing off the future and by turning it into a repetition of the past-present. This commitment to an immutable present is one of the reasons the announcement of the end of history was gleefully received amongst conservatives, just as they welcomed Bell's announcement of the end of ideology in the 1960s.[14] Consequently, the fact that it is now alright to see SI and Kaprow, and even the Independent Group, as having been able 40 years ago to elaborate and intervene in the cultural/aesthetic and political discourses of their time by employing the alternatives that seemed to be available to them, does not make them prescient, but only contemporary. Today, however, their practices, rather than being the roots of a living heritage, are material waiting to be transformed into the historical/monumental – that is, they are to be fixed and made immutable – offered up as yet another rehearsal.

Accordingly, we must now ask ourselves in the face of both the recurring vision of cultural resistance, as evidenced by Benjamin's hypotheses, Kaprow's gratuitous acts, and Debord's acts of intervention, what we might do to prevent turning this struggle for a political aesthetic into nothing more than a fetishized, self-propitiating proposition. It does not seem possible to recuperate Kaprow and SI to the project of art without losing them. If this is the conundrum that we face, then Benjamin, Debord, and Kaprow's importance to us is in this sense theoretical, for their respective aesthetic responses to the cultural crisis of capital they faced take prominence over their deeds – which now mythically exist only in the most mutable of forms, the anecdote.

> The history of the SI will someday be of use in a new project. What that project will be like is guesswork. It will certainly have to reconceive the tentacular unity of its enemy; hence, it will need to articulate the grounds of unity capable of contesting it. And it will want to know the past.[15]

Or, as Kaprow pointed out in 1958, 'only the changing is really enduring and all else is whistling in the dark'.[16]

Notes

INTRODUCTION

1   Klossowski has discussed his translation and offered a short reflection on the text in 'Lettre sur Walter Benjamin' in Pierre Klossowski, *Tableaux vivants: Essais Critiques 1936–1983* (Paris: Le Promenur, 2001), pp 86–7.
2   For an excellent overview of the text and an interpretation of what occurs in the differing formulations and reformulations see Howard Caygill, *Walter Benjamin: The Colour of Experience* (London: Routledge, 1998), pp. 98–117.
3   Martin Heidegger, 'The Origins of the Work of Art', trans. David Farrell Krell in *Basic Writings* (San Francisco: Harper, 1993), pp. 139–213. While this book contains important engagements with the complex relationship between Heidegger and Benjamin, it is envisaged that a future volume of Walter Benjamin Studies will engage the question of that relationship outside of a concern limited by their respective 'art work' essays'.
4   Heidegger, ibid., p. 144.
5   I wish to thank Dimitris Vardoulakis for his help in the preparation of the manuscript. His intellectual generosity and keen editorial eye made the final part of editing both collaborative and a pleasure.

CHAPTER 1

1   Reference is to the third version of the 'Das Kunstwerk im Zeitalter seiner technischen Reproduzierbarkeit' ('The Work of Art in the Age of its Technological Reproducibility'), composed 1936–1939. My attention was first drawn to the theme of distraction in Benjamin's work by Lindsay Waters' essay, 'Walter Benjamin's Dangerous Idea' (manuscript, 58–61).
2   Bertolt Brecht, *Schriften zum Theater* (cited in the text as *ST*), ed. Siegfried Unseld (Frankfurt: Suhrkamp, 1957), p. 170/*Brecht on Theatre* (cited in the text as *BT*), trans. John Willett (New York: Hill and Wang, 1964), p. 203.
3   See, on this point, Norbert Bolz and Willem van Reijen, *Walter Benjamin*, trans. Laimdota Mazzarins (Atlantic Highlands, New Jersey: Humanities Press, 1996), pp. 41–2.
4   William Shakespeare, *The Tempest*, ed. Robert Langbaum (New York: New American Library, 1964), pp. 95–6, 111 (III. ii. 88–90 and 95; V. i. 61). In Prospero's Epilogue, the spell of art entails freedom for artist and audience alike.
5   Concerning the difference between Benjamin and Brecht on this point, see Miriam Hansen, 'Benjamin, Cinema and Experience: The Blue Flower in the Land of Technology', *New German Critique* 40 (1987), pp. 218–19.
6   This applies *a fortiori* to the way in which the improvising jazz musician himself listens to the improvisations of the others in the group – both *as* a group and as other individuals – and responds to the surprises. The musician must have at his disposal a set of (variable) moves, to paraphrase Benjamin, in order to perform this task, which involves equal measures of spontaneity and knowledge, or receptivity and productivity.

The deflection of attention here is manifold and concentrated, for the player is both carried away and in control.

7 Benjamin's own word for the 'Work of Art' essay was *'programmatisch'* (*GB* 5:193, 209), or *Programmschrift* (*GB* 5:200, 230). On Benjamin's conception of the artwork as reflecting historical changes in the mode of human sense perception, a conception deriving in part from the art historian Alois Riegl, see Michael W. Jennings, *Dialectical Images: Walter Benjamin's Theory of Literary Criticism* (Ithaca: Cornell University Press, 1987), pp. 156–8.

8 In *Walter Benjamin: Zwischen den Stühlen* (Frankfurt: Fischer, 1981), p. 273, Werner Fuld associates the motif of distraction with the idea of freedom.

9 Siegfried Kracauer, 'Kult der Zerstreuung' (1926), in *Das Ornament der Masse* (Frankfurt: Suhrkamp, 1977), p. 313/ 'Cult of Distraction', in *The Mass Ornament*, trans. Thomas Y. Levin (Cambridge, MA: Harvard University Press, 1995), p. 325. Subsequent references to this essay and its translation appear in the text in parentheses.

10 S. M. Eisenstein, *Towards a Theory of Montage* [1937–1940], trans. Michael Glenny (London: British Film Institute, 1991), p. 231.

11 I am quoting here from Jacques Rivière's description of the choreography of Vaslav Nijinsky. See *'Le Sacre du Printemps'* [1913] in *The Ideal Reader*, trans. Blanche A. Price (New York: Meridian, 1960), p. 138. Rivière says that Nijinsky approached 'each object according to its own orientation … The way in which Nijinsky has treated the movements of groups shows the same effort to espouse details, to discover and bring out individual orders … By breaking the movement and bringing it back to the simple gesture, Nijinsky has put expression back into dance … Acid and hard … its contours have been … dulled by no culinary art … there are no … poetic blendings; there is no trace of atmosphere' (pp. 136, 137, 139, 125).

12 See Sergei Eisenstein, 'Perspectives' [1929] and 'The Dynamic Square' [1931], both translated by Jay Leyda, in *Film Essays*, ed. Jay Leyda (1968; rpt. Princeton: Princeton University Press, 1982), pp. 41, 61.

13 Eisenstein, 'The Unexpected' [1928], in *Film Form*, trans. Jay Leyda (New York: Harcourt, 1949), p. 27. On montage as the unity of sequence and simultaneity, see Eisenstein, *Towards a Theory of Montage*, p. 86; on the problem of (continuous) transition, p. 192.

14 The privileged position of the cinema *vis-à-vis* other contemporary arts has to do with its intrinsically technological nature: 'Film: unfolding [*Auswicklung*] <result [*Auswirkung*]?> of all the forms of perception, the tempos and rhythms, which lie preformed in today's machines, such that all problems of contemporary art find their definitive formulation only in the context of film' (K3,3).

15 Louis Aragon, *Paysan de Paris* [1926] (Paris: Gallimard, 1953), p. 60 (cited in the text as *Paysan*)/*Paris Peasant*, trans. Simon Watson Taylor (Boston: Exact Change, 1994), p. 47 (cited in the text as *Peasant*).

16 On the 'nominalist' context for montage theory, see Theodor W. Adorno, *Ästhetische Theorie* (Frankfurt: Suhrkamp, 1970), pp. 231–4 (*Stimmigkeit und Sinn*, 'Krise des Sinns')/*Aesthetic Theory*, trans. Robert Hullot-Kentor (Minneapolis: University of Minnesota Press, 1997), pp. 154–6 (*'Coherence and Meaning'*, 'The Crisis of Meaning'). Compare Ernst Bloch's reflections on montage, understood as 'Wege im Einsturz' (paths in the midst of collapse) and 'Hohlraum mit Funken' (hollow space with sparks), in *Erbschaft dieser Zeit* (1935; rpt. Frankfurt: Suhrkamp, 1962), p. 22, also pp. 17, 224, 369/*Heritage of Our Times*, trans. Neville Plaice and Stephen Plaice (Berkeley: University of California Press, 1991), p. 8, also pp. 3, 205, 335.

17 In a conversation with Benjamin in 1928, André Gide speaks of Proust's obsession with 'processes of the cinema, with superimpositions, dissolves' ('Gespräch mit André Gide',

GS 4.2:505/'Conversation with André Gide', trans. Rodney Livingstone, *SW* 2:94). The original French is printed in *GS* 7.2:621.

18   This stratified inscription has affinities with the Baudelairean conception of *modernité*, of a present day worthy of becoming antiquity, as reflected in Convolute J of the *Passagen-Werk* and in the essay produced directly from the materials of Convolute J in 1938, 'Das Paris des Second Empire bei Baudelaire'. At stake in this citation (that is, appropriation and [re]enactment) of the poet's theory is an idea of allegory, understood as a form of superimposition and interpenetration. See, for example, the discussion of Charles Meryon in the context of this Baudelairean problematic: 'For in Meryon, too, there is an interpenetration of classical antiquity and modernity, and in him, too, the form of this superimposition [*Überblendung*] – allegory – appears unmistakably' (*GS* 1.2:591/*SW* 4:54). See also *GB* 6:65.

19   Benjamin's theory of reading, as conditioned on the primacy of the present, echoes Nietzsche in particular. On the necessity of interpreting the past from out of the highest energy of the present, see section 6 of 'Vom Nutzen und Nachteil der Historie für das Leben' [1874], part 2 of *Unzeitgemässe Betrachtungen*, in vol. 1 of Friedrich Nietzsche, *Werke*, ed. Karl Schlechta (Frankfurt: Ullstein, 1980), pp. 250–1/*On the Advantage and Disadvantage of History for Life*, trans. Peter Preuss (Indianapolis: Hackett, 1980), pp. 37–8. See also Henri Bergson, *Matière et mémoire* (1896; rpt. Paris: Presses Universitaires de France, 1939), p. 170/*Matter and Memory*, trans. N. M. Paul and W. S. Palmer (New York: Zone, 1991), p. 153. For Benjamin, the present moment wakes to itself only insofar as it awakens in itself a past. This dialectic is elucidated by Irving Wohlfarth in an unpublished paper, 'Erwachen aus dem zwanzigsten Jahrhundert?', delivered at Barcelona in September 2000. 'It is *his own* day and age', writes Wohlfarth, 'that makes it possible for the historian to focus his lens on the past ... and only by this roundabout way back into the past does his own day and age come into view ... To write history is to determine the present day; both activities are forms of dream interpretation' (my translation). The Benjaminian conception of awakening out of and into the dream may be compared to the Heideggerian conception of *Entwachen*. See Martin Heidegger, *Zur Sache des Denkens* (Tübingen: Niemeyer, 1976), p. 32: '*So ist das Erwachen aus der Seinsvergessenheit zu ihr das Entwachen in das Ereignis*'.

20   The term 'Bildraum' appears at the end of Benjamin's 1929 essay 'Der Sürrealismus' (*GS* 2.1:309–10/*SW* 2:217–18).

CHAPTER 2

1   I should like to take this opportunity to thank Bob Eaglestone for inviting me to present this paper to the Institute for English Studies, at the University of London, and Ullrich Haase and Keith Crome for the invitation to deliver a draft of it at the Manchester Human Sciences Seminar. Thanks are due to Roxana Baiasu and Gary Banham, for their customarily perspicacious questions in response to hearing that first version of the paper, which has benefited as a consequence. All translations from *Das Passagen-Werk* are my own.

2   Ernst Cassirer in his contemporaneous study *The Philosophy of Enlightenment* [1932], trans. F. C. Koelln and James P. Pettigrew (Princeton, NJ: Princeton University Press, 1951) analyses the complementary roles of Kant as theorist of the concept and of Goethe as practitioner in his last chapter: 'Fundamental Problems of Aesthetics'. While Goethe as the younger man was aware of Kant's decisive role in relation to analysis of art, Kant was not so attuned to that of Goethe and died in 1804, only half way through Goethe's life.

3 Gillian Rose in her path-breaking essay 'Hermann Cohen: Kant among the Prophets' lays the basis for a discussion of the connection between Rosenzweig and Cohen, and between Cohen and Kant. See Gillian Rose, *Judaism and Modernity: Philosophical Essays* (Oxford: Blackwell, 1993), pp. 111–25. In the same volume is her essay 'Walter Benjamin: Out of the Sources of Modern Judaism', in which Rose discusses the problem status of Jewish theology: 'Strictly speaking there is no Judaic theology – no logos of God', she writes. 'Now if there is strictly speaking no Judaic theology there can be no theological notions of creation, revelation, and redemption' (pp. 182–3). Rose also obliquely draws attention to the manner in which Cohen's reading of Kant might stand as an exemplary case of destructive reading.

4 For Bergson, see *The Two Sources of Morality and Religion* [1932], trans. R. Ashley Audra and Cloudesley Brereton (New York: Doubleday and Co., 1935). For Kant see *Religion within the Bounds of Reason Alone* [1794], trans. and ed. Allen Wood (Cambridge: Cambridge University Press). In the first section of the latter, Kant identifies and analyses the notion of radical evil in human nature as the capacity for forming a maxim for action not in accordance with the categorical imperative.

5 There are three previous occasions on which Derrida writes about Benjamin: there are remarks on Benjamin in *Truth in Painting* (1978) trans. by Geoffrey Bennington and Ian Mcleod (Chicago: Chicago University Press, 1987); there is an essay on Benjamin's 'The task of the translator', 'Des Tours de Babel' from 1984 trans. Joseph F. Graham, in Joseph F. Graham (ed.) *Difference in Translation* (Ithaca: Cornell University Press, 1987), in which the full extent of a disagreement between Benjamin and Derrida on the nature of language and meaning begins to come to the fore, and there is the now notorious reading of Benjamin's Critique of Violence in Derrida's paper from 1989, 'The Force of Law and the Mystical Foundation of Authority' in Drusilla Cornell, Michel Rosenfeld and David Gray Carlson (eds.) *Deconstruction and the Possibility of Justice* (New York and London: Routledge, 1992), pp. 3–67, where Benjamin is bizarrely construed as responsible for the incineration of European Jewry in the Nazi camps. Derrida has returned to these issues in his reply 'Marx and Sons' printed in conclusion to the volume, *Ghostly Demarcations: A Symposium on Derrida's Spectres of Marx*, ed. Michael Sprinker (London: Verso 1999). These readings would be the topic for another paper. For Derrida's relation to Kant see Joanna Hodge: 'Kant par excellence', introduction to Philip Rothfield, ed., *Kant after Derrida* (Manchester: Clinamen Press, 2003).

6 In their book, *Walter Benjamin*, [1991] trans. Laimdota Mazzarins (New Jersey: Humanities Press, 1996), Norbert Bolz and Willem van Reijen argue that the destruction and resurrection coincide in Benjamin's idea of reconciliation that is put forward in the essay on the *Elective Affinities*. 'I suspect I had some dim recollection of this as I started planning this paper. I should like to acknowledge here that my interest in Benjamin philosophically goes back to my good fortune in attending some classes given by Norbert Bolz at the Free University, Berlin in 1980.'

7 Derrida, 'Faith and Knowledge: The Two Sources of "Religion" at the Limits of Reason Alone' (trans. Samuel Weber) in Jacques Derrida and Gianni Vattimo (eds.), *Religion* (Oxford: Polity Press, 1998) p. 17.

8 Derrida, 'Marx and Sons', pp. 249–50.

9 For the beginnings of this discussion of Benjamin's interest in antinomy, see Joanna Hodge, 'Aesthetics and Politics: between Adorno and Heidegger', in *The New Aestheticism*, eds. John Joughin and Simon Malpas (Manchester: Manchester University Press, 2003).

10 A number of important articles on this are gathered together in Beatrice Hanssen and Andrew Benjamin (eds.), *Walter Benjamin and Romanticism* (London: Continuum, 2002).

11   Derrida, *The Gift of Death* [1992], trans. David Wills (Chicago and London: University of Chicago Press, 1995).

12   This is the challenge Derrida poses to Benjamin in his controversial analysis of Benjamin in 'Force of Law'. This is an outline of a possible response to that challenge, which would require more careful development in the wider context of Derrida's readings of Benjamin already mentioned.

13   J. W. Von Goethe, *Dichtung und Wahrheit* in *Goethe's Werke* ed. Lieselotte Blumenthal (Muenchen: Beck Verlag, 1978, two volumes), also trans. Minna Steele Smith (London: Bell & Sons, 1973) Part III, Book XIV 1774–1775, p. 166.

14   Goethe continues: 'The article on Spinoza excited me with displeasure and distrust. To begin with, the philosopher is represented as an atheist, and his opinions as highly reprehensible; but immediately afterwards it is admitted that he was a calm thinker, devoted to his studies, a good citizen, a sympathizing neighbour, and a peaceable individual. The writer seemed to me to have quite forgotten the words of the Gospel: By their fruits ye shall know them, for how could a life pleasing in the sight of God and man spring from corrupt principles?' (Part iv, Book XVI, 1775, p. 204)

15   The relation between pre-predicative experience and an intuition of essences is one analysed by Edmund Husserl throughout his inquiries, but perhaps most emphatically in *Experience and Judgment: Investigations for a Genealogy for Logic* [1939] ed. Ludwig Landgrebe, trans. James S. Churchill and Karl Ameriks (London: Routledge, 1973). Derrida's reading of Husserl in Jacques Derrida: *The Problem of Genesis in Husserl's Philosophy* [1990] trans. Marion Hobson (Chicago and London: University of Chicago Press, 2003), analyses this difficulty at some length. For 'the dignity of an experience that is ephemeral', see Gerhard Richter: *Walter Benjamin and the Corpus of Autobiography* (Detroit Michigan; Wayne State University Press, 2000), throughout and esp. p. 15.

16   Immanuel Kant, *Critique of Judgement* [1790] trans. Werner S. Pluhar (Indianapolis: Hackett Publishing Company 1987), p. 221.

17   Ibid., p. 193.

18   See Irving Wohlfarth, 'Resentment Begins at Home: Nietzsche, Benjamin and the University' in Gary Smith, ed., *On Walter Benjamin: Critical Essays and Recollections* (Cambridge, MA: MIT, 1988). Wohlfarth too stands out for his refusal to align himself in the either/or of theology versus historical materialism.

CHAPTER 3

Translations from the *Passagenwerk*, the essay on the *Elective Affinities* are the author's. Further, the author has often modified the referenced English translations.

1   Theodor Adorno, *Negative Dialektik* (Frankfurt: Suhrkamp, 1966), p. 207/*Negative Dialectics*, trans. E. B. Ashton (New York: Continuum, 1973), p. 207.

2.   On some of the medieval controversies concerning the role of the body in the *visio Dei*, see Carolyn Walker Bynum, *The Resurrection of the Body 200–1336* (New York: Columbia University Press, 1995), pp. 279–317.

3   See Jaroslav Pelikan, *Christianity and Classical Culture: The Metamorphosis of Natural Theology in the Christian Encounter with Hellenism* (New Haven: Yale University Press, 1993), pp. 120–35, 280–95, 311–26. On the 'economy' of resurrection, see pp. 153, 289f. For the metaphor of the wax seal or stamp in Patristic theology (sometimes related to the parable of the lost coin in Luke 15:10), see pp. 126–8 and Pelikan, *The Christian Tradition: A History of the Development of Doctrine*, 5 vols. (Chicago: University of Chicago Press, 1971–1989) 2:96.

4   *Babylonian Talmud*, Sanhedrin 91a–91b, trans. I. Epstein (London: Soncino Press,

1935). On the various senses of resurrection in rabbinic Judaism, see George W. E. Nickelsburg, *Resurrection, Immortality, and Eternal Life in Intertestamental Judaism* (Cambridge: Harvard University Press, 1972); George Foot Moore, *Judaism in the First Centuries of the Christian Era: The Age of Tannaim* (Cambridge: Harvard University Press, 1927, reprinted 1966); Shaye J. D. Cohen, *From the Maccabees to the Mishnah* (Philadelphia: Westminster, 1987).

5   See my 'Mourning Work and Play', in *Research in Phenomenology* 23 (1993).

6   Benjamin, 'Theological-Political Fragment', trans. Edmund Jephcott, in *Reflections: Essays, Aphorisms, Autobiographical Writings*, ed. Peter Demetz (New York: Harcourt Brace Jovanovich, p. 313, hereafter cited as *R*).

7   Theodor Adorno, *Prismen* (Frankfurt: Suhrkamp, 1955)/*Prisms*, trans. Sam Weber and Shierry Weber (Cambridge: MIT, 1981). Here pp. 286/270–1.

8   'The absolute experience is not disclosure [*dévoilement*] but revelation [*révélation*]'. Emmanuel Levinas, *Totality and Infinity*, trans. Alphonso Lingis (Pittsburgh: Duquesne University Press), p. 65f.

9   Notwithstanding Benjamin's somewhat perverse claim to have pored over Cohen's *Ästhetik* and to have failed to come up with anything of value. See letter of 26 March 1921 to Gershom Scholem (*GB* 2:146/*C*, p. 177).

10   Thus the inevitable link between the prohibition against graven images and the prohibition against incest. See, for example, Jean-Joseph Goux's influential reading of the Mosaic injunction as directed in the first place against fusion with the mother, in *Les iconoclastes* (Paris: Seuil, 1978).

11   G. W. F. Hegel, *Phenomenology of Spirit*, trans. A. V. Miller (Oxford: Oxford University Press, 1977), pp. 79–103.

12   'Perhaps there is no sublimer passage in the Jewish law than the command, "Thou shalt not make to thyself any graven image"'. Kant, *Critique of Judgment*, trans. J. H. Bernard (New York: Hafner, 1951), §29, 'General Remark on the Exposition of the Aesthetic Reflective Judgment'.

13   Maurice Blanchot, 'Interruptions', in Eric Gould, ed., *The Sin of the Book: Edmond Jabès* (Lincoln: University of Nebraska Press, 1985), p. 49.

14   Hegel, *Phenomenology*, p. 344.

15   Ibid., p. 332.

16   See letters of Scholem to Benjamin of 9 July 1934 and 17 July 1934, in Gershom Scholem, ed., *The Correspondence of Walter Benjamin and Gershom Scholem*, trans. Gary Smith and André Lefevere (New York: Schocken, 1989), pp. xxx, 123, 127. Contrast Adorno, 'Notes on Kafka', *Prisms*, esp. pp. 259f., 268.

17   Max Horkheimer and T. Adorno, *Dialektik der Aufklärung* (Frankfurt: Suhrkamp, 1984), p.45; *Dialectic of Enlightenment*, trans. John Cumming (New York: Continuum, 1972), p. 28.

18   Nietzsche, *Will to Power*, §603.

19   Theodor Adorno, *Kierkegaard: Konstruktion des Ästhetischen* (Frankfurt: Suhrkamp, 1962), pp. 190ff.; *Kierkegaard: Construction of the Aesthetic*, trans. Robert Hullot-Kentor (Minneapolis: University of Minnesota Press, 1989), pp. 134ff.

20   *Quasi una fantasia*, trans. Rodney Livingstone (London: Verso, 1992), p. 241.

21   Gershom Scholem, *Walter Benjamin: The Story of a Friendship* (London: Faber and Faber, 1981).

22   Werner Fuld, *Walter Benjamin: Zwischen den Stühlen* (Munich: Hanser Verlag, 1979).

23   Cf. Jürgen Habermas, 'Walter Benjamin: Consciousness-Raising or Rescuing Critique', in Gary Smith, ed., *On Walter Benjamin: Critical Essays and Reflections* (Cambridge, Mass.: MIT, 1988), p. 114.

24   See Rabbi Hiyya b. Abba's representation of Rabbi Johanan's proscription of any prophetic vision of the world 'to come' (by way of an idiosyncratic rendering of

Isaiah 64:5 – 'the eye hath not seen, oh Lord, beside thee, what he hath prepared for him that waiteth for him') in Sanhedrin 99a, *Babylonian Talmud*, together with Maimonides' related critique of eudaimonism in *Mishnah Torah*, 'Laws of Repentance', and Hermann Cohen's denunciation of the 'utopia of mythic belief' in *Religion der Vernunft aus den Quellen des Judentums* (Wiesbaden: Fourier Verlag, 1928, reprint 1988), pp. 361–3. The scope of prophecy is here rigorously limited to the messianic (in contrast to the afterlife 'to come'). See also Emmanuel Levinas' commentary on the rabbinic subtext *Difficult Freedom: Essays on Judaism*, trans. Sean Hand (Chicago: University of Chicago Press, 1994), pp. 59-68.

25   Marx, 'Afterword' to the second German edition of *Capital* (Moscow: Progress Publishers, 1959), 1: 26.

26   G. W. F. Hegel, *Grundlinien der Philosophie des Rechts* (Frankfurt: Suhrkamp, 1970), p. 27.

27   Letter of 19 October 1877 to Sorge, in Marx and Engels, *Selected Correspondence 1846–95*, trans. Dona Torr (New York: International Publishers, 1942).

28   Karl Korsch, *Karl Marx* (Frankfurt am Main: Europäische Verlagsanstalt, 1967), p. 53.

29   Immanuel Kant, *Critique of Practical Reason*, trans. Lewis White Beck (Indianapolis: Bobbs Merrill, 1956), p. 146.

30   'God and eternity in their awful majesty would stand unceasingly before our eyes (for that which we can completely prove is as certain as that which we can ascertain by sight)'. *Critique of Practical Reason*, p. 152.

31   Ibid., p. 153.

32   Nietzsche, *Thus Spoke Zarathustra*, 'On the New Idol', in Walter Kaufman, trans., *The Portable Nietzsche* (New York: Viking, 1968), p. 162.

33   See Susan Buck-Morss, *The Dialectics of Seeing: Walter Benjamin and the Arcades Project* (Cambridge, Mass.: MIT, 1989).

34   Cf. Wolfgang Schivelbusch, *Disenchanted Night: The Industrialization of Light in the Nineteenth Century* (Berkeley: Unversity of California Press, 1988).

35   Cf. Jacques Lacan, 'The gaze as *objet a*', *Four Fundamental Concepts of Psychoanalysis* (New York: Norton, 1978).

36   See the proverbial definition – not actually penned by Hegel himself – of beauty as the 'sensuous appearance of the Idea'. G. W. F. Hegel, *Aesthetics*, trans. T. M. Knox (Oxford: Oxford University Press, 1975), 2 vols. Ironically, Hegel's own determination of the symbol, in the *Aesthetics*, would correspond more precisely to Benjamin's notion of allegory, insofar as it exemplifies the gap or discrepancy between 'meaning' and 'shape', *Bedeutung* and *Gestalt* – in Benjamin's terms, the 'abyss between visual being and meaning' (*GS* 1.1:342/*OT*, p. 165) – and thus stands as a cipher of radical non-reconciliation.

37   See 'Some Motifs in Baudelaire' (*GS* 1.2:646/*SW* 4:338). For a discussion of some of the ambiguities of this transaction, see my 'Framing Redemption: Aura, Origin, Technology in Heidegger and Benjamin', in Arleen Dallery and Charles Scott, eds., *Ethics and Danger* (Albany: SUNY, 1992), and 'Facies Hippocratica', in Adriaan Peperzak, ed., *Ethics as First Philosophy: The Thought of Emmanuel Levinas* (New York: Routledge, 1995).

38   See Irving Wohlfarth's comments on this passage, 'Resentment Begins at Home: Nietzsche, Benjamin, and the University', in Gary Smith, ed., *On Walter Benjamin* pp. 225f.

39   'You never look at me from the place from which I see you'. Lacan, *Four Fundamental Concepts*, p. 103.

40   Cf. *GS* 1.1:343/*OT*, p. 166. It is perhaps for this reason that Lacan associates Holbein's skull with the melting watches of Salvador Dali: the anamorphic distortion would correspond to the allegorical disruption of the temporal continuum, exemplified by the

revolutionary shooting of the clock-towers, as described in Benjamin's 15th thesis on history. See *Four Fundamental Concepts*, p. 88.

41 Christine Buci-Glucksmann, *La folie du voir: de l'esthétique baroque* (Paris: Galilée, 1986). Cf. *La raison baroque: de Baudelaire à Benjamin* (Paris: Galilée, 1984).

42 Cf. Marcel Proust, *Remembrance of Things Past*, trans. C. K. Scott Moncrieff and Terence Kilmartin (London: Penguin, 1983), 2: 35ff.

43 Louis Aragon, *Paris Peasant*, trans. Simon Watson Taylor (London: Cape, 1971), p. 28.

44 The convergence of '*voir*' and '*désirer imiter*' (*GS* 2.1:318/*SW* 4:243) will be observed to extend to Proust's eventual stage-management of his own illness (*GS* 2.1:322/*SW* 4:246).

45 Karl Marx and Frederick Engels, *Werke* (Berlin: Dietz, 1962), 23: 15.

46 Cf. Philippe Ivornel, 'Paris, Capital of the Popular Front or the Posthumous Life of the 19th Century', *New German Critique* 39 (1986): 61–84.

47 Charles Baudelaire, 'Salon de 1859', in *Œuvres complètes* (Paris: Gallimard, 1979), 2: 614–19.

48 Benjamin, *Briefe*, eds. Gershom Scholem and Theodor W. Adorno (Frankfurt: Suhrkamp, 1978), 2:627, hereafter cited as *Br.*

49 Cf. Sigmund Freud, *Interpretation of Dreams*, *Standard Edition of the Complete Works of Sigmund Freud*, trans. ed. James Strachey (London: Hogarth Press, 1953), 5: 621.

50 Letter of 23 February 1927 to Buber. Also in *Moscow Diary*, trans. Richard Sieburth (Cambridge, Mass.: Harvard University Press), p. 126. Benjamin is here citing Simmel's own citation of Goethe in his *Goethe* (Leipzig: Klinkhardt und Biermann, 1913, reprint 1918), p. 57.

51 Compare here Benjamin's comments on Leskov. 'The hierarchy of the creaturely world, which has its apex in the righteous man, reaches down into the abyss of the inanimate through many gradations. In this connection, one particular circumstance must be noted. This whole creaturely world speaks not so much with the human voice as with what could be called "the voice of Nature", after the title of one of Leskov's most significant stories' (*GS* 2.2:460/*SW* 3:159).

52 Benjamin's interest in Goethe's morphological writings is evidenced as early as in a fragment of 1918 on 'Symbolism' (*GS* 6:38f.), is expressed further in the dissertation on Romanticism (*GS* 1.1:110–19), in *Goethes Wahlverwandtschaften* (*GS* 1.1:147), and in a discarded passage of the *Trauerspielbuch* (*GS* 1.1:953), and appears finally in the *Passagenwerk* (N2a,4), where Simmel's presentation in his 1913 *Goethe* plays a decisive role.

53 Simmel, *Goethe*, p. 56, quoted by Buck-Morss, *The Dialectics of Seeing*, p. 72.

54 '"To study this period, at once so close and so remote, I compare myself to a surgeon operating with a local anaesthetic; I work in places which are numb, dead; the patient, however, is alive and can still talk". Paul Morand: 1900 Paris 1931 p. 6/7' (N2a,5).

55 See Irving Wohlfarth's astute comments on this passage in 'Et Cetera? The Historian as Chiffonier', *New German Critique* 39 (1985), p. 163.

56 Cf. *Dialectic of Enlightenment*, pp. 43–80.

57 Roland Barthes, *Camera Lucida: Reflections on Photography*, trans. Richard Howard (New York: Hill and Wang, 1981).

58 Cf. Jacques Derrida, *Spectres of Marx*, trans. Peggy Kamuf (New York: Routledge, 1994).

59 Jean-François Lyotard, 'Adorno as the Devil', *Telos* 19 (1974): 127–38; Giorgio Agamben, 'Le prince et le crapaud', in *Enfance et histoire: Dépérissement de l'expérience et origine de l'histoire* (Paris: Payot, 1978); Peter Bürger, *The decline of Modernism*, trans. Nicholas Walker (University Park: Pennsylvania State University Press, 1992).

60 Such a point is argued forcefully by Agamben in 'Le prince et le crapaud'.

61 See the neo-Leninist avowals in the letter of 18 March 1936. *GS* 1.3:1003 and *GS*

1.3:1005; trans. Ronald Taylor *Aesthetics and Politics* (London: Verso, 1977), pp. 122, 125.

62 Adorno, *Noten zur Literatur* (Frankfurt: Suhrkamp, 1974), p. 571/trans. Shierry Weber Nicholson, *Notes to Literature*, vol. 2 (New York: Columbia University Press, 1972), p. 224.

63 Cf. H. D. Kittsteiner, 'Walter Benjamin's Historicism', *New German Critique* 39 (1986): 179–215.

64 'An introduction [to the Baudelaire essay] will establish the work's methodological relationship to dialectical materialism in the form of a confrontation of "saving" [*Rettung*] with the customary "apologia"'. Benjamin to Horkheimer, April 16, 1938 (L 556).

65 Cf. Rolf Tiedemann, 'Historical Materialism or Political Messianism', in Gary Smith, ed., *Walter Benjamin: Philosophy, History, Aesthetics* (Chicago: University of Chicago Press, 1989), p. 201.

66 Franz Rosenzweig, 'The True and the False Messiah: A Note to a Poem by Judah he-Levi', in Nahum N. Glatzer, *Franz Rosenzweig: His Life and Thought* (New York: Schocken, 1961), p. 350.

67 Adorno, *Minima Moralia: Reflections from Damaged Life*, trans. E. F. N. Jephcott (London: NLB, 1974), sec. 153.

CHAPTER 4

1 Unless otherwise indicated, I cite from the second version of the 'Artwork' essay, published in the seventh volume of the *Gesammelte Schriften*. All translations are my own.

2 Karl Marx, *Zur Kritik der politischen Ökonomie* (1859), in Karl Marx and Friedrich Engels, *Werke* (Dietz: Berlin, 1971), 13:9.

3 Immanuel Kant, *Gesammelte Schriften*, ed. Königlich Preußische [later Deutsche] Akademie der Wissenschaften (Berlin: Reimer; later, De Gruyter, 1900–), A, vii; all further references to Kant in this volume are in parentheses ('Ak'), except for the *Critique of Pure Reason*, as in this case, which refers to the 1781 edition ('A') or the 1787 edition ('B'). For an analysis of the Kantian direction of Benjamin's essay – which is differently oriented than this one – see Rodolphe Gasché, 'Objective Diversions: On Some Kantian Themes in Benjamin's "The Work of Art in the Age of Mechanical Reproduction",' in *Walter Benjamin's Philosophy: Destruction and Experience*, ed. Andrew Benjamin and Peter Osborne (London: Routledge, 1994), 183–204.

4 The passages of the *Critique of Pure Reason* to which the above comments refer are especially A293–309; B249–366.

5 The first instance of the technical term *aesthetics* can be found in the penultimate paragraph of Alexander Baumgarten's treatise, *Meditationes philosophicae de non-nullis ad poema pertinentibus* (Halle, 1735), § 116; *Reflections on Poetry*, trans. Karl Achenbrenner and William Holther (Berkeley: University of California Press, 1954), p. 78.

6 For a nuanced reading of this passage, see Samuel Weber, 'Art, Aura and Media in the Work of Walter Benjamin', in *Mass Mediauras: Form, Technics, Media*, ed. Alan Cholodenko (Stanford: Stanford University Press, 1996), pp. 76–107.

7 See, for example, Kant's utter rejection of the nobility in the *Metaphysics of Morals*, Ak, 6:329.

8 See, for example, Heidegger, *Nietzsche* (Pfullingen: Neske, 1961), 1:91–109.

9 See in particular Benjamin's letter to Gershom Scholem of January 1920, reprinted in *GB* 2: 109.

10 See Jürgen Habermas, 'Bewußtmachende oder rettende Kritik – Die Aktualität Walter Benjamins', in *Kultur und Kritik* (Frankfurt am Main: Suhrkamp, 1977), esp. p. 316.

CHAPTER 5

1 Hannah Arendt, 'Introduction – Walter Benjamin: 1892–1940', in Walter Benjamin, *Illuminations* (New York: Schocken, 1969), p. 46. For a reference to Arendt's work for the Paris office of the Youth Aliya, which helped send refugee children to Palestine, see Gershom Scholem, *Walter Benjamin: The Story of a Friendship* (New York: Schocken, 1981), p. 213.

2 See note N3,1: 'Heidegger seeks in vain to rescue history for phenomenology abstractly through "historicity"'. For an analysis of this cryptic Heidegger reference in the context of Benjamin's theory of 'natural history', see my *Walter Benjamin's Other History: Of Stones, Animals, Human Beings and Angels* (Berkeley, Los Angeles, London: University of California Press, 1998, 2000), p. 22.

3 See his letter to Scholem of 25 April 1930 (*C*, p. 365). It should be noted that Benjamin's critical attitude towards Heidegger is well documented in the six-volume German edition of his collected letters, which, regrettably, have not yet appeared in a complete English edition. For example, in 1935 Dolf Sternberger, author of *Der verstandene Tod*, asked Benjamin to write a review of this study. Benjamin first encouraged Sternberger to write a brief synopsis of *Der verstandene Tod*, explaining how the study's theses, implicitly or explicitly, differed from Heidegger's philosophy (letter of 29 July 1935). However, in a follow-up letter, Benjamin distanced himself from the 'repulsive' object of Sternberger's study, as he realized that the latter followed Heidegger's path of thinking. Benjamin added that he had studied Heidegger's dissertation on Duns Scotus early on; however, after reading Heidegger's 1916 essay on historical time (as part of preparatory work for the *Trauerspiel* study), he had decided to ignore Heidegger's philosophy henceforth. The fame that Heidegger had acquired at the beginning of the 1930s appeared threatening to him. See *GB* 5:134–5, 156–7.

4 The original titles in German are: 'Der Ursprung des Kunstwerkes' (Heidegger) and 'Das Kunstwerk im Zeitalter seiner technischen Reproduzierbarkeit' (Benjamin). The terms 'mechanical' and 'reproduction', to be found in some English translations of Benjamin's essay, do not appear in the essay's original title. Unless otherwise noted, all further citations are from the 'third version' of Benjamin's essay: 'The Work of Art in the Age of its Technological Reproducibility', in *SW* 4:251–83/*GS* 2:471–508; Martin Heidegger, 'Der Ursprung des Kunstwerkes (1935/36)', in Martin Heidegger, *Holzwege* (Frankfurt a. M.: Vittorio Klostermann, 1950), pp. 1–74; for the English translation, see Heidegger, 'The Origin of the Work of Art', in Martin Heidegger, *Basic Writings from Being and Time (1927) to The Task of Thinking (1964)*, revised and expanded edition, ed. David Farrell Krell (New York: Harper Collins, 1993), pp. 139–212.

5 See 'Spiegel-Gespräch mit Martin Heidegger (23. September 1966)', in Martin Heidegger, *Reden und andere Zeugnisse eines Lebensweges, 1910–1976*, vol. 16 of the *Gesamtausgabe* (Frankfurt a. M.: Vittorio Klostermann, 2000), p. 663. See also 'Zeittafel', ibid., 826. The *Spiegel* interview is reprinted in English as '"Only a God Can Save Us": *Der Spiegel's* Interview with Martin Heidegger (1966)', in Richard Wolin, *The Heidegger Controversy: A Critical Reader* (Cambridge, MA: MIT, 1991), pp. 91–116. However, Hermann Heidegger – Heidegger's son and editor – notes that the German interview in the *Gesamtausgabe* is a reconstruction of the original interview and as such different from the version published earlier (see note by Hermann Heidegger, in vol. 16, pp. 815–18).

6   Martin Heidegger, 'Antrag auf die Wiedereinstellung in die Lehrtätigkeit (Reintegrierung)', in Heidegger, *Gesamtausgabe*, vol. 16, pp. 397–404. An English version of the text, 'Letter to the Rector of Freiburg University, November 4, 1945', appears in Wolin, *The Heidegger Controversy*, pp. 61–6. It is in this letter that Heidegger made the distinction between his own allegiance to *Geist* and Rosenberg's 'biologism'. Defending his own use of language in the rectorial address, Heidegger claimed that it was not the expression of a biological-racist essence of humanity, but of *Geist* – reminiscent of Valéry's *La crise de l'esprit* (ibid, p. 398). See also Jacques Derrida, *Of Spirit: Heidegger and the Question* (Chicago and London: University of Chicago Press, 1989), *passim*.

7   Heidegger, 'Antrag', 398; in Wolin, *The Heidegger Controversy*, pp. 61–2 (modified translation).

8   Corrected translation of the phrase '*die wissende Entschlossenheit zum Wesen des Seins*', in Martin Heidegger, *Die Selbstbehauptung der deutschen Universität: Rede gehalten bei der feierlichen Übernahme des Rektorats der Universität Freiburg i. Br. am 27.5.1933; Das Rektorat 1933/34: Tatsachen und Gedanken* (Frankfurt a. M.: Vittorio Klostermann, 1983), p. 15; see Martin Heidegger, 'The Self-Assertion of the German University', in Wolin, *The Heidegger Controversy*, p. 33.

9   Heidegger, 'Antrag', p. 402; Wolin, *The Heidegger Controversy*, p. 65.

10   'Letter from Heidegger to Marcuse of January 20, 1948', in Wolin, *The Heidegger Controversy*, p. 162.

11   'Letter from Marcuse to Heidegger of May 12, 1948', in Wolin, *The Heidegger Controversy*, p. 164.

12   Martin Heidegger, *Nietzsche* (Pfullingen: Günther Neske, 1961), pp. 99ff.; English translation: Martin Heidegger, *Nietzsche: Volume I: The Will to Power as Art*, trans. David Farrell Krell (San Francisco: Harper Collins, 1991), pp. 83ff.

13   See Jürgen Habermas, *The Philosophical Discourse of Modernity: Twelve Lectures* (Cambridge, MA: MIT, 1993), pp. 18–19.

14   Heidegger, 'Der Ursprung des Kunstwerkes', p. 26; Heidegger, *Basic Writings*, p. 166.

15   Heidegger, 'Der Ursprung des Kunstwerkes', pp. 64ff.; Heidegger, *Basic Writings*, pp. 200ff.

16   See Susan Buck-Morss's excellent article, 'Aesthetics and Anaesthetics: Walter Benjamin's Artwork Essay Reconsidered', *October* 62 (1992): 3–41. Buck-Morss here pursues the connections that Benjamin established between political manipulation, phantasmagoria, intoxication, and anaesthetics in elucidating detail. She also describes how Benjamin's 'technoaesthetics' departed from the Kantian aesthetic and its hostility to the senses.

17   See, for example, 'On Some Motifs in Baudelaire', in which Benjamin explicitly analyses Freud's *Beyond the Pleasure Principle* (*SW* 4:313–55). See also Anton Kaes's recent work, forthcoming in *Shell Shock: Trauma and Film in Weimar Germany* (Princeton: Princeton University Press), and Jeffrey Herf, *Reactionary Modernism: Technology, Culture, and Politics in Weimar and the Third Reich* (Cambridge: Cambridge University Press, 1985).

18   Benjamin's use of the term *Zerstreuung* here differs markedly from Heidegger's coinage of the term. In the German language, *zerstreuen* can have the following meanings: to scatter or disperse; to divert someone; and, in the reflexive form, to take one's mind off something or to amuse oneself. (See, for example, *Collins German Dictionary*.) In Heidegger's thought *Zerstreuung* almost always evokes the negative condition of dispersal, which is to be undone by the thinking force of re-collection and collecting (*Versammlung*); in Benjamin's cultural theory, *Zerstreuung* refers either to the new condition of dispersal that typified modernity or to the culture of leisure and distraction. As his artwork essay suggested, the new 'reception in distraction', facilitated by

film and its shock effects, made 'cult value recede into the background' and turned the audience into 'an examiner, but a distracted one' (*SW* 4:268–9).

19 While neither Kant nor Schopenhauer are explicitly mentioned in section 15 of Benjamin's artwork essay, their spectral presence can be sensed in the term 'contemplation' (*GS* 1.2:505/*SW* 4:268).

20 Martin Heidegger, 'Bauen Wohnen Denken' in Heidegger, *Vorträge und Aufsätze, Gesamtausgabe* (Frankfurt a. M.: Vittorio Klostermann, 1976), pp. 147–64; Heidegger, 'Building Dwelling Thinking', in *Basic Writings*, pp. 343–63.

21 Philippe Lacoue-Labarthe analyses the predicament entailed in Winckelmann's statement in great detail. See his *Heidegger, Art and Politics: The Fiction of the Political* (Oxford: Basil Blackwell, 1990), *passim*.

22 For a critique of *Wissenschaft*, see also 'Der Ursprung des Kunstwerkes', pp. 49–50.

23 See especially the account of the rectorial address provided in the *Spiegel* interview, *Gesamtausgabe*, vol. 16, p. 656 and 663, where Heidegger noted that he wanted to oppose the 'technische Organisation der Universität'. Similar remarks appeared in 'Das Rektorat 1933/34 – Tatsachen und Gedanken (1945)', in *Gesamtausgabe*, vol. 16, pp. 373–4.

24 Martin Heidegger, 'Das Ding', in *Vorträge und Aufsätze*, p. 167.

25 As for the avant-garde, 'consciousness-raising' use of 'shock' or 'montage', celebrated in Brecht's epic theatre or Benjamin's artwork essay, Heidegger only recognized one sort of 'montage', that of mere machine assembly, consisting of 'rods, pistons and chassis'. Heidegger, 'Die Frage nach der Technik', 21; Heidegger, *Basic Writings*, 325.

26 Heidegger, 'Der Ursprung des Kunstwerkes', 5, 10, 11; Heidegger, *Basic Writings*, 147, 152.

27 In fact, 'To the Planetarium', the final section of Benjamin's *One-Way Street* (*Einbahnstraße*), published in 1928, already presented the theory of instrumental reason *in nuce*; that is, it decried how World War I was a manifestation of the 'the immense wooing of the cosmos [...] enacted for the first time on a planetary scale – that is, in the spirit of technology'. Criticizing the imperialists' belief that the purpose (or 'end') of technology was the 'mastery of nature', the final lines of the essay, in highly suggestive, somewhat 'apocalyptic' language, opened up the possibility that the proletariat might replace the 'frenzy of destruction' with a new 'ecstasy of procreation'; it would do so informed by the deeper insight that technology consisted in a novel mastery of humans' relation to nature. In many ways, the later artwork essay further developed and corrected the half-fledged insights of 'To the Planetarium' (see *SW* 1:486–7).

28 'About the attempts to take second nature, which once let first nature step forth, back into first nature: blood and soil' (*GS* 1.3:1045).

29 The original text states: '*das Technische im heutigen Sinne*'; Heiddeger, 'Der Ursprung des Kunstwerkes', p. 46; Heidegger, *Basic Writings*, p. 184.

30 Heidegger, 'Der Ursprung des Kunstwerkes', p. 47; Heidegger, *Basic Writings*, p. 184.

31 See W. J. T. Mitchell's analysis of iconophobia in the Western theories and philosophies, in *Iconology: Image, Text, Ideology* (Chicago: University of Chicago, 1986), as well as Martin Jay's *Downcast Eyes: The Denigration of Vision in Twentieth-Century French Thought* (Berkeley, CA: University of California Press, 1993).

32 Martin Heidegger, 'Die Frage nach der Technik', in Heidegger, *Vorträge und Aufsätze*, pp. 7–36; Heidegger, 'The Question Concerning Technology', *Basic Writings*, pp. 307–41.

33 Heidegger, 'Die Frage nach der Technik', pp. 16–21; Heidegger, *Basic Writings*, pp. 321–6.

34 Heidegger, 'Die Frage nach der Technik', pp. 16–17; Heidegger, *Basic Writings*, p. 321.

35 Heidegger, 'Die Frage nach der Technik', p. 14; Heidegger, *Basic Writings*, p. 318.

36 Heidegger, 'Der Ursprung des Kunstwerkes', p. 49; Heidegger, *Basic Writings*, p. 186–7.
37 Heidegger, 'Der Ursprung des Kunstwerkes', pp. 40–1; Heidegger, *Basic Writings*, pp. 179–80.
38 In the later addendum to the artwork essay, Heidegger underscored the distinction between 'Ge-Stell' as used in that essay and as thematized in his later thought. However, he at once consolidated his conservative critique of technology, suggesting that his postwar criticism of the *Gestell* still needed to be read against the foil of the 1935 essay. Moreover, technology was never just a human praxis nor a mere instrument, as anthropology would have it. Heidegger, 'Der Ursprung des Kunstwerkes', p. 72; Heidegger, 'The Origin of the Work of Art', pp. 209–10.
39 Heidegger, 'Der Ursprung des Kunstwerkes', p. 49; Heidegger, *Basic Writings*, pp. 186–7.
40 Heidegger, 'Die Selbstbehauptung', p. 16; Wolin, *The Heidegger Controversy*, p. 36.
41 The original passage reads as follows: '*Was heute als Philosophie des Nationalsozialismus herumgeboten wird, aber mit der inneren Wahrheit und Größe dieser Bewegung (nämlich mit der Begegnung der planetarisch bestimmten Technik und des neuzeitlichen Menschen) nicht das geringste zu tun hat, das macht seine Fischzüge in diesen trüben Gewässern der "Werte" und "Ganzheiten"*'. These lines are from *Einführung in die Metaphysik*, a course held in 1935 and published in 1953; see vol. 40 of the *Gesamtausgabe*, p. 208; for the English translation, see Martin Heidegger, *Introduction to Metaphysics* (New Haven: Yale University Press, 2000), p. 199. Hannah Arendt referred to the lines in her 'For Martin Heidegger's Eightieth Birthday', originally published in *Merkur*, 10 (1969): 893–902, reprinted in Günther Neske and Emil Kettering (eds), *Martin Heidegger and National Socialism: Questions and Answers* (New York: Paragon House, 1990), p. 284n. However, she placed the passage in the context of Heidegger's so-called 'error'. His sympathies for the National Socialist cause expressed a fleeting moment of 'temptation', right at the moment when he left his habitual 'abode', that of thinking, 'to involve himself in the world of human affairs' (ibid., p. 216). As her endnote stated: 'The contents of this error differed considerably from the "errors" that were then common. Who else but Heidegger came up with the idea that National Socialism was "the encounter between planetarily determined technology and human beings" – except perhaps those who read, instead of Hitler's *Mein Kampf*, some of the Italian futurists' writings, which fascism, in contrast to National Socialism, referred to here and there' (p. 284). Arendt then went on to argue in the note that the error was less serious than that of others, those who ignored the existence of the Gestapo and concentration camps.
42 Ernst Jünger, 'Total Mobilization', in Wolin, *The Heidegger Controversy*, p. 126.
43 Jünger, 'Total Mobilization', p. 127.
44 Jünger, 'Total Mobilization', p. 128.
45 Ibid.
46 Ibid.
47 Walter Benjamin, 'Theorien des deutschen Faschismus: Zu der Sammelschrift "Krieg und Krieger"'. Herausgegeben von Ernst Jünger', *GS* 3:239–40; 'Theories of German Fascism: On the Collection of Essays *War and Warriors*, edited by Ernst Jünger', *SW* 2:313–14.
48 Benjamin's language here is clearly inspired by his *Origin of the German Tragic Drama*, that is, his theory of natural history and the allegorical reading of nature.
49 Heidegger, 'Die Selbstbehauptung', p. 15; Wolin, *The Heidegger Controversy*, p. 35; see also Heidegger's reflections in the *Spiegel* interview, vol. 16, p. 657.
50 'Das Rektorat 1933/34 – Tatsachen und Gedanken', first published in Germany in 1983, together with the new edition of *Die Selbstbehauptung der deutschen Universität*. According to Hermann Heidegger, this overview text was written shortly after the

'collapse' ('Zusammenbruch') of 1945. Heidegger gave the manuscript to his son with the specification to publish it in due course. Reprinted in Heidegger, *Gesamtausgabe*, vol. 16, pp. 372–94. English translation in Neske and Kettering, *Martin Heidegger and National Socialism*, pp. 15–32.

51 Above quotations are from Heidegger, 'The Rectorate 1933/34: Facts and Thoughts', pp. 17–18; see Heidegger, 'Das Rektorat', pp. 375–6.

52 Martin Heidegger/Karl Jaspers, *Briefwechsel 1920–1963*, ed. Walter Biemel and Hans Saner (Munich: Piper, 1992), p. 256.

53 Jünger, 'Total Mobilization', p. 129.

54 Ibid.

55 Heidegger, 'Die Selbstbehauptung', p. 14; Wolin, *The Heidegger Controversy*, p. 34, mod. trans.

56 Heidegger, 'Das Rektorat', p. 378; 'The Rectorate', p. 20.

57 Heidegger, 'Das Rektorat', p. 379.

58 Heidegger, 'Die Selbstbehauptung', p. 11; Wolin, *The Heidegger Controversy*, p. 31.

59 Ibid.

60 Friedrich Nietzsche, *On the Genealogy of Morals and Ecce Homo* (New York: Vintage Books, 1969), p. 108. As the editors of Benjamin's *Gesammelte Schriften* observe in their editorial comments, Benjamin's Latin phrase referred to Ferdinand I's '*Fiat iustitia et pereat mundus*', cited in Johannes Manlius, Loci communes, Basileae, 1563 (*GS* 1.3:1055). Yet, it is much more likely that Benjamin based his own transformation of the phrase on Nietzsche's *Genealogy of Morals*. In the context of the artwork essay, the Nietzsche reference is far more important, since he was the first to thematize the peculiar spectatorial dialectic at the heart of Greek tragedy; both Greek religion and Greek tragedy, he claimed, had invented the gods as the privileged spectators of human foibles – a claim inspired by the left-Hegelian critique that religion was the mere fulfilment of (anthropological) needs. It is this very reversal of the relationship between spectator and spectacle that Benjamin has in mind, when he takes the model one step further, noting how through the new technology of war '[humankind], which once, in Homer, was an object of contemplation for the Olympian gods, has now become one for itself. Its self-alienation has reached the point where it can experience its own annihilation as a supreme aesthetic pleasure' (*SW* 4:270).

CHAPTER 6

1 'Das Werkwerden des Werkes ist eine Weise des Werdens und Geschehens der Wahrheit'. 'Die Kunst ist das Ins-Werk-Setzen der Wahrheit'. Martin Heidegger, *Der Ursprung des Kunstwerkes* (Stuttgart: Reclam 1960), pp. 60 and 79 (my trans.).

2 I am quoting from Harry Zohn's translation of the third version of the artwork essay, sometimes adjusted according to the German original in *GS* 1.2:471–508. References will be given to the quoted section.

3 Karlheinz Stierle, *Ästhetische Rationalität: Kunstwerk und Werkbegriff* (München: GmbH & Co. Verlags-KG, 1997).

4 Heidegger, *Der Ursprung des Kunstwerkes*, p. 74f.

5 Ibid., p. 56.

6 Jean-Paul Sartre, *The Psychology of Imagination*, trans. Mary Warnock (London, Methuen, 1972). All quotes from the first part of chapter 5, 'Conclusion'.

7 *Der Meridian und andere Prosa* (Frankfurt: Suhrkamp 1988), p. 48. All further quotes from p. 53ff. (my trans.).

8 *Der Begriff der Kunstkritik in der deutschen Romantik. GS* 1.1:103 (my trans.).

CHAPTER 7

1   Walter Benjamin, 'Theories of German Fascism: On the Collection of Essays *War and Warriors*, edited by Ernst Jünger', *SW* 2:321.

2   For a very astute analysis of this theme, see Ubaldo Fadini, *Sviluppo tecnologico e identità personale: Linee di antropologia della tecnica* (Bari: Dedalo, 2000).

3   See Kant's statements to this effect in the essay 'The End of All Things', in Immanuel Kant, *Religion within the Boundaries of Mere Reason and Other Writings*, trans. and eds. Allan Wood and George Di Giovanni (Cambridge: Cambridge University Press, 1998), p. 197.

4   In the second version of his essay on the *Kunstwerk* (which is the version we are reading here) Benjamin characterizes the modern significance of technology in these terms, in opposition to a magical-ritual significance. While the 'first technology' is oriented towards appropriative identification, the 'second' (the modern or in any case de-ritualized) technology aims to distance human beings from nature. But for Benjamin in precise terms this is a condition for understanding technological activity as cooperative in relation to nature: a playing with nature. It is precisely through the mimetic-expressive attitude of play that human beings distance themselves from nature 'by an unconscious ruse' (*SW* 3:107). This is obviously the point at which Benjamin is most distant from Heidegger's diagnosis. For a comparison with Heidegger's essay 'On the Origin of the Work of Art', see Fabrizio Desideri, *La porta della giustizia: Saggi su Walter Benjamin* (Bologna: Pendragon, 1995), pp. 101–17.

5   Precisely to the extent that – as Aristotle maintains in the *Physics*, II, 199b 26ff. – *techne*, like *physis*, is not governed by a deliberative will, which represents rather the external cause of its productive process. This process is governed, then, by a law inherent to its self-production (its internal finalism) which assimilates it to nature's self-production. On this topic, see Margherita Isnardi Parente, *Techne: Momenti del pensiero greco da Platone a Epicuro* (Firenze: La Nuova Italia, 1966), pp. 153ff. In these pages, Parente also clearly explains how the Aristotelian dimension of the *automaton* corresponds to the sense of necessity (*ananke*) Plato speaks of in the *Timaeus*.

6   Martin Heidegger, 'The Question Concerning Technology', trans. David Farrell Krell, *Basic Writings* (London: Routledge, 1993), pp. 311–41.

7   Ibid., p. 339.

8   Something of this sort could also hold true for Benjamin's distinction between a magical-sacred and a modern sense of technology. But in this case the diachronic succession loses its rigidity and is synchronized in the actuality of a political conflict surrounding the fate of technology, the catastrophic outcomes of which Benjamin perceives ahead of time.

9   For the development of this idea in Adorno see Fabrizio Desideri, *Il fantasma dell'opera* (Genoa: Il melangolo, 2002), pp. 155–68.

10 Ingenuous readings of Benjamin's essay in a 'materialist' key have failed to see that this passage, marked by the loss of a magical-sacred conception of art, is closely connected with the liberation of its mystical character (in exactly the sense that the mimetic truth of the artwork lies in perception). In Benjamin's own words '*die Auffassung der Kunst umso mystischer wird, je mehr die Kunst von echter magischer Brauchbarkeit sich entfernt; je größer dagegen diese magische Brauchbarkeit ist (und in der Urzeit ist sie am größten), desto unmystischer ist die Aufassung von der Kunst*' (*GS*, 1.3:1050). 'The conception of art becomes that much more mystical the more art distances itself from genuine magical usefulness; on the other hand, the greater this magical usefulness (and in primitive times it is at its greatest) the less mystical the conception of art'.

11 '*Die Kunst ist ein Verbesserungsvorschlag an die Natur, ein Nachmachen, dessen verborgenstes Innere ein Vormachen ist. Kunst ist, mit andern Worten, vollendende Mimesis.*' On the same manuscript page, Benjamin explains the modern significance of the relation-

ship between technology and politics: *'Die befreite Technik schließt die Bewältigung der gesellschaftlichen Elementarkräfte als Voraussetzung für die der natürlichen ein. (In der Urzeit liegt die umgekehrte Beziehung vor: die Beherrschung der natürlichen Kräfte schließt die Beherrschung von gewissen gesellschaftlichen Elementarkräften ein.)'* 'Liberated technology includes the emergence of elementary social forces as a condition for the emergence of natural forces. (In primitive times the inverse relationship applies: the domain of natural forces includes that of certain elementary social forces.)' *GS*, 1.3:1047.

12   Benjamin, 'On the Mimetic Faculty', *SW* 2:720–2.

13   What Benjamin does not underline in this respect, perhaps because of a Fourierian influence undoubtedly present in his reflection on technology, is the measure of violence implicit in this play. It does emerge, however, in a note from 1936 which constitutes an important variation on his 1933 theory of *mimesis*: 'The knowledge that the first material in which the mimetic faculty tested itself was the human body should be used more fruitfully than hitherto to throw light on the primal history [*Urgeschichte*] of the arts. We should ask whether the earliest mimesis of objects through dance and sculpture was not largely based on imitation of the performances through which primitive man established relations with those objects. Perhaps Stone Age man produced such incomparable drawings of the elk because the hand guiding the implement still remembered the bow with which it felled the beast' (*SW* 3:253).

14   For a precise definition of the concept of aura see Josef Fürnkäs, 'Aura', in *Benjamins Begriffe*, eds. Michael Opitz and Erdmut Wizisla (Frankfurt: Suhrkamp, 2000), 1: pp. 95–146.

15   Benjamin, 'On Some Motifs in Baudelaire', *SW* 4:333.

16   For the development of this theme in Kant see Fabrizio Desideri, *Il passaggio estetico: Saggi kantiani* (Genoa: il Melangolo, 2003).

17   Benjamin, 'The Currently Effective Messianic *Elements*', *SW* 1:213.

18   Plato, *Protagoras* 322b.

19   Plato, *Protagoras* 356d.

20   Plato, *Protagoras* 356e.

21   For a discussion of this theme, see Fabrizio Desideri, *L'ascolto della coscienza: Una ricerca filosofica* (Milano: Feltrinelli, 1998), pp. 80–104.

22   For the relation of this thesis to Plato's *Protagoras*, see David Roochnik, *Of Art and Wisdom: Plato's Understanding of Techne* (Pennsylvania: University of Pennsylvania Press, 1996), pp. 211–31.

CHAPTER 8

For their responses to early drafts of this chapter and/or assistance with translations, I am indebted to Russell A. Berman, Jay M. Bernstein, Adam Casdin, Howard Eiland, Hal Foster, Lydia Goehr, Geoffrey Galt Harpham, Stephen Hinton, Robert Hullot-Kentor, Martin Jay, Tamara Levitz, and Arthur Strum. Earlier versions of some portions of this article have appeared in *Das Brecht-Jahrbuch/The Brecht Yearbook*, *European Romantic Review*, and *Romantic Circles Praxis*.

1   See, for example, Walter Benjamin, 'The Work of Art in the Age of Mechanical Reproduction' and, especially, 'On Some Motifs in Baudelaire', as well as 'The Paris of the Second Empire in Baudelaire', all in volume 4 of *SW*; 'Das Kunstwerk im Zeitalter seiner technischen Reproduzierbarkeit', 'Das Paris des Second Empire bei Baudelaire', and 'Über einige Motive bei Baudelaire' in *GS* 1.2:431–654; see also Benjamin, *Charles Baudelaire: Ein Lyriker im Zeitalter des Hochkapitalismus. Zwei Fragmente.*, ed. and with an afterword by Tiedemann (Frankfurt: Suhrkamp, 1969).

And see Theodor Adorno, 'On Lyric Poetry and Society' in Adorno, *Notes to Literature*, ed. Rolf Tiedemann, trans. Shierry Weber Nicholsen, 2 vols. (New York: Columbia University Press, 1991–1992), 1: 37–54, and *Aesthetic Theory*, ed., trans., and with a translator's introduction by Robert Hullot-Kentor (Minneapolis: University of Minnesota Press, 1997), *passim*; 'Rede über Lyrik und Gesellschaft', *Noten zur Literatur*, ed. Tiedemann, 4 vols. (Frankfurt am Main: Suhrkamp, 1958–1974), 1: 73–104, and *Ästhetische Theorie*, vol. 7 of *Gesammelte Schriften*, ed. Gretel Adorno and Tiedemann (Frankfurt: Suhrkamp, 1970), *passim*.

See too Adorno, Benjamin, *Briefwechsel 1928–1940*, ed. Henri Lonitz (Frankfurt: Suhrkamp, 1994), pp. 138ff., 364ff. , and 388ff.; in English, *CC*, pp. 104ff., 280ff., and 298ff.

2   For more sustained discussions of the distinction, and of Adornian constructivism in relation to the history of poetics and critical theory, see Kaufman, 'Red Kant, or The Persistence of the Third *Critique* in Adorno and Jameson', *Critical Inquiry* 26 (2000): 682–724, and 'Negatively Capable Dialectics: Keats, Vendler, Adorno, and the Theory of the Avant-Garde', *Critical Inquiry* 27 (2001): 354–84.

3   Adorno develops this argument from the late 1930s onwards, although probably never in so sustained a manner as in *Aesthetic Theory*; see, for example, pp. 33, 79, 167–8, 173–4, 204, 209, 245, and 269; *Ästhetische Theorie*, pp. 57, 122–4, 249–52, 258–60, 303–4, 311, 363–4, and 401.

4   It should be emphasized that the linkage between aura and labour-otherness is meant, in Frankfurt School terms, critically to distinguish *via negativa* aura from official culture's blithe or 'affirmative' attempts (in the Marcusean sense) falsely to re-enchant and reconcile a world still scored by profound exploitation and stark inequality.

5   *Aesthetic Theory*, pp. 269, 245; *Ästhetische Theorie*, pp. 401, 364. On 'second-reflection', see 'Red Kant', pp. 718–19.

6   As with much contemporary experimental poetry, the work of the poets listed above has often been published by smaller presses whose books may sometimes prove difficult to find. I should therefore add that most of these poets' work is available through the (non-profit) Small Press Distribution, the leading such distributor in the United States, at 1341 Seventh Street, Berkeley, CA 94710, (510)524–1668 or (800)869–7553, fax (510)524–0852, orders@spdbooks.org, <http://www.spdbooks.org>.

7   For Adorno's quite Benjaminian diagnosis of lyric's 'go-for-broke game' ('*va-banque-Spiel*'), and of lyric's relation to conceptuality and objective reality, see 'On Lyric Poetry and Society', pp. 44, 43; 'Rede über Lyrik und Gesellschaft', pp. 87, 85. On the more general relationship between aesthetic quasiconceptuality and conceptual thought proper (a relationship that Benjamin, Adorno, and countless artists and critics find dramatized with special intensity in lyric), see 'Red Kant', esp. at pp. 710–24.

8   For an important reconsideration of the 'crisis of experience' theory standing behind Benjamin's and Adorno's thoughts about the loss of aura in modernity, see Martin Jay, 'Is Experience Still in Crisis? Reflections on a Frankfurt School Lament', *Kriterion* 100 (1999): 9–25.

9   On Whitney's work, see, for example, Raphael Rubinstein, 'Nine Lives of Painting', *Art in America* 86 (1998): 90–9, and Geoffrey Jacques, 'Complicated Simplicity: The Work of Stanley Whitney', *Nka: Journal of Contemporary African Art* 4 (1996): 10–1.

10 See Whitney's discussion of Mondrian in 'Complicated Simplicity'.

11 For the most recent volume of her own poetry, see Norma Cole, *Spinoza in Her Youth* (Richmond, CA: Omnidawn Press, 2002). For her most recent translations from the French, see *Crosscut Universe: Writing on Writing from France*, ed. and trans. Cole (Providence, RI: Burning Deck Press, 2000), and the rendering of the poet Anne Portugal's *Le plus simple appareil* (Paris: P.O.L., 1992), trans. Cole under the title *Nude* (Berkeley, CA: Kelsey St. Press, 2001).

12 See, for example, Jess's front-and-back-cover 'paste-up' (the term he has long preferred to

'collage') for Cole's *Mars* (Berkeley: Listening Chamber, 1994); see too Jess's and Cole's folio *Catasters* (Edinburgh: Morning Star Editions (Folio Series) 1995–1996). On Jess, see, for example, Michael Duncan, 'Maverick Modernist', *Art in America* 82 (1994): 92–7, and the essays in *Jess: A Grand Collage 1951–1993*, ed. Michael Auping (Buffalo, NY: Albright-Knox Art Gallery, 1993).

13 From Cole, 'Singularities: The Painting of Stanley Whitney' (Dayton, OH: University of Dayton Rike Center Gallery, 1991). See too Cole's 'Stay Songs', dedicated to Whitney, written for his Spring 2001 show of new work, and published with reproductions of several of his paintings in *Stanley Whitney: 'Stay Songs'*, Norma Cole (New York: Bill Maynes Gallery, 2001).

14 Cole, *My Bird Book* (Los Angeles: Littoral Books, 1991). *My Bird Book* continues the investigation into how painting and poetry speak to each other about lyric; see, for example, the untitled poem dedicated to Whitney and to the painter Marina Adams, ibid., pp. 58–9.

15 Ibid., p. 7.

16 Mzwhake Mbuli, untitled elegy for Kippie Moeketsi; recorded in *Songololo: Voices of Change*, prod. Marianne Kaplan and Cari Green, dir. Marianne Kaplan, Telefilm Canada and MSK Productions, 1990. (Mbuli seems not to have published the elegy elsewhere; it does not appear in any volumes of his poetry, nor on any of his CDs.) Moeketsi is almost ritually described in music and musicology circles as 'the legendary saxophonist Kippie Moeketsi'; in 1959, together with Dollar Brand (later known as Abdullah Ibrahim), Hugh Masekela, and Jonas Gwangwa, Moeketsi formed The Jazz Epistles. The Jazz Epistles, deeply influenced by Ellington and Monk, named their group after another touchstone, Art Blakey and The Jazz Messengers; The Jazz Epistles became known as South Africa's first 'modern' jazz ensemble.

17 From 'After Arthur, or please let me be misunderstood', *My Bird Book*, p. 30.

18 See *Une Saison en enfer* in Arthur Rimbaud, *Œuvres*, ed. Suzanne Bernard (Paris: Garnier, 1960), and cf., for example, the sections 'Matin', p. 239 (*'Quand irons-nous, par delà les grèves et les monts ... ?'*) and 'Mauvais Sang', p. 213 (*'–Quel siècle a mains! –Je n'aurai jamais ma main ...'*).

19 For these last several excerpts from 'After Arthur', cf. again *Une Saison en enfer*: 'Mauvais Sang', pp. 213 (*'J'ai horreur de tous les métiers ...'*), 217 (*'Connais-je encore la nature? me connais-je? – Plus de mots. J'ensevelis les morts dans mon ventre ...'*); and 'Délires II', p. 234 (*'O saisons, ô châteaux!/Quelle âme est sans défauts?/... O saisons, ô châteaux!'*).

20 See Kristin Ross, *The Emergence of Social Space: Rimbaud and the Paris Commune* (Minneapolis: University of Minnesota Press, 1988), pp. 11, 29 n.11, quoting Bertolt Brecht, 'On the Formalistic Character of the Theory of Realism', *Aesthetics and Politics*, ed. Rodney Livingstone, Perry Anderson, Francis Mulhern, and Ronald Taylor, trans. Anya Bostock, Stuart Hood, Rodney Livingstone, Francis McDonagh, and Harry Zohn, Afterword by Fredric Jameson (London: New Left Books, 1977), pp. 70–6; for the German text, see 'Über den formalistischen Charakter der Realismustheorie', Bertolt Brecht *Werke: Grosse kommentierte Berliner und Frankfurter Ausgabe*, ed. Werner Hecht, Jan Knopf, Werner Mittenzwei, and Klaus-Detlef Müller, 30 vols. (Berlin and Frankfurt: Aufbau/Suhrkamp, 1989–1998), 22.1 (*Schriften* 2.1): 437–45, and 22.2 (*Schriften* 2.2): 1038–40. In Brecht's text the question about lyric actually reads, *'Was ist es mit dem Realismus in der Lyrik ...?'* (p. 437); *Aesthetics and Politics* translation reads: 'But what about realism in lyric poetry ...?' (p. 70). Unless otherwise indicated, all further references to Brecht's German texts are to the *Werke: Grosse kommentierte* edition and are cited by volume and page. All translations of Brecht, unless making specific reference to Bertolt Brecht, *Poems: 1913–1956*, ed. John Willett and Ralph Manheim, trans. Willett, Manheim, *et al.* (London and New York: 1987), or to other published translations, are my own.

21 The editors of *Aesthetics and Politics* and a kindred text, *Die Expressionismusdebatte:*

Materialien zu einer marxistischen Realismuskonzeption, ed. Hans-Jürgen Schmitt (Frankfurt: Suhrkamp, 1973), and other commentators, have asserted that Brecht was only a figurehead for, or, at most, nominally involved in editing *Das Wort*. See, for example, *Aesthetics and Politics*, p. 62. Brecht's journals and letters, as well as some of Benjamin's recollections (and Benjamin's own contributions to *Das Wort*) show this to be an inadequate overall analysis. In fact, Brecht's attitudes towards his participation in *Das Wort* ranged from frustration, cynicism, and disgust, to cautious enthusiasm and energetic determination to shape the journal more towards his liking (including through active solicitation of manuscripts from writers around the world).

See Brecht's correspondence about *Das Wort* in the Brecht *Werke* 28 [*Briefe* 1] (1998): 562 and 569, and 29 (*Briefe* 2) (1998) (both *Briefe* volumes ed. Günter Glaeser, in cooperation with Wolfgang Jeske and Paul-Gerhard Wenzlaff): 9, 13, 19, 20, 21, 25–6, 36, 38, 64, 77, 81, 83–4, 101, 106–7, 126, and 147–8. (Most of these letters can be found in the English translation of an earlier edition of Brecht's letters, *Brecht Briefe* (Frankfurt: Suhrkamp, 1981); see *Bertolt Brecht Letters*, trans. Ralph Manheim and ed., with commentary and notes, by John Willett (London: Methuen, 1990), pp. 163, 235, 239, 240, 246, 247, 248, 256, 259, 260, 271, 276, 279, 289, 290, 295, 315, 607, 610, and 611.)

See too, for further evidence of Brecht's ambivalent attitudes towards, and dealings with, *Das Wort*, the Brecht journal entries cited in my n.30 below.

For a measured assessment of the relevant materials and controversies, see David Pike, *German Writers in Soviet Exile, 1933–1945* (Chapel Hill: University of North Carolina Press, 1982), esp. Chapter 8, 'The Literary Popular Front, Part I: *Das Wort*'.

22   Until the publication of Brecht's *Arbeitsjournal* (Frankfurt: Suhrkamp, 1973), the best-known evidence was probably the June–August 1938 section of 'Gespräche mit Brecht' in Benjamin, *Versuche über Brecht*, ed. and with an Afterword by Tiedemann (Frankfurt: 1966), pp. 117–35; 'Conversations with Brecht' in Benjamin, *Understanding Brecht*, trans. Anna Bostock, Introduction by Stanley Mitchell (London: New Left Books, 1973), pp. 105–21. The Brecht *Werke*'s generous editorial notes add a good deal to the picture; see citations in my n.30 below.

23   They are now all available, with ample editorial notes, in the Brecht *Werke* 22.1 and 22.2 (*Schriften* 2.1 and 2.2), ed. Inge Gellert and Werner Hecht in cooperation with Marianne Conrad, Sigmar Gerund and Benno Slupianek (1993).

24   See Walter Haenisch's essay 'Percy Bysshe Shelley', *Das Wort* 1 (1938): 96–110; and see the account of Haenisch's fate given by his widow in *Gut angekommen, Moskau: Das Exil der Gabriele Stammberger, 1932–1954. Errinerungen und Dokumente*, written with and ed. Michael Peschke (Berlin: Basis Druck, 1999). Also on Haenisch, see Hans-Albert Walter, *Deutsche Exilliteratur 1933–1950*, (Stuttgart: J. B. Metzler, 1978–1984) 6 vols., II (*Europäisches Appeasement und überseeische Asylpraxis*) (1984): 525–6 n. 4, and IV [*Exilpresse*] (1978; 1984), p. 422.

25   *Werke* 22.1, p. 423–34 and 22.2: 1035–7nn. 'Weite und Vielfalt' was first published, some sixteen years after its composition, in the series *Brecht Versuche*, Heft 13 (Berlin, 1954): 97–107. The essay was also published – before the 1989–1998 *Werke*'s appearance – in Brecht's *Gesammelte Werke* 8 (*Schriften* 2), ed. Werner Hecht (1967): 340–9.

26   Brecht is of course often described, by others and himself, as the Left's *plumpes Denken* (*crude-thinking*, *crude-thought*, '*vulgar*') poet, over against Left writers like Wolfenstein who exhibit a penchant for visionary, sometimes arcane or delicate, symbolist esotericism. It therefore seems entirely natural that Brecht chooses to render Shelley's lines far more literally than had Wolfenstein. Yet paradoxically, it is Wolfenstein's translation that yields the familiar Popular Front verse cadence of ringing hammerbeat, along with a rhetorical thematics that quickly thins to weak abstraction. Meanwhile, Brecht's scrupulously literal, generally unrhymed translation somehow manages – no doubt due to Brecht's terrific feel for other poets' language, and, more specifically, his obvious sympathy with the

Mask – to convey Shelley's startling ways of simultaneously condensing and exfoliating image, phrase, and line. Brecht, that is, powerfully grasps and identifies with Shelley's manner of marrying rhythmic propulsion to textural density, whereby through syntax, cadence, diction, and tone, an intense forward movement and stingingly precise denotation coexist with an imagistic counter-impulse that, with understated elegance, deftly builds back into the poem a cumulatively thickening self-reflection. The inspired and brilliant literalism of Brecht's translation – Brecht's ability to see (and then to render into an impressive construction of energy, concretion, and transparency) the *Mask*'s interanimation of the material and the ideational, of grit and philosophically oriented intellection – results in stanzas notably more literary and poetic than Wolfenstein's. In that sense, Brecht seizes on something in Shelley's *Mask* that had already long proved congenial to Brecht: the effort of an essentially lyric practice to assimilate the social-popular materials of the ballad form. If lyric is thereby 'refunctioned' (to use the favoured term in the Brechtian lexicon), it is likewise true that there is no real getting back behind modern lyric autonomy. As Brecht indicated time and again, ballad or other popular forms and materials, recast by the progressive or radical poet, are henceforth 'literary' (which, in Brecht's view, by no means necessitates their subsequent isolation from sociopolitical *engagement*).

For Benjamin's implicit, and Adorno's and Elizabeth Hauptmann's explicit, assessments of Brecht's Shelley translations (as well as Brecht's later, possibly ambivalent attitude towards the translations), see my nn. 46 and 47 below.

27 See Percy Bysshe Shelley, *The Mask of Anarchy*, in *Shelley's Poetry and Prose*, ed. Donald H. Reiman and Sharon B. Powers (New York: Norton, 1977), pp. 301–10. Unless otherwise indicated, all further references to Shelley's writing are to this edition.

Wolfenstein's translation of the *Mask* stanzas had been the first text in the 'Übersetzungen [Translations]' section of *Das Wort*'s June 1937 issue 6, pp. 63–5. The translated *Mask* excerpt was titled 'Sie Sind Wenige – Ihr Seid Viel!' ('They are Few – You are Many!'); an introductory note told *Das Wort* readers that the stanzas came from the last part of Shelley's *Mask*, and that they had been translated by Wolfenstein.

In the Wolfenstein translation, the German title (and text) translates but reverses the sequencing within the *Mask*'s celebrated, twice-repeated sentence addressing English workers (a sentence Shelley simultaneously intends as description, incantation, and exhortation/inspiration): 'Ye are many – they are few'. (In Shelley's text, these words appear at l.155 and again in the poem's final line (l. 372).) Wolfenstein apparently changes Shelley's word order in an attempt to preserve, in German, what he perceives as the essence of the *Mask*'s rhyme-scheme, syntax, and overall rhythm. The reversed sequencing may also reflect Wolfenstein's and *Das Wort*'s political judgement about the importance of ending – that is, ending first the bold-faced, all-capitalized, exclamatory title given to the *Mask*-excerpt; then, the repeated phrase within the translated stanzas; finally, the translated text as a whole – with the 'many', rather than the ruling class's 'few'.

See also Wolfenstein's 'Nachwort' to his earlier Shelley translation, the *Dichtungen* of Shelley (Berlin: Paul Cassirer, 1922), pp. 87–94; reprinted as 'Nachwort zu *Dichtungen von Shelley*' in Alfred Wolfenstein, *Werke*, ed. Hermann Haarmann and Günter Holtz (Mainz: Hase & Hoehler, 1982–1993) 5 vols., 4 (*Vermischte Schriften: Ästhetik, Literatur, Politik*, ed. Hermann Haarmann, Karen Tieth, and Olaf Müller (1993), pp. 210–15. The *Vermischte Schriften*, along with the poems, short stories, novels, and plays collected in the other volumes of Wolfenstein's *Werke*, reveals Wolfenstein's writings to have been thoroughly saturated by his readings in, and responses to, Shelley. For a valuable discussion of how Shelley infuses Wolfenstein's attempts to couple, or put into dialogue, an experimental poetics and a committed Left politics, see Klaus Siebenhaar, 'Ästhetik und Utopie: Das Shelley-Bild Alfred Wolfensteins: Anmerkungen zum Verhältnis von Dichtung und Gesellschaft im Spätexpressionismus', in *Preis der Vernunft: Literatur und*

Kunst zwischen Aufklärung, Widerstand und Anpassung. Festschrift für Walter Huder, ed. Klaus Siebenhaar and Hermann Haarmann (Berlin: Medusa Verlag, 1982), pp. 121–33. See too Peter Fischer, *Alfred Wolfenstein: Der Expressionismus und die verendende Kunst* (Munich: Wilhelm Fink Verlag, 1968), and Russell E. Brown, 'Alfred Wolfenstein', in *Expressionismus als Literatur: Gesammelte Studien*, ed. Wolfgang Rothe (Berne and Munich: Francke Verlag, 1969), pp. 264–76.

28 'Weite und Vielfalt', *Werke* 22.1: 424–5, 430, 432–3 (emphasis in original ('*den grossen revolutionären englischen Dichter P.B.* Shelley')).

29 *Werke* 14 (*Gedichte* 4), ed. Jan Knopf and Brigitte Bergheim, in cooperation with Annette Ahlborn, Günter Berg, and Michael Duchardt (1993): 404–5, 662n. Brecht worked on both the *Mask* and *Peter Bell* translations with his close collaborator Margarete Steffin; see *Werke* 14: 662–3nn., and 22.2: 1035–6nn.

The *Werke* presents Brecht's *Peter Bell* translation as part of a larger text entitled 'Hölle' ('Hell'), *Werke* 14: 404–9, 662–3nn. 'Hölle' begins with the nine *Peter Bell* stanzas, and then segues directly into the 25 *Mask of Anarchy* stanzas translated – and otherwise appearing only in – in 'Weite und Vielfalt'. The textual history provided in the *Werke*'s notes leads one to deduce that publication of the *Peter Bell* translation occurred only in (and then after) 1972, when the translation appeared in Benjamin's posthumously-organized-and-published *Passagenwerk*; see my n.30 below.

See also Shelley, *Peter Bell the Third*, 'Part Third: Hell', p. 330, l.147 and ff.

30 Brecht's translated *Peter Bell* stanzas appear in Benjamin's *Passagenwerk* (*AP* M18).

The sequence of this sharing of ideas and manuscripts, and copying out of translations, can be reconstructed by coordinating Brecht's *Arbeitsjournal* entries for the period in question, along with the June–August 1938 sections of 'Gespräche mit Brecht' in Benjamin's *Versuche über Brecht*, pp. 128–35 ('Conversations with Brecht' in *Understanding Brecht*, pp. 114–21), as well as Benjamin's correspondence (particularly with Adorno; see my n.46 below). In addition to the Benjamin texts just cited, see the Brecht *Werke* 26 (*Journale* 1), ed. Marianne Conrad and Werner Hecht, in cooperation with Herta Ramthun (1994): 312–23, esp. 315, 317, and 319; these entries can be found in English in *Bertolt Brecht Journals* (part of the series *Bertolt Brecht: Plays, Poetry and Prose*, ed. John Willett and Ralph Manheim), ed. John Willett, trans. Hugh Rorrison (London: New York, 1993), pp. 6–19, esp. pp. 10, 13, and 14.

31 See Brecht, '(Notizen über Baudelaire)' and '(Zu *Les fleurs du mal*)', *Werke* 22.1 and 22.2 (*Schriften* 2.1 and 2.2): 451–53 and 1044–5nn. Brecht had left these Baudelaire-fragments untitled (though the manuscript explicitly indicates that he has taken some of the materials from Benjamin's essay); 'Notizen über Baudelaire (Notes on Baudelaire)' and 'Zu *Les fleurs du mal*' ('On *The Flowers of Evil*') are the bracketed titles supplied by the *Werke*'s editors. For Brecht's notably ambivalent *Arbeitsjournal* entries about Benjamin's notion of aura ('there is good stuff' in the essay, it 'is useful to read', and Brecht clearly is intrigued by what he regards as the essay's odd articulation of aura's strangeness; but it is also all 'a load of mysticism, although his [Benjamin's] attitude is against mysticism'), and for Brecht's self-identification with Shelley, see *Werke* 26 (*Journale* 1): 315, 610–11nn., and 319, 618n.; *Bertolt Brecht Journals*, pp.10, 463n, and 14. See also 'The Paris of the Second Empire in Baudelaire' (*GS* I.2:562, n.51/*SW* 4:81, n.155). For the Benjamin–Adorno disagreements over 'Das Paris des Second Empire bei Baudelaire', see my n.45 below.

32 Benjamin (*AP* J81,6; translation slightly amended; emphasis in the original).

33 As Benjamin, Adorno, and various commentators and artists will go on to elaborate, 'distance from auratic distance' entails the baleful negation of a previously generative, protocritical experience of suspension-negation. In other words, distance from auratic distance involves a movement *away* from experiences of formal suspension or negation (away from experiences of a provisional, enabling distance from the reigning concepts of presently existing society) and *towards* affirmation, positivity, and – especially in terms of

art and aesthetic experience – immediacy vis-à-vis ruling concepts and the social status quo. The governing notion is that the age of art's technical-mechanical reproducibility is characterized not by the artistic-aesthetic aura that operates via charged distance, suspension, or negation, but by the commodity-form's version of aura, which actually is the photo-negative of the critical negation formally enacted by aesthetic aura. The commodity attempts positively to sell auratic luminosity in, or as, immediacy. The commodity-form does not present aura in or as charged distance; which is to say, the commodity-form does not really proffer its aura via *the aesthetic*'s thought-and-felt *as-if*. Rather, the commodity presents aura through aesthetic*ization*, and the commodity does so in lockstep with aestheticization's march towards its (aestheticization's) logical endpoint: the collapse into pure immediacy of the *as-if*'s constitutive distance, not to mention the collapse of the reflective judgement-experience and of the critical agency that depend on such provisional distance. On aesthetic experience as a provisional, formal suspension-negation of extant ruling concepts, and therefore as a basis for the construction of materials for new concepts (and for the sociopolitical praxis and dispensations that can spring from them), see 'Red Kant' and 'Negatively Capable Dialectics'.

34 'Nachenkend über die Hölle' directly paraphrases and adapts lines from *Peter Bell the Third* that Brecht had previously translated. See the Brecht *Werke* 15 (*Gedichte* 5): 46, and *Poems*, p. 367. In the Brecht *Werke*, the poem is known by its first words, 'Nachdenkend, wie ich höre', whereas in the older *Gesammelte Werke* 4 (*Gedichte*): 830, it is formally titled 'Nachdenkend über die Hölle', by which title it is still often discussed in the critical literature, even where the later (*Werke*) edition is cited.

35. Some, but by no means all of these poems (not to mention the drafts printed in the *Werke* notes) have been published in the English *Poems*. See the poems gathered under the titles *Hollywoodelegien* and *Gedichte im Exil*, *Werke* 12 (*Gedichte* 2: *Sammlungen 1938–1956*), ed. Jan Knopf (1988): 115–25; in *Poems*, see *Hollywood Elegies*, pp. 380–1, and the texts in the section 'American Poems 1941–1947'. See too 'An Walter Benjamin, der sich auf der Flucht vor Hitler Entleibte', 'Die Verlustliste', 'Nachdenkend, wie ich höre' ('Nachdenkend über die Hölle'), and 'Zum Freitod des Flüchtlings W.B.', *Werke* 15 (*Gedichte* 5): 41, 43, 46, 48; in *Poems*, see 'On Thinking About Hell' and 'On the Suicide of the Refugee W.B.', pp. 367, 363.

See also the *Werke*'s reprinting of the remarkable 1942 typescript draft that Brecht had provisionally titled 'Die Hölle' (which is distinct from the *Werke* text combining the *Mask* and *Peter Bell* translations and titled 'Hölle', discussed in my n.29 above); this 'Die Hölle' typescript is clearly a preliminary stage of the *Hollywoodelegien*. This 1942 'Die Hölle' typescript, moreover, unmistakably arises from the Shelley-matrix, reworking, in fact, the same ideas and even words about '*mein Bruder Shelley*' (and the figuration of London and Los Angeles as competing versions of Hell) that appear in the 1941 'Nachdenkend über die Hölle'. Both 'Nachdenkend über die Hölle' and the 'Die Hölle' typescript should be traced, of course, back to the Summer 1938 translations, analyses, and discussions of Shelley, particularly to the *Peter Bell* translation. See *Werke* XII: 399–400nn. (The 1942 'Die Hölle' typescript may well have emerged from what would have been a previous, manuscript sketch – evidently not possessed by the Brecht Archive, nor elsewhere known – that would have served as the basis for 'Nachdenkend über die Hölle', the *Hollywoodelegien*, and related poems.) See too the discussion in my n.44 below of Brecht's 1947 rewriting of *The Mask of Anarchy*.

36 From Brecht's draft version of 'Die Verlustliste' ('The Casualty List'), *Werke* 15: 338–9nn.

37 See, most recently, James Chandler's magisterial *England in 1819: The Politics of Literary Culture and the Case of Romantic Historicism* (Chicago: University of Chicago Press, 1998), pp. 483–554; Jeffrey N. Cox's brief but very suggestive comments in *Poetry and Politics in the Cockney School: Keats, Shelley, Hunt and Their Circle* (Cambridge and New York: Cambridge University Press, 1998), pp. 211–16; and Steven E. Jones, *Shelley's*

Satire: Violence, Exhortation, and Authority (DeKalb: Northern Illinois University Press, 1994), pp. 49–69, 149–64.

38 *Aesthetic Theory*, pp. 321–2; *Ästhetische Theorie*, pp. 476–7.

39 *Bertolt Brecht Journals*, pp. 257–8 (translation amended) ('*wenn er von diesen Kompositionen spricht, nicht wenn er komponiert*', *Werke* 27 (*Journale* 2), ed. Werner Hecht (1995): 125). See too the editors' notes, *Werke* 12 (*Gedichte* 2): 399–403, and the note in *Poems*, p. 586.

40 *Bertolt Brecht Journals*, p. 258; *Werke* 27 (*Journale* 2): 125. Eisler's 1942 comments on the Brecht poems may not have been as judgemental as Brecht had initially believed, nor, in any case, do they appear to have represented Eisler's final opinion on the texts: Eisler subsequently observed that the *Hollywoodelegien* were his favourite works among all Brecht's poetry. See Hans Bunge, *Fragen Sie mehr über Brecht. Hanns Eisler im Gespräch* (Leipzig: 1975), p. 244, cited in the Brecht *Werke* 12 (*Gedichte* 2): 402.

41 The texts have a staggered publication and reception history, dating from Eisler's 1950s recordings of the *HollywoodLiederbuch* (*Hollywood Song-Book*) (which includes the *Hollywoodelegien* and other Brecht poems), and the volumes of Brecht's later poetry, in German and in translation, that appear from the late 1940s onwards. With the Brecht volumes in particular, it happens that a significant number of the early 1940s poems from and around the Shelley-Baudelaire-critical-lyric matrix become readily available in German only in the 1950s and 1960s, and in some cases are not translated until the 1960s and 1970s.

42 Here I use *avant-gardist* and *anti-aesthetic* in the very specific sense drawn out by Peter Bürger's *Theory of the Avant-Garde*, trans. Michael Shaw (Minneapolis: University of Minnesota Press, 1984). For related thoughts about how currents within today's experimental poetry complicate the usual narrative of postmodernism's superannuation of modernism, see Kaufman, 'A Future for Modernism: Barbara Guest's Recent Poetry', *American Poetry Review* 29 (2000): 11–16, and 'Everybody Hates Kant: Blakean Formalism and the Symmetries of Laura Moriarty', *Modern Language Quarterly* 61 (2000): 131–55.

43 See Kaufman, 'Legislators of the Post-Everything World: Shelley's *Defence* of Adorno', *English Literary History* 63 (1996): 707–33, esp. 731 n.29.

44 *Werke* 26 (*Journale* 1, 24 August 1940): 417–18, 661n; *Bertolt Brecht Journals*, pp. 90–1 (emphases in original German text and in original English translation). The lines that Brecht copies into his *Arbeitsjournal* are from Wordsworth's 'She Was a Phantom of Delight'.

Brecht's wildly unexpected receptivity to Wordsworthian lyric aura – Brecht and *Wordsworth?* – certainly offers powerful evidence of a willingness to think autonomously, and of a consequent ability to understand the fundamental relationality (rather than the allegedly inherent individualist separatism) of artistic, intellectual, and political autonomy themselves. But how does an artist – how does Brecht – go on to *make art* whose autonomy is the sign of its capacity for engagement, whose aura and autonomy are conceived in opposition to an archaic-dictatorial mode of domination-and-command that Brecht calls *autarchy?* The answers may be countless and always provisional, yet one fascinating place to begin looking is at the dynamics of autonomy not just between art (here, Brecht's art) and the sociopolitical, but *within* art (Brecht's art). The crucially nondeterminative relationship between art and the social is perhaps mirrored, or even projected from, nondeterminative relations inside art itself. And again, there may be no better place to focus than on Brecht's strong impulse to think with or through Shelley. For if, in the late 1930s and early 1940s, Brecht finds indispensable lessons for his critical and lyric work in Shelley's *Mask of Anarchy* and related Shelley texts, and if those Shelleyan lessons inflect Brecht's writing until his 1956 death, Brecht is nonetheless perfectly able, in the later 1940s, to read what he views as the autonomous and therefore *available* imaginative power of the Shelleyan lyric-ballad genre-mix into a Brechtian project that, while making some use of lyric skills, intends momentarily to emphasize the more populist registers within ballad-form. The case in point is Brecht's inspired, scabrous, and entirely explicit 1947 rewriting (in a Cold-War, Marshall-Plan context, where the poem's manifest content includes the much-advertised 'economic miracle' in what Brecht deems a far-from-denazified Federal Republic of Germany) of Shelley's *Mask of Anarchy*. See Brecht's 'Freiheit und Democracy', in *Werke* 15 (*Gedichte* 5), ed. Jan Knopf and Brigitte Bergheim, in cooperation with Annette Ahlborn, Günter Berg, and Michael Duchardt (1993): 183–8, 422–4nn. (published in Brecht's previous *Gesammelte Werke* under the overtly Shelleyan title, 'Der anachronistische Zug oder Freiheit und Democracy', and still often referred to by that title in the critical literature); in English, see 'The Anachronistic Procession or Freedom and Democracy' in *Poems: 1913–1956*, pp. 409–14, 593–94nn. Although not focusing on lyric aura and artistic-aesthetic autonomy, various commentators have briefly traced the ways that Brecht models 'Der anarchronistische Zug oder Freiheit und Democracy' on *The Mask of Anarchy* (the latter's title, in the published German Shelley-translations that began appearing in 1844 – *Der Maskenzug der Anarchie* – makes immediately apparent Brecht's echoing of Shelley's poem). See, for example, S. S. Prawer, *Comparative Literary Studies: An Introduction* (London: Duckworth, 1973), pp. 92–6; Richard Cronin, *Shelley's Poetic Thoughts* (New York/London: St. Martin's/MacMillan, 1981), pp. 39–42; and, again, Steven E. Jones, *Shelley's Satire*, pp. 103–5, as well as Jones's 'Shelley's Satire of Succession and Brecht's Anatomy of Regression: "The Mask of Anarchy" and *Der anachronistische Zug oder Freiheit und Democracy*" in *Shelley: Poet and Legislator of the World*, ed. Betty T. Bennett and Stuart Curran (Baltimore and London: The Johns Hopkins University Press, 1996), pp. 193–200.

45   In his February 1 1939 letter to Benjamin about 'The Paris of the Second Empire in Baudelaire', Adorno questions the fidelity to Shelley of the Brecht *Peter Bell* translation that Benjamin's essay quotes; Adorno wonders whether such 'directness and bluntness' ('*Direktheit und Härte*') can really be found in the original. See Adorno and Benjamin, *Briefwechsel*, p. 397; *CC* p. 304. An editor's note in *Complete Correspondence*, though not indicating that the rest of Brecht's *Peter Bell* translation appears in the *Passagenwerk*, does provide Shelley's stanza in English, and comments that 'Brecht's translation does follow the English of Shelley's original very closely', p. 308 n. 32.

Adorno for his part really may subsequently have changed his mind – at least somewhat – about the *Peter Bell* translations, which he in all likelihood would have continued to read, preserved as they were in the Benjamin texts that Adorno helped to edit after Benjamin's death. Significantly, the first line of those *Peter Bell* stanzas reappears, as noted in my text above, in one of Adorno's most important discussions of modern poetics, 'Parataxis' (1963). As if at once conceding and yet contesting the same old point, Adorno (here constellating Shelley, Baudelaire, and Hölderlin) quite laudatorily gives the first line from those *Peter Bell* stanzas: but he presents the first half of Shelley's line in German, the second half in English! 'Wie Hölderlins Wahlverwandtem Shelley die Hölle eine Stadt ist, much like London …' ('Just as for Hölderlin's kindred spirit Shelley Hell is a city, much like London …'). See 'Parataxis. Zur späten Lyrik Hölderlins', *Noten zur Literatur* 3: 174 (*Gesammelte Schriften* 11: 462); 'Parataxis: On Hölderlin's Late Poetry', *Notes to Literature* 2: 122.

For several years beginning in 1935, Benjamin had gone back and forth with Adorno (who usually also represented Horkheimer in these colloquies) about Benjamin's Baudelaire texts and related writings (the texts that would become the *Passagen-Werk* and its spin-off, *Charles Baudelaire*). Some of these discussions involved the question of which versions of Benjamin's texts or analyses would appear in the Institut für Sozialforschung's (Institute of Social Research's) house organ, the *Zeitschrift für Sozialforschung* (*Journal of Social Research*). In autumn 1938, Benjamin submitted 'The Paris of the Second Empire in Baudelaire', the essay that quoted and briefly discussed one of the *Peter Bell* stanzas.

Adorno and Benjamin had sharp interchanges over the essay; Adorno and Horkheimer did not publish the essay in the *Zeitschrift für Sozialforschung.*

Adorno contended (probably believing that Brecht's influence was to blame) that 'The Paris of the Second Empire in Baudelaire' had capitulated to facile determinist theory, that it tried to establish one-to-one, directly causal relationships between aesthetic (or cultural) and economic phenomena. (The charge noticeably, if unfairly, parallels Adorno's unjustified complaint about the 'directness and bluntness' of Brecht's Shelley translations. The dispute over whether Brecht had accurately rendered Marx's favorite nineteenth-century English poet – and thus, the dispute over Left poetics from Shelley and Marx to Brecht and Benjamin and Adorno – was really, for Adorno, another argument about whether Marx was a 'blunt' economic determinist or, for that matter, a determinist of *any* sort.)

Adorno essentially claimed that in 'The Paris of the Second Empire in Baudelaire' Benjamin had retreated from his own previous refusals of false immediacy, from his own prior commitment to analyses that foregrounded the dialectical mediation of economic and aesthetic-cultural phenomena through an entity or matrix never directly present to any one person, and which therefore could appear only 'negatively': the social totality. In Adorno's view, 'The Paris of the Second Empire in Baudelaire' correctly emphasized the relationships between loss-of-aura and capitalist development, but the essay itself slipped into a Left version of 'positivism' and uncritical, illusionist 'magic' (the bad version of aura) when it directly, unproblematically conjoined economics and poetry.

Benjamin contested these charges, but agreed to undertake a different treatment of the subject. The result was Benjamin's 'Über einige Motive bei Baudelaire' ('On Some Motifs in Baudelaire'), which Adorno and Horkheimer published in the *Zeitschrift für Sozialforschung* in early 1940 (see some of the essay's more recent publication history in my n.1). 'Über einige Motive bei Baudelaire' has come to be seen as one of the great twentieth-century essays on modern poetry, social analysis, and critical theory, and as a *locus classicus* for the analysis of lyric aura. It is generally thought also to lead directly into Benjamin's 'On the Concept of History' (Über den Begriff der Geschichte'), a text that achieved the rare feat of being lauded by Adorno and Horkheimer *and* Brecht (though Brecht, again characteristically eschewing what he saw as Benjamin's sometimes overly hermetic literariness and too-voiced-in-religion messianism, lamented the Theses' meta-phoricity and use of Judaica).

For the Adorno–Benjamin exchanges about the Baudelaire texts and related matters, see *CC*, pp. 104ff., 280ff., and 298ff. (Some of these letters previously appeared in *Aesthetics and Politics*'s section on the Adorno–Benjamin debates.) For 'On the Concept of History' see *SW* 4:389–400; 'Über den Begriff der Geschichte', *GS* 1.2:693–704. For Brecht's comments on Benjamin's Theses, see the Brecht *Werke* 27 (*Journale* 2) (1995): 12, and *Bertolt Brecht Journals*, p. 159. For a lucid, compressed history of the initial controversies over Benjamin's Baudelaire writings, see Martin Jay, *The Dialectical Imagination: A History of the Frankfurt School and the Institute of Social Research, 1923–1950*, 2d. ed. (1973; Berkeley and Los Angeles: University of California Press, 1996), pp. 197–212, esp. 206–11.

46 Adorno's initial doubts concerning the translations' fidelity or quality are later echoed, for example, by Brecht's close collaborator and influential editor Elisabeth Hauptmann, who observes too that Brecht himself had seriously doubted the Shelley-translations' merit; see the Brecht *Werke* 14 (*Gedichte* 4): 662–3nn. However, there is no corroborating evidence, from Brecht or others, that Brecht ever publically ratified Hauptmann's view or held the one she attributes to him; Brecht's 1954 publication of the *Mask* translation-essay (in the *Brecht Versuche* series) would seem to count as contrary evidence.

47 See Adorno, 'On Lyric Poetry and Society', p. 46; 'Rede über Lyrik und Gesellschaft', p. 90. This assessment of Brecht's status as poet is echoed throughout *Aesthetic Theory*.

48 For a preliminary sketch of Adorno's thinking about these relationships among nine-

teenth- and twentieth-century poetry, modern aura, and critical thought, see Kaufman, 'Negatively Capable Dialectics'.

49   For valuable explications of Benjamin's and Adorno's development of the force-field and constellation, see the introduction in Martin Jay, *Force Fields: Between Intellectual History and Cultural Critique* (New York and London: Routledge, 1993), esp. pp. 1–3 and 8–9; see also the introduction to Jay's *Adorno* (Cambridge, MA: Harvard University Press, 1984), esp. pp. 14–23.

50   See, for example, Howard Caygill, *Walter Benjamin and the Colour of Experience* (London and New York: Routledge, 1998).

51   For discussion see, for example, Anthony J. Cascardi, *Consequences of Enlightenment* (Cambridge: Cambridge University Press, 1999); Frances Ferguson, *Solitude and the Sublime: Romanticism and the Aesthetics of Individuation* (New York: Routledge, 1992); Caygill, *Art of Judgment* (Oxford: Blackwell, 1989); and Kaufman, 'Red Kant' and 'Negatively Capable Dialectics'.

52   See the fourteenth of Benjamin's 'theses' in 'On the Concept of History' (*GS* 1.2:727/*SW* 4:395). Cf., for its applicability to the making of constellations, Benjamin's fascinating distinction between *Jetztzeit* and *Jetztsein* ('waking-being') in the *Passagenwerk* (K2,3).

53   For a key treatment of the concept and form of constellative thought and writing within criticism, and for the constellation's relationship to the nonarbitrary yet nonargumentative forms of modern art, see Robert Hullot-Kentor, 'Foreword: Critique of the Organic', in Adorno, *Kierkegaard: Construction of the Aesthetic*, trans. Hullot-Kentor (1933; Minneapolis: University of Minnesota Press, 1989), pp. x–xxiii. For related discussions of how mimesis informs Adorno's modes and styles of writing, see Jameson, *Late Marxism: Adorno, or, The Persistence of the Dialectic* (New York and London: Verso, 1990) (at, for example, p. 68); and Jay, 'Mimesis and Mimetology: Adorno and Lacoue-Labarthe', in *The Semblance of Subjectivity: Essays in Adorno's Aesthetic Theory*, ed. Tom Huhn and Lambert Zuidervaart (Cambridge, MA: MIT, 1997), pp. 29–54, reprinted in Jay, *Cultural Semantics: Keywords of Our Time* (Amherst, MA: University of Massachusetts Press, 1998), pp. 120–37.

54   See, for example, Adorno, 'On Lyric Poetry and Society', esp. pp. 38–42, 43–6, 53–4; 'Rede über Lyrik und Gesellschaft', esp. pp. 75–83, 84–91, 103–4; and see *Aesthetic Theory*, pp. 55, 99, 133, 122–4, 167–8; *Ästhetische Theorie*, pp. 88, 152–3, 201–2, 185–8, 249–52. For a parallel critique of various modernist and postmodernist composers' attempts to create an art of sheer materiality and construction (effectively and uncritically leaving expression and aura behind), see Adorno, 'Das Altern der Neuen Musik', *Dissonanzen*, ed. Tiedemann, *Gesammelte Schriften* 14 (1973): 143–67; trans. Hullot-Kentor and Fredric Will under the title 'The Aging of the New Music', *Telos* 77 (1988): 95–116. For indications about how such musical questions translate back into problems of literary art, see Adorno's treatment of sheerly constructivist play with 'protocol sentences' and conventions, *Aesthetic Theory*, pp. 154–7, 203–6; *Ästhetische Theorie*, pp. 231–6, 302–7.

55   See T. J. Clark, 'In Defense of Abstract Expressionism', *October* 69 (1994): 23–48, reprinted in Clark's *Farewell to an Idea: Episodes from a History of Modernism* (New Haven and London: Yale University Press, 1999), pp. 371–403. Clark's remarkable sketch of later modern petit-bourgeois vocation vis-à-vis the bourgeoisie – crossed or melded, in Clark's telling, with the enormously self-conscious audaciousness (the enormously self-conscious *vulgarity*) of later modernist lyric painting's expressive ambition and its potential ability crassly to turn aura's endgame into a cultural-capital cash-cow of endlessly postauratic aura – may have an even more surprising analytical yield when applied (all over again, as it were) to foundation stones and adjacent rocks of the Critical-Theory and estrangement-effect canons. Brecht's decades-long insistence, even during his most apparently anti-aestheticist periods, on his commitment to lyric practice, together with his obvious delight in his *plumpes-Denken* (crude-thinking, '*vulgar*') Marxist reputation

(and his delight in some of that reputation's less public vagaries and contradictions), cry out to be thought together not only with Brecht's hostility towards Horkheimer's and Adorno's intellectualism (and towards what Brecht deemed Benjamin's embarrassing religious mysticism). That is, the rich and productive tensions generated from the Brechtian lyric stance need also to be thought together with Adorno's and Horkheimer's ungenerous but not entirely dismissable gibes that Brecht was not a Marxist so much as – what else? – a petit bourgeois with genuinely radical intentions and extraordinary artistic abilities who peddled populist misconceptions about Marx having been an economic determinist. In a manner at once grudgingly respectful, scornfully triumphant, and meant to throw back at Brecht what he was certainly throwing at them, Adorno and Horkheimer were happy to affirm that Brecht was, when all was said and done, truly great: a great lyric poet.

CHAPTER 9

The translations of the convolute passages which are the research notes for Benjamin's unwritten book *Passagenwerk* (*GS* 5), are my own.

1   Georg Lukács, *History and Class Consciousness*, trans., Rodney Livingstone (Cambridge, MA.: MIT, 1971).

2   Jeffrey Mehlman, *Walter Benjamin for Children: An Essay on the Radio Years* (Chicago, IL: University of Chicago Press, 1993), p. 80.

3   Mitchell Schwarzer, 'Ontology and Representation in Karl Bötticher's Theory of Tectonics', *Journal of the Society of Architectural Historians*, 53 (1993): 267–80.

4   Karl Bötticher, 'Das Prinzip der hellenischen und germanischen Bauweise hinsichtlich der Übertragung in die Bauweise unserer Tage', *Allgemeine Bauzeitung*, 2 (1846): 111–25; Carl Gottlieb Wilhelm Bötticher, 'The Principles of the Hellenic and German Ways of Building', *In What Style Should We Build? The German Debate on Architectural Style*, trans. Wolfgang Herrmann (Santa Monica, CA : The Getty Center for the History of Art and Humanities, 1992), pp. 147–67.

5   Translation taken from Bötticher, 'Principles'.

6   Alfred Gothold Meyer, *Eisenbauten: Ihre Geschichte und Ästhetik* (Esslingen: Paul Neff, 1907, reprint: Berlin, Gebr. Mann Verlag, 1999).

7   In his introduction to the English translation of Sigfried Giedion's *Bauen in Frankreicht*, Sokratis Georgiadis observed that 'What Meyer experienced as non-aesthetic, he actually described in terms of an aesthetic of the sublime' (p. 35). See note 8.

8   Sigfried Giedion, *Bauen in Frankreich: Bauen in Eisen – Bauen in Eisenbeton* (Leipzig and Berlin: Klinkhardt and Biermann, 1928); *Building in France: Building in Iron – Building in Ferro-Concrete*, trans. J. Duncan Berry (Santa Monica, CA: The Getty Center for the Study of Art and the Humanities, 1995).

9   For a more detailed treatment of Benjamin's reading of Giedion and Meyer, see Detlef Mertins, 'The Threatening and Enticing Face of Prehistory: Walter Benjamin and the Utopia of Glass', *Assemblage*, 29 (1996): 7–23.

10   Sigmund Freud, *The Psychopathology of Everyday Life*, trans., Alan Tyson (New York: W. W. Norton, 1960).

11   I have altered the translation of this passage to render Benjamin's use of '*durchwirken*' as 'interweaving' rather than 'inform'.

12   Walter Benjamin, 'Benjamin an Kraft. Paris, 28.10.1935' (*GS* 5.2:1151).

13   Eduardo Cadava has given a more precise reading of this in 'Words of Light: Theses on the Photography of History', *Diacritics* 22 (1992): 84–114.

14   The significance of these notes was first recognized by Susan Buck-Morss in *The*

Dialectics of Seeing: Walter Benjamin and the Arcades Project (Cambridge, MA: MIT, 1989).

15 See exhibition catalogue, *Le pont Transbordeur et la Vision Moderniste* (Marseille: Musées de Marseille, 1991).

16 Giedion, *Building*, Note 8 above, p. 147.

17 See Giedion, *Bauen in Frankreich*, pp. 83–96.

18 Emphasis added. I have altered the translation by Edmund Jephcott and Kingsley Shorter by using the more palpable phrase 'interwoven with consciousness' instead of their 'informed by'.

19 Karl Blossfeldt, *Kunstformen der Natur* (Berlin: Ernst Wasmuth, 1928); *Art Forms in Nature* (New York: E. Weyhe, 1929).

20 Karl Nierendorf, 'Art Forms in Nature', in Blossfeldt, *Nature*, pp. iii–xiii.

21 Walter Benjamin, 'Doctrine of the Similar', trans. Michael Jennings (*SW* 2:694–8)/'Lehre vom Änlichen' (*GS* 2.1:204–10). 'On the Mimetic Faculty', trans. Edmund Jephcott (*SW* 2:720–2)/'Über das mimetische Vermögen' (*GS* 2.1:210–13).

22 See Detlef Mertins, 'Playing at Modernity', in *Toys and the Modernist Tradition* (Montreal: Canadian Centre for Architecture, 1993), pp. 7–16.

23 J. J. Grandville, 'Une Autre Monde', in *Bizarreries and Fantasies of Grandville* (New York: Dover Press, 1978).

24 Walter Benjamin, 'Karl Kraus', in, *GS* 334–67.

25 Walter Benjamin, 'Paul Scheerbart: Lesabéndio', *GS* 2.2: 618–20.

CHAPTER 10

I would like to thank David Campany, Béatrice Han, and Maggie Iversen for their comments and correspondence on this chapter in draft. I would also like to acknowledge the time made available by the support of a Leverhulme Trust Research Fellowship while working on this paper.

1 For examples of this postmodern reception of Benjamin see: Craig Owens, 'The Allegorical Impulse: Towards a Theory of Postmodernism Parts I/II', reprinted in *Beyond Recognition: Representation, Power and Culture* (Berkeley and LA: University of California Press, 1994); Douglas Crimp, 'The Photographic Activity of Postmodernism' and 'This Is Not a Museum of Art', reprinted in *On The Museum's Ruins* (Cambridge, MA: MIT, 1993); and Andreas Huyssen, 'The Hidden Dialectic: Avant-Garde–Technology–Mass Culture', in *After the Great Divide: Modernism, Mass Culture, Postmodernism* (Bloomington and Indianapolis: Indiana University Press, 1986). Peter Wollheim set out to retrieve Benjamin's work from this postmodern appropriation in 'The Politics of Memory: Re-Reading Walter Benjamin', *Vanguard* (February/March, 1986): 22–6, by resituating the concept of 'aura' in the context of Benjamin's conflicted understanding of memory, perception and experience more generally. More recently, original contributors to the debate, such as Rosalind Krauss, have begun reflecting on the afterlife of Benjamin's concept of aura in art theory; see 'Reinventing the Medium', *Critical Inquiry* 25 (1999): 289–305, in the special issue of *Critical Inquiry* entitled *Angelus Novus: Perspectives on Walter Benjamin*.

2 The latter distinction is my own and, so far as I know, has not previously been presented in this way. The former distinction is a point of contention in the literature. For an exemplary account of this aspect of Benjamin's thought, see John McCole, *Walter Benjamin and the Antinomies of Tradition* (Ithaca: Cornell University Press, 1993), especially section 1, chapter I, 'Benjamin on Tradition', 1–10. Here McCole portrays Benjamin's double-edged response to the destruction of aura as a key to interpreting his work as a whole. See also Rainer Rochlitz, *The Disenchantment of Art: The Philosophy*

of Walter Benjamin (New York: Guilford Press, 1996), chapter II, parts 2 and 3. Susan Buck-Morss is also attentive to this tension in Benjamin's work; see *The Origin of Negative Dialectics: Theodor Adorno, Walter Benjamin and the Frankfurt Institute* (New York: Free Press, 1977), chapters 9–10 on 'The Adorno–Benjamin Debate'.

3   On this point, see Howard Caygill's reading of the artwork essay in terms of Kant's understanding of the concept of experience in chapter 3 of *Walter Benjamin and the Colour of the Experience* (London and New York: Routledge, 1998). For an interpretation that puts more emphasis on where Benjamin departs from Kant, while still reading the artwork essay as a crypto-Kantian text, see Rodolphe Gasché, 'Objective Diversions: On Some Kantian Themes in Benjamin's "The Work of Art in the Age of Mechanical Reproduction"', in eds. Andrew Benjamin and Peter Osborne, *Walter Benjamin's Philosophy: Destruction and Experience* (2nd edition, Manchester: Clinamen, 2000). Both Caygill and Gasché would contest the double-edged reading of Benjamin's response to the withering of the aura put forward here. For a fine reconstruction of Benjamin's account of the relation between particular art forms and transformations in the structure of perception, see Joel Snyder, 'Benjamin on Reproducibility and Aura: A Reading of "The Work of Art in the Age of its Technical Reproducibility"', in Gary Smith, ed., *Benjamin: Philosophy, Aesthetics, History* (Chicago: University of Chicago Press, 1989).

4   See Hal Foster, 'Postmodernism: A Preface' in Hal Foster, ed., *The Anti-Aesthetic: Essays in Postmodern Culture* (Seattle: Bay Press, 1983). On a more critical note, Foster was already referring to an orthodoxy of the 'purloined image' in postmodern theories of photographic appropriation by 1982 in 'Re: Post', reprinted in Brian Wallis, ed., *Art After Modernism: Rethinking Representation* (New York: New Museum of Contemporary Art, 1984).

5   Both Roland Barthes' 'The Death of the Author' and Michel Foucault's 'What is an Author?' appeared in widely read translations in 1977: Barthes' *Image, Music, Text* (London: Fontana, 1977), and Foucault's *Language, Counter-Memory, Practice* (Ithaca: Cornell University Press, 1977), respectively.

6   See, for example, Douglas Crimp's critique of Barbara Rose's explicitly anti-photographic defence of contemporary painting in 'The Photographic Activity of Postmodernism', pp. 114–15.

7   The show itself included the work of Troy Brauntuch, Jack Goldstein, Sherrie Levine, Robert Longo and Phillip Smith; only Sherrie Levine remains prominent among the group in retrospective accounts of the period. Today it is just as likely that Cindy Sherman, Richard Prince, Louise Lawler, or Barbara Kruger would be associated with this way of working.

8   Crimp, 'The Photographic Activity', p. 112.

9   Ibid., 113.

10   See, for example, Benjamin's claim in 'Little History of Photography' that 'what is again and again decisive for photography is the photographer's attitude to his techniques' (*SW* 2:517).

11   See Roland Barthes, *Camera Lucida* (London: Fontana, 1984). For an overview of Barthes' theory of the photographic 'punctum' and 'studium', as well as the parallels between Barthes' and Benjamin's views of photography, see Maggie Iversen, 'What is a Photograph?', *Art History*, 17:3, September 1994.

12   Benjamin further notes of the slow optics of early photography that 'the low light-sensitivity of the early plates made prolonged exposure outdoors a necessity. This in turn made it desirable to take the subject to some out-of-the-way spot where there was no obstacle to quiet concentration ... The procedure itself caused the subject to focus his life in the moment' (*SW* 2:514).

13   Adorno was the first to point this out, in his correspondence with Benjamin concerning the essay's prospective publication in the Institute's journal. See letter II of

'Presentation III' in Theodor Adorno, Walter Benjamin, Ernst Bloch, Bertolt Brecht, Georg Lukács, *Aesthetics and Politics*, (London: NLB, 1977, pp. 121–2).

14 Cf. *SW* 4:255. For all the Kantian overtones of this passage, which I bring out below, it also echoes Valéry's account of listening to music: '[it] weaves us an artificial span of time by lightly touching the keys of our real life', allowing us 'to live again in a vibrant milieu not very different from that in which it was created'; see 'Conquest of Ubiquity', reprinted in Paul Valéry, *Collected Works* ('Aesthetics') ed. J. Matthews (London: Routledge & Kegan Paul, 1964) 13: 226–7, from which Benjamin takes his epigraph for the 'Work of Art' essay. Valery's paper originally appeared in 1928 in *La Musique Avant Tout Chose*, prior to its collection in *Pieces Sur L'Art*, 1934. 'Little History', in which Benjamin invokes this 'strange weave of space and time' for the first time, was written in 1931.

15 On space and time as the *a priori* forms of intuition, see the 'Transcendental Aesthetic', in Immanuel Kant, *Critique of Pure Reason*, trans. Norman Kemp-Smith (London: Macmillan, 1929). Gasché's 'Objective Diversions' focuses explicitly on the way in which Benjamin is recasting Kant's forms of intuition in his description of aura. On the significance of Kant for Benjamin's thought more generally, see Caygill, *The Colour of Experience*.

16 For a contrasting critique of Benjamin's periodization of art, see chapter II of Peter Bürger, *Theory of the Avant-Garde*, trans. Michael Shaw (Minneapolis: University of Minnesota Press, 1984).

17 The same passage appears in Benjamin, 'Little History of Photography' (*SW* 2:519).

18 On the experience of city crowds as an experience of shock, see 'On Some Motifs in Baudelaire' (*SW* 4:324–9).

19 Benjamin claims these new ends are political, in §IV of 'The Work of Art' essay, but does not offer an argument for the claim (*SW* 4:256–7).

20 Caygill, *The Colour of Experience*, pp. 93–117.

21 I come back to this point below. As to the cogency of Benjamin's central – and massive – claim in the artwork essay that the very *structure* of experience is being transformed as a result of the new reproductive technologies, notably film, see Joel Snyder's 'Benjamin on Reproducibility and Aura', for a defence; and chapter II of Noël Carroll's *A Philosophy of Mass Art* (Oxford: Clarendon Press, 1998), for a sceptical reply.

22 Adorno appealed to his own experience as a composer, when corresponding with Benjamin about his essay: '[d]ialectical though your essay may be, it is not so in the case of the autonomous work of art itself; it disregards an elementary experience which becomes more evident to me every day in my own musical experience – that precisely the uttermost consistency in the pursuit of the technical laws of autonomous art changes this art and instead of rendering it into a taboo or fetish, brings it close to the state of freedom, of something that can be consciously produced and made'. See Adorno *et al.*, *Aesthetics and Politics*, 121–2.

23 See also §IX of Susan Buck-Morss's 'Aesthetics and Anaesthetics: Walter Benjamin's Artwork Essay Reconsidered', *October* 62 (1992), a highly original re-reading of the artwork essay, where she comments:

> The medical practice was professionalized in the mid-nineteenth century, and doctors became prototypical of a new elite of technical experts. Anaesthesia was central to this development. For it was not only the patient who was relieved from pain by anesthesia. The effect was as profound upon the surgeon. A deliberate effort to desensitize oneself from the experience of the pain of another was no longer necessary. Whereas surgeons earlier had to train themselves to repress empathic identification with the suffering patient, now they had only to confront an inert, insensate mass that they could tinker with without emotional involvement. (pp. 27–8)

24   See Adorno: 'What nature strives for in vain, artworks fulfil: They open their eyes',
     and 'An artwork opens its eyes under the gaze of the spectator when it emphatically
     articulates something objective', in *Aesthetic Theory*, trans. Robert Hullot-Kentor
     (Minneapolis: University of Minnesota Press, 1997), pp. 66, 275. In effect, Adorno
     concurs with Benjamin's characterization of aura in the 'Work of Art', but not with its
     consignment to cult, hence nor with Benjamin's willingness to dispense with it. This
     is apparent in the 'Paralipomena' to *Aesthetic Theory*, pp. 273–5, in which Adorno uses
     the idea of aura (*contra* Benjamin) to contest Hegel's idealist conception of the work of
     art as *thoroughly* permeated by mind.
25   See, in this regard, Susan Buck-Morss's discussion of eyes that *look* but no longer *see*,
     having been anaesthetized through over stimulation, in 'Aesthetics and Anaesthetics',
     §§VI–VIII, especially p. 18.
26   I take this way of characterizing Benjamin's double-edged response to the withering of
     aura from John McCole's *Walter Benjamin and the Antinomies of Tradition*, pp. 1–10
     in particular.
27   Benjamin is here invoking Proust's idea of 'involuntary memory', which he regards as a
     modern phenomenon. For Benjamin, the fact that voluntary and involuntary memory
     should have come apart, and that retrieving the richness of the latter thereby become
     a matter of chance, is a product of the fact that once consciousness is forced to func-
     tion as a shield against excessive stimulation, only what circumvents consciousness *can*
     lodge itself within our experience in a deep sense. Thus Benjamin characterizes 'the
     associations which, at home in the *mémoire involuntaire*, seek to cluster around the
     object of perception' as auratic (*SW* 4:337).
28   This conception of experience is predicated, specifically, on Freud's work on con-
     sciousness as shock-defence and, more generally, on Freud's view of the mind as a
     dynamic, self-regulating system that functions by deflecting or discharging excitations
     and stimuli that threaten its own equilibrium. See, for example, 'Beyond the Pleasure
     Principle', in Sigmund Freud, *On Metapsychology*, Penguin Freud Library, vol. 11,
     trans. James Strachey (London: Penguin, 1991), pp. 275–338.
29   Thus Benjamin cites in 'Little History' Dauthendey, a contemporary of Daguerre,
     remarking:

> We didn't trust ourselves at first to look long at the first pictures he devel-
> oped. We were abashed by the distinctness of these human images, and
> believed that the little faces in the picture could *see us*, so powerfully was
> everyone affected by the unaccustomed clarity and unaccustomed fidelity
> to nature of the first daguerreotypes. (*SW* 2:512)

     'At first', that is, when photography was still a truly startling invention, looking for
     too long would have felt akin to *staring* at another person who was looking back. This
     impression that the subjects of early photography were looking back gave it an uncanny
     quality for its contemporaries, not least because it gave rise to the feeling that the
     inanimate objects of their gaze were alive, imbued with a subjective interiority of their
     own.
30   For an account of the relation between aura, intersubjectivity and transcendence
     consonant with that put forward here see Andrew Benjamin, 'The Decline of Art:
     Benjamin's Aura', *Art, Mimesis and the Avant-garde: Aspects of a Philosophy of Difference*
     (London: Routledge, 1991), pp. 147–8 and 150–1. Despite our different starting-
     points, Benjamin's remarks on the 'inexhaustibility' and 'primordial presence' of
     the face, the fact that it remains distant and other despite proximity – what I call
     its 'transcendence' – his stress on its ability to look back, returning the gaze, and his
     claim that this confers an *ethical* significance on aura anticipates my argument here.
     See also Andrew Benjamin's discussion of the 'cleavage of experience' in 'Tradition
     and Experience: Walter Benjamin's "On Some Motifs in Baudelaire"', in Andrew

Benjamin, ed., *The Problems of Modernity: Adorno and Benjamin* (London: Routledge, 1989), pp. 122–40 (pp. 132–3 in particular), for the parallels in our discussions of Benjamin's concept of 'experience' relevant to our respective accounts of aura.
31 See 'Interview with Rineke Dijkstra' in *Rineke Dijkstra*, Exhibition Catalogue (London: The Photographers Gallery, 1997), n.p.

CHAPTER 11

1 Quoted in Friedrich A. Kittler, *Gramophone, Film, Typewriter* [1986], trans. Geoffrey Winthrop-Young and Michael Wutz (Stanford, CA: Stanford University Press, 1999), p. 39.
2 Cf. Michael André Bernstein, *Five Portraits: Modernity and the Imagination in Twentieth-Century German Writing* (Evanston, IL: Northwestern University Press, 2000), p. 80.
3 Martin Heidegger, 'The Origin of the Work of Art' [1936], *Martin Heidegger: Basic Writings*, ed. David Farrell Krell (New York: HarperCollins, 1977, rev. 1993), p. 165.
4 Cf. Jeremy Tambling, *Opera and the Culture of Fascism* (Oxford: Clarendon Press, 1996), pp. 234–5.
5 Adorno to Benjamin, 18 March 1936:

> It neglects a fundamental experience which daily becomes increasingly evident to me in my musical work, that precisely the uttermost consistency in the pursuit of the technical laws of autonomous art actually transforms this art itself, and instead of turning it into a fetish or taboo, brings it that much closer to a state of freedom, to something that can be consciously produced and made ... You underestimate the technical character of autonomous art and overestimate that of dependent art; put simply, this would be my principal objection. (*CC*, p. 129, 131; cf. *Aesthetic Theory* [1970] ed. Gretel Adorno and Ralf Tiedmann, trans. Robert Hullot-Kentor (London: The Athlone Press, 1999), pp. 33, 45, 56, 66, 311, 320)

6 Quoted in a note, without comment, by Terry Eagleton, *Walter Benjamin, or, Towards a Revolutionary Criticism* (London: Verso, 1981), from Brecht's *Arbeitsjournal*, vol. 1 (Frankfurt-am-Main, 1973), p. 16.
7 At one extreme, it evoked the oddest associations, as when he wrote to Ernst Schoen on 10 September 1917, that he was affected by the sight of a hump that had developed on the back of a friend he had not met for several years: 'This hump suddenly seemed to me to be a characteristic of most modern people who devote themselves to music ... This "hump" and everything connected to it is a particular form of the Socratism I despise, a form of the modern, of "beauty in ugliness"' (*C*, p. 95). Adorno confirms this prejudice in *Alban Berg: Master of the Smallest Link* [1968], trans. Julianne Brand and Christopher Hailey (Cambridge: Cambridge University Press, 1991), pp. 25–6: 'Benjamin ... was rather indifferent to music and ... in his youth had nursed a certain animosity towards musicians.' (Cf. Theodor W. Adorno, *Essays on Music*, selected, with an introduction, commentary and notes by Richard Leppert, trans. Susan H. Gillespie, Berkeley, CA: University of California Press, 2002, p. 625.)
8 Theodor Adorno and Hans Eisler, *Composing for Films* [1947], reprinted with an introduction by Graham McCann (London: The Athlone Press, 1994), p. lii. The book has not fared well with later theorists. See Peter Kivy, 'Music in the Movies', *Film Theory and Philosophy*, ed. Richard Allen and Murray Smith (Oxford: Clarendon Press, 1997), pp. 314–19.

9   Michael Chanan, *Musica Practica: The Social Practice of Western Music from Gregorian Chant to Postmodernism* (London and New York: Verso, 1994), p. 229.

10   Cf. Rajeev S. Patke, 'Benjamin's Aura, Stevens's "Description without Place"', *Benjamin's Blindspot: Walter Benjamin and the Premature Death of Aura*, ed. Lise Patt (Topanga, CA: Institute of Cultural Inquiry, 2001), pp. 81–98.

11   Mikhail Bakhtin, *The Dialogic Imagination*, trans. Caryl Emerson and Michael Holquist, ed. Michael Holquist (Austin: University of Texas Press, 1981), writes of the chronotope as holding space and time in a single continuum, 'functioning as the primary means of materializing time in space' (p. 250).

12   Theodor Adorno, *Sound Figures*, [1978] trans. Rodney Livingstone (Stanford: Stanford University Press, 2002), p. 75.

13   In 'The Opera *Wozzeck*'(1929), Adorno remarks: 'Walter Benjamin correctly remarked on the analogy between Berg's method and Karl Kraus's treatment of the lyrics of Matthias Claudius' (*Essays on Music*, p. 620). In 'Berg's Discoveries in Compositional Technique' (1961), he writes: 'freedom is intimately connected with the quality which ... originally attracted me to Berg, as well as to Benjamin's philosophy. This was the quality of inexhaustibility, of a profusion of ideas which constantly regenerates itself and flows in superabundance', *Quasi una Fantasia: Essays on Modern Music* [1962], trans. Rodney Livingstone (London and New York: Verso, 1992), pp. 194–5.

14   The affinity between Benjamin and the temperament ascribed to Berg is evident, as remarked by Bernstein, *Five Portraits*, p. 93.

15   'Webern shared with Walter Benjamin a penchant for the micrological and the confidence that the concrete concentration of a fulfilled moment is worth more than any amount of development that is merely ordained abstractly from outside' (Adorno, *Sound Figures*, p. 94).

16   Adorno, *Beethoven: The Philosophy of Music*, ed. Ralf Tiedemann, trans. Edmund Jephcott (Stanford: Stanford University Press, 1998), p. 7.

17   Ibid., p. 9.

18   Jacques Derrida, *Of Grammatology* [1967], trans. Gayatri Chakravorty Spivak (Baltimore: The John Hopkins Press, 1974), p. 46.

19   Ibid. p. 199.

20   Alastair Williams, *New Music and the Claims of Modernity* (Aldershot and Brookfield: Ashgate, 1997), p. 57.

21   Ashok D. Ranade, *Essays in Ethnomusicology* (New Delhi: Munshiram Manoharlal, 1998), p. 245. From a contrary perspective, Roger Scruton, *The Aesthetics of Music* (New York: Oxford University Press, 1997), inverts the Derridean emphasis: 'Written signs owe their life to the thing which is *written down*' (p. 439). Despite his rejection of Adorno's view of the bourgeoisie in the decline of culture, Scruton's idea of music as 'the thing' prior to its transcription and performance is not very different from that developed by Adorno.

22   Williams, *New Music and the Claims of Modernity*, pp. 74–5.

23   Philip Auslander, *Liveness: Performance in a Mediatized Culture* (New York and London: Routledge, 1999), p. 84.

24   Ibid. p. 35.

25   Kittler, *Gramophone, Film, Typewriter*, pp. 24–5.

26   *Essays on Music*, p. 274. Cf. Barbara Engh, 'Of Music and Mimesis', in *Adorno: Culture and Feminism*, ed. Maggie O'Neill (London, Thousand Oaks, CA, New Delhi: Sage Publications, 1999), p. 171.

27   William Gaisberg, one of the earliest recording engineers in India, wrote in 1918 of his experiences of 1906: 'The most appreciated singers are the young women with very high voices ... One rarely hears a male singer, except when his voice resembles a woman's', in 'Romance of Recording', *The Voice* (House magazine of The Gramophone Company, Ltd, Hayes, England) [1918], reprinted in *The Record News* (The Journal

of the Society of Indian Record Collectors, Bombay), with notes by Michael Kinnear, 17 (January 1995), p. 40i. Cf. Gerry Farrell, *Indian Music and the West* (Oxford: Clarendon Press, 1997): 'some of the greatest male vocalists of the century . . . emulated the performance practices of the *tawā'ifs'* (women who sang and danced as professional entertainers) (p. 121).

28 *Essays on Music*, p. 271.
29 Ibid., pp. 279–80.
30 Theodor W. Adorno, *Mahler: A Musical Physiognomy* [1971] trans. Edmund Jephcott (Chicago, IL: University of Chicago Press, 1991), p. 38. See also Theodor W. Adorno, 'The Schema of Mass Culture', *The Culture Industry: Selected Essays on Mass Culture*, ed. J. M. Bernstein (London: Routledge, 1991), p. 80; cf. Barbara Engh, 'Of Music and Mimesis', p. 170.
31 *Essays on Music*, p. 315.
32 Ibid., p. 312.
33 Adorno, *Mahler*, p. 38.
34 Cf. Eva Geulen, 'Under Construction: Walter Benjamin's "The Work of Art in the Age of Mechanical Reproduction"' [1992], reprinted in *Benjamin's Ghosts: Interventions in Contemporary Literary and Cultural Theory*, ed. Gerhard Richter (Stanford: Stanford University Press), p. 135:

> The aura, as the distinguishing feature of traditional art, becomes visible only to the extent that art has lost this character. The manifestation of the aura arises out of its loss . . . Authenticity is a belated effect. In the beginning was not the original, but rather the reproduction, which makes the concept of authenticity possible in the first place . . . The decline does not happen to, but rather constitutes the aura.

35 Wallace Stevens, *Collected Poems* (New York: Knopf, 1956), p. 70.
36 Andrew Benjamin, *Present Hope: Philosophy, Architecture, Hope* (London and New York: Routledge, 1997), p. 52.
37 Ibid. pp. 158, 160.
38 *Essays on Music*, p. 288.
39 *Beethoven*, p. 163.
40 Fredric Jameson, *Late Marxism: Adorno, or, The Persistence of the Dialectic* (London and New York: Verso, 1990), p. 185.
41 Sam Weber, 'The Virtuality of Media', *sites* 4 (2000): 297–318.
42 Gilles Deleuze, *Difference and Repetition* [1968], trans. Paul Patton (London: The Athlone Press, 1994), p. 208. Weber, 'Virtuality of Media', links the notion of virtuality to Heidegger's discussion of 'possibility' and 'being towards death' in §53 of *Being and Time* (1927), and stresses the importance of mediation to the concept of a medium of reproducibility: 'the Hegelian notion of mediation as an infinite process of becoming other in order to become the same, presents a strategy of safeguarding finitude from an alterity, and a future, that would not come full-circle and not simply be a return of the same' (p. 316).
43 Pierre Lévy, *Becoming Virtual: Reality in the Digital Age* (New York and London: Plenum Trade, 1998), p. 26. Cf. L. L. Yong., 'Shakespeare as Virtual Event', *Theatre Research International* 28 (2003), p. 49.
44 Philippe Lacoue-Labarthe, 'Poetry's Courage', *Walter Benjamin and Romanticism*, eds. Beatrice Hanssen and Andrew Benjamin (New York and London: Continuum, 2002), p. 170; Beatrice Hanssen, '"Dichtermut" and "Blödigkeit": Two Poems by Friedrich Hölderlin, Interpreted by Walter Benjamin', in the same book: 'At a second level of specification, the poetized took on the meaning of a limit-concept (*Grenzbegriff*), a demarcating sphere between two concepts, those of the poem and of life' (p. 151). David Wellbery reads *das Gedichtete* as 'an overcoming of the mythic, a negation of

the mythic conflict in a structure that brings that conflict … to rest', in 'Benjamin's Theory of the Lyric', in *Benjamin's Ground: New Readings of Walter Benjamin*, ed. Rainer Nägele (Detroit: Wayne State University Press, 1988), p. 50.

45   *Mahler*, p. 68.

46   Ibid., p. 108.

47   Scruton, *The Aesthetics of Music*, p. 442.

48   Deleuze, *Difference and Repetition*, p. 209.

49   Cf. Weber, 'Virtuality of Media', p. 311: 'all actualization of the medial, whether linguistic or other, tends to mediate the linguistic aspect of the medial, its impartability, by institutionalizing and codifying it. Such codification is exemplified in the work, and in particular, in the artwork.'

50   The practice of concluding a 78rpm record by announcing the vocalist's name can be treated as a token of resistance to this separation, a literal inscription of identity into the grooves of a record, as in 'My name is Gauhar Jan!' Farrell, *Indian Music and the West*, p. 140, accounts for the practice on the more mundane grounds of novelty and advertising, but Suresh Chandvankar's explanation in 'Presenting First dancing girl, Calcutta', *The Indian Express* (15 November 2002), is even more mundane and plausible: 'Gaisberg requested her to sing for three minutes and to announce her name at the end of the recording. She announced: "My name is Gauhar Jan". This was necessary, since the wax masters were sent to Hanover in Germany for pressing the records, and the technicians would make proper labels and confirm the name by listening to these announcements at the end of the performance.' Source: <http://www.indianexpress.com/full_story.php?content_id=13037> Accessed 24 May 2003.

51   Daniel M. Neuman, *The Life of Music in North India: The Organization of an Artistic Tradition* [1980], (2nd edn, London and Chicago, IL: The University of Chicago Press, 1990), p. 223.

52   Farrell, *Indian Music and the West*, p. 113.

53   Ranade, *Essays in Ethnomusicology*, p. 21.

54   Bonnie Wade, *Music in India: The Classical Traditions* (Englewood Cliffs, NJ: Prentice-Hall, 1979), pp. 24–5: 'in India, written transmission has been seen as unnecessarily restrictive: since improvisation is the heart of the tradition'.

55   William Gaisberg writes from his experience of recording music in India in 1906: 'one never finds written music for these songs; they are handed down from father to son, and this has been going on for hundreds of generations' (p. 40i). For the role of the musicologist and the use of notation in teaching, see Sobhana Nayar, *Bhatkhande's Contribution to Music: A Historical Perspective* (New Delhi: Sangam Books, 1989).

56   *The Raga Guide: A Survey of 74 Hindustani Ragas*, ed. Joep Bor (London: Zenith Media for Nimbus Records with the Rotterdam Conservatory of Music, 1999), p. vii. Cf. Ashok Ranade, *Essays in Ethnomusicology*, 'Indian music does not accept concepts of absolute time and pitch. As a corollary, the three basic tempi, namely slow, medium and fast are defined with reference to one another' (p. 203). He also stresses the Heraclitan and aleatory persuasion of Indian music: 'Indian music lays special emphasis on improvisation. Consequently, there is an ever-present theoretical possibility that no music can be performed twice' (p. 157).

57   *Nāda* connotes the primordial manifestation of energy in vibration. It embodies recognition of several orders of duality within its unitariness: breath (*prāna*) against non-being; the audible (*ahat*) against the inaudible (*anahat*); and its metaphorical equivalent, the expressible against the ineffable, the former finding its realization in music, the latter in the yogic discipline of the *kundalini*, in which energy spirals back to its origins. In *nāda*, therefore, music as sound is closely allied to silence.

58   Bonnie C. Wade, *Khyal: Creativity within North India's classical music tradition* (Cambridge: Cambridge University Press, 1984) (reprinted New Delhi: Munshiram

Manoharlal Pvt Ltd, 1997), p. 2. Her earlier work, *Music in India: The Classical Traditions* (1979), comments on the concept of the *rāga*:

> The idea of 'scale' is alien to many Hindustani *rāgas*, because melodic shape, rather than an abstract scale, accounts for the difference between one *rāga* and another ... It may involve ... other characteristic turns of melody (*pakad*) that make a *rāga* immediately recognizable to a listener. (pp. 59, 63)

59 Cf. Michael Kinnear, *The Gramophone Company's First Indian Recordings, 1899–1908* (Bombay: Popular Prakashan, 1994), p. 28: 'many great vocalists and musicians in India ... were left unrecorded, either because they were not approached to do so or had declined to have their talents recorded, as was often the case'. Farrell, *Indian Music and the West*, notes: 'in the early days many performers of Indian music refused to be recorded' (p. 137), citing the example of the singer Chandra Prabhu as recounted by A. H. Fox-Strangways in *The Music of Hindostan* (1914). Even if the following anecdote were to prove apocryphal, one would like to believe it. The great vocalist Alladiya Khan (1855–1946) is reported to have turned his back on Bhatkhande's request that the vocalist allow the scholar to transcribe his singing. As he walked away from the crestfallen scholar on Chowpatti Beach in Bombay, Alladiya Khan is supposed to have hummed the beginning of *rāga* Tilak Kamod, whose lyric ('*Sur sangat rāga vidya ...*') commemorates music as alive only in the moment of its singing.
60 Cf. Kinnear (1994), p. 3.
61 Cf. Suresh Chandvankar, 'Centenary of Indian Gramophone Records', *The Record News* (The Journal of the Society of Indian Record Collectors, Bombay, TRN Annual 2000), p. 83. Gaisberg remarked in 1918, 'we went out to India to furnish records for the natives, not for Europeans' (p. 40i).
62 Ibid. p. 92.
63 Kinnear (1994), p. 29.
64 Michael Kinnear, *The Gramophone Company's Indian Recordings 1908–1910* (Heidelberg, Victoria, Australia: Bajakhana, 2000), pp. 22–3.
65 Chandvankar, 'Centenary of Indian Gramophone Records', p. 99.
66 Ibid. pp. 85, 95.
67 Adorno, *Essays on Music*, p. 301. Cited in Neuman, *The Life of Music in North India*, p. 224.
68 The Indian scene provides confirmation for the more general claim made by Chanan, *Musica Practica*, that reproducibility had 'marked effects on both performance and listening. The former began to lose its spontaneity and became the art of the repeated take. The latter turned attention away from the excitement and risk of the act of performance, towards the reproduction and its surface sheen' (pp. 250–1).
69 William Gaisberg writes in 1918: 'In recording we experienced great difficulty in getting the singers to sing their songs out of proper time of day' (p. 43i).
70 V. V. Navelkar and Suresh Chandvankar, 'Zohrabai Agrewali, a literature survey', *The Record News* (The Journal of the Society of Indian Record Collectors, Bombay, TRN Annual 2001), pp. 23–31, brings together many published acknowledgments by noted musicians of their debt to her recordings.
71 *Sound Figures*, p. 94.
72 Ibid., p. 201.
73 Farrell, *Indian Music and the West*, p. 112.
74 *Essays on Music*, p. 298.
75 Farrell, *Indian Music and the West*, pp. 140–1.
76 Neuman, *The Life of Music in North India*, p. 224.
77 Cf. Farrell, *Indian Music and the West*, p. 124: 'Music and musicians stigmatized as immoral and degenerate by large sections of the population ... came to gain status as

carriers of classical musical culture. The gramophone industry played an important role in this process'.

78 Ibid. p. 119: 'Gauhar Jan charged 1,000 rupees for a recording session, and Jankibai 3,000.'

79 Neuman, *The Life of Music in North India*, explains: 'A musician's identity is always defined in part by the identity of his teacher who, in turn, is identified by the identity of *his* teacher back through the line. This taken as a whole comprises a given 'school,' called a *gharānā* (lit., 'of the house'), distinguished from other gharānās on the basis of its unique history, pedigree, and style of performance' (p. 31).

80 Wade, *Music in India*, p. 25.

81 Chanan, *Musica Practica*, p. 251.

82 Cf. Auslander, *Liveness: Performance in a Mediatized Culture*, p. 159: 'I have described the relationship between the live and the mediatized as competitive, conflictual and agonistic ... however ... It is not an opposition rooted in essential differences between the live and the mediatized.'

83 Neuman, *The Life of Music in North India*, p. 224.

84 Edward Said, *Musical Elaborations* (New York: Vintage, 1991), p. 22: 'he only played concerts in public for about ten years – between the mid-1950s and the mid-1960s – and after retiring from concert life permanently devoted himself to making records', until his death in 1982.

85 'MacMoutal's RagPage': <http://homepage.mac.com/patrickmoutal/macmoutal/rag. html>.

86 Neuman, *The Life of Music in North India*, p. 225.

CHAPTER 12

1 This description of Mikami's work is cited from: http://red.ntticc.or.jp/preactivities/ ic95/profile/mikami-e.html, accessed February 2000 (the site appears no longer to exist). Another gloss on this work can be found at: http://web.canon.jp/cast/artlab/ archives/artlab5/main.html, accessed April 2004. The work itself is to be found at: http://web.canon.jp/cast/artlab/artlab5/, accessed April 2004.

2 Ziarek, *The Historicity of Experience: Modernity, the Avant-Garde, and the Event* (Evanston: Northwestern University Press, 2001).

3 'Real denunciation is probably only a capacity of form, which is overlooked by social aesthetic that believes in themes'; Theodor W. Adorno, *Aesthetic Theory*, trans. Robert Hullot-Kentor (Minneapolis: University of Minnesota Press, 1997), p. 230.

4 While Benjamin does not think about the issue of the 'aestheticization' of art in these terms, in 'Program for Literary Criticism', he remarks briefly about the end of aesthetics: 'Criticism has failed to notice that the time for aesthetics in every sense, and especially in the sense practised by Friedrich Theodor Vischer, is gone forever.' In place of traditional aesthetic criticism, Benjamin calls for a new materialist aesthetics 'that would situate books in the context of their age. Such criticism would lead to a new, dynamic, dialectical aesthetics' (*SW* 2:282, 284).

5 Art appears to be less than praxis because it is not 'action' and seems ineffectual from the perspective of pragmatic action. 'Art, however, is more than praxis because by its aversion to praxis it simultaneously denounces the narrow untruth of the practical world' (Adorno, *Aesthetic Theory*, p. 241).

6 Ibid.

7 This is already evident in 'The Origin of the Work of Art', where Heidegger detaches art from the idea of aesthetics, with its foundation in the metaphysical oppositions of matter/form, subject/object, truth/falsehood, etc.; see *Basic Writings*, ed. David Farrell

Krell (New York: Harper Collins, 1993), especially pp. 152–62. At the end of 'The Question Concerning Technology', Heidegger remarks that it is precisely what he calls 'our sheer aesthetic-mindedness' about art that makes it extremely difficult to understand how art unfolds and works (ibid., pp. 340–1).

8   The key element of Genesis is an 'artist's gene', a synthetic gene created by translating a sentence from the biblical book of Genesis into Morse Code, and converting the Morse Code into DNA base pairs. The sentence reads: 'Let man have dominion over the fish of the sea, and over the fowl of the air, and over every living thing that moves upon the earth'. This sentence was chosen for what it implies about the dubious notion – divinely sanctioned – of supremacy over nature. Crucial in Genesis is the way Kac interpreted the meaning of the word 'dominion' from the biblical passage, creating, through viewer participation, a powerful symbol for change. According to Kac, Morse code was chosen because, as the first example of the use of radiotelegraphy, it represents the dawn of the information age – the genesis of globalcommunication. The 'Genesis' gene is incorporated into glowing bacteria and projected as live video in the gallery and streams over the Internet, where the public is encouraged to intervene and monitor the evolution of the work. Original Genesis DNA music by composer Peter Gena accompanies the installation.
     The full text from which this excerpt comes can be found on Eduardo Kac's web page: http://www.ekac.org/osthoffldr.html (accessed April 2004).

9   Heidegger, *Basic Writings*, pp. 337–40.

10   '*In photography, exhibition value begins to drive back cult value on all fronts*' (*SW* 4:257, emphasis in the original).

11   This anxiety looks similar to the one discussed by Lyotard, but in fact is less ontological; it is not a matter of the sublime but, rather, of a more ordinary historical situation in which art finds itself fretting over its demise, more and more paralysed by the disseminating technicization of being.

12   See Ziarek, 'The Turn of Art: The Avant-Garde and Power', *New Literary History* 33 (2002): 96–7.

13   I discuss the relation between aesthetics and globalization in more detail in 'Is All Technological: Global Power, Aesthetic Forces', *The New Centennial Review* 2 (2002): 139–68.

CHAPTER 13

1   There are three versions of 'The Work of Art in the Age of its Technological Reproducibility'. This text is premised in the main on the second version which was written in 1935–6 and was unpublished during Benjamin's lifetime. Published in *SW* 3: 101–33, trans. Edmund Jephcott and Harry Zohn.

2   Donald Judd, 'Specific Object', *Art Yearbook* 8 (1965): 74–82.

3   Phil Leider, 'Literalism and Abstraction: Frank Stella Retrospective', *Artforum* 8 (1970): 44–51.

4   See Andreas Huyssen, 'The Hidden Dialectic: Avantgarde-Technology-Mass Culture' in *After The Great Divide: Modernism, Mass-Culture, Postmodernism* (Bloomington: Indiana University Press, 1986), pp. 3–15.

5   Allan Kaprow, 'The Education of the Un-Artist, part 1', *Art News* 69.10 (1971): 28–31; 'The Education of the Un-Artist, part 2', *Art News* 71.3 (1972): 34–9; 'The Education of the Un-Artist, part 3', *Art in America* 62.1 (1974): 85–9.

6 Susan Buck-Morse, *The Dialectics Of Seeing: Walter Benjamin and the Arcades Project* (Cambridge, Mass.: MIT, 1991).

7 See Howard Caygill, *Walter Benjamin: The Colour of Experience* (London: Routledge, 1998): 80–117.

8 'Culture' emerged in the era of postwar consensus as a refuge for the left to pursue a sublimated form of critique, which was appropriated by more conservative forces such as Bell. In international relations, culture became the way to explain the development of societies in what was known as the 'modernization' thesis. Briefly, this view held that 'advanced' industrial nations were at the end of social evolution (at the end of history, as it were) and that so-called lesser developed nations were further down the ladder, but would eventually climb up given the proper circumstances (which the advanced nations would graciously provide in the form of foreign aid). This is not unlike the traditional ethnographic model that saw so-called primitive cultures as primordial residues of modern societies, preserved in pristine form due to their isolation. The reason given wasn't the asymmetrical relationships of a world capitalist system (as defined, for example, by Immanuel Wallerstein), but as the function of cultural factors such as literacy rates, welfare state services, urbanization, etc. In this context, so-called high culture (in the visual arts, specifically abstract expressionism) became the epitome of the evolutionary model. As Herbert Gans (in 'Popular Culture and High Culture: An Analysis and Evaluation of Taste') notes, it's in this period that Dwight MacDonald, Clement Greenberg, Lionel Trilling, etc. took center stage as essentially new mandarins, protecting the purity of high culture from the great unwashed of the popular mass of society. Gans's notion of 'taste cultures' is echoed in Pierre Bourdieu's construction of the field of cultural production, which establishes so-called disinterested taste (i.e., pure aesthetics) as the head of the leviathan of bourgeois social relations. In this system, 'aesthetic criteria' are purported to be objective and transcendent, but are in actually neither. They reflect a privileged social position that provides distance, first and foremost, from economic need (see 'Distinction: A Social Critique of the Judgment of Taste', among other writings by Bourdieu). Simply put, it's a lot of work, not to mention expense, to acquire the proclivities of taste at that level. It takes time, a conducive social environment, and a network of interactions and opportunities of a very particular sort. It's important to note that Bourdieu's solution is not to dump the universal aesthetic condition, but to make the conditions of the universal universally available, primarily through access to education and other methods of acquiring the habitus (i.e., personal habits, tastes, proclivities, abilities to judge, etc) needed to participate on equal footing in this highest rung of taste culture. From a purely political perspective (i.e., that the great unwashed know what they are in the eyes of the dominant elite and resent the hell out of it as they have every right to), the so-called lowbrow has a point.
E-mail Vince Carducci, aesthetics-l@LISTSERV.INDIANA.EDU
Subject: [AE] Dave Barry writes off modern art
Date: Sat, 3 Apr 2004 10:08:21 −0800

9 'Editorial Notes: The Meaning of Decay in Art', *Internationale Situationiste* 3 (1959): 3–8.

10 It is for this reason I chose Kaprow over the example of Joseph Beuys. Although Beuys proposed a social vision of art that embraced all forms of contemporary practice, he seemed committed to the anaesthetized politics that Benjamin attributes to Fascism in as much as his popularity in the 1970s and 1980s, like Anselm Keifer a generation

later, was based on the appeal of shamanism and mysticism and a nostalgia for art's diminished aura.

11   Allan Kaprow, 'The Legacy Of Jackson Pollock', *Art News* 57.6 (1958): 24–6, 55–7.
12   Allan Kaprow, 'Notes on the Creation of a Total Art', in *Essays on the Blurring of Art and Life*, ed. Jeff Kelley (Berkeley: University of California Press, 1993), pp. 10–14.
13   Guy Debord, 'One More Try If You Want To Be Situationists', *Potlach* 29 (1957): n.p.
14   Daniel Bell, *The End of Ideology: On the Exhaustion of Political Ideas in the Fifties* (New York City: Collier Books, 1960).
15   T. J. Clark and Donald Nicholson-Smith, 'Why Art Can't Kill the Situationiste Internationale', *October* 79 (1997): 15–31.
16   Allen Kaprow, 'Notes on the Creation of a Total Art', in catalogue for Environment (New York: Hansa Gallery, November 1958).

CONTRIBUTORS

Andrew Benjamin has taught philosophy and architectural theory in both Europe and the US. He is currently Professor of Critical Theory in Design and Architecture at University Technology, Sydney and Adjunct Professor at Monash University, Australia. His past books include *The Plural Event* (1993), *Present Hope: Philosophy, Architecture, Judaism* (1997), and *Philosophy's Literature* (2001). His forthcoming book is *Disclosing Spaces: On Painting* (Clinamen Books, 2004). He is co-editor of the series Walter Benjamin Studies (Continuum).

Rebecca Comay is Professor of Philosophy at the University of Toronto. She has published extensively in areas of European philosophy, and particularly on the work of Walter Benjamin, Martin Heidegger, Hegel, and contemporary French thought.

Diarmuid Costello is Senior Lecturer in the Theory of Art and Leverhulme Trust Research Fellow in the School of Arts and Humanities at Oxford Brookes University, UK. He has published articles on various philosophers and art theorists relevant to recent debates in art theory and aesthetics including: Clement Greenberg, Jean-François Lyotard, Martin Heidegger, Arthur C. Danto, and Ludwig Wittgenstein. He is at present working on a monograph contesting the marginalization of aesthetics in theories of art after modernism.

Fabrizio Desideri is Professor of Aesthetics at the Florence University (Italy). He is author of several books, including: *Walter Benjamin: Il tempo e le forme* (Roma, 1980); *Quartetto per la fine del tempo: Una costellazione kantiana, Marietti* (Genova, 1991); *La porta della giustizia: Saggi su Walter Benjamin* (Bologna, 1995); *Il velo di Iside: Coscienza, natura e messianismo nella filosofia romantica* (Bologna, 1997); *L'ascolto della coscienza: Una ricerca filosofica* (Milano, 1998); *Il fantasma dell'opera: Benjamin, Adorno e le aporie dell'arte contemporanea* (Genova, 2002); and *Il passaggio estetico: Saggi kantiani* (Genova, 2003). He has also edited in Italian works of Benjamin, Kant, Nietzsche, Novalis, Scheerbart, and Simmel. His forthcoming book is *Estetica: un percorso. Dall'esperienza del bello al problema dell'arte.*

Howard Eiland is co-editor of Volumes 2, 3, and 4 of Benjamin's *Selected Writings*, and co-translator of his *Arcades Project*. He has also published articles on Heidegger and Nietzsche. He is currently working with Michael W. Jennings on a short biography of Benjamin. He teaches literature at the Massachusetts Institute of Technology.

Peter Fenves is the author of *A Peculiar Fate: Metaphysics and World-History in Kant* (1991), *'Chatter': Language and History in Kierkegaard* (1993), *Arresting Language: From Leibniz to Benjamin* (2001), and *Late Kant: Towards Another Law of the Earth* (2003). He is editor of *Raising the Tone of Philosophy: Late Essays by Kant, Transformative Critique by Derrida* (1993) and translator of Werner Hamacher's *Premises: Literature and Philosophy from Kant to Celan* (1996). He is currently completing a study entitled *The Messianic Reduction: Walter Benjamin and the Abstention from Philosophy*.

Beatrice Hanssen is Professor of German at the University of Georgia, Athens. She is the author of *Walter Benjamin's Other History: Of Stones, Animals, Human Beings, and Angels* (University of California Press, 1998, 2000), and *Critique of Violence: Between Poststructuralism and Critical Theory* (Routledge, 2000). She is co-editor of *The Turn to Ethics* (Routledge, 2000). Together with Andrew Benjamin, she is also co-editor of the series Walter Benjamin Studies, which includes the volumes *Walter Benjamin and Romanticism* (Continuum, 2002) and *Walter Benjamin and the Arcades Project* (Continuum, forthcoming).

Joanna Hodge is Professor of Philosophy at Manchester Metropolitan University, UK. She did her doctoral work in Oxford, Heidelberg, and Berlin on Martin Heidegger, and in 1995 published her study *Heidegger and Ethics* with Routledge. She has also worked over the years on the thought of Benjamin, of Hegel, and of Husserl. She is currently completing a manuscript on Derrida's rethinking of time, in the context of his reception of critical philosophy and of phenomenology. Her next project is to continue to explore the connection between ethics and phenomenology in relation to a phenomenological reconstruction of the thinking of time. She has a long essay preliminary to this forthcoming in *Diacritics*, entitled 'Ethics and Time: Levinas, Husserl, Kant'.

Robert Kaufman is Assistant Professor of English and Affiliated Assistant Professor of German Studies at Stanford University. His essays on nineteenth- and twentieth-century poetry, poetics, aesthetics, and critical theory have appeared in various journals and collections, including *Critical Inquiry, October, American Poetry Review, Modern Language Quarterly, The Cambridge Companion to Adorno, The Brecht Yearbook,* and *Studies in Romanticism*. He is at present completing *Negative Romanticism, Almost Modernity: Keats, Shelley, and Adornian Critical Aesthetics,* and is at work on a related study, *Experiments in Construction: Frankfurt School Aesthetics and Contemporary Poetry*.

Arne Melberg was born and educated in Sweden and has been Professor in Comparative Literature at the University of Oslo since 1987. He has published widely within literary history and literary theory, e.g. *Theories of Mimesis* (Cambridge, 1995), and, in his own language, monographs on *Hölderlin* (1994), *Rilke* (1997), *Montaigne* (1999, also in German, 2003), and *Nietzsche* (2002). He is currently the leader of the research project 'Aesthetics at Work'.

Detlef Mertins is Professor and Chair of the Architecture Department at the University of Pennsylvania. He has published extensively on the history and theory of architectural modernity, including a critical introduction to the English edition of Walter Curt Behrendt's 1927 functionalist polemic, *The Victory of the New Building Style* (2000). He is the editor of *The Presence of Mies* (1996) and is currently completing a monograph on Ludwig Mies van der Rohe (Phaidon Press, 2005). He is also co-editing a translation of the 1920s avant-garde journal *G: Material zur elementaren Gestaltung* (Monacelli, 2005). From 2001 to 2003, he was Canada Research Chair in Architecture at the University of Toronto and in 2003 he won the Konrad Adenauer Prize of the Alexander von Humboldt Foundation and the Royal Canadian Society.

Saul Ostrow is Dean of Fine Arts and Chair of Painting at the Cleveland Institute of Art. Trained as an artist and receiving his MFA from the University of Massachusetts, since 1996 he has worked primarily as a critic, an organizer of exhibitions. He is currently the Art Editor for *Bomb Magazine*, co-editor of Lusitania Books (publishing anthologies focusing on cultural issues), and editor of the book series: Critical Voices in Art, Theory and Culture. His writings have appeared in *Flashart International*, *ArtPress* (France), *Neue Bilde Kunst* (Germany) the *International Review of Art* (Columbia, SA), *Arts Magazine*, *World Art*, and the *New Art Examiner* (USA). He has interviewed artist such as Brice Marden, Barry LeVa, Olu Oguibe and Sol Lewitt among others for *Bomb Magazine*. He has also written numerous exhibition catalogues and has organized and participated on panels whose topics have ranged from the education of the artist to perspectives on multi-culturalism and the politics of culture. Since 1987 he has curated over 40 exhibitions in the US and Europe, half of which have dealt with Abstract Art, the rest with issues inherent in other forms of representation.

Rajeev S. Patke is Associate Professor at the Department of English Language and Literature, National University of Singapore. He is the author of *The Long Poems of Wallace Stevens: An Interpretative Study* (Cambridge: Cambridge University Press, 1985). He has co-edited *Institutions in Cultures: Theory and Practice* (Amsterdam and Atlanta, GA: Rodopi, 1996), and *Complicities: The Literatures of the Asia-Pacific Region* (Bern: Peter Lang, 2003). His publications on Benjamin include 'Benjamin's Aura, Stevens's

"Description without Place"', in *Benjamin's Blindspot: Walter Benjamin and the Premature Death of Aura*, ed. Lise Patt (Topanga, CA: Institute of Cultural Inquiry, 2001); 'Benjamin in Bombay? An Extrapolation', *Postmodern Culture* 12.3 (May 2002); 'Benjamin's *Arcades Project* and the Postcolonial City', *Diacritics* 30.4 (Winter 2000), and 'Benjamin and Bakhtin: The Possibility of Conversation', *Journal of Narrative Theory* 33.1 (Winter 2003).

Krzysztof Ziarek is Professor of Comparative Literature at the University at Buffalo. He is the author of *Inflected Language: Toward a Hermeneutics of Nearness* (1994), and *The Historicity of Experience: Modernity, the Avant-Garde, and the Event* (2001). His newest work, *The Force of Art*, is forthcoming from Stanford University Press. He has also published numerous essays on Coolidge, Stein, Stevens, Heidegger, Benjamin, Irigaray, and Levinas, and co-edited a collection of essays, *Future Crossings: Literature Between Philosophy and Cultural Studies*. A volume of his poems in Polish, *Zaimejlowane z Polski*, was published in 2000. He has won NEH and ACLS fellowships. He is currently working on aesthetics and globalization.

Index